Arthur Devine

The creed explained

Or, An exposition of Catholic doctrine

Arthur Devine

The creed explained
Or, An exposition of Catholic doctrine

ISBN/EAN: 9783741183058

Manufactured in Europe, USA, Canada, Australia, Japa

Cover: Foto ©Lupo / pixelio.de

Manufactured and distributed by brebook publishing software
(www.brebook.com)

Arthur Devine

The creed explained

Nihil Obstat.

PHILIPPUS COCHLAN, C.P.,

Censor Deputatus.

Imprimatur.

DANIEL GILBERT,

VICAR. CAPITUL. WESTMONAST.

Die 28 Aprilis, 1892.

THE CREED EXPLAINED;

OR,

An Exposition of Catholic Doctrine,

ACCORDING TO

THE CREEDS OF FAITH

AND THE

CONSTITUTIONS AND DEFINITIONS OF THE CHURCH.

BY THE

REV. ARTHUR DEVINE,

PASSIONIST,

AUTHOR OF "CONVENT LIFE" AND "HISTORY OF THE PASSION."

SECOND EDITION.

R. WASHBOURNE,
18 PATERNOSTER ROW, LONDON.

DUBLIN: M. H. GILL & SON, 50 UPPER O'CONNELL STREET.
BENZIGER BROS.: NEW YORK, CINCINNATI AND CHICAGO.

1897.

PREFACE.

THE following work, which I am now giving to the public, has for its object to promote Catholic truth by explaining Catholic doctrine as contained in the " Creeds," and as it is defined and interpreted by the Church.

It contains the summary and substance of lectures and instructions which for several years I have been accustomed to give to students and pupils ; and in it I have endeavoured to explain the twelve Articles of the Creed, as well as the more recent definitions and declarations of the Church on matters of faith as contained in the decrees of the Vatican Council, and the constitutions of the Sovereign Pontiffs.

I have not thought it necessary to make the work in any sense a controversial one, because I believe that a clear and accurate exposition of Catholic doctrine is the best means of promoting its knowledge, and the best remedy against misrepresentations, and the dishonest criticisms of our adversaries ; and also the best refutation of the many false theories of Christianity against which we have to contend, in order to guard the true doctrine of Christ, and make it known to the people.

In the manner of treating the subject, I first give an introductory treatise on the virtue of faith, together with the full text of all the " Creeds " that are approved by the Church, and professed by the faithful. Afterwards, I give the text of the " Apostles' Creed " and of the " Nicene Creed " at the head of each Article as the subject of the instructions and explanations which follow. In the explanation of the Articles I state the doctrine, explain its meaning, and then give the proofs of its truth, taken from the usual Theological sources— Sacred Scripture, Tradition, the definitions of the Church, the authority of Fathers and Theologians, and reason.

Article IX of the Creed, which embraces all that concerns the Church and the Sovereign Pontiff, has demanded several chapters in order to deal with it fully, and to explain in detail all the points of doctrine that affect Catholic claims, Catholic policy, and Catholic teaching and authority. There are therefore separate chapters in this Article on the Church:—The Primacy of St. Peter; the Sovereign Pontiff and his infallibility; General Councils and their authority; and a concluding chapter on the legislative authority of the Church, and her relations to civil society. It would have saved much controversy and misunderstanding at the time of the publication of Mr. Gladstone's "Expostulation on the Vatican Decrees," had the doctrine of the Church been better known and understood by the English public on the question of Catholic allegiance, Catholic policy, and Catholic teaching, which the Expostulation attacked with such vehemence and severity. Men who were then disturbed by the controversy may now, with calm and dispassionate reason, read and understand the sense in which all these questions are held and taught in the Catholic Church, without any fear of their believing that "the Church of Rome is arrogant in her claims, dishonest in her policy, shallow and ignorant in her teaching." (a)

From this outline of the work, it will appear that it covers a large field of study, common to ecclesiastical students, to teachers in schools, colleges and convents, to whom I hope it may be specially useful in their religious studies and examinations; and many a hard worked priest may find it a convenient hand-book for the subject-matter of his pastoral sermons and instructions.

On the part of the Catholic laity, there is always to be found amongst them an earnest and laudable desire to read and to study doctrinal works, as they deem it necessary, in the midst of their Protestant friends and relations, to be well instructed in their Creed, in order to be able to assign a reason

---

(a) Dean Nevill's "Comments on the Expostulation." (*Page* 6.)

for the faith that is in them, and to instruct others in the Christian doctrine when required.

And it seems that amongst the people of this Country in general there is a sincere and ever increasing spirit of research and inquiry into religious truth and doctrine, as is evident from the publication and large circulation of numerous works, even of fiction, all tending in this direction, as for example "Robert Elsemere," and others of a like class.

For these reasons I am led to hope that the work, which I now publish, may find a place in the religious and doctrinal literature of the day. It is intended as a help to Catholic students and teachers; as a safe and secure guide to the laity in matters of Catholic belief; and as a convenient hand-book for priests, on the mission, for the preparation of their sermons and instructions. And all non-Catholics may learn from it a correct knowledge of the Christian doctrine as held and taught in the Catholic Church. To these individually we must give the full benefit of the excuse derived from invincible ignorance with regard to the truths of faith which they do not know, or which they are prevented from knowing through no fault of theirs. At the same time, we must remember the words of the prophet Isaias, which St. Jerome applies to the Catholic Church:—*And in the last days the mountain of the house of the Lord shall be prepared on the top of mountains, and it shall be exalted above the hills, and all nations shall flow into it.* (a) The Church of Christ is therefore as a city placed on the top of a mountain, which cannot be hidden from view, and which can be seen by all, as expressed in the words of St. Augustine :-- *Extat Ecclesia cunctis clara atque conspicua, quippe civitas, quæ abscondi non potest supra montem constituta.* (b)

Throughout the work, I have taken many quotations and extracts from various authors whenever I have found that they expressed my meaning clearly and correctly; and I have en-

---

(a) II. 2. (b) Lib. 2., Contra Creson, C. 86.

deavoured to acknowledge my obligation to them in the several places in which the references are given.

From amongst Protestant works, I have used in many instances that of Pearson on the Creed, (a) and I consider it, to a great extent, the work of a man who has carefully studied and followed the teaching of Catholic Theology. In the narrative of the events of our Saviour's life, sufferings and death, I have made much use of the publications under the title of the "Cambridge Bible for Schools and Colleges," on account of the clearness and brevity with which these events are narrated, and the Scriptural knowledge and erudition carefully acquired, and evidently possessed, by the authors of these manuals.

Apart from these, throughout the whole work I have used and followed the usual standard works of Catholic Theology; and in all the various subjects of which I treat I have endeavoured faithfully to follow and to adhere to the teaching of that science, as it interprets the doctrine of faith and morals. After having spent most of the years of my life in its study and teaching, I have learned to love it for its own sake, and to esteem it as the highest, the most excellent, and the most useful of all sciences.

St. Joseph's Retreat,
  Highgate, London, N.

Feast of the Assumption, 1892.

(a) "Analysis of Pearson on the Creed," by Rev. J. Gorle, M.A.

CONTENTS.

CONTENTS.

THE CREED EXPLAINED.

INTRODUCTORY TREATISE ON FAITH.

CHAPTER I.

PAGES

CHAPTER II.

CHAPTER III.

CHAPTER IV.

A 2

THE CREED EXPLAINED.

INTRODUCTORY TREATISE ON FAITH.

CHAPTER I.

FAITH, ITS DEFINITION AND DIVISION.

1. Faith, its various meanings.—2. Its definition as a Supernatural virtue.
—3. The virtue of faith resides in the intellect.—4. It is the first
of Supernatural virtues, but not the first grace.—5. The division of
faith.—6. The difference between divine faith and divine-Catholic
faith.

BEFORE explaining the Articles of our faith as contained in
the Apostles' Creed, I think it necessary to give an explanation
of the faith itself, and the Catholic motives of credibility, so that
all may be able to give a reason for the faith which is in them.

1. Faith as used in Holy Scripture has many significations:—
(a) It signifies confidence :* *Let him ask in faith nothing
wavering.*
(b) Fidelity to promises :† *For what if some of them have not
believed? shall their unbelief make the faith of God
without effect? God forbid.*
(c) Conscience :‡ *For all that is not of faith is sin.*
(d) The doctrine and object of faith :§ *And thou holdest fast
my name and hast not denied my faith.*

Here, however, I take the word *faith* in its strict sense,
namely, for the assent or belief which we give to truths on the
authority of another. If the authority is divine, the faith is called
divine ; if human, the faith is only human.

Faith is different from science, because what we know and

---

*S. James i. 6.   ‡Romans xiv. 23.
†Romans iii. 3.   §Apoc. ii. 13.

B

assent to by science rests on intrinsic evidence, and what is known and believed by faith rests on external authority.

2. Here there is question of divine and supernatural faith; and this faith is defined in the Catechism: "A supernatural gift of God, which enables us to believe without doubting whatever God has revealed." Or it may be defined more fully: "A supernatural virtue, inclining the intellect to assent to the truths revealed by God, because of the authority of God revealing them."

It is described by the Vatican Council: "A supernatural virtue, by which, through the grace of God inspiring and helping us, we believe as true all that God has revealed, not on account of their truth as perceived by natural reason, but on account of the authority of God revealing them* ' Who can neither deceive nor be deceived.'"

Hence the question and answer in the Catechism: "Why must you believe whatever God has revealed?" "I must believe whatever God has revealed, because God is the very truth, and can neither deceive nor be deceived."

This faith is called supernatural, inasmuch as it is a virtue infused into the soul by God, and cannot be acquired by our own natural powers; and, also, because it is supernatural in its motive, that is, it must rest on the authority of God revealing. This is the only true divine faith, that faith which is necessary for justification.

We have to believe that neither this salutary faith, nor even its beginning, can be obtained without the grace of God. This was defined in the Council of Orange against the Pelagians and the Semi-pelagians; and in the Council of Trent.† Faith is therefore the gift of God, and the *beginning* of all true belief must be through the grace of God.

Some of the objects of faith are said to be supernatural, not only in the sense that they are believed on the authority of God, in which sense all the objects of faith may be considered supernatural; but, also, because we could never come to their knowledge without the supernatural medium of revelation. Such, for example, are the dogmas of the Holy Trinity and the Incarnation.

3. The virtue of faith resides in the intellect as in its subject; because to believe is immediately the act of the intellect,

---

*Const. dog. de fide Catholica. Cap. iii.
†Sess. vi. Can. 3.

inasmuch as its object is truth, which belongs to the intellect. It is, however, the will that moves the intellect to elicit an act of faith, and to assent to truths which, in themselves, are not evident. Hence the assent of faith is a free act of the will, as we shall explain more fully later on.

4. Faith is the first of all the virtues in the supernatural order, and hence it is called by the Council of Trent,* *the beginning of human salvation, the foundation and root of all justification.*

Some natural virtues, such as humility removing the pride of intellect, and other such virtues, may exist before it, but in the natural order.

Faith is not the first grace, because that grace which moves the will before the assent of faith must precede the faith itself. This is of course actual grace; but the state of sanctifying, or habitual grace, cannot be found in a soul without faith, as this virtue is the foundation of all the supernatural qualities of the soul.

The light of faith does not give a vision of the object, but only a certain knowledge of it on the testimony of God.

5. *The division of faith.* Faith may be (a) *habitual* or *actual*, (b) *internal* or *external*, (c) *explicit* or *implicit*. *Explicit* faith is that which is given to a truth which, in itself, is proposed to the mind. *Implicit* faith is that which is given to a truth which is contained in another truth, and not in itself proposed to the mind or known to it. Thus, he who *explicitly* believes that there are two natures in Christ, *implicitly* believes that there are in Him also two wills and two operations ; and again, he who *explicitly* believes all that the Church teaches as of faith, *implicitly* believes in the Seven Sacraments, although he may not know them.

(d) Faith is either *formata*, that is, united with Charity and sanctifying grace ; or *informis*, that is, faith without sanctifying grace. (e) *Living* or *dead*. *Living* faith is that which is accompanied with good or salutary works. *Dead* faith is that which is not accompanied by good works, which does not produce them, or does not produce them in the proper way. This division does not differ much from the preceeding, namely, faith *formata* and *informis* ; there is, however, some difference, for *dead* faith can exist with a certain spiritual languor, which does not immediately and of necessity expel grace, and yet does no good.

---

*Sess. vi. c. 8.

(*f*) Faith is divided into *divine* and *divine-Catholic* faith. *Divine* faith is that which is given to truths revealed by God, even though not yet proposed by the Church to all to be believed. *Divine-Catholic* faith is that which is given to truths revealed by God, and proposed by the Church to all to be believed.

6. The only difference between these two is, that what is simply revealed by God is believed by divine faith, and if a truth revealed by God be proposed by the Church to all to be believed, it is called *divine-Catholic* faith. Thus, the Immaculate Conception of the Blessed Virgin, and the Papal Infallibility, were believed by *divine* faith, and were of *divine* faith always; but it was only after they were defined to be so, that the faithful were obliged to believe them, and that they were numbered among the Church's dogmas as the objects of *divine-Catholic* faith. This distinction between *divine* and *divine-Catholic* has reference only to the manner in which the word of God is made known to man, and the difference in the faith is only accidental, yet it is of great importance to know it, as it serves to explain Catholic doctrine and practice; and I shall have reason to refer to it more fully later on.

CHAPTER II.

THE OBJECT AND MOTIVE OF FAITH.

1.—The primary object of faith.—2. The formal object of faith, or the motive of faith.—3. The material object of faith.—4. The Decree of the Vatican Council as to the object of faith.—5. The Summary of the truths that are the object of *divine-Catholic* faith.—6. Propositions and conclusions deduced from revealed truths.—7. The rule by which we may know whether such conclusions belong to the object of faith or not.

PASTORS of souls are obliged to teach the people not only what they are to believe, but also the *why* or reason of their belief. We have, therefore, to explain the object of our faith and its motive, that is, the reason why we give our assent to the truths of faith.

1. The *primary* object of faith is God Himself, considered as the Deity. Faith primarily intends or regards the knowledge of the true God as He is in Himself, and all the other truths of revelation are ordained to the more perfect knowledge of God. Hence, as St. Paul says, "*Accedentem ad Deum oportet credere quia est*": "*He that cometh to God must believe that He is.*"*

2. The *formal* object of faith, or that which we may call the motive of faith, is the veracity of God, arising from His infinite knowledge and wisdom. It is the authority of God which consists in His infinite wisdom, through which He cannot be deceived; and in His infinite veracity and truth, through which He cannot deceive us. Hence the answer in the Catechism to the question, " Why must you believe whatever God has revealed?" " I must believe whatever God has revealed because God is the very truth, and can neither deceive nor be deceived."

There is, therefore, no other answer to be given by a Catholic for his belief in general, or the belief in any particular dogma, than the reason—because God has said it or revealed it. If a Catholic is asked, Why do you believe in the Catholic

*Heb. xi. 6.

Church? Why do you believe in the Incarnation of Christ? or, Why do you believe in the Blessed Eucharist, or in the Papal Infallibility? the answer to all such questions is one and the same: I believe on the authority of God, and because God has said or told me these things by revelation or inspiration. He has revealed or inspired tnem to His Church, and hence I believe them because He is the very truth, and can neither deceive nor be deceived.

3. The *material object* of faith is all and every truth revealed or inspired by God. That anything be believed by faith, two conditions are required: (a) That it be revealed or inspired by God; (b) That it be certainly known to be revealed or in-spired.

That about which something is believed may be called the *subject* of faith in an objective sense. Thus the Church is the subject about which we believe *unity, infallibility, &c.* The primary subject of all faith in this sense is God Himself.

4. The Vatican Council declares,* "*Fide divinâ et Catholicâ ea omnia credenda sunt, quae in verbo Dei Scripto vel tradita continentur, et ab Ecclesia, sive solemni judicio, sive ordinario et universali magisterio, tanquam divinitus revelata proponuntur*": " By divine and Catholic Faith are to be believed all those things which are contained in the Word of God, written or handed down by tradition, and proposed by the Church as divinely revealed, either by her solemn judgments, or by her ordinary and universal teaching."

It may be asked, What are the truths that we must receive as revealed by God, and as proposed by the Church, and that we have to believe by divine-Catholic faith?

5. These truths may be classed under the following heads:—

(a) All those truths that are so clearly contained in Sacred Scripture that no one can doubt or mistake their meaning, viz., the Nativity of Christ, His death and resurrection, &c.

(b) The truths that are obscurely contained in the Sacred Scriptures, but declared by the Church to be therein contained, such as the definition or declaration of the true sense of any text of Scripture.

(c) Those truths that are expressly defined by.the Church to be of faith, or whose contradictories are condemned

---

*Const. de fide. Cap. iii.

as heretical, viz., That there are Seven Sacraments of the New Law ; That we cannot merit beatitude or perform salutary works without the aid of God's grace.

(d) The truths that are handed down to us by *divine tradition*, and which the Church has always held and declared, or manifested by her doctrine and practice, such as her doctrine regarding Guardian Angels, Infant Baptism, the Canonical Books of Scripture, &c.

All the truths contained under these heads are revealed or inspired by God, and declared or defined by the Church ; and, therefore, to be believed by divine-Catholic faith. It is not necessary to have an explicit definition of the Church for every text of Scripture, and for those portions of the Sacred Scriptures whose sense can be clearly known to any one who reads them ; neither is there need of an explicit definition in regard to those truths which are known to all as handed down by divine tradition. When a doubt has arisen with regard to any proposition, as to whether it is contained in Scripture or tradition, the Church, through the divine assistance, defines the truth of its revelation, or condemns it if it is opposed to revelation. This she has done whenever she has judged it necessary for the preservation of the deposit of faith committed to her by her Divine Founder. She has defined what we have to believe as divinely revealed, and condemned errors opposed to revealed doctrine whenever this was necessary for the preservation of faith and morals.

6. How are we to regard propositions that are deduced from revealed premises, and that are, therefore, necessarily connected with our faith and its preservation? For example :—

(a) Propositions or Conclusions drawn from two revealed premises by evident reasoning, viz.: All the Apostles received the Holy Spirit ; but St. John was an Apostle, therefore St. John received the Holy Spirit.

(b) Propositions or Conclusions deduced from one premise revealed, and the other only evident to reason, viz. : A baptized child is sanctified ; but this child is baptized, therefore this child is sanctified. Or again : A consecrated host is to be adored ; but this host is consecrated, therefore this host is to be adored. Or again : Whatever is defined by an Ecumenical Council is to be believed ; but the Council of Trent

was an Ecumenical Council, therefore its definitions
are to be believed.

Are these conclusions to be considered as coming under the
object of faith? And again, what are we to hold in connection
with the object of faith, with regard to singular propositions
contained in revealed universal propositions, or propositions
virtually contained in revealed truths?

A conclusion as such is not an object of faith, but merely the
result of human reasoning. And a proposition, to be of faith,
must be immediately revealed by God, and received on His
authority. Propositions or conclusions such as are here given,
may be said to be more certain than the conclusions arrived at
by mere natural science, because they are founded on and
deduced from revealed dogmas; and they have, therefore, a
certain amount of divine authority, as they are so closely
connected with revealed truths.

7. A rule is laid down for deciding whether a conclusion of
this kind belongs to faith or not, namely : If the conclusion be
formally and immediately contained in the premises, or in the
premise which is of faith as a part is contained in the whole or
a singular in a universal, and if the deduction be only a further
explanation of the premises, and does not introduce any new
idea into the definition, such a proposition or conclusion would
be the object of faith, and is to be believed as such. If it be not
formally, but only *virtually* contained in the premises as an effect
in a cause, the conclusion is not to be believed by divine faith
because it is not the object of faith, but a deduction of reason.
It is, however, often said to belong to faith indirectly, in as
much as by denying a conclusion of this kind the revealed
premises from which it is deduced are indirectly denied.

Other propositions, which are not clearly and immediately
revealed by God, or which are not deduced by reason from divine
truths, but are taught by the Fathers and Theologians as certain
and true, are said to be received on ecclesiastical faith. They
are not the objects of divine faith, and they are received by
something more than mere human faith, and may be said, therefore, to be believed by a certain ecclesiastical faith. This
faith is sometimes called *divine* (though in reality it is not
divine), because its act may proceed from the divine virtue
which is in us, and the dispositions which it creates in the
soul.

As to these few questions which I have here introduced,
we have no definition of the Church, and I only state the received

teaching of Theologians on such points for the purpose of meeting captious objections, after the manner of Dr. Littledale's "Plain Reasons," that may, from time to time, be urged against the Catholic faith and doctrine. For this purpose, it is necessary to explain even critical questions from a Catholic point of view that the enemies of the Church may not be credited with inventing objections that she has long ago considered and rejected, and thereby do harm to the faithful and others.*

CHAPTER III.

THE CERTITUDE AND OBSCURITY OF FAITH.

1. The two-fold certitude of faith.—2. God cannot reveal anything false.—
3. What is false cannot be the object of faith.—4. The subjective
certitude of faith.—5. The assent of faith more certain and firm
than the assent of science.—6. Obscurity of faith, its meaning.—
7. The object of faith essentially obscure.—8. Two acts, one of
faith, and one of science, may be elicited about the same truth, but
one and the same act cannot be one of faith and of science.—9. The
acts of mental knowledge which precede faith.—10. The obscurity
of faith illustrated.

1. THE certitude of faith may be two-fold : (a) The objective certitude of faith. (b) The subjective certitude of faith. By
the objective certitude of a dogma or proposition is meant its truth.

Concerning this certitude two things may be stated :

2. (a) God cannot reveal anything false, as this would be
against His infinite perfection and veracity ; and, in the words
of St. Paul, " It is impossible for God to lie."*

3. (b) Falsehood cannot come under faith. That is, a man,
by virtue of divine faith, cannot believe falsehood ; or, in other
words, that which is false cannot be the object of divine faith.
This is clearly affirmed in the 9th Chapter of the VI. Sess. of the
Council of Trent. Even though a particular person might think
that which is false to be a revealed truth, it could not be believed
by the virtue of faith. For example : A man who would consider
every priest speaking from the pulpit as infallible as the Pope,
and would bring himself to believe it, does not do this by virtue
of his faith, nor does the act of belief proceed from the habit or
virtue of divine faith which is in him ; because this virtue only
reaches that which is true and divinely revealed ; and falsehood
cannot be attained by it, or in any sense come under it, or become
its object.

The assent, however, which is given in such cases, in as
much as it proceeds from a good pious intention of the soul, may
be praiseworthy and even meritorious.

*Heb. vi.

4. *The subjective certitude of faith.* This is the certitude of faith as it exists in the soul. It is the firm adhesion of the mind to the object proposed to it, through a sufficient and proper motive. If it were an adhesion without a sufficient reason or motive, it should be called pertinacity rather than certitude.

Innocent III. condemned a proposition which stated that "The assent of faith, which is supernatural and useful (or necessary) for salvation, can remain with a knowledge of revelation which is only probable, or even with a fear that God has not revealed or spoken." From which condemnation, it follows (*a*) that probable revelation is not sufficient for supernatural and salutary faith, the facts of revelation must be certain; and (*b*) a doubtful assent is not sufficient for faith, it must be firm and certain. The assent which is not firm is not the assent of divine faith; and, such is the nature of faith in the present order or dispensation of divine things, that God will not accept a faith which is not firm and certain.

5. This assent of faith should also, in a certain sense, be more firmly given, and held with greater certainty than the assent given to scientific truths; inasmuch as the knowledge of faith should be more certain and firm than any scientific knowledge, or any knowledge received through the senses in the natural order. This may need some further explanation. It means that the assent of faith, at least in appreciation or in estimation, can and ought to be above and more firm than any other assent. It can be so through God's supernatural grace, by which it is given, and ought to be so by reason of the truths revealed, and the motives of credibility.

The faithful, however, are not obliged or advised to make comparisons; and, in fact, it is impossible to have real comparisons, as the one is in the supernatural, and the other in the natural order. We know that natural and supernatural truths cannot in any way be opposed to each other, as they have one and the same Author.

Faith may be real, even though it be weak, provided that the assent be without doubt, and no comparison be made in respect of other truths; and, it may be well to remember that the assent to faith may be more certain and firm in itself (*quoad se*), but not in the impression which it makes upon the mind (*quoad nos*).

It may also be said that we can profitably give the assent of divine faith to a truth which we may already know by natural reason, or on human authority.

THE OBSCURITY OF FAITH, OR OF THE TRUTHS OF FAITH.

6. That is said to be obscure which is not known by intrinsic evidence. That is, any truth which cannot be demonstrated by reason, may be said to be obscure.

Obscurity in the matter of faith may be two-fold : *Absolute (simpliciter)* and *mixed (secundum quid)*. The former is in regard to those truths which can be known only by authority, viz., the Mystery of the Holy Trinity, and of the Incarnation of the Son of God. The latter is in regard to those truths which, although known by and believed on the authority of God, may also be known by natural reason, and demonstrated ; such as " the existence of God," the " Immortality of the Soul," &c.

7. The object of faith *as such* is essentially obscure, as expressed in the words of St. Paul : " *Now faith is the substance of things to be hoped for, the evidence of things that appear not.*"* Besides, an assent given on account of evidence is an assent of science, and not of faith, which must be the assent of the mind, because of the authority of the person who speaks or tells us the truth.

Obscurity in regard to faith does not enter into its intrinsic nature, but is only a condition required for it, without which an act of faith cannot be made.

As to whether a man can, by two distinct acts, elicit an act of faith and of science about one and the same truth, viz., the existence of God, or the immortality of the soul, is not certain. One School of Doctors (the Thomists) hold that this is not possible.

8. According to the teaching of some recent authors, it may, however, be asserted that this can be the case, and I see no contradiction or impossibility in eliciting two acts of this kind. I know the reasons that prove the existence of God, and the Immortality of the Soul ; but I also believe these truths with a firmer conviction of faith than human reason or human knowledge could create. Faith and science are in two different spheres, and one need not necessarily exclude the other. It is, however, denied by all that one and the same act can be at the same time an act of faith and an act of science.

9. It may be well here to enumerate the acts of knowledge, or of the mind, which usually precede faith. They are the following :—

---

*Heb. xi. 1.

(a) The perception and the knowledge of the truth itself which is proposed to be believed together with the motives of credibility.

(b) An examination of the motives of credibility to the extent of understanding their force and value.

(c) A judgment formed as to the credibility of the truths, and the obligation of believing them.

(d) The authority of the will determines the intellect to give its assent. From which authoritative motion of the will

(e) The intellect elicits an act of faith.

10. The obscurity of faith may be illustrated in the following manner : An unbeliever said to a priest one day, " Sir, I believe nothing but what I can understand." " Then," replied the priest, " you do not believe that light shines ; that fire burns ; that the wind blows ; for these are things that you cannot fully comprehend." " Yes," he replied, "but I see and feel these things." The priest said, " Even if you did not see or feel them they would be no less true." That night the man had a dream, in which it appeared to him that he was in a lovely forest, and there met a man who was born blind. Speaking to the man who had never seen the light of day, he told him about the sun, and the beauties of nature. The blind man said, " I do not understand, but I believe all that you say ; I believe that the sun is beautiful and ravishing, &c. If I should refuse to believe you because I do not understand or comprehend all that you see, you would think me very unreasonable." Then the blind man seemed to change his countenance, and to say to him in a tone of authority, " You should follow my example, and know that there are many things most excellent, and most wonderful which surpass our vision and understanding, that are none the less true and desirable although we can neither comprehend or imagine them.'

It is by no means unreasonable to believe the mysteries of faith. " If you place," says Bourdaloue, " a blind man before a mirror, and explain to him the phenomena which he produces : that in that glass there is another blind man just like him, who does not occupy any space there, and who imitates all his movements, would not the blind man be astonished at hearing these things? He might stretch out his hand to touch the other man, but would only feel the glass ; he would not be able to understand it ; but being a man of common sense, he would not refuse to believe what you tell him. We are in the position of that blind man with regard to the mysteries which God has revealed."

CHAPTER IV.

THE NECESSITY OF FAITH FOR SALVATION.

1. The necessity of means (*necessitas medii*) and the necessity of precept (*necessitas præcepti*) in the matter of salvation.—2. Faith necessary as a means to salvation.—3. The four dogmas necessary to be believed by explicit faith.—4. The precept of faith negative and affirmative, and the obligations arising from it.—5. The precept in regard to the external profession of faith.—6. The application of the doctrine concerning the necessity of faith.

1. NECESSITY in the work of salvation is two-fold : *necessity of means* (necessitas medii), and *necessity of precept* (necessitas præcepti). The first is that necessity without which the end cannot be attained. That is, a thing is said to be necessary as a means of salvation, when without it salvation cannot possibly be obtained. The *necessity of precept* is that which is ordained by the command of a Superior as necessary to be fulfilled in order to attain the end. Thus, in the matter of salvation, that is necessary by the *necessity of precept* which God has commanded us under sin to fulfil. Salvation may, absolutely speaking, be obtained without fulfilling the precepts, inasmuch as this may be morally, or physically, impossible ; and under such circumstances, precepts do not oblige.

2. Faith is necessary for salvation both by the *necessity of means* and by *precept*.

It is necessary as a *means* to salvation for all men : *Habitual* faith for infants and for those who have never attained the use of reason ; *actual* and *habitual* for adults. Faith, considered as a habit or virtue, is called *habitual*; as it is an act or the assent of the mind, it is called *actual*. By this obligation, it was always necessary to believe in God, and that He is the Remunerator, that is, that He will reward the good hereafter in heaven, and punish the wicked in hell, according to the words of St. Paul : " *But without faith it is impossible to please God. For he that cometh to God must believe that He is, and is the rewarder to them that seek Him.*"*

---

*Heb. xi. 6.

That faith is the gift of God, and that it is necessary for salvation, may be clearly proved from several places of Holy Scripture : " *For by grace you are saved through faith, and that not of yourselves, for it is the gift of God.*"* " *Think of the Lord in goodness, and seek Him in simplicity of heart. For He is found by them that tempt Him not ; and He sheweth Himself to them that have faith in Him.*"† " *He who believeth not shall be condemned.*"‡

It is also clear from the Scriptures that some faith in Christ was always necessary ; thus : (*a*) " *And in thy seed shall all the nations of the earth be blessed.*"§ (*b*) " *No one cometh to the Father except through Me.*"° (*c*) " *Neither is there salvation in any other. For there is no other name under heaven given to men whereby we must be saved.*"** (*d*) " *But knowing that man is not justified by the works of the law, but by the faith of Jesus Christ.*"‖ (*e*) " *Who is he that overcometh the world, but he that believeth that Jesus is the Son of God ?*"†*

3. In the Christian dispensation, and under the New Law, it is necessary to have explicit faith in the following four dogmas :—

(*a*) That there is one God.
(*b*) That in this one God there are three divine Persons (the Trinity).
(*c*) That God the Son, the Second Person of the Blessed Trinity, became Man, and died on the Cross to redeem and save us.
(*d*) That God will reward the just, and punish the wicked

In the New Law, these four truths have to be believed explicitly as a means of salvation ; that is, no one who is ignorant of them can be saved. This is the opinion to be followed in practice, and which is certainly the safest. At the same time, many Theologians hold it, as a probable opinion, and some, as the more propable, that explicit faith in the Trinity and the Incarnation is not so absolutely necessary, and that some may be ignorant of these mysteries through no fault of theirs.

The doctrine of the necessity of faith by reason of *precept*, may be summed up in the following propositions :—

---

*Ephes. ii. 8.
†Wisdom i. 1, 2.
‡St. Mark xvi. 16.
§Gen. xxii. 18.

°St. John xiv. 6.
**Acts iv. 12.
‖Gal. ii. 16.
†*1 St. John v. 5.

4. The precept of faith is two-fold; to wit, *affirmative* and *negative*.

(a) The *negative* precept, that is, the precept of not rejecting or disbelieving any dogma sufficiently proposed to the mind, binds all *sub gravi;* that is under a grave obligation, and, as Theologians say, *semper* and *pro semper;* that is at every moment of their lives. This negative precept urges always, and at every moment.

(b) By the *affirmative* precept, all are obliged to believe *implicitly* all the truths revealed by God.

(c) By the *affirmative* precept, all are obliged to know and to believe explicitly, not only those truths which are necessary *necessitate medii,* but also the following : (1) All the articles of the Apostles Creed; (2) the commandments of God and of the Church; (3) the Lord's Prayer; (4) the Sacraments necessary to be received, namely, Baptism, the Holy Eucharist, and Penance, and the other Sacraments when they are to be received.

This portion of the Christian doctrine must be known to all who have an opportunity of being instructed, at least in its substance, but not necessarily as to all the words of the Catechism, or any other set form of words.

(d) By reason of the *affirmative* precept, all those to whom the faith has been sufficiently proposed are obliged *per se,* that is, by the very precept itself, to make an explicit act of faith (1) when they attain the use of reason; (2) at the hour of death; (3) sometimes during life. As to how often this precept binds *per se* during life, Theologians do not agree. Cardinal Lugo says, " That he who has once embraced the Christian faith (and it may be added, lives in a Christian way, at least by complying with his Easter duty), need not doubt but that he has satisfied the precept of faith; and the same is to be understood of the precept of hope."*

At the same time we are all admonished and exhorted frequently to make acts of the Theological virtues. Benedict XIV. has attached many Indulgences to the recital of these acts, and has declared that each person may, in their recital, make use of

_____

* St. Alph. *Homo Apostolicus,* tract 4, num. 13.

any formula of words he pleases, provided that in it the special motives of each of the Theological virtues be expressed.

Per accidens ; that is, by reason of some other precept or obligation, all are obliged to make an act of faith (*a*) when strongly tempted against faith, or tried by any temptation which they cannot overcome except by an act of faith ; (*b*) when some other precept has to be observed which requires faith, such as the precept of confession and communion ; (*c*) after one has fallen into heresy, and denied the faith, it is necessary to make an act of faith in order again to turn to God, and to receive back His gift of faith.

5. As to the external profession of faith, St. Thomas teaches that it is not necessary for salvation to profess our faith always and in every place, but in some place and time ; that is, when the omission of such a profession would take away from the honour due to God, or be injurious to our neighbour ; as for example, if, when interrogated about the faith by one in authority, a person should remain silent under circumstances in which it would be thought that either he had no faith, or that his faith was not true or real ; and when others, by reason of his silence, might be turned away from the faith ; then the profession of faith would be necessary for salvation ; and it would be a grave sin not to make that profession.

The negative precept, that which is binding always and at all times, prohibits three things which are unlawful in every place and at every time, namely, (*a*) to deny the faith, (*b*) to profess a false religion, and (*c*) to simulate a false religion. Sometimes it is lawful to conceal or hide one's faith ; for example, by using the garments and other external signs of infidels that are merely profane, or in accordance with the national customs or usages independent of their religion ; as, for example, a man living in Turkey dressing as a Mohammedan. But it would not be lawful to use those things which are specially characteristic of their religion, and which those only use who belong to the false religion.

To fly in the time of persecution is quite lawful of itself, but by accident it might be unlawful in case the faithful would be scandalized, or God dishonoured ; it might also be obligatory to fly, when a priest would be required to preserve his life for the sake of others.

6. The doctrine of the necessity of faith may be applied in the following manner :

" All men are bound to believe whatever they know to have been in any way revealed by God."

c

Some men have only the light of reason to guide them; but even these, by the grace of Him " *Who enlighteneth every man that cometh into this world*,"* may know at least that God is, and that He is the Rewarder of good and evil.

Others, as those brought up amongst Jews and heretics, may have reason and grace (*a*) to believe in detail many revealed truths that are plainly taught in the Scripture, and (*b*) to believe many more truths implicitly, if they believe that whatever Scripture teaches is true.

Such men as these are bound to believe according to their knowledge; and they are also bound to increase their knowledge as soon as they become conscious of their defectiveness.

And, lastly, those who have means of knowing that the Christian Church is the divinely appointed teacher of truth, are bound to believe that all things whatsoever pertaining to salvation, which God has made known to the Church, either by direct revelation, as the mystery of the Incarnation, or by natural means providentially employed, as the facts of sacred history are true.

And they are bound to know and believe those truths in detail, one by one, so far as they need to know them in order to do God's will and to save their souls.

The obligation of faith is not difficult to comply with, for faith is the gift of God. That is to say, all men are moved and assisted by grace to believe what God has taught. And especially to Christians there is given at their Baptism a permanent power, disposition, and inclination to believe, which is called the infused virtue of faith. And the virtue of faith remains in the soul until it is destroyed by some contrary mortal sin, as for example, wilful doubt or disbelief."†

---

*St. John i. 9.
†See a work entitled "Facts of Faith," compiled by the Rev. A. Bromley Crane., pp. 7, 8.

CHAPTER V.

THE LIBERTY OF FAITH.

1. The assent given to the truths of faith is voluntary and free.—2. The freedom of faith illustrated, and shown from the object and obscurity of faith.—3. No one can be forced to believe.

1. By the liberty of faith I mean that it is in our power to receive or to reject the faith—that the assent to faith is voluntary and free. Not that we are, morally speaking, free to believe or not, to receive or reject the truth of faith at will. On the other hand, no one is forced to believe against his will, and those who have the faith are not under any physical necessity, but entirely free in their acts either of faith or infidelity. In this sense we are exposed to the danger of committing sins against faith as we are exposed to the danger of other sins, and the will may consent to them as in the case of other sins.

This freedom may be proved from Holy Scripture : " *Go ye into the whole world,*" says our Saviour, " *and preach the Gospel to every creature. He that believeth and is baptized shall be saved ; but he that believeth not shall be condemned.*"* And again : " *He that believeth in Me is not judged. But he that doth not believe is already judged, because he believeth not in the name of the only begotten Son of God.*"

As no one can be rewarded or punished according to the designs of God, unless for voluntary and free acts, it follows that our faith is free in the sense I have explained, as we are to be rewarded or punished in the next life as believers or unbelievers. We have also to bear in mind that the obligation of faith is imposed upon us by command or precept ; and a command is given only in regard to things that depend upon our free will, inasmuch as it would be useless to command that which of necessity must be.

2. The freedom of faith may be illustrated from the sixth chapter of St. John's Gospel.† When Christ had taught or

---

*St. Mark xvi. 15, 16.   †Verses 6-8.

announced the mystery of the holy Eucharist, and many of the
Jews had left Him on that account, He turned to the *twelve* and
said, " *Will you also go away ?*" He thus signified that they had
full freedom to go or stay, to believe or not, but that they must
take the consequences both here and hereafter.

This freedom of will, in regard to faith, may be further
explained from what has already been said in regard to the
object and the obscurity of our faith. Its object is not evident ;
the mysteries and truths of faith are obscure. Neither is the
fact of revelation itself evident, therefore the human mind is not
necessarily drawn, by any intrinsic evidence, to assent to the
truths of faith ; nor is it forced by extrinsic evidence, namely, the
motives of credibility. These motives do not remove the obscurity of faith. Although they rest on a first principle that is
metaphysically certain, yet their connection with that principle
is a moral and not a physical one, and only begets evidence in
the moral order of things ; that is, from the consideration of
various facts, relations and principles, we are shown that things
are so, and that they cannot be otherwise in the present state of
human nature, although, absolutely speaking, they could be
otherwise under another hypothesis or in another state. Thus,
the nature of the evidence is moral, and, as such, cannot of
necessity compel the mind to assent to it, as in the case of
metaphysical evidence, viz., " the same thing cannot at the same
time be and not be, exist and not exist ;" "the whole is greater
than its part " where the mind is obliged to give its assent, and
cannot refuse it.

In matters of faith and in the divine order of things we must
not look for, or expect to find, metaphysical evidence. This is
not possible here on earth, and we must be satisfied with moral
evidence of the motives of credibility which lead us up to faith.

3. It follows, therefore, from this teaching, that people
cannot be compelled to embrace the faith ; and no amount of
human influence and industry can make a man believe against
his will ; and that the assent given to the Catholic faith must be
voluntary and free.

It follows also that evil passions and inclinations may overcome us in the duty of faith, as in the duties imposed by other
virtues. The mind may be drawn away from the examination
and consideration of divine truths and the obligations of religion,
and our judgment may be misled by false and erroneous opinions.
Hence, the virtue of faith may be lost after it has been received
and professed even for years ; or it may be rejected and refused

altogether, as in the case of those who wilfully remain in error. Of this our Lord Himself complained when He said, "*The light is come into the world, and men love darkness rather than the light, for their works were evil. For everyone that doth evil hateth the light, and cometh not to the light, that his works may not be proved.*"*

Everyone is conscious of this freedom within himself notwithstanding the grave obligation of faith. There is, therefore, no danger whatever of anyone being forced or deceived into embracing the faith ; and no one can be received into the communion of the faithful unless they willingly receive, and freely profess, that true Catholic faith which is necessary for salvation.

CHAPTER VI.

THE INTEGRITY OF FAITH.

1. What is meant by the integrity of faith.—2. A former habit or inclination of heresy is not necessarily and all at once destroyed by the virtue of faith.—3. Any act of formal heresy destroys entirely and immediately the virtue or habit of faith in the soul.—4. A heretic cannot elicit an act of divine or supernatural faith in any revealed truth.—5. A man who rejects or denies even one truth of faith, cannot elicit an act of true faith in any dogma whatever.

1. THAT is entire which is one and unbroken; and by the integrity of faith, I mean, that it cannot be mixed with heresy or unbelief, and it must not exclude any revealed truth.

On this subject it will be sufficient to examine the three following questions: (a) Whether the habit of faith, and the habit of heresy, can exist at the same time in a soul? (b) Whether every sin of heresy expels the habit of faith? (c) Whether a heretic can elicit an act of divine faith in any one revealed dogma, say, the Divinity of Christ, for example?

2. The meaning of the first question is whether one who has been a heretic, or a non-Catholic, on his conversion to the faith, loses entirely the habit of mind or inclination towards heresy or his former errors? It must be answered that the former habit or inclination is not necessarily, and, all at once, destroyed by the virtue of faith. Like all other vices and evil habits, it may remain for a time with its former aversions and inclinations. This may be perceived in the case of some converts who retain many of their former tendencies and inclinations after their reception into the Church; and some never entirely get rid of all the former habits and dispositions. It is for this reason that the Church has ordained that neophytes should not be admitted to Sacred Orders, or to the exercise of ecclesiastical functions. There is reason to fear about their perseverance, because of their propensity to, and habit of, unbelief, which, as I have said, is not always entirely eradicated. It is also advisable that, after conversion, they should not immediately begin to preach, and to teach, and, I might add, to write and publish.

Let them remain in silence and solitude, as far as their religious opinions are concerned, for some years, unless called upon by the proper ecclesiastical authority to speak. They have much to learn as to the Church's practices, and they have to give themselves time to acquire Catholic ways of thinking and acting. It is unnecessary to publish the reasons of their conversion to the world, or to write a book on some point of doctrine, new, indeed, to them, but which every Catholic is familiar with since the time of their first Communion, or first Confession. These publications, as a rule, do very little good. Recent converts are not trusted by the members of the sect which they have abandoned, because of what is regarded as their ungrateful desertion ; and they are not yet qualified as safe guides and teachers of Catholic doctrine.

I know there may be exceptions, in which cases the Church dispenses with neophytes, and permits them to receive Sacred Orders ; and, in cases where talent and grace supply for time and experience, such converts render invaluable help ; and by their influence and example, become the instruments through which many others are gained over to the true faith. Neither should we forget the sacrifices which such souls make in renouncing their errors, and becoming Catholics, and their self-denying and zealous labours amongst us ; but in all cases it will, I believe, be better for themselves, and without any great injury to others, if they remain quiet, hidden, and unknown to the world at large, for at least a few years after their reception into the Church.

Not only is it true of faith, but also of the infused virtues of hope and charity, that they do not always, and immediately, extinguish the natural habits and inclinations contrary to them, which have been previously acquired and retained.

3. Second question, namely, whether every act of heresy destroys entirely the virtue or habit of faith in the soul ? To this question, it may be answered, that any one act of heresy expels from the soul immediately the divine virtue of faith. This is the opinion of all Theologians against Durandus. And it is so certain, according to the learned Suarez, that it cannot be denied without error. As to the manner in which it expels the habit of faith, whether physically or by a positive decree of God, we do not know, and no definite opinion can be given on the point.

4. The Third question, that is, whether a heretic can elicit an act of divine faith in any revealed dogma ? This must be answered in the negative. This question is implied in the preceding one, and it comes into the question as to whether a person denying wilfully one article of faith, can have any faith as to the

others? It is certain that any one who rejects or denies one dogma of faith, cannot have the habit of faith, or make an act of divine faith in any other revealed truth. Thus, those that deny the supremacy of the Pope, or his infallibility, as defined by the Church, cannot believe with true and Catholic faith the mystery of the Incarnation, or the resurrection of the body, or any other revealed truth. The reason of this is, because the man who wilfully denies even one truth of faith thereby denies and rejects the authority of God, which is the one sole motive of divine faith. There is only one and the same authority for all the truths of faith, and that authority once questioned or denied, the foundation of faith is destroyed. It must be all or none, as far as the truths of faith are to be received on the authority of God. I do not say that a man may not have natural faith and human and imperfect faith in some other truths after he has rejected one; but in such a case there can be no divine faith whatever.

Besides, as I have already stated, divine faith ought to be appreciatively, or in estimation, the highest; that is, it should be received with the will, entirely and absolutely subjecting our judgment and mind to the divine authority, and receiving all the divine truths when sufficiently proposed to us. If we believe with our whole heart, as it is written in the Acts of the Apostles,* this must be with the will of accepting entirely all that God has said or revealed when it is sufficiently proposed and known to us. How, for example, can John be said to believe with absolute and entire faith in Peter, if he denies some of the things which Peter tells him, or some statements which he knows have been made by Peter? In the same way, how can there be absolute and entire faith in God when some of His truths are rejected by one professing to believe the others? In such a case, it is in our own selection of the truths we place our faith, and we may be said to believe in ourselves rather than in the Word of God, or by the authority of God.

In further illustration of this doctrine, let us take the example of a *formal* heretic, K——, who nevertheless professes to be a Christian, and to believe in the Divinity of Jesus Christ. The faith which he has in the one dogma is not divine, but human. He believes in this one dogma of the Divinity of our Lord, either on the authority of his parents, or teachers, or pastors; or because he has had it impressed on his mind from childhood; or

* viii. 37.

because he has studied the question ; or on the testimony of God, but not with the assent which is entire and supreme. He cannot receive entirely and with perfect assent the testimony and authority of God in this case whilst he rejects that authority in other things, and therefore rejects the motive or formal object of faith, which is the veracity of God, or the truth of God in speaking.

The Council of Trent* has declared—"That the grace of justification is lost, not only by infidelity, by which *faith itself is lost*, but also by any mortal sin, even though faith itself be not lost."

5. If a heretic or infidel could elicit an act of faith, it would not be said absolutely by the Council of Trent that faith is lost by *infidelity ;* infidelity understood, in this place, as the sin of denying an article of faith.

I may therefore conclude by stating that a person who rejects or denies one truth of faith, cannot elicit a true and perfect act of divine faith in any dogma, and by this denial the virtue or habit of faith is entirely expelled from the soul. This is a conclusion certain, according to the common opinion and consent of Theologians, and founded on the declaration of the Council of Trent, as already given.

Durandus, as stated by Dr. Murray, seems to have held an opinion that a person denying one dogma of faith could make an act of divine faith in other dogmas. Durandus is not a safe authority to follow on many points of Catholic doctrine. His opinions are often erroneous, and on the very verge of heresy.

---

* Sess. vi., c. 15.

CHAPTER VII.

ON HERESY.

1. Heresy here referred to as the principal sin against faith amongst Christians.—2. What is meant by heresy.—3. Heresy objectively taken, or an heretical proposition.—4. Heresy subjectively taken or considered as a sin in the soul.—5. Ignorance excuses from *formal* heresy.

1. THERE are many sins against faith which may be explained more in detail under the First Commandment.

Here, it is only necessary to refer to the sin of *infidelity* ; or rather to the species of it, called heresy. I have used the word so frequently in explaining the nature and qualities of faith, that I consider it necessary to explain the nature of the sin of heresy itself. A clear understanding of the meaning of heresy will be a great help to secure right ideas as to our faith, and a protection against error.

I must call attention, in the first place, to the distinction given above, between *divine faith* and *divine-Catholic faith.* We give *divine faith* to every truth revealed by God ; but that it may be the object of *divine-Catholic faith*, it must be proposed by the Church to be believed by all as the word of God.

2. Heresy is an error against *divine-Catholic faith*, as it consists in the denial of some truth revealed by God and proposed by the Church. Thus, for example, Gallicans who denied the Papal Infallibility before the definition of the Vatican Council, were not guilty of heresy, because, although that truth was revealed by God, and could be believed by divine faith, it had not been defined or proposed by the Church as the object of faith. Any one wilfully denying or disbelieving in the truth since its definition, becomes guilty of the sin of heresy, as the Papal Infallibility as defined in the Vatican Council is now the object of *divine-Catholic faith.*

3. *Heresy objectively taken.* An heretical proposition is that which is directly opposed to a dogma of Catholic faith ; thus the proposition, "Christ is not man," is heretical because it is directly opposed to the dogma, "Christ is truly man."

If a proposition be only indirectly opposed to a dogma of faith, it is not to be considered heretical, but it may fall under some other ecclesiastical censure, such as *proximate to heresy* or *erroneous.*

The malice of an heretical proposition, as distinguished from other censured and condemned propositions, consists in this, that being directly opposed to divine revelation, it expressly denies the word of God, and immediately destroys Catholic faith as it exists in the soul of one who, up to that time, has believed with true faith.

It is necessary to impress upon the minds of the faithful the two things that are required for a Catholic dogma, namely, that it be revealed by God, and that it be proposed by the Church to be believed by all. All who are Catholics must hold that such a dogma is truly revealed, and that it is necessary to believe it with divine and Catholic faith.

These dogmas are made known by the Church (a) by the definitions of Ecumenical Councils, confirmed by the Pope; (b) by the definitions of the Pope himself teaching *ex cathedra :* (c) by the manifest faith of the Church, as held and taught by her pastors; in such a manner, that any one who should dare to deny the particular truth thus universally held, would immediately be regarded by all as a heretic, as in the case of Nestorius; (d) by the manifest sense of the Sacred Scriptures and divine tradition, as universally admitted and received in the Catholic Church. If the sense of a particular passage of Scripture, or some teaching of tradition, be not clear, or if disputed amongst Theologians, the matter thus disputed, or not clearly manifested, would not be the object of faith, inasmuch as it is not yet proposed by the Church to be believed by all.

The proposition of the Church, in one or other of the foregoing ways, is necessary that a dogma may be the object of Catholic faith, and that its opposite may be heretical, because the whole body of Catholic doctrine, revealed through Christ and His Apostles, was entrusted to the Church and to her teaching, and to her alone. She was instituted in this world by our divine Lord, that she might preserve, diffuse, teach and inculcate that doctrine until the end of time.

It is therefore the Church, and she alone, that can authoritatively and infallibly teach what is and what is not revealed truth, and what is injurious to, or at variance with, the doctrine of Christ.

It is certain that it would be heresy to deny, not only a

revealed truth proposed by the Church, but even to deny the
fact of its revelation after the Church's definition. It generally
happens that a man who denies a revealed truth, denies at the
same time the fact of its revelation, but not necessarily; for a
man might admit that Moses worked miracles, and that Christ
was truly man, and yet deny that these were revealed truths.
In such a case, by the very fact of denying that the dogma is
revealed, he denies that it is to be believed by faith and on
divine authority, and that, therefore, it can be rejected without
injury to, or taking away from, the divine authority; which would
be a heretical assertion or proposition.

4. *Heresy subjectively taken. Heresy in this sense is a voluntary error of a Christian against some truth of Catholic faith.*
That, therefore, a Christian may be called a heretic it is necessary
(*a*) that he err, (*b*) that he err in faith, and (*c*) that he err in
faith knowingly and willingly.

    (*a*)   Error is contained in the judgment, hence an act of
judgment is required for an act of heresy. As to
doubt, if the doubt be positive, viz., " perhaps our
Lord was not born of a virgin "; it is heretical, inasmuch as one thereby judges that a truth which
God has revealed is not certain. If the doubt be
negative, that is, without affirming or denying anything either by word or thought, it is not heretical,
because there is no act of judgment formed.

    (*b*)   The error must be in those things which belong to faith;
that is, those things that are contained in the Word of
God, *written* or *unwritten*, and which are proposed to
us by the Church to be believed as explained
already.

    (*c*)   The error must be known and wilful; that is, the per-
tinacity of the will is required for *formal* heresy.

5. Therefore one who errs through ignorance, even vincible
ignorance, is not a *formal* heretic. If the ignorance is vincible,
the man has sinned against the precept of learning his faith; but
his error is not heretical, as it is not accompanied by that pertinacity of will which belongs essentially to an act of heresy; so
that, Christians outside the Church, and living in ignorance of the
truth, cannot individually be called heretics, or pronounced guilty
of heresy, even if the ignorance be *vincible*, and even if it be so
grave as to be what Theologians call *affectata*. Although they
may be sinners, they cannot be called heretics as long as they are
in a state of ignorance. Those who are in invincible ignorance.

and live according to their conscience, are not only free from heresy, but even from sin in their errors.

That a man incur the excommunication of the Church, as the penalty inflicted for the sin of heresy, it is necessary that he manifest externally his error by some human act, either in word or deed. If, thinking of the mystery of the Holy Eucharist, he should disbelieve the *real presence* in his mind, he would be guilty of the sin of heresy; but, if he should express that by saying "I do not believe that Christ is really present in the Blessed Sacrament", he would incur the penalty of excommunication, and this, even though no one might be present to hear the expression.

CHAPTER VIII.

THE CREDIBILITY OF FAITH, AND THE MOTIVES OF ITS CREDIBILITY

1. The fact of revelation; and Catholic dogmas are evidently credible.—
2. The same amount of knowledge of the motives of credibility is not
required in all.—3. In order to accept revealed religion, the motives
of credibility should be examined.—4. Prophecy, its nature and
object.—5. The three conditions required for a true prophecy.—6.
Prophecy is possible.—7. God alone is the Author of prophecy.—
8. The rules by which we may distinguish true from false prophecies.
—9. Prophecies are motives of the credibility of the Christian
religion.—10. Miracles, their nature and the conditions of a true
miracle.—11. The possibility of miracles.—12. God alone is their
efficient cause.—13. The divinity of the Christian religion proved by
miracles.—14. Especially by the miracle of Christ's Resurrection.

THAT is said to be evidently credible, that is, morally speaking and excluding all rational doubt, which is proved by trustworthy witnesses, signs, and other extrinsic arguments.

1. The fact of revelation, and Catholic dogmas are evidently
credible.

This, according to the learned Saurez, is an assertion which
no Catholic can doubt or call in question. Faith is reasonable,
and therefore a man's assent is not given to its truths unless on
reasonable grounds of credibility. The motives of the credibility
of our faith are distinct from the motives of faith itself, and the
two must not be confounded.

The Psalmist has said, "*Testimonia tua credibilia facta sunt
nimis*"—"*Thy testimonies are become exceedingly credible.*"*

According to the ordinary Providence of God, and putting
aside a miraculous intervention, it is required that the motives
of credibility be perceived and understood, and that a firm
judgment be formed as to the credibility of the dogmas, before
the assent of faith be given to them.

2. The same amount of knowledge of these motives is not
to be expected from the simple and illiterate people as from the
learned and wise. The former can depend on the tradition of
the Church, as known in their midst, as a sufficient motive for
the credibility of their faith. They hear of the Christian religion
and its tenets from their pastors, their teachers, and their

---

* xcii. 5.

parents, &c. ; and they hear that it has been divinely confirmed by prophecies, miracles, and examples of sanctity, &c. ; and these proofs, in respect of such people, are sufficient to make the Christian doctrine evidently credible to them. For the learned and more intelligent, a wise and careful examination of the motives of credibility is required, and they ought to be satisfied and sufficiently instructed on this head before admitted into the communion of the faithful.

God can, in an instant, in an extraordinary manner, enlighten the mind of a person, so that, without any of our motives of credibility, or with them, but without any external means proposing them, revelation and the whole Christian doctrine may become immediately evident, or rather evidently credible, as in the case of St. Paul.

3. In order to accept revealed religion, the motives of credibility must be examined. These motives are numerous. Some of them are intrinsic, arising out of the very nature of the truths themselves, that is the excellence of the doctrine ; and some of them are extrinsic, as the witnesses of revelation. There are also supernatural motives or signs, or rather facts and signs in the supernatural order, that claim our special attention ; these are *prophecies* and *miracles*, on which two subjects some explanation may be needed.

PROPHECIES.

4. Prophecy is derived from the Greek word προφητεία, which signifies foretelling. It is defined as " The certain foretelling of a future contingent event which cannot be foreseen from any natural cause."

The prediction ought to be certain and precise, and not a vague, hazardous, and equivocal conjecture.

The object of the prophecy ought to be a future event, free and contingent, and depending on the will of God or the will of men.

We cannot regard as prophecies the predictions of the natural effects either of physical or moral causes, such as the approach of a storm, the crisis of a malady, a political revolution.

In the physical order, these things may be predicted with certainty, as judgments formed from certain phenomena, which, as known by experience from the principles of induction, usually produce such effects.

In the moral order, as it is subject to the free will of men, there cannot be the same amount of certainty. When one knows the character of a man, the customs, the inclinations, and the morals and ideas of a people, one can form a judgment as to this man and this people, but only in a general way, and without being able to decide upon anything precisely, or with any certainty.

When future events depend for their cause on the Divine liberty, or human liberty, they are beyond the knowledge of every created intelligence. The demon, whose knowledge of things is more perfect than ours, may conjecture better than we can, and make superhuman predictions, but he cannot tell with any certainty future contingent events, for he does not know the will of God, and he has not power over our free will.

5. There are, therefore, three conditions required for a true prophecy: (a) That it be certain, and not a mere conjecture; (b) that it be of a future contingent event; (c) that what is predicted cannot be foreseen from any natural cause.

6. Prophecy, as it is here understood, is possible, because it is not impossible either on the part of God or on the part of men. God knows future contingent events, and He can manifest them to men. That He knows such events is certain from His Omniscience. The knowledge of God is perfect and infinite. It embraces in an adequate manner all that can be known, all that exists or can exist, all that is, and all that will be. If God were to know things simply after the manner of our knowledge, His intelligence would not be perfect; it would be subject to succession and mutation, which is contrary to the very nature of an Infinite and Supreme Being.

Furthermore, the Providence of God, in this supposition, would be almost annihilated, as it would not be possible for Him to dispose or ordain to their proper end, infallibly and for eternity, the free actions of man.

As God necessarily knows the future, He can communicate that knowledge to man, either by revelation or inspiration, or by vision, or by exterior signs or apparitions.

The possibility and the fact of prophecies are shown also by the belief of mankind. Not to speak of Jews and Christians, whose books contain so many prophecies, there have been no people, in any age of the world, who did not believe in the divine foreknowledge of things, and make use of some means to discover that knowledge. Hence the consultation of oracles, divinations, by necromancy, auguries, astrologies, &c.

7. God alone is the Author of prophecy. This is certain from the fact that God alone can know future contingent things, that is, those things that depend on the free will of man. This is admitted by the common consent of Jews and Christians, and even of Pagans and Mohammedans. In the Sacred Scripture we find that prophecy is given as a proof of divine knowledge. *" Shew the things that are to come hereafter, and we shall know that ye are gods."** And again: *" Remember the former age, for I am God, and there is no God beside, neither is there the like to Me. Who shew from the beginning the things that shall be at last, and from ancient times the things that as yet are not done."*‡ From the fact that God alone is the Author of prophecy, it follows that prophecies form a conclusive argument in favour of divine revelation.†

8. We must, however, know how to distinguish true from false prophecies. The truth of a prophecy may easily be proved by applying the conditions required, namely: (a) that it be of some future event; (b) that the event afterwards take place in the manner foretold; and (c) that it cannot be known from natural causes.

Prophecies are certainly true if confirmed by miracles; and, also, if the effect takes place at the time and in the manner in which it was foretold. The prediction, and the realization of the event, are sensible facts to which one can apply the ordinary rules of historical criticism; and by the examination of the circumstances in connection with them, one can easily judge whether the prevision, or foreknowledge, could be obtained by natural means, or whether the effect takes place by accident or chance.

Prophecies are certainly false that have not the above conditions; and, also, if they are proved to be false by contrary miracles, and when opposed to true doctrine.

They are to be suspected (a) if put forth by unworthy men; (b) if they are ambiguous and obscure in every respect; (c) if the prophet, at the time of ennunciating his prediction, is without the use of reason or liberty.

St. John Chrysostom says that it is the sign of a false prophet when the mind is disturbed, when the man who predicts is agitated, and behaves in any way like a lunatic or senseless person;

---

*Isa. xli. 28.   ‡Isa. xlvi. 9, 10.
†Prophecy in the sense here explained, is in the intellectual order a true miracle. It can come only from God; and as a miracle in the physical order, it is an invincible argument in favour of the truth and divinity of a doctrine.

D

on the other hand, a true prophet is always self-possessed, temperate, modest, and knows what he is saying.

9. Prophecies are therefore motives of the credibility of the Christian religion. By the prophecies of the Old Testament, it is proved that Christ is the true Messiah, especially by the prophecies of Jacob,* of Daniel,† of Aggeus,‡ and of Malachias§, all of which, speaking of the Messiah, were verified in Jesus of Nazareth.

The prophecies which predicted the abrogation of the law of Moses were fulfilled in Christ Jesus, as were also all the prophecies concerning the nativity, family, and the circumstances of the life and death of the Messiah, and His exaltation after death.

Christ Himself made many prophecies, all of which have been clearly verified before the world.

(a) He predicted many things about Himself.‖
(b) He predicted many things about His disciples which came to pass, viz., the betrayal of Judas, the fall of Peter, the descent of the Holy Ghost, &c.
(c) He predicted the obstinacy of the Jews, and the calamities that befell them afterwards.
(d) He predicted the spread of the Gospel throughout the whole world.

All these prophecies prove the divine origin of the Christian religion, and are therefore the motives of the credibility of our faith. For, we conclude, that as Christ made true prophecies, He must have been God or one filled with the spirit of God; therefore He must necessarily be believed when He tells us that He was sent by His Father, and in all His other words and deeds.

With the prophecies are closely connected the Death and Resurrection of Christ, which are the foundations of our faith.

MIRACLES.

10. A miracle, according to St. Thomas, is that which is produced by God outside the established order of created nature. It is a supernatural act or fact caused immediately by God, in the place of a natural fact. When I say, immediately caused by God, it must not be understood that God, in the working of miracles, does not use the instrumentality of His creatures;

---

*Gen. xlix. ‡Ag. ob., ii
†Dan. ch., ix. §Mal. ch., iii.
‖St. Matt. xvi. 17, 20, and 36. St. Mark x. St. Luke xvii.

but these, in miraculous facts, act only as instruments in the hands of God.

There are four conditions required for a true miracle :

(*a*) That it be a sensible work, or a work that can be perceived by the senses.

(*b*) That it be a work which cannot be done by any created cause.

(*c*) That it be out of the ordinary course of nature, or not a thing that usually happens.

(*d*) That it lead us to God, or be ordained for this purpose.

Miracles are divided into miracles *quoad substantiam, quoad subjectum et modum*. They are likewise divided into those that are wrought *above, beside,* and *contrary* to nature (*supra, præter, et contra naturam*).*

11. *The possibility of miracles.* A miracle is possible if it is not repugnant to our nature, to the nature of things, or to God.

A miracle is not repugnant to our nature, because in every age mankind believed in miracles. This belief is proved (*a*) by prayer, which supposes that God interferes directly in the government of the universe, and that He rules all the powers of nature which He can direct as He judges fit, either in their usual course or in another way. (*b*) By the great number of prodigies narrated in the Sacred Scriptures, and handed down by religious traditions. If miracles were impossible, this belief would be inexplicable. It may be said that humanity is credulous and superstitious, and admits a great number of false miracles, but this does not weaken the authority of miracles ; because, as Pascal says, instead of concluding that there are no true miracles because false ones are admitted, we should rather conclude that, from the fact that there are so many false ones, there must have been true ones.

Miracles are not repugnant to the nature of things. This would be the case if the physical order of things were necessary ; but God, having freely created the world, and freely ordained its laws, can, in His wisdom and power, change these laws.

Amongst all the laws of nature there is this great law, that all things be subject in their existence and movement to the Supreme power ; and a miracle is only the execution of this law.

In rejecting the possibility of miracles, we should have to admit the absolute independence of nature, and, in the place of Providence, an inexorable fatality. There would be nothing to believe, or nothing to hope for from the Supreme Judge ; there

---

* Benedict XIV., de beat. et Canoniz. Sancts., bib. iv. p. 1., c. 1. et seq.

would be no moral responsibility, and no distinction between good and evil. In fact, the negation of miracles would imply *Atheism.*

Miracles are not repugnant to the nature of God. It is not repugnant to His *power* to work a miracle, because, as St. Thomas says, God has not limited or enchained His power by creation in such a way that He cannot depart from and act outside the usual course of things. It is not repugnant to His *wisdom,* that is to say, His love of order, for He can have, and always has, very wise and good reasons for working miracles. It is not against the *immutability* of God, for as God is a pure act, and essentially One, He places the exception at the same time that He makes the rule, and the particular departure at the same time that He establishes the general law. The miracle which He works in time He has foreseen and ordained from eternity. There is, therefore, no change in His will when He acts outside the usual course of nature.* God is the Author of nature, and rules over its species and *genera,* and also over individuals. He makes the laws, and can therefore make the exceptions.

12. He alone is the efficient cause of miracles, as is clear from the very definition of a miracle. This is also evident from proofs of Scripture : " *Blessed be the Lord, the God of Israel, who alone doth wonderful things.*"† " *God also bearing them witness by signs and wonders, aud divers miracles, and distributions of the Holy Ghost according to His own will.*"‡ This has been the belief of all nations, and is admitted by the common consent of mankind.

The force of miracles as an argument, or a motive of credibility in favour of a doctrine or creed, may be understood from what has been said in this explanation.

A miracle, having God for its Author, demonstrates directly the marvellous order of nature, the power, the wisdom, the goodness, and sometimes the justice of God. Indirectly, when it is worked in favour of a doctrine, it manifestly demonstrates the truth of that doctrine, for it is not possible that God would work a miracle to favour imposture or error. A miracle does not make revealed mysteries comprehensible, and does not assign a reason for the divine precepts imposed upon men ; but it makes us accept these mysteries and these precepts as coming from God and from Him alone. It is the seal which He im-

---

* *Demonstration de la divinité du Catholicisme* par l'Abbé Moulin.
†Psalm lxxi. 18.   ‡Heb. ii. 4.

presses upon His revelation, the letter which He entrusts to His ambassadors.*

13. The divinity of the Christian religion is proved by the miracles of Christ. He worked many miracles, as the Evangelists narrate many wondrous works performed by Him, which surpass all the powers of nature; viz., He turned water into wine, opened the eyes of one born blind, multiplied bread, raised the dead to life, &c.

He worked these miracles in proof of, or in confirmation of, His doctrine, according to the words of our Saviour, given by St. John: "*But I have a greater testimony than that of John: for the works which the Father hath given me to perfect: the works themselves which I do, give testimony of me that the Father hath sent me.*"† And again: "*If I do not the works of my Father, believe me not. But if I do, though you do not believe me, believe my works, that you may know and believe that the Father is in me, and I in the Father.*"‡

The Apostles, during the lifetime of Christ, and after His death, worked miracles in confirmation of the Christian doctrine, as may be proved from innumerable places in the Acts of the Apostles, in which many particular facts are narrated, as well as the general statement: "*Multa prodigia et signa per Apostolos in Jerusalem fiebant*": "*Many wonders also, and signs, were done by the Apostles in Jerusalem.*"

MIRACLES IN THE MORAL ORDER.

Besides the miracles in the physical order, which are used as motives of the credibility of the Christian religion, we have also to consider the miracles in the moral order, that have been manifested to the world in confirmation of that religion.

By miracles in the moral order, I mean those extraordinary events, which, considering the manners and customs of men, and the natural course of things, could not happen but by the divine power. The arguments of this kind in proof of the Christian religion may be briefly enumerated.

(a) The wonderful propagation of the Gospel. This was a wonderful miracle, whether we consider the rapidity with which the faith was spread, the difficulties in the way of its propagation by reason of the habits

---

*See *Demonstration de la divinité du Catholicisme* par l'Abbé Moulin.
†St. John v. 86.   ‡Ibid. x. 87, 88.

and lives of men, the nature of the doctrine itself, or
the means that were used for its propagation.

(b) The great efficacy of the Christian doctrine in changing
the morals of men.

(c) The fortitude and the constancy of the martyrs.

(d) The cessation of oracles.

(e) The effusion of the gifts of the Holy Spirit on the first
Christians, and their continuation in the Church
afterwards.

(f) The punishment of God falling upon the Jews, and the
preservation of these people still in the world.

(g) The death of persecutors.

(h) The constant stability of the Christian religion.

(i) To these may be added the argument of "the safer
way," that is, according to the wise rule of Moralists
in things regarding salvation *Tutior pars est eligenda ;*
it is safer to be a Catholic than anything else.
Amabius and Pascal have used this argument, but it
requires some explanation to be taken and used in a
Catholic sense.

14. There is one miracle to which I think it well, even in
this place, to draw special attention, as it is the foundation of
our faith, and of our hope in the future resurrection of the dead,
according to the words of St. Paul : " *But if there be no resurrection of the dead, then Christ is not risen again. And if Christ be
not risen again, then is our preaching vain, and your faith is also
vain.*"*

Our argument from the resurrection may be thus framed :
" If Christ rose from the dead, His religion and His doctrine
are divine ; but Christ rose again from the dead, therefore His
religion and doctrine are divine."

The first of these propositions is true ; because, if Christ rose
from the dead, it must have been by His own power, or by the
power of God ; if by His own power, by that very fact He would
prove Himself God ; if by the power of God, this would prove
beyond doubt His divine mission. God could not, by such a
miracle, approve the sayings and doctrine of an impostor.
Christ, during His life, foretold that He would rise again,
so that it might be known to all that He came forth from
God.

The second proposition, namely, but Christ rose again, only

---

*1 Cor. xv. 13, 14.

asserts one of the most certain historical facts; and one whose witnesses *could not be deceived themselves; would not be deceived even if they could; and could not be deceived even if they would.* These were the witnesses of the Resurrection. There could be no deception in the matter; for Christ, after His Resurrection, showed Himself resuscitated from the dead, in broad daylight, to many, viz., to 500 at one time.* This He did often to His disciples and friends, and in close proximity to them, so that He eat and conversed with them, and allowed Himself to be touched by them.†

The Apostles were unwilling to be deceived, for they could have no reason to wish for such a deception, and every reason to protect them against it. By such a lie and imposture, they could not hope to gain any advantage either from God, or from Christ, or from men, from whom they had nothing to expect but contempt and persecution even to death. Everything was against such a deception: the honest character of the Apostles themselves; the difficulties and dangers of the situation; the nefarious nature of such a fraud, and the impossibility of creating it. Besides, because of the guard and the precautions taken by the Jews, the body of our Lord could not be stolen from the tomb if the Apostles had wished it. And had the Resurrection not really happened, how could the Apostles have persuaded the whole world of its truth, and confirmed it by miracles?

"The Resurrection of Christ," says the Abbé Moulin, "is the miracle *par excellence;* the miracle of His *power,* for He resuscitated Himself; the miracle of His *goodness,* for His Resurrection is the cause and model of the glorious resurrection of those who have believed in Him; the miracle of His *wisdom,* for He has made it as it were the corner-stone of Christianity. It is on the fact of the Resurrection that our faith, our hope, our worship, and our history rest."

This miracle is the object of the attacks of all the incredulous, for this once admitted, no one could deny the divine Mission and the Divinity of Jesus Christ.

The Apostles, according to these, were either impostors or men labouring under hallucinations; but one or other of these hypotheses would be as extraordinary a miracle as could be conceived. But suppose that the Apostles were deceived, or wished, as our enemies say, to be deceived, would it not have

---

*1 Cor. iv.
†Acts i. 3.

been easy for the enemies of Christ to refute that lie, and such folly, by exhuming, and presenting before the people, our Lord's body, which, they said, was risen from the dead? Will they say that the Apostles stole the body, or concealed it? Admitting even this unlikely and impossible hypothesis, will they explain how a small band of false deceivers would dare to affirm the fact of the Resurrection; how they could make millions of men believe in that fact, and found upon it a religion which alone is worthy of the respect and the love of mankind?

CHAPTER IX.

THE ARTICLES AND CREEDS OF FAITH.

1. What is meant by an Article of Faith.—2. The conditions required for an Article of Faith as understood in the "Creeds."—3. The reason why the truths of faith are divided into Articles.—4. In what sense have the Articles of Faith increased?—5. The "Creeds," the meaning of a Creed or Symbol of faith.—6. The Apostles' Creed : why so called.—7. The reason why the Apostles composed it.—8. The division of the Creed : its twelve Articles.—9. The Feasts of the Church, on which certain Articles of the Creed are commemorated.—10. The obligations of Catholics in regard to the "Creed."

1. ARTICLE is derived from the Greek, and means a little joint It gives the idea of small parts, that, united together, go to make up a whole body. Hence, those things which we have to believe are distinguished by *Articles*, inasmuch as they are divided into parts that fit into one another, and thus compose one whole Creed, or body of faith.

The Catechism of the Council of Trent tells us, that the sentences of the "Creed" are called *articles* by a sort of comparison frequently used by our forefathers ; for as the members of the body are divided by joints (*articulis*), so in this profession of faith, whatever is to be believed distinctly and separately from anything else, is appositely called an *article*.

2. Theologically speaking, not all the truths of faith are divided into Articles (although commonly speaking, any revealed truth may be called an Article of Faith), but only those which have the following two conditions : (*a*) That they primarily and principally appertain to faith, as are those truths of which we shall have the vision in heaven, and through which we may obtain the Beatific Vision. (*b*) That they have some special and distinct difficulty in being believed. Thus, that *Christ died and rose again from the dead* forms two *articles*. It is a distinct difficulty to rise again after dead ; whilst, *suffered under Pontius Pilate, was crucified, dead and buried*, is only one *article*, because no distinct difficulty arises between the different propositions.

If a man be crucified he will naturally die, and the natural consequence of death is burial. In the same way, *He ascended into heaven, and sitteth at the right hand of God the Father*

Almighty, is only one Article, although it contains two propositions; but yet we have between the two no distinct difficulty, because the proper and natural place for Christ in His Father's Kingdom, after His Ascension, is at the right hand of God the Father Almighty. An Article of Faith may therefore be defined: "A Catholic proposition primarily appertaining to faith, and having some special difficulty in being believed."

3. It is most useful and convenient to have the truths of faith divided into Articles, as has been done by the Apostles and by Councils. (a) It facilitates the instruction of the faithful. (b) It preserves uniformity of faith amongst us. (c) It enables us to have a profession of faith in readiness against tyrants and heretics.

The twelve Articles of the Apostles' Creed are those that are in common use, and the best known amongst the faithful.

Concerning the Articles of Faith, it may be asked whether they have increased with time, or whether they have been multiplied?

4. Increase in matters of this kind may be two-fold. (a) By the revelation of a new truth; or (b) by the clearer manifestation of a truth already revealed. This manifestation may be (a) by interpretation; (b) by application; or (c) by the proposition of the truth which the Church has made from time to time to meet the errors of different ages and different places.

Now, in answer to the question, it is necessary to distinguish the various ages of the world. From Adam to Christ the two principal Articles, namely, that God is, and that He is the Remunerator of the good and bad, did not increase in substance, but they did in explanation and application. The dogmas of the Trinity and the Incarnation were made more clearly known, especially in the life-time of our Lord.

Other Articles of Faith increased as often as new revelations were made. New revelations were made to the Prophets and Apostles, and by Christ.

Since the time of the Apostles, although the Articles of Faith have increased by reason of their clearer manifestation in the above three-fold manner, they have not increased as to substance; inasmuch as no new Article has been revealed to the Church since the time of the Apostles. This is proved from the words of Christ, given in St. John's Gospel: "*I will not now call you servants; for the servant knoweth not what his lord doth; but I have called you friends, because all things whatsoever I have* *heard of my Father I have made known to you.*"* And again: "*But when He, the Spirit of truth, is come, He will teach you all truth. For He shall not speak of Himself; but what things soever He shall hear He shall speak: and the things that are to come He shall show you.*"†

The same is also proved by the authority of the Council of Trent, as it clearly teaches, in its 4th and 6th Sessions, that the Catholic doctrine is contained in the Sacred Scriptures and tradition. Thus the definitions of the Church, from time to time, are the declarations and explanations, or applications of truths contained in the deposit of faith; and the notion that these definitions are of the nature of divine revelation or inspiration is not in accordance with Catholic teaching.

THE CREEDS OR SYMBOLS OF FAITH.

5. The chief things which God has revealed, and the truths of salvation, are contained in an abridged form in the formula of faith composed by the Apostles.

This formula is called a *Creed* or *Symbol.* It is called *Creed* from the Latin word *Credo*, I believe, and inasmuch as it contains the principal Articles of our faith or belief. It is called the *Symbol* from the Greek word Σύμβολον, a sign or mark. The recital of the *Symbol* of the Apostles, like the sign of the Cross, is the mark of a Christian, and the pass-word of a soldier of Christ. The word *Symbol* also signifies a collection, an assemblage or reunion, and, in this sense, it is rightly used to signify the abridged *formula* of our faith, that is, a collection of the principal truths which every Christian should know and believe.

"A Creed may therefore be defined as a summary or rule of faith made up of various Articles of faith, and proposed to the faithful as a sign of their profession."

According to Benedict XIV., the *Symbol* of faith is a certain sign by which the faithful are discernable from infidels; the simile being taken from the military sign by which soldiers of different countries are distinguished.

THE APOSTLES' CREED.

6. The first Creed or *Symbol* of faith is that of the Apostles. It is called the *Apostles'* Creed because it was composed by the Apostles before their dispersion, and attributed to them by the

---

* St. John xv. 15.   † Ibid. xvi. 13.

whole Church (some say ten years after our Saviour's Passion,
but they were dispersed long before that time). That we have
the Creed from the Apostles may be proved, first, from the Sacred
Scripture. We find in the Epistles of St. Paul passages which
clearly refer to the Creed. He writes in his Epistle to the
Romans : " *But thanks be to God, that you were the servants of
sin, but have obeyed from the heart unto that* FORM OF DOCTRINE
UNTO *which you have been delivered.*"* And in his Epistle to
Timothy he tells him to " *Hold the* FORM OF WORDS *which thou
hast heard from me in faith, and in the love which is in Christ
Jesus.*"†
St. Paul, in his first Epistle to the Corinthians, gives a short
outline of the Creed in the words : " *For I delivered unto you first
of all which I also received, how that Christ died for our sins
according to the Scriptures ; and that He was buried, and that He
rose again the third day according to the Scriptures.*"‡
Also I may notice from the Acts of Apostles, that St. Philip
required a profession of faith from the Ethiopian before he
admitted him to Baptism: "*And Philip said, if thou believest
with all thy heart, thou mayst* (be baptised). *And he answering
said, I believe that Jesus Christ is the Son of God.*"§
There was, therefore, a *formula* of faith in use in the time of
the Apostles, and used by them, which we hold ; and this must
have been the same as the *Apostles' Creed*, which, tradition tells
us, the Apostles composed and agreed upon as the *formula* of
faith before their dispersion.
It has been in use from the very time of the Apostles even
to our own day. St. Clement, Pope and Martyr, and disciple
of the Apostles, tells us that the Apostles composed the Creed
which the faithful had to profess in his day. St. Irenæus, an
Apostolic man, who lived near the time of the Apostles, and was
taught by the immediate disciples of the Apostles, cites the Creed
and the arrangement of its Articles as the work of the Apostles ;
and Tertullian speaks of it as the *rule of faith* common to all
Christians, and says, that this divine work has preceeded all
heresies.
St. Cyprian, St. Ambrose, St. Jerome, and St. Augustine,
and all the Fathers and Doctors of the Church after them, regard
it as a fact, established by the clearest and most invincible tradition, that the Apostles assembled, and, full of the Holy Spirit,

---

*Rom. vi. 17.   ‡1 Cor. xv. 3, 4.
† 2 Tim. i. 13.   §Acts viii. 37, et seq.

composed this summary or *formula* of Christian doctrine, which has been taught in the Church ever since.

It is not, however, certain that each of the Apostles composed a separate and single Article, as for example, St. Peter, the first ; St. Andrew or St. John, the second ; St. James, the third ; and so on. This, as I have said, is not known with any certainty, and it is not a matter of much importance. What is of importance is, that which we know for certain ; viz. : that the Creed is the work of the Apostles, and that we can consider it the work of God Himself, as the Apostles were inspired by God, and the truths were interiorly dictated by the Holy Spirit, the Teacher of all truth ; those same truths which they had heard from Jesus Christ Himself, and learned from His teaching.

7. This Creed was composed by the Apostles for the following reasons : (*a*) That they might have one and the same rule of faith to propose to the people ; (*b*) that the faithful, individually, might have a short form of faith which they could learn by heart, and remember ; (*c*) that the faithful might be preserved from false teachers, who would try to pervert the faith.

THE DIVISION OF THE CREED.

8. Cardinal Bellarmine divides the Apostles' Creed into two parts. In the first, he places the eight Articles which regard God ; and in the second, the four which regard the Church.

Most other authors, in imitation of the Catechism of the Council of Trent, divide the Creed into three parts, referring each part to one of the Three Persons of the most Holy Trinity. According to this division, the first part treats of the Eternal Father, His Divinity, His Omnipotence, the creation of the world and of mankind, and all things visible and invisible. The second part treats of God the Son, and the marvellous work of Redemption, the Incarnation of this divine Person, His Birth, His Passion, His Death, His Resurrection, and Ascension into heaven, and His coming at the end of time to judge the world.

The third part treats of the Holy Ghost, and the works which He performs through His Spouse, the Church, which are principally these : the Communion of Saints, the Forgiveness of sins, and the Resurrection of the body ; all these in order to the possession of Life Everlasting.

The Apostles' Creed is also divided into twelve Articles, as follows :—

 I. I believe in God the Father Almighty, Creator of heaven and earth.

 II. And in Jesus Christ, His only Son, our Lord ;

 III. Who was conceived by the Holy Ghost, born of the Virgin Mary,

 IV. Suffered under Pontius Pilate, was crucified, dead, and buried.

 V. He descended into hell; the third day He rose again from the dead ;

 VI. He ascended into heaven, and sitteth on the right hand of God the Father almighty ;

 VII. From thence He shall come to judge the living and the dead.

 VIII. I believe in the Holy Ghost,

 IX. The Holy Catholic Church, the Communion of Saints,

 X. The forgiveness of sins,

 XI. The resurrection of the body, and

 XII. Life Everlasting. Amen.

9. " The following Articles of the Creed are commemorated by the Church on special Festivals, viz. :—

Christmas Day. Art. III. Who was conceived by the Holy Ghost, born of the Virgin Mary,

Good Friday. Art IV. Suffered under Pontius Pilate, was crucified, dead and buried ;

Easter. Art. V. He descended into hell ; the third day He rose again from the dead ;

Ascension Day. Art. VI. He ascended into heaven, and sitteth at the right hand of God the Father almighty ;

Advent. Art. VII. From thence He shall come to judge the living and the dead.

Whit Sunday. Art. VIII. I believe in the Holy Ghost,

All Saints Day. Art. IX. The Holy Catholic Church, the Communion of Saints."*

---

*I have taken this arrangement from Gill's *Church Catechism.*

THE OBLIGATIONS OR DUTIES OF CATHOLICS WITH REGARD TO THE CREED.

10. Our duties in regard to the Creed are (besides the obligation of believing firmly the truths it contains, and professing them), to know it, and to recite it often.

(*a*) We should learn the Creed and know it. The Apostles composed it in order that the faithful might learn and know it. The Church has on this account ordered, all along, that her children should be instructed in the Creed, that her Pastors should explain it, and that parents should teach it to their children.

All are therefore obliged to learn and know the Creed. St. Leo says that no one is allowed to be ignorant of it. St. Maximus, in his day, reckoned amongst the greatest enemies of the faith, those amongst the baptized who were ignorant ; and, in our day, we may reckon amongst the greatest enemies of the faith, Catholics who, without any excuse, are ignorant of the doctrine of their religion.

St. Thomas regards, as a mortal sin, wilful ignorance of the Creed. St. Charles Borromæo considered a person ignorant of the Articles of the Creed, at least as to their substance, unworthy of absolution.

(*b*) We should recite the Creed often, in order to keep it impressed upon our memory, to nourish and strengthen our faith, to profess our faith, and preserve it against dangers and temptations. It forms part of our morning and evening prayers.

It is said by priests and religious in the Divine Office before Matins and Prime in the morning, and after Complin in the evening.

St. Ambrose exhorts his sister to recite the Creed often. He advises her to say it every morning and every evening ; and to look into it, as into a mirror, often during the day, that she may therein see her faith, and know whether she be truly faithful.

St. Augustine, in addressing his Catechumens, says to them, " Receive, my dear children, this rule of faith which we call the *Symbol* or *Creed* ; engrave it on your hearts ; carry it about always with you that it may be your defence, and that your memory may be an open book wherein you can read it continually."

The custom of saying the Creed frequently is the means of preserving the faith amongst the people. I believe it was one of the great means which the people of Ireland used, for the preservation of their faith in the days of persecution. The Creed is said amongst her people more often than amongst any other people. They generally say it either before or after the Rosary, and in some places both before and after; and the Creed forms a part of all their public devotions, and the private and family devotions which are said by the people in their own homes.

Besides the Apostles' Creed, the Church makes use of three other Creeds, or Professions of Faith—namely, the Nicene Creed, the Athanasian Creed, and the Profession of Faith, edited by Pope Pius IV. Of these we shall speak in the next chapter.

CHAPTER X.

THE OTHER CREEDS OF FAITH.

1 The Nicene Creed—its history, and its additions to the Apostles' Creed.
—2. Its introduction into the Liturgy of the Mass, and why recited
on certain days.—3. The full text of the Nicene Creed.—4. The
Athanasian Creed—its object, its authorship, and its use in the
Church.—5. The full text of the Athanasian Creed.—6. The Profession
of Faith of Pope Pius IV.—7. A Shorter Form of Profession of Faith.

THE NICENE CREED.

1. ARIUS denied the *divinity* of the Word, and taught that
Christ, the Son of God, was only a creature. Against this heresy
a General Council was held at Nice in Bithynia, A.D. 325, at which
there were 318 bishops present. They resolved to draw up a
Creed to determine, and explain more fully, the faith of the Church
with regard to the Second Article of the Apostles' Creed, *and
in Jesus Christ His only Son our Lord.* The Council expressed
clearly the Catholic faith by these words : *We believe in one
Lord Jesus Christ, the only begotten Son of God, born of the
Father before all ages, God of God, Light of Light, true God
of true God, begotten not made, consubstantial with the Father ;
by Whom all things were made.* This was the principal addition
made by the Council of Nice.

To the profession of faith of the Council of Nice, another
addition was made by the first Council of Constantinople, A.D.
381. In this the error of Macedonius, who was bishop of
Constantinople, and who denied the divinity of the Holy Ghost,
was condemned, and the doctrine of the Church in regard to the
Holy Ghost was more clearly defined and explained in the
following terms : *We believe also in the Holy Ghost, the Lord and
Life-giver ; Who proceedeth from the Father and the Son, Who
together with the Father and the Son is adored and glorified ;
Who spoke by the Prophets.* The Nicene Creed, on this account,
is sometimes mentioned as the Creed of Constantinople.

After the Councils of Nice and Constantinople, all
Catechumens were required to recite this Creed in the Eastern
Church before they were admitted to Baptism

E

2. About the middle of the fifth century it was introduced into the Liturgy of the Mass in the Eastern Church. In the Western Church it was established as part of the Liturgy of the Mass in the Pontificate of Benedict VIII., A.D. 1014, although for many years before that date it was used in the churches of Spain and France. It was not introduced before this time in all the Western Church, for the reason that there was no pressing necessity for it, as the Western Church was not invaded by these heresies up to that time. It is now said in the holy Sacrifice of the Mass after the Gospel, but not on all days.

The reasons for saying the Creed on some days are assigned as three ; namely, mystery, doctrine, or celebration. By reason of the mysteries of our religion, it is said on all the festivals of our Lord, and of His blessed Mother ; by reason of the doctrine of the faith delivered to us by scripture and tradition, it is said on all the Feasts of the Apostles and the Doctors of the Church ; and by reason of celebration, it is said on the Feasts of Patrons and other Feasts of the first and second class, when the people are supposed to attend Mass in greater numbers. These are the general rules laid down by Liturgists as to when the Creed has to be said at Mass.

3. The following is the full text of the Nicene Creed :—

" I believe in one God, the Father Almighty, maker of heaven and earth, and of all things visible and invisible.

" And in one Lord, Jesus Christ, the only begotten Son of God, and born of the Father before all ages ; God of God, Light of Light, true God of true God, begotten, not made ; consubstantial to the Father, by Whom all things were made. Who, for us men, and for our salvation, came down from Heaven, and became incarnate by the Holy Ghost of the Virgin Mary, AND WAS MADE MAN.* He was crucified also for us, suffered under Pontius Pilate, and was buried. And the third day He rose again, according to the Scriptures, and ascended into heaven ; sitteth at the right of the Father ; and He is to come again with glory, to judge both the living and the dead ; of Whose Kingdom there shall be no end.

" And in the Holy Ghost, the Lord and Giver of life, Who proceedeth from the Father and the Son ; Who together with the Father and the Son is adored and glorified ; Who spoke by the prophets. And One, Holy, Catholic and Apostolic Church. I confess one Baptism for the remission of sins. And I expect the

_____

*All kneel at these words, in reverence of Christ's Incarnation.

resurrection of the dead, and the life of the world to come. Amen."

THE ATHANASIAN CREED.

4. This is the Creed attributed to St. Athanasius, and bearing his name. He was the great Bishop of Alexandria, and the great defender of the faith against all the heretics of his day, especially the Arians. It contains a wise, clear and profound exposition of the doctrine of the Holy Trinity and of the Incarnation, and admirably states the doctrine of the one Person and the two natures in Christ. It is called the Creed of St. Athanasius, not that it was composed by that holy bishop, but because it propounds the truths which he so heroically defended, and because it is taken from the writings of this Father. It is generally believed that it is the work of a bishop of Tapse, in Africa, called Vigilius. But some say that it was composed in Latin by Hilary of Arles in Gaul, A.D. 429. At a Council held at Autun in Gaul, in the year 800, we find it mentioned. By Ayton, bishop of Bale, it was prescribed to be said at the Office of Prime by the Clerics. Ratherius, bishop of Verone, desired all the priests of his diocese to learn by heart, not only the Apostles' Creed and the Nicene Creed, but also the Creed of St. Athanasius. Nowadays it forms part of the divine Office, to be said by priests and religious at the Office of Prime on all Sundays.

5. The following is the full text of the Athanasian Creed :—

" Whosoever will be saved, before all things it is necessary that he hold the Catholic faith.

" Which faith, except every one do keep entire and inviolate, without doubt he shall perish everlastingly.

" Now the Catholic faith is this : that we worship one God in Trinity, and Trinity in Unity.

" Neither confounding the Persons, nor dividing the substance.

" For there is one Person of the Father, another of the Son, another of the Holy Ghost.

" But the Godhead of the Father and of the Son and of the Holy Ghost is all one ; the glory equal, the majesty co-eternal.

" Such as the Father is, such is the Son, and such is the Holy Ghost.

" The Father uncreate, the Son uncreate, the Holy Ghost uncreate.

"The Father incomprehensible, the Son incomprehensible, and the Holy Ghost incomprehensible.

"The Father eternal, the Son eternal, the Holy Ghost eternal.

"And yet they are not three eternals, but one eternal.

"As also they are not three uncreates, nor three incomprehensibles; but one uncreate, and one incomprehensible.

"In like manner, the Father is almighty, the Son almighty, and the Holy Ghost almighty.

"And yet they are not three almighties, but one almighty.

"So, the Father is God, the Son God, and the Holy Ghost God.

"And yet they are not three Gods, but one God.

"So, likewise, the Father is Lord, the Son is Lord, and the Holy Ghost is Lord.

"And yet they are not three Lords, but one Lord.

"For like as we are compelled by the Christian verity to acknowledge each Person by himself to be God and Lord :

"So we are forbidden by the Catholic religion to say there are three Gods, or three Lords.

"The Father is made of none, neither created nor begotten.

"The Son is from the Father alone, not made, nor created, but begotten.

"The Holy Ghost is from the Father and the Son, not made, nor created, nor begotten, but proceeding.

"So there is one Father, not three Fathers; one Son, not three Sons; one Holy Ghost, not three Holy Ghosts.

"And in this Trinity there is nothing before or after, nothing greater or less; but the whole three Persons are co-eternal together, and co-equal.

"So that in all things, as is aforesaid, the Unity is to be worshipped in Trinity, and the Trinity in Unity.

"He, therefore, that will be saved, must thus think of the Trinity.

"Furthermore, it is necessary to everlasting salvation that he also believe rightly the Incarnation of our Lord Jesus Christ.

"Now the right faith is, that we believe and confess that our Lord Jesus Christ, the Son of God, is both God and man.

"He is God of the substance of His Father, begotten before the world ; and He is man of the substance of His Mother, born in the world :

"Perfect God and perfect man; of reasonable soul and human flesh subsisting.

"Equal to the Father according to His Godhead ; and less than the Father according to His manhood.

"Who, although He be both God and man, yet He is not two, but one Christ :

"One, not by the conversion of the Godhead into flesh, but by the taking of the manhood unto God.

"One altogether, not by confusion of substance, but by unity of person.

"For as the reasonable soul and the flesh is one man, so God and man is one Christ.

"Who suffered for our salvation, descended into hell, rose again the third day from the dead.

"He ascended into heaven ; He sitteth at the right hand of God the Father Almighty ; from whence He shall come to judge the living and the dead.

"At Whose coming all men shall rise again with their bodies, and shall give an account of their own works.

"And they that have done good shall go into life everlasting ; and they that have done evil, into everlasting fire.

"This is the Catholic faith, which except a man believe faithfully and steadfastly, he cannot be saved.

"Glory be to the Father and to the Son and to the Holy Ghost.

"As it was in the beginning, is now, and ever shall be world without end. Amen."

The Profession of Faith of Pope Pius IV.

6. This Profession of Faith or Creed was published during the Pontificate of Pius. IV., on the 9th Dec., 1564, a short time after the conclusion of the Council of Trent. This Creed, similar to the Nicene Creed in its articles, solemnly expounds the doctrine of the Church against the heresies of those times, those of Luther, Calvin, &c., and their followers.

According to the injunction of the Council, the following persons are required to make this Profession of Faith, namely, all those who are promoted to the Episcopate, to Canonship, to a Benefice to which is attached the cure of souls, or to the government of a monastery ; also all Lectors and Professors are obliged to make this Profession of Faith ; and all converts from the Greek Church, and from Protestantism, have to recite this Creed on

being admitted into the Catholic Church.* The following is the
text of this Creed.

"I, N. (Christian name), with a firm faith believe and profess
all and every one of those things which are contained in the
Creed which the Holy Roman Church maketh use of, namely:—
I believe in one God, the Father Almighty, maker of heaven and
earth, of all things visible and invisible. And in one Lord, Jesus
Christ, the only-begotten Son of God, born of the Father before
all ages. God of God; Light of Light; true God of True God;
begotten, not made, consubstantial to the Father; by Whom all
things were made. Who, for us men, and for our salvation, came
down from heaven, and was incarnate by the Holy Ghost of the
Virgin Mary, AND WAS MADE MAN. He was crucified also for us,
under Pontius Pilate, He suffered and was buried, and the third
day He rose again according to the Scriptures. He ascended
into heaven, and sitteth at the right hand of the Father; and He
shall come again with glory to judge the living and the dead:
of Whose Kingdom there shall be no end And I believe in the
Holy Ghost, the Lord and Life-giver, Who proceedeth from the
Father and the Son, Who, together with the Father and the Son
is adored and glorified; Who spoke by the Prophets. And I
believe One, Holy, Catholic and Apostolic Church. I confess one
Baptism for the remission of sins; and I look for the resurrection
of the dead, and the life of the world to come. Amen.†

"I most steadfastly admit and embrace the Apostolical and
Ecclesiastical Traditions, and all other observances and constitutions of the same Church.

"I also admit the Holy Scriptures, according to that sense
which our holy Mother the Church has held, and does hold, to
whom it belongs to judge of the true sense and interpretation of
the Scriptures; neither will I ever take and interpret them otherwise than according to the unanimous consent of the Fathers.

"I also profess that there are truly and properly seven
Sacraments of the New Law, instituted by Jesus Christ our
Lord, and necessary for the salvation of mankind, although not
all of them necessary for every one; namely, Baptism, Con-
firmation, the Eucharist, Penance, Extreme Unction, Order and
Matrimony; and that they confer grace; and that of these,
Baptism, Confirmation, and Order, cannot be repeated without

* A few supplementary words were added by Pope Pius IX. to this Creed,
referring to the Supremacy and infallibility of the Roman Pontiff.
† So far this is word for word the Nicene Creed.

the sin of sacrilege. I also receive and admit the received and approved ceremonies of the Catholic Church used in the administration of the aforesaid Sacraments.

"I embrace and receive all and every one of the things which have been defined and declared in the holy Council of Trent, concerning original sin and justification.

"I profess likewise, that in the Mass there is offered to God a true, proper, and propitiatory Sacrifice for the living and the dead; and that in the most holy Sacrament of the Eucharist, there is truly, really and substantially, the Body and Blood, together with the Soul and Divinity of our Lord Jesus Christ, and that there is made a conversion of the whole substance of the bread into the Body, and of the whole substance of the wine into the Blood; which conversion the Catholic Church calls Transubstantiation. I also confess, that under either kind alone, Christ is received whole and entire, and a true Sacrament.

"I steadfastly hold that there is a Purgatory, and that the souls therein detained are helped by the suffrages of the faithful. Likewise that the Saints reigning together with Christ are to be honoured and invocated; and that they offer prayers to God for us, and that their relics are to be held in veneration.

"I most firmly assert that the images of Christ, of the Mother of God ever Virgin, and also of other Saints, ought to be had and retained, and that due honour and veneration are to be given them.

"I also affirm that the power of granting Indulgences was left by Christ in the Church, and that the use of them is most wholesome to Christian people.

"I acknowledge, the Holy, Catholic, Apostolic, Roman Church for the mother and mistress of all Churches; and I promise true obedience to the Bishop of Rome, successor of St. Peter, Prince of the Apostles, and Vicar of Jesus Christ.

"I likewise undoubtingly receive and profess all other things which the Sacred Canons and General Councils, and particularly the holy Council of Trent, and the Ecumenical Vatican Council, have delivered, defined, and declared, and in particular, about the supremacy and infallible teaching of the Roman Pontiff. And I condemn, reject, and anathematize all things contrary thereto, and all heresies which the Church has condemned, rejected, and anathematized.

"I, N. (Christian name), do, at this present, freely profess and sincerely hold this true Catholic Faith, out of which no one can be saved; and I promise most constantly to retain and confess the same entire and unstained, with God's assistance, to the end of my life."

7. We have now in use a shorter form of Profession of Faith, authorised by the Holy See, for the whole of Christendom, and which is the form used constantly in Rome for the reception of Protestants and Schismatics into the Catholic Church.

The following is the text of this short form of Profession of Faith.

" I, (name), son (or daughter) of (name and surname of the father), born in (place of birth, and whether married or single), kneeling before you, Rev. Father, duly authorized by the Bishop of (name), having before my eyes the holy Gospels which I touch with my hand, and knowing that no one can be saved without that faith which the Holy, Catholic, Apostolic, Roman Church holds, believes, and teaches, against which I grieve that I have greatly erred, inasmuch as I have held and believed doctrines opposed to her teaching.

" I, now enlightened by divine grace, profess that I believe the Holy, Catholic, Apostolic, Roman Church to be the only true Church established on earth by Jesus Christ, to which I submit myself with my whole heart. I believe all the Articles that She proposes to my belief, and I reject and condemn all that She rejects and condemns, and I am ready to observe all that She commands me, and especially I profess that I believe—

"One only God, in three Divine Persons, distinct from, and equal to, each other, that is to say—the Father, the Son, and the Holy Ghost ;

" The Catholic doctrine of the Incarnation, Passion, Death, and Resurrection of our Lord Jesus Christ, and the Hypostatic (personal) union of the two natures, the divine and the human ; the divine maternity of the Most Holy Mary, together with her Immaculate conception and most spotless virginity ;

"The true, real, and substantial presence of the Body, together with the Soul and Divinity, of our Lord Jesus Christ in the most Holy Sacrament of the Eucharist;

" The seven Sacraments instituted by Jesus Christ for the salvation of mankind ; that is to say—Baptism, Confirmation, Eucharist, Penance, Extreme Unction, Order, Matrimony ;

" Purgatory, the Resurrection of the Dead, Everlasting life ;

" The Primacy, not only of honour, but also of jurisdiction of the Roman Pontiff, successor of St. Peter, Prince of the Apostles, Vicar of Jesus Christ ;

" The veneration of Saints and of their images ;

"The authority of the Apostolic and Ecclesiastical Traditions, and of the Holy Scriptures, which we must interpret and understand only in the sense which our Holy Mother, the Catholic Church, has held and holds;

"And everything else that has been defined and declared by the Sacred Canons, and by the General Councils, especially by the Council of Trent, and by the Ecumenical Vatican Council.

"With a sincere heart, therefore, and with unfeigned belief, I detest and abjure every error, heresy and sect, opposed to the said Holy, Catholic and Apostolic Roman Church. So help me God, and these, His holy Gospels, which I touch with my hand."

The Author of "Catholic Belief" proposes a short Form or Profession of Faith to be used only in cases of very grave and urgent necessity; as Theologians teach, that in case of an urgent necessity, as of grave illness, a short comprehensive Form may be used in receiving Converts into the Church. This Form may be as follows:—

"I, (name), do sincerely and solemnly declare that, having been brought up in the Protestant Religion (*or other Religion as the case may be*), but now, by the grace of God, having come to the knowledge of the Truth, I firmly believe and profess all that the Holy Catholic and Roman Church believes and teaches, and I reject and condemn whatever she rejects and condemns."

THE APOSTLES' CREED.

I SHALL give for the explanation of the Creed, the text of the Nicene Creed together with that of the Apostles' Creed.

ARTICLE I.

APOSTLES' CREED.	NICENE CREED.
"I believe in God the Father Almighty, Creator of heaven aud earth."	"I believe in one God, the Father Almighty, Maker of heaven and earth, *and of all things visible and invisible.*"

By this Article we profess our faith in one God, and in the three Divine Persons, one of whom is named in particular; and we also profess that this Almighty God, of His own power, has created (that is, made out of nothing) heaven and earth and all things that are in them.

In this Article we do not say, "I believe in a God," or "I believe God," but, "I believe in God"; because to believe *in a God* is simply to believe that there is a God, which the devils do, and tremble. To *believe God* is simply to believe His words, and submit our understanding to His. To *believe in God* means not only that there is a God, and that we believe His Word and submit to Him our intellect. but it means likewise to give Him our whole hearts, and offer our entire beings to Him in the words of the Psalmist, "*Lord, what have 1 in heaven, and besides Thee what do I desire upon earth ?   Thou art the God of my heart and my portion for ever.*" *

---

* Psalm lxxii. 25, 26.

SECTION 1.   (ARTICLE I.)

THE NAME OF GOD AND HIS NATURE OR ESSENCE.

1. The Name of God.—2. The Nature of God.—3. Three revelations regarding the nature of God.—4. Errors condemned by the Vatican Council in regard to the existence and nature of God.

THE NAME OF GOD.

1.   God, properly speaking, can have no name ; for as He is one, and not subject to those individual qualities which distinguish men, and on which the different names given to them are founded, He needs not any name to distinguish Him from others, or to mark a difference between Him and any, since there is none like Him.   Hence, when Moses asked His name, He answered : I AM WHO AM : *He said, Thus shalt thou say to the children of Israel, He who is, hath sent me to you.**   The names, therefore, which we ascribe to Him, are descriptions or epithets which express our sense of His divine perfections, in terms necessarily ambiguous, because they are borrowed from human life and conceptions, rather than true names which justly represent His nature.†

God is in English the common name for the Supreme Being. It is derived from the German *Gott*, which is allied with *gut*—good.

The Hebrews designated God by various names, such as *El*, which means *might* or *strength*; *Eloah* or *Elohim*, which signifies *lord* and *master*.   Elohim is the plural of Eloah, and is more frequently used, for which reason some understand it to include the Trinity in its meaning ; but it is used here for the purpose of enlarging and intensifying the idea expressed in the singular.   It is the plural of magnitude.   Taken in its full meaning, Elohim designates God as the infinitely great and glorious One, having in Himself all divine perfections in their manifold variety of powers and operations.

Adonai, the Hebrew word for *Lord*, is frequently substituted for the name of God in the Hebrew Scriptures.

---

* Exod. iii. 14. † See Calmet's Dictionary. *God.*

Jehovah is the name of God in most frequent use in the Hebrew Scriptures. Both Adonai and Jehovah are translated in the English Bible as *Lord.*

Jehovah is the ineffable and mysterious name of God by which He revealed Himself to Moses. It means the self-existent, and He who gives being and existence to others. This name was pronounced only by the high-priest, and that, once a year, when he entered into the Holy of Holies.

It is said by Calmet that "the Jews, after the captivity of Babylon, out of superstitious respect for this holy name, ceased to repeat it, and forgot its true pronunciation." He also is of opinion that the LXX, or seventy Interpreters or Translators, were not accustomed to pronounce it, since they generally render it Κύριος, as our English—*the Lord.*

The modern Hebrews affirm that Moses, by virtue of the word Jehovah engraven on his rod, performed all his miracles; and that Christ also, while in the temple, obtained this ineffable name, and performed all His miracles through it. They add, that we might do as much as they did, if we could attain the perfect pronunciation of that name; and they flatter themselves, that the Messiah, whom they erroneously expect, will teach them this secret.

The same author gives us the characteristics of this name, to show its full import and signification: (*a*) Although it signifies the state of being, yet it forms no verb. (*b*) It never assumes a plural form. (*c*) It does not admit an article, or take an affix. (*d*) Neither is it placed in a state of construction with other words, though other words may be in construction with it. It seems to be a compound of *essence*, and *always existing*; whence the word eternal appears to express its import; or as it is rendered in its full meaning, *He who is, and who was, and who is to come*; that is eternal, as the Schoolmen speak, both *a parte ante* and *a parte post.*

THE NATURE OF GOD

2. In answer to the question in the Catechism: "What is God?" it is said, "God is the Supreme Spirit, who alone exists of Himself, and is infinite in all His perfections."

We therefore understand by God a Spiritual Being, existing of Himself from all eternity, everywhere present, of infinite power, knowledge, and holiness; Creator of heaven and earth, and Sovereign Lord of all things.

The nature and the essence of God is beyond the power of our mind. He is incomprehensible. For this reason St. Paul says : *Who only hath immortality, and inhabiteth light inaccessible, whom no man hath seen or can see.**

But if we cannot, ourselves, speak of God in a just and worthy manner, let us hear how God speaks of Himself in the Holy Scriptures ; and let us direct our thoughts and our language by the revelations which He has made to us.

3. We have principally three revelations concerning the nature of God.

The first was made to Moses, when this great legislator received from God the commission to lead the Children of Israel out of Egypt into the land of Canaan. When Moses asked what answer he was to give, should the Children of Israel demand by what authority he acted ; *Lo,* he says, *I shall go to the Children of Israel, and say to them, the God of your fathers hath sent me to you. If they should say to me, What is His name ? what shall I say to them ? God said to Moses,* I AM WHO AM. *He said, Thus shalt thou say to the Children of Israel :* HE WHO IS *hath sent me to you.*

This revelation tells more than any other, that in which the essence of God consists, namely, His *asseity* (self existence) or His being of Himself—*a se. He always was, He is, and always will be.* It is this which we first apprehend in God, and which cannot flow from any of His other perfections. It is that from which all other perfections flow, and are more easily understood as belonging to Him ; and it is that which primarily and essentially distinguishes God from every other being : God is of Himself self-existent ; all others are from Him.

The divine essence may therefore be said to consist in the *asceitas,* or His being *a se* (self-existent), rather than in any other perfection. It is true that God is infinite, but infinity belongs to all His perfections, and is rather the mode of their being than anything constituting them. Again, God is the highest intelligence, but He *must be* before He can be thought of as understanding or exercising intelligence. Hence, in the words, *I am who am,* God makes known to us that which primarily constitutes His divine essence after our manner of knowing Him.

The second revelation, by which God manifests His nature, is included in that which Christ refers to in St. John's Gospel (cap. xiv. 6.) when He says *I am the life.* This revelation is not

---

* 1 Tim. vi. 16.

made, in words, at the first creation, but God makes it by a very
significant act in the formation of man : *" And the Lord God formed
man of the slime of the earth ; and breathed into his face the breath
of life ; and man became a living soul."** From this we form the
notion that God is *Life.* We, as well as other men, live, but we
are not *life,* we have only a *breath* of life in us, a life which is not
our own, but which we have received from God.

The third revelation of the nature of God is that given by
our divine Saviour, in His conversation with the Samaritan
woman, at the fountain or well of Sichar. *God is a spirit,* He
says.†

We thus learn that God has no body, nor the form, size,
colour, or any other qualities of bodies, and, therefore, He cannot
be seen. He is pure intelligence, and in no sense composed of
parts ; and hence, the Council of the Vatican declared—" The
Holy, Catholic, Apostolic, Roman Church believes and professes
that there is One true and living God...... Who, being a *spiritual
substance,* One absolutely simple and immutable, must be regarded as really and essentially distinct from the world."

Dr. Lingard, in his Catechism says : " We are not to question
His existence because we see Him not. Matter alone is the
object of sight ; and yet we continually believe in the existence
of immaterial, and therefore invisible beings. When I speak to
another man, it is not to his body, or to any visible part of his
body, that I address myself, but to something invisible, which I
believe to dwell in that body, though I cannot see it. That
something is the soul, which, being a spirit, is invisible. In the
same manner, God, being a Spirit, cannot be seen with the eyes
of the body."

4. In accordance with this explanation of the nature of
God, and in confirmation of the doctrine, we have the following
errors condemned by the Vatican Council :

" If any one deny that there is one true and only God,
Creator and Lord of all things, visible and invisible : let him be
anathema.

" If any one dare to affirm that there is nothing outside
matter : let him be *anathema.*"‡

" If any one say that there is only one and the same substance of God and all the other things : let him be *anathema.*

" If any one say that finite things, whether corporal or

---

*Gen. ii. 7.   †St. John iv. 24.   ‡*Const. Dei Filius*, c, 1.

spiritual, or at least spiritual, are emanations of the divine substance : let him be *anathema.*

"Or that the divine essence, by its own manifestation or evolution, becomes all things—

"Or in fine, that God is the universal and indefinite Being, Who, in determining Himself, constitutes the universality of things in genus, species and individuals : let him be *anathema.*"*

This, then, is the faith of the Church in regard to the nature of God : He is a Spirit, subsisting and existing by and of Himself and distinct from all other things.

We shall be able to learn more of the nature and essence of God from the explanation of His attributes and perfections. After explaining the meaning of His name, and what that name implies, we come to the consideration of the existence of God; namely, that such a Being exists.

---

*Const. Dei Filius, o. l. n. 1-4.

SECTION 2. (ARTICLE I.)

THE EXISTENCE OF GOD.

1. Human knowledge can come with certainty to the knowledge of the existence of God.—2. The proofs of the existence of God are *a posteriori* arguments, that is, from the effects to the cause.—3. The first argument may be taken from the fact that things *exist.*—4. The second argument is from *motion* : existing things move.—5. The third is taken from *Life.*—6. The fourth from the order which we observe in the Universe.—7. Three arguments in favour of the existence of God taken from the spiritual order, namely, *intelligence, heart,* and *will.*—8. No one can be invincibly ignorant of the existence of God.—9. The propositions containing the doctrine of faith in regard to the existence of God.

1. THE human reason, by the consideration of created things, can come, with certitude, to the knowledge that there is one true and only God. God has so manifested Himself in the works of nature, that every nation and people, even the most savage, have ever and always acknowledged a divinity to whom they owed worship.

The proofs of the existence of God are very numerous, and it would, in some sense, be impossible to give them all. The multiplicity of proofs in regard to a well-known truth of this kind would only cause inconvenience, and engender weariness and confusion in our minds. I shall therefore confine myself to a few of the principle arguments or proofs.

In proving the existence of God, by the light of reason, I have first to note that demonstration is two-fold, one called *a priori*, that is, proving the effects by the cause ; the other is called *a posteriori*, that is, proving the cause by the effects. The existence of God cannot be proved by *a priori* arguments, inasmuch as God has no cause, and His existence is absolute and necessary, and not an effect flowing from any cause.

2. Our arguments, therefore, in proof of the existence of God, must all be taken *a posteriori*, that is, deriving from the effects a knowledge of their cause. Having in mind the truth of faith expressed by St. Paul, *Without faith it is impossible to please God : for* HE THAT COMETH TO GOD MUST BELIEVE THAT

He is, *and is a rewarder to them that seek Him,** we may, for the sake of order, arrange the proofs of the existence of God as they may be derived (*a*) from the *material*, and (*b*) from the *spiritual* world.

In the material world or order of things, we can consider these proofs as taken from *existence, motion, life*, and *order*.

EXISTENCE.

3. Matter exists composed of indivisible elements called *atoms*. These atoms have neither life, intelligence, or liberty. If we suppose them existing of themselves, no one could limit them, and they would have all perfections. They depend, therefore, on some one who made them, and this one Being who gave them existence is no other than God, Who exists of Himself, and who is infinitely perfect.

Under this head may also be considered the necessity of a first cause of all things, and this first cause can be no other than God. Also the existence of a necessary Being, inasmuch as contingent things exist. The first cause of all things is God; because a first cause is infinite, and cannot be limited. A necessary Being is also God; because such a Being is infinite, and cannot be destroyed or diminished, because it is *necessary*.

MOTION.

4. Matter cannot put itself in motion, and it requires a motive power to bring about its movements from the state of inertness. To explain the forces and motions which take place in the Universe, it is necessary to refer them to some first all-powerful Agent, to a first universal Mover, Who remains Himself immovable, and such a Being is the infinite and supreme Lord of all things. We see everything changing and moving; and there could be no motion whatever were it not that there exists a first Mover Who is immovable. Because, in motions or movements, we cannot have an infinite series, as the infinite cannot be passed over; and we could not therefore ever arrive at any present motion were the series before it infinite. The first Mover must be a *pure act*, or reality, and an absolutely perfect being, because if He were capable of acquiring or losing anything, He would thereby be capable of motion itself, and not the first Mover immovable.

---

*Heb. xi. 6.

F

LIFE.

5. The most perfect bodies are those that are living, such as plants, animals, and man. But these bodies cannot live of themselves. It is necessary that there be a principle of life distinct from the atoms which constitute these bodies, otherwise all bodies would be alive, stones as well as plants. But that which puts the principle of life into certain bodies must be the fountain of all life, and the first living Being, who is essentially *Life*, and this is no other than God, Whose existence can be proved from the leaves of the trees, the birds of the air, the beasts of the field, and from the body and soul of man.

THE ORDER OR THE ARGUMENT FROM DESIGN.

6. In the whole Universe, and in each of its parts, a wonderful order is established and preserved. All is done according to wise laws, and nothing is left to chance or hazard. The same causes, in the same circumstances, always produce the same effects. Thus, the heat of the sun on the surface of the earth, draws from water the vapours that form the clouds, which, afterwards, send down the rain upon the earth. Plants and animals are produced from the like germs and kind.

Each being has a fixed and determined end, and means proportionate to the attainment of that end. The human body, for example, is a marvellous machine, whose organs are adapted for life, for motion, and for the perception of external things. There is more art in one work of nature than the skill of men can ever equal or reproduce.

The Universe, including this earth and the heavenly bodies, in their movements and revolutions, supposes a plan, a design. Who has conceived and executed this design? It can be no other than an infinite, intelligent cause. As to chance or accident bringing about this admirable order of things, is a matter that is unworthy of consideration. Who would think of the Crystal Palace, with its grand original exhibition, being a work of the fortuitous accumulation of atoms? Or who could suppose an ordinary globe, either of the earth or of the heavens, to be the work of accident or chance?

7. In the *spiritual* order of things we can consider arguments taken from *intelligence*, *heart* and *will*, in order to raise our minds up to God, and to realise His existence.

INTELLIGENCE.

(a) Men have always agreed upon certain truths, as for example, that the whole is greater than its part; everything that is, must have a cause; that it is good to be faithful to one's word, and bad to break a promise, &c. This proves that there is a Supreme Intelligence, who communicates His own light to reasonable beings, and makes them admit these principles. The very light of reason, therefore, through which the human mind thinks and acts, brings to it the knowledge of a higher intelligence, and a more perfect Being: of that Being who is infinitely perfect and intelligent.

THE HEART.

(b) All men aspire to some perfect good, which they cannot find here on earth. They have desires which cannot be satisfied by any created or finite thing. They conceive an ideal truth, an ideal beauty, an ideal good, the possession of which would render them completely happy. Who has put this love into their heart but God—infinite Truth, infinite Beauty, infinite Goodness? There is, then, some Being who has implanted in us this desire of eternal life, this capacity tending towards an object which is infinite, and which alone can satisfy the human heart.

THE WILL.

(c) All men acknowledge that they are bound by a moral law, which commands some things, and forbids others. When they obey this law, they are at rest and happy; when they violate it, they are filled with remorse and interior trouble. There is, therefore, a universal and supreme Legislator, Who obliges the human will to do good, and avoid evil; there is, therefore, a Witness to all our actions, an infallible and inevitable Judge, Who recompenses, or punishes us by peace or torment of conscience. This is God. To this the Royal Prophet alludes when He says: " *The light of Thy countenance, O Lord, is signed upon us: Thou hast given gladness in my heart.*"*

The hand of God, which has engraven on all creatures the name of their Author, has impressed this in an indelible manner on the heart of man. The first thing which we discover in our-

*Ps. iv. 7.

which can be acquired by Him; and because He is a necessary Being, He cannot lose anything which He has; hence, He cannot change.

Mutation may be in a three-fold way: (a) By passing from non-existence to existence, or by beginning to be, or exist, or by ceasing to exist. (b) By receiving or losing some perfection. (c) By operation.

7. God, in this three-fold respect is immutable; for, as He has Himself said, "*I am the Lord, and I change not.*"*

He cannot change as to nature or existence : *I am who am.* From all that has been said concerning the nature of God, we may easily conclude that He is not only immutable in nature as to His existence, but in every other respect. He is a pure act, and the first Mover of all things. He is of Himself, and necessarily exists, and, therefore, cannot pass from non-existence to existence, or *vice versa.* He is infinitely perfect, and, therefore, no change can be effected in Him either by acquiring or by losing any perfection. Neither can He change as to His operations, or His actions, or the reasons of them. Every change of judgment or counsel would imply an imperfection in God, because it would be a sign of inconstancy, or levity, to revoke decrees once made without having some new reason or motive for doing so ; but no new motive or reason can come to Him who knows all things from eternity.

8. There may be a special difficulty in regard to the work of God. The creation of the world is an act of God ; and, it may be asked, was this action in God from eternity? It is certain that the world was created in time, and it is certain that God is immutable, and cannot receive into Himself any new action, as this would be against His simplicity. To explain the difficulty, we may regard, or view, creation (a) inasmuch as it is the action of God ; and in this light it is identified with His omnipotence, and is, therefore, not distinct from God Himself, and is as eternal as His own nature. (b) As to its termination, inasmuch as out of that creative action, and through it, all things began to be. In this sense creation is attributed to God in time, namely when things began to be. But, because of this, no new perfection can be attributed to God, He would be the same infinite and perfect Being even though he had never created or caused anything else. The title of Creator is given to Him in reference to time, because the termination of His creative action is in time.

---

*Mal. iii. 6.

The immutability of God is defined as a dogma of faith by the Council of Nice, as quoted by St. Ambrose,* and also by the Council of Lateran,† in whose profession of faith God is asserted *immutable.*

This attribute is incommunicable, and, in a strict sense, belongs alone to God, because all other things are made by Him, and depend upon Him for their existence. All other things are contingent and finite, and may, therefore, absolutely speaking, receive new perfections, or lose those which they have; and, as they are not gifted with immensity, they may be changed from place to place.

THE ETERNITY OF GOD.

9. God is eternal, that is to say, He has no beginning or end, or succession of instants in His life. If God could have a beginning or end, He would not be a necessary Being; and if any succession of instants could be in His life, He would not be immutable. In His divine life there is neither past, nor future, but all is present, and always the same. By the mouth of the prophet, He has said: "*I, the Lord, I am the first and the last.*"‡ And St. Peter, in his Epistle, signifies this truth: "*But of this one thing be not ignorant, my beloved, that one day with the Lord is as a thousand years, and a thousand years as one day.*"§ And St. Paul, in his Epistle to Timothy, says of God: "*Who only hath immortality.*"‖ The eternity of God is expressed in the Athanasian Creed: "*The Father eternal, the Son eternal, the Holy Ghost eternal; and yet there are not three eternals, but one eternal.*"

10. Let us endeavour to form some correct idea of eternity. It is defined by the Philosopher Boetius: *Interminabilis vitæ tota simul et perfecta possessio*—"An entire, and at once a perfect possession of endless life." This definition is generally admitted, although there are authors who say that eternity is successive duration, or infinite time; but the idea of time and infinitude exclude each other, and the terms are contradictory.

Eternity is duration, because duration is nothing else than the permanence of a thing in being or existence. This permanence or duration is three-fold: (*a*) As to being or existence and operation, which belongs to God alone. And this is the duration which, properly speaking, is called eternity. (*b*) Permanence as to being or existence, but subject to change as to operation. This permanence is called *ævum*, and it belongs to our souls and

---

*De Fide., Lib. 1. c. 18, n. 120.   †Cap. firmiter.   ‡Isa. xli. 4.
§2 St. Peter iii. 8.   ‖1. Tim. vi. 16.

SECTION 3 (ARTICLE I.)

THE PERFECTIONS AND ATTRIBUTES OF GOD.

1. The common notion of the Deity, and the particulars in which it consists.
—2. The perfections of God, and what is meant by them.—
3. Three sorts of perfections.—4. The difference between perfections
as applied to creatures and to God, and the manner in which all
perfections of creatures are contained in God.—5. The first of the
divine perfections, namely, *Aseitas* or self-existing.—6. The Attributes of God, and how are they distinguished?—7. The unity of
God, and why God is one.—8. The simplicity of God, and the sense
in which God is said to be simple.—9. Errors opposed to the simplicity of God.

1. GOD, as we have said in the preceeding Sections, is described as, *He who is*; that is to say, He is self-existing, and
cannot but exist. He is necessary. He has the plenitude of
being. He is infinite, that is, without limits. He is perfect, that
is, wanting in nothing. In God there is no shadow, even of imperfection, for He possesses all perfections in an infinite degree.
Deus est id quo magis aut melius cogitari non potest : God is that,
than which a greater or a better cannot be thought of. (St.
Anselm.)

Before explaining the Attributes of God, it is necessary to
understand what is meant by saying that God is infinitely perfect. This means that God, in an infinite degree, possesses all
imaginable perfections.

THE PERFECTIONS OF GOD.

2. The word *perfection* excludes the idea of imperfections
and faults of any kind, and includes the idea of gifts or qualities.
In a general way, that is said to be perfect which is com-

---

in cognoscendo. Nam, ut ait St. Thomas (1 P. q. 88, a 3). ' Deus non
est primum quod a nobis cognoscitur sed magis per creaturas in Dei cog-
nitionem pervenimus'." (a). Lafosse, tr. *de Deo.* q. 1. a. L; et Schouppe
Elementa Theol. Dog. tr. 5., cap. 1. n. 39 et 44.

plete, and has all that its nature requires. In this sense, some created things may be said to be perfect; as, for example, a man whose body is entire and without spot or mark, and whose soul has all its faculties sound and healthy, may be said to be perfect, inasmuch as he has all that his nature requires or demands.

Since, however, God is the absolute Being, and exists of Himself, and is the Being from whom all others proceed as from their first cause, in order that He be perfect, it is necessary that He should have all the perfections and all the realities that can be thought of in creatures.

3. There are three sorts of perfections, according to our way of understanding them. The first are those which involve no imperfection in their concept, and are better to have than not to have; these are called by Theologians *simpliciter simplices*. The second are called *pure simplices*; and those do not involve in their notion any imperfection, but their possession does not make one being better than another, nor their non-possession make one being worse than another. Such are the relations which exist in the three Divine Persons. The third (*secundum quid simplices*) are those which, in their notion, involve an imperfection, and are opposed to a greater perfection; thus, seeing, hearing, reasoning, &c., may be said to be perfections of this kind. It would be better for some beings to have them than not to have them; but not for every being, inasmuch as they would be an obstacle to greater perfection.

4. Perfection in creatures is not the same as their essence and nature, but something superadded to that nature. But as God is a Being absolute and of Himself, whatever is in Him is God, and His perfections are not really distinct from His nature, but one and the same with it. Hence, the perfection of God is one and indivisible, namely, the Divine nature itself. But as our limited capacity cannot understand this one perfect Divine nature, we consider separately, and distinguish from one another the Divine perfections and attributes, that thus we may obtain a better knowledge of our Lord and Creator.

As to the manner in which God possesses the perfections of His creatures, we must remember the distinctions between the perfections that involve no imperfection, and those that do. The former are in God *formally* and really, but in a more eminent manner than they are to be found in creatures; as, for example, goodness, wisdom, &c. The latter, namely those that involve an imperfection, are not really in God as they are in creatures; but they are in Him virtually, inasmuch as He produces them as their first cause, and in a higher and more eminent way He does what these perfections enable creatures to do. Thus, the Royal Prophet has said: "*Qui plantavit aureum non audiet ? aut qui finxit oculum non consideret ?*"* "*He that planted the ear, shall He not hear ? or He that formed the eye, shall He not consider ?* And St. Augustine conveys the same truth by the words *Intelligamus Deum sine loco, ubique totum, sine tempore sempiternum,* &c. "Let us understand that God is everywhere without place, and eternal or everlasting without time."

5. The first divine perfection, according to our manner of speaking, and that which sustains and includes all the others, and which represents the nature of God, is Self-existence, *Aseitas, ens a se*—a Being necessarily existing of Himself. This name gives to the infinite Being that which is proper to Him, and to Him alone, namely, that He exists of Himself, by Himself, and by virtue of His own essence.†

THE ATTRIBUTES OF GOD.

6. The attributes of God are the perfections which are attributed to Him, as if they were *proper* to Him, and hence they are called also, Divine properties,

After the *Aseitas*, the principal attributes of God may be divided into *absolute* and *relative*, as they regard things outside God, or have no reference to, or connection with them.

The following are the absolute attributes which we select out of innumerable others, as to explain in detail the attributes of God would be an endless labour: *Unity, Simplicity, Inte.ligence, Love, Life, Immutability, Eternity, Immensity.*

THE UNITY OF GOD.

7. Although the unity of God is included in the words, *I believe in God*, as expressed in the Apostles' Creed, the Nicene Creed expresses it more explicitly in the words, *I believe in one God.*

---

*Ps. xcii., 9.

†Aseitas et intellectualitas actualis simul requiruntur ad conceptum seu constitutionem essentiæ divinæ. (Schnell. part 1, p. 16.) Etenim essentia metaphysica seu metaphysicum constitutivum ex communi sententia quatuor haec complectitur, necesse est. 1. Ut sit quidpiam intrinsicum enti. 2. Ut ipsum ab quolibet secernat. 3. Ut primo concipiretur. 4. Ut caeterarum omnium perfectionum spetari possit veluti fons et origo. Jam vero quatuor in *aseitate* reperiuntur. Perrone, Tr. *de Deo Uno*, p. 1, o. 3.

Oneness may be taken in a twofold sense. (*a*) *One* means that which is undivided in itself, and distinct from everything else. In this sense, every *individual man* is one, but there are others. The *sun* is one, and there is no other ; but there might have been another. (*b*) *One* may be taken exclusively to signify a being which cannot be numerically multiplied, and which excludes the existence of another equal to itself. It is in this exclusive sense that God is *one*. There is one true and only God, and there cannot be more Gods than one.

No other being can have existence but from God ; and anything that receives its existence from another cannot be God.

There is only one God. This is the first dogma of the Mosaic and of the Christian revelation. It is the first commandment of the law : " *I am the Lord thy God ; thou shalt not have strange Gods before me.*"* " *Hear, O Israel : the Lord thy God is one God.*" †

This is also clear by reason. (*a*) That which is Supreme, or the Infinite Being, cannot have an equal or a superior. (*b*) That which is a simple and pure act cannot be communicated to another. (*c*) It is manifested by the unity and order of worldly or created things. Those things which are opposed and different could not be directed to one end and order unless guided by some *one* Being. God is a God of order, and therefore a God of unity. (*d*)He is the First Cause of all things, and their Last End. Two first causes are unimaginable. It is a contradiction to say that all things depend on One, and yet that more than one independent Being exists. If there were more Gods than one, then all perfection could not be in *One*.

The two Pagan systems of Dualism (two Gods or first principles) and Polytheism (many Gods) are opposed to this attribute of God. Those who taught the former were chiefly the Manicheans ; the arguments that refute Dualism serve as a refutation of Polytheism.

THE SIMPLICITY OF GOD.

8. God is absolutely simple ; that is to say, without any composition. He is not made up of parts.

Composition is threefold, *metaphysical, physical* and *logical. Metaphysical* is that which is made up of *power* (potentiality) and *act* (actuality, *potentia et actus*), *essence* and *existence, nature* and *personality. Physical* is that which is made up of parts really distinct, such as that which results from *matter* and

---

*Exod. xx. 2, 3. †Deut. vi. 4.

form, substance and *accident. Logical* is that which arises from *genus* and *differentia* (specific difference).

Now we cannot admit composition of either kind in God. Physical composition is not in God, because it belongs only to bodies, and God is a pure spirit. *"God is a spirit, and they who adore Him must adore Him in spirit and truth."**

Metaphysical and *Logical* compositions do not belong to God.† In the Sacred Scriptures God is said to be wisdom, justice, the way, the truth, and the life ; and these abstract names are given to Him as subsisting things. It is not said that God has wisdom, justice, &c., which would be required for metaphysical and logical compositions.

This truth may also be proved from the nature of God, and from His attributes. As to His nature. God being (*a se*) of Himself, and a necessary being, is essentially whatever He is. Every composite thing is such, after a certain manner, by accident and by participation. Hence, according to the saying of the Fathers, *God is all or whatever He has* ; that is, whatever is in God, is God. Again, whatever is composed of parts is imperfect, for the parts composing a thing, in mutually perfecting each other, must be supposed in themselves imperfect. In man, for example, the soul has need of the body, and the body of the soul. Neither is the soul perfect without the body, nor the body without the soul ; and hence man, the composition which results from these two imperfect things, is not completely or entirely perfect. God is absolutely perfect, and must therefore be a pure spirit.

God is the first Being, but a composite being would be after its component parts. Hence the Council of Lateran says : *" The essence of God is one substance or simple nature."*

9. Against the simplicity of God, all those err who attribute to God a corporeal nature. These are all idolaters, as those who worship the sun, the moon, or heavenly bodies. Also a sect of men called *Anthropomorphites*, who affirmed that God has a human corporeal form, with the head, hands and feet like us, and that it was in this sense, namely, as to His body, that man was made to the image and likeness of God. Also, those who place a real distinction between the essence and the attributes of God, or between the attributes themselves. And the Pantheists, who say that God is this visible universe, or at least has come forth from it.

---

*St. John iv. 24.

†St. Thomas and the Scholastics expressed this briefly by saying, that in no created thing are essence and existence the same ; and, that every created thing is composed of essence and existence, or of potentiality and actuality. (*Potentia and actus*).

SECTION 4 (ARTICLE I).

NTELLIGENCE, LOVE AND LIFE IN GOD, AND OTHER ABSOLUTE ATTRIBUTES.

1. The Intelligence, Love and Life in God.—2. The Divine intellect, and the extent of the knowledge of God.—3. What is meant by Love as attributed to God, and what is its object?—4. God does not love all things equally; and His love for intelligent beings is different from that which He has for His other creatures.—5. Life as attributed to God, and the sense in which God is Life.—6. What is meant by immutability? —7. God is immutable.—8. The special difficulty in regard to the immutability arising from the work of God, viz., Creation.—9. God is eternal.—10. The idea which we form of eternity, and how it is distinguished from *aevum* and *tempus.*—11. What is meant by immensity, and how distinguished from Omnipresence.—12. God is immense and everywhere present; and in a special manner present: (a) in the souls of the just; (b) in the humanity of Christ; (c) in His temples and Churches; (d) in the assemblies of the faithful; (e) the three Divine Persons present to each other by circuminsession.

1. MAN is endowed with understanding and will. He is capable of knowing truth and loving good; and, it is in this knowledge and in this love that his intellectual life consists. God, who is the Author of man's existence, eminently possesses these attributes. He is in the highest degree *Intelligence, Love* and *Life.* "He knows Himself in an infinite manner as the infinite truth. He loves Himself infinitely as the infinite good. He loves all things that it pleased Him to create, and He lives the most perfect and happy spiritual life."*

The intelligence in God, which is the same as the divine Intellect, is nothing else than the divine knowledge, one, infinite and eternal. In this divine knowledge, no memory is required, for all things are present to Him; and reasoning or reflection is not required, for this would imply an imperfection in the manner of knowing. Holy Job tells us : " *With Him is wisdom and strength, he hath counsel and understanding.*"†

---

*l'Abbé A. R. Moulin, *Premier Article du Symbole.*
†Job xii. 13.

LIFE.

5. The most perfect bodies are those that are living, such as plants, animals, and man. But these bodies cannot live of themselves. It is necessary that there be a principle of life distinct from the atoms which constitute these bodies, otherwise all bodies would be alive, stones as well as plants. But that which puts the principle of life into certain bodies must be the fountain of all life, and the first living Being, who is essentially *Life*, and this is no other than God, Whose existence can be proved from the leaves of the trees, the birds of the air, the beasts of the field, and from the body and soul of man.

THE ORDER OR THE ARGUMENT FROM DESIGN.

6. In the whole Universe, and in each of its parts, a wonderful order is established and preserved. All is done according to wise laws, and nothing is left to chance or hazard. The same causes, in the same circumstances, always produce the same effects. Thus, the heat of the sun on the surface of the earth, draws from water the vapours that form the clouds, which, afterwards, send down the rain upon the earth. Plants and animals are produced from the like germs and kind.

Each being has a fixed and determined end, and means proportionate to the attainment of that end. The human body, for example, is a marvellous machine, whose organs are adapted for life, for motion, and for the perception of external things. There is more art in one work of nature than the skill of men can ever equal or reproduce.

The Universe, including this earth and the heavenly bodies, in their movements and revolutions, supposes a plan, a design. Who has conceived and executed this design? It can be no other than an infinite, intelligent cause. As to chance or accident bringing about this admirable order of things, is a matter that is unworthy of consideration. Who would think of the Crystal Palace, with its grand original exhibition, being a work of the fortuitous accumulation of atoms? Or who could suppose an ordinary globe, either of the earth or of the heavens, to be the work of accident or chance?

7. In the *spiritual* order of things we can consider arguments taken from *intelligence, heart* and *will*, in order to raise our minds up to God, and to realise His existence.

may be applied to God in the same sense as love, although they are, in a way, distinguished from it. Love tends to good absolutely, abstracting from the fact of its possession or non-possession. Joy or pleasure is *quies in bono possesso*—rest in the possession of good. Delight is applied to the good which we have intrinsically united to us; joy or pleasure may be applied to any external good. God delights in His own internal perfection, and rejoices over the good which He communicates to us His creatures. *"For thou lovest all things that are, and hatest none of the things which Thou hast made."**

4. God does not love all things equally. The love of God is the cause of goodness in things; and as all things are not equally good, so His love for all is not equal. Some things are better than others because God wishes them more good, and, therefore, they are more loved by Him.

We have to distinguish the love of God for His intelligent creatures from that which He has for the irrational creatures. The former may be called the love of friendship, and may be mutual; that is, a return of love on the part of His creatures, and only intelligent beings are capable of this return of love.

The love for irrational creatures is a love of complacency; that is, a love of them because they are useful, and serve to manifest God's goodness, without any possibility of a return of love on their part. It is in this sense, also, that our love is directed towards inanimate things and irrational beings.

LIFE.

5. When speaking of the Divine nature, I explained the sense in which we understand the *Life* of God. This may be numbered also amongst His perfections. He is *the way*, and *the truth*, and *the life*. The difference between a living being and one without life is, that the former can move itself, and act by itself, and the latter requires to be moved by another, and does not act of itself. Inasmuch, therefore, as a being acts of itself, so much the more perfectly does it live. Now God not only acts and moves, but is the first Mover and pure Act, and, therefore, the most perfect life belongs to Him.

THE IMMUTABILITY OF GOD.

6. When we say that God is immutable, we mean that He cannot change. Because He is infinitely perfect, there is nothing

*Wisdom xi. 25.

which can be acquired by Him; and because He is a necessary Being, He cannot lose anything which He has; hence, He cannot change.

Mutation may be in a three-fold way: (a) By passing from non-existence to existence, or by beginning to be, or exist, or by ceasing to exist. (b) By receiving or losing some perfection. (c) By operation.

7. God, in this three-fold respect is immutable; for, as He has Himself said, "*I am the Lord, and I change not.*"*

He cannot change as to nature or existence : *I am who am.* From all that has been said concerning the nature of God, we may easily conclude that He is not only immutable in nature as to His existence, but in every other respect. He is a pure act, and the first Mover of all things. He is of Himself, and necessarily exists, and, therefore, cannot pass from non-existence to existence, or *vice versa.* He is infinitely perfect, and, therefore, no change can be effected in Him either by acquiring or by losing any perfection. Neither can He change as to His operations, or His actions, or the reasons of them. Every change of judgment or counsel would imply an imperfection in God, because it would be a sign of inconstancy, or levity, to revoke decrees once made without having some new reason or motive for doing so; but no new motive or reason can come to Him who knows all things from eternity.

8. There may be a special difficulty in regard to the work of God. The creation of the world is an act of God; and, it may be asked, was this action in God from eternity? It is certain that the world was created in time, and it is certain that God is immutable, and cannot receive into Himself any new action, as this would be against His simplicity. To explain the difficulty, we may regard, or view, creation (a) inasmuch as it is the action of God; and in this light it is identified with His omnipotence, and is, therefore, not distinct from God Himself, and is as eternal as His own nature. (b) As to its termination, inasmuch as out of that creative action, and through it, all things began to be. In this sense creation is attributed to God in time, namely when things began to be. But, because of this, no new perfection can be attributed to God, He would be the same infinite and perfect Being even though he had never created or caused anything else. The title of Creator is given to Him in reference to time, because the termination of His creative action is in time.

---

*Mal. iii. 6.

The immutability of God is defined as a dogma of faith by the Council of Nice, as quoted by St. Ambrose,[*] and also by the Council of Lateran,[†] in whose profession of faith God is asserted *immutable*.

This attribute is incommunicable, and, in a strict sense, belongs alone to God, because all other things are made by Him, and depend upon Him for their existence. All other things are contingent and finite, and may, therefore, absolutely speaking, receive new perfections, or lose those which they have; and, as they are not gifted with immensity, they may be changed from place to place.

THE ETERNITY OF GOD.

9. God is eternal, that is to say, He has no beginning or end, or succession of instants in His life. If God could have a beginning or end, He would not be a necessary Being; and if any succession of instants could be in His life, He would not be immutable. In His divine life there is neither past, nor future, but all is present, and always the same. By the mouth of the prophet, He has said: "*I, the Lord, I am the first and the last.*"[‡] And St. Peter, in his Epistle, signifies this truth: "*But of this one thing be not ignorant, my beloved, that one day with the Lord is as a thousand years, and a thousand years as one day.*"[§] And St. Paul, in his Epistle to Timothy, says of God: "*Who only hath immortality.*"[||] The eternity of God is expressed in the Athanasian Creed: "*The Father eternal, the Son eternal, the Holy Ghost eternal; and yet there are not three eternals, but one eternal.*"

10. Let us endeavour to form some correct idea of eternity. It is defined by the Philosopher Boetius: *Interminabilis vitæ tota simul et perfecta possessio*—"An entire, and at once a perfect possession of endless life." This definition is generally admitted, although there are authors who say that eternity is successive duration, or infinite time; but the idea of time and infinitude exclude each other, and the terms are contradictory.

Eternity is duration, because duration is nothing else than the permanence of a thing in being or existence. This permanence or duration is three-fold: (*a*) As to being or existence and operation, which belongs to God alone. And this is the duration which, properly speaking, is called eternity. (*b*) Permanence as to being or existence, but subject to change as to operation. This permanence is called *ævum*, and it belongs to our souls and

---

to the Angels. It is the same as their immortality. *Ævum* is also said to be in regard to beings who have a beginning and will have no end. (c) The succession of things, rather than any permanence as to their being and their operations, as in material substances, and especially in *accidents*. This succession or duration is called *time*.

Eternity is therefore to be distinguished from *avum* and time, not only because it has neither beginning nor end, but because it is not subject to mutation. It is *tota simul et perfecta possessio*. Eternity is infinite, because it is the duration of an infinite being. It is simultaneous and in act always present, because it is the duration of an immovable and immutable God. It contains eminently and surpasses all the duration of time, and is present to every moment of it. No *before* or *after* in eternity. It is wholly and entirely present to every part of time, without ceasing to be present wholly to every other part.

God alone is eternal. As St. Augustine says : "He alone has no beginning." Other things are said to be eternal, because they are immortal, and participate in everlasting life. But because they may be changed or destroyed by God at any moment, they cannot, strictly speaking, be said to be eternal. Although some things may be, as to their substance, immortal, inasmuch as they will never have an end or cease to live, nevertheless they all had a beginning except God, Who alone is eternal.

THE IMMENSITY OF GOD.

11. The immensity of God is that attribute by which He is substantially present in each and everything ; as the human soul is whole in the entire body, and whole in each part of it. If God were not present everywhere, He would be circumscribed by limits, and would therefore be deprived of one of His infinite perfections.

This immensity, as defined by Theologians, is the aptitude or perfection by which God, of His own nature, is intimately present in everything by His essence.

Immensity is not exactly the same as Omnipresence or Ubiquity. God was immense before He created ; but after Creation, by His Immensity, He is present in everything and in every place. His immensity therefore signifies more than His omnipresence.

12. God may be considered present in many ways. (a) God is everywhere by His *power*, as a King in his kingdom. (b) He

is everywhere by His *presence*, as a King in his court or hall. (c) He is everywhere by His *substance*, as a King on his throne. He is substantially present in everything, without being circumscribed by any space. He is whole in everything, in every place, and yet without place.

Besides His general presence with all His creatures, God is in a special manner present to some :

(a) God, as a friend, is present by His grace in the souls of the just. "*If any one love Me, the Father will love him ; and we shall come to him, and take up our abode with him.*"*

(b) He is specially present in Christ by reason of the hypostatic or personal union ; and according to the words of St. Paul : "*For in him dwelleth all the fulness of the Godhead corporally.*"†

(c) In some places He is specially present, as in His temples. Thus Jacob spoke after his vision : "*Indeed the Lord is in this place ; and I knew it not. And trembling, he said, How terrible is this place ! this is no other but the house of God, and the gate of heaven.*"‡ He is present in a more special manner in heaven, according to the words of Isaias : "*Heaven is my throne, and the earth my footstool.*"§

(d) He is also present, in a special manner, by His assistance at the assemblies of the faithful in prayer, at the Councils of the Church, and with the Sovereign Pontiff when teaching the whole Church.

(e) The three divine Persons are most intimately present with each other, by a special in-dwelling called circuminsession ; according to the words of Christ : "*I am in the Father, and the Father in me.*"

God is present, in these several ways, with particular persons, and in particular places, and by particulars means ; but by His immensity He is everywhere. "*Shall a man be hid in secret places, and I not see him, saith the Lord ? Do not I fill heaven and earth, saith the Lord ?*"= "*That they should seek God, if happily they may feel after Him or find Him, although He be not far from every one of us. For in Him we live and move and*

---

*St. John.　　　　†1 Coll. ii. 9.
‡Gen. xxviii, 16, 17.　　§Isa. lxvi. L.
=Jer. xxiii. 24.

have our being." Immensity is a perfection of the Deity alone. All things depend on the Will of God; all things are governed by His direction; by His power 'hey are moved. Therefore He must be intimately present with them, as the power of God and His operation are not distinct from His substance or essence.

SECTION 5 (ARTICLE I.)

THE RELATIVE ATTRIBUTES OF GOD.

1. The relative Attributes of God—goodness, power and providence.—
2. The sense in which God is free to create or not to create.—
3. Goodness in its three-fold sense—natural, moral and relative.—
4. This three-fold goodness is in God in the highest degree.—5. The answer to the difficulty : why it is that so many evils exist, God being infinitely good ?—6. The meaning of God's Omnipotence.—7. The meaning of the word Almighty, and the extent of God's dominion over all His creatures.—8. Why God is called Omnipotent, and the object of His Omnipotence.—9. What is meant by the Providence of God ? —10. God disposes and governs all things by His Providence.— 11. The special Providence of God for rational beings, and the answer to the difficulty, why the just are afflicted, and the wicked prosper in this world ?

1. AFTER explaining the absolute Attributes of God; namely, those divine attributes that are thought of in Him, without any reference to creatures, I have now to explain some of the relative attributes, or those divine perfections which have reference to creatures. Of these, I select the following : *The goodness of God, His power and His providence.*

God has in Himself the *ideal* of all things. His essence can be represented in His creatures, and His creatures are all formed according to the designs which He has of them in His divine mind : as an artist has in his mind the model of those things which he afterwards reproduces in his works.

2. God is under no necessity to realize any of these ideas outside Himself. Being in Himself infinitely perfect and infinitely happy, He is sufficient for Himself, and, therefore, He has no need of things other than Himself. He is and was free to create or not to create. We must give that perfect freedom to God in His external works, for we cannot deny to Him full liberty, which is a perfection we ourselves enjoy. By the liberty of God is meant, that His Will is perfect and independent. It is independent, because God acts of Himself, and is not necessitated or influenced by any external cause. It is perfect, because

whatever is in God is perfect. The freedom of His Will must not be extended to those things that would be against the perfections of God, and, therefore, He is not free in His internal actions, which are one and the same thing as God Himself; and there is not in Him the power of evil, or of doing what is wrong, as this does not belong to liberty, but rather implies something wanting. All His external actions are free, although His decrees in regard to them are eternal. As we do not know fully the nature of human liberty, we must not pretend to know all about the freedom of God in His actions, and, therefore, it is sufficient to bear in mind that God's Will is perfect and independent, and also perfectly free, according to the doctrine of faith : " *The Lord is the God to whom revenge belongeth; the God of revenge hath acted freely.*"*

The Goodness of God.

God's goodness determined Him to create, in order to manifest His perfections through His creatures. Created things participate, more or less, of the divine perfections, according to the degree of entity and goodness that He has impressed upon them. He has made them, as it were, copies or pictures of His own beauty, more or less perfect, according to the designs of His wisdom.

3. Goodness is three-fold. It may be *natural, moral,* and *relative. Natural* goodness consists in the very nature and perfection of a thing, by which it is desirable (*quod est appetibile*).

Moral goodness consists in the conformity of the will with right reason, or with the law of God, viz. : A man who lives according to the dictates of right reason and the law of God, is called good. This goodness is to be found only in rational creatures, and those gifted with a will. In God, it is His incomparable Sanctity.

Relative goodness is the inclination or desire to impart good to others, and to raise them up to a state of perfection. In God, it is His will for the salvation of men, and to render them blessed and happy. This goodness is known by different names, according to the various ways in which it is manifested. When it imparts good to creatures who cannot of themselves merit it, it is called grace; when it is extended to the wretched and the needed, it is called mercy; and when it tolerates evil, and punishment is withheld from evil-doers, it is called patience or longanimity.

*Ps. xciii.

4. This three-fold goodness is in God, and in the highest degree : therefore God is good. *" Give glory to the Lord, for He is good, for His mercy endureth for ever."** *" Thou art just, O Lord, and thy judgment is right."*† *" None is good but God alone."*‡ And St. James says : *" Every best gift, and every perfect gift, is from above, coming down from the Father of lights, with Whom there is no change, nor shadow of alteration."*§

God's goodness follows from what we have said about His perfection ; and it is unnecessary to develop more in detail the ways in which He communicates goodness to His creatures.

5. In connection with the goodness of God, it may be asked, Why it is, as God is infinitely good, that so many evils exist ? To this, the usual answer may be given : Evil is nothing else than the want (*carentia*) of good, or of some perfection ; and because it is nothing positive, but a want of something, it is not from God, but it arises from the very nature of created things. Finite and contingent things cannot have all perfections ; and inasmuch as they have wants or defects, they may be said to be bad, as the whole reason of evil consists in a defect or want. Moral evils are the works of men ; and their malice arises from their defect or want of conformity to right reason, and the law of God.

Physical evils, inasmuch as they indicate a defect, flow from the natural condition or state of created things. Inasmuch as they are positive things, they are good; and inasmuch as they are troublesome to human nature, they are not evils, but salutary penalties for sins, and indications of God's goodness and clemency ; for *He afflicts those whom He loves.*

This short explanation ought to suffice to account for the origin of evil. We cannot, as the Manicheans imagined, have two principles of things : one of good, and the other of evil. All things are good as to their entity, and have God for their Author ; evil is of its own nature a nothing and a defect, and cannot, therefore, be attributed to God as such, but to the imperfections of His creatures.

THE OMNIPOTENCE OF GOD.

6. God is Almighty and all-powerful, that is, He can do all that is possible, as His power is as infinite as His essence. He works or acts with independence, and does not stand in need either of matter, or of any instrument. The beings He wishes

---

*Ps. cvi. 1.   †Ps. cxviii. 137.
‡St. Luke xviii.   §St. James i. 17.

to produce, He takes not out of His own substance, or out of any other substance, but out of nothing; He makes them from nothing, that is, by a simple act of His Will He causes them to come into existence from a state of pure possibility.*

7. We may include under this head the *dominion* which God has over all; and the *power* by which He can do all things. The word *Almighty* is sometimes interpreted, *The Lord of Hosts.* This power of God may be considered (a) as the right of making and framing anything which He wills, and in the manner He wills; (b) the right of having and possessing all things so made by Him, as His own, properly belonging to Him as their Lord and Master, by virtue of direct dominion. This right is (1) *independent* both in its origin, for God receives no authority from any, because He has all power originally in Himself, and has produced all things by the authority of His free will alone; and in its exercise, as being liable to no direction or regulation by any other, nor to the exaction of any account of His administration as He is unlimited, absolute and supreme, and the fountain whence all dominion is derived. (2) This right is *infinite* in its object, as shown by those names attributed to God : *Lord of heaven, Lord of the whole earth, Lord of heaven and earth, King of kings, and Lord of lords. Infinite* in the manner in which He possesses that power in Himself, that is, subjectively considered; and infinite in duration, which must be eternal as things are immortal. (3) He has the right to the *use* of all things in His possession, and this, by virtue of His absolute dominion over them. God, indeed, is all-sufficient and infinitely happy in, and of Himself; and He cannot receive any real benefit from the creature; yet, He rejoiceth at the effects of His wisdom, power and goodness, and taketh delight in the works of His hands. Thus doth He order and dispose of all things, to His own glory, which redounds from the demonstration of His attributes.

8. Besides dominion, we have to consider the *power* of the Almighty. God is called *Omnipotent*, (a) because all power whatsoever, in any creature, is derived from Him ; (b) because there can be no resistance made to His power, no opposition to His Will ; and, (c) because His own active power, as I have said above, extends itself to all things ; nor is there anything imagi-nably possible which He cannot do.

The object of God's power is whatsoever is simply and absolutely possible *in itself,* such that it may be ; and *so* possible

---

*l'Abbé Moulin.

is everything which does not imply a contradiction. Again, whatever implies a contradiction is impossible. For, that is said to imply a contradiction which, if it were, it would necessarily follow that the same thing would be and not be at the same time, and in the same respect ; which is impossible, and consequently not within the power of God, because *impossibility* is a contradiction of all power : (*a*) In respect to the *object* that implies a contradiction which, plainly and in terms, signifies a repugnancy, and so destroys itself, viz., as for the same thing to be or not to be, to have been and not to have been. (*b*) In respect to the *agent*, that implies a contradiction which is repugnant to His essential perfection ; for since every action flows from the essence of the agent, whatsoever is totally repugnant to that essence must involve a contradiction as to the agent ; viz., God cannot sleep, want, die, being essentially spiritual, all-sufficient, self-existent. Nor can that be a diminution of His omnipotence, the contrary whereof would be a proof of His *impotence*. Thus, it is impossible for God to *lie*, because a lie is repugnant to the perfection of *veracity*, which is essential to God, as necessarily following from His infinite *knowledge*. That knowledge cannot be deceived, and His infinite *sanctity* which cannot deceive. It being, therefore, manifestly contradictory to say that God can lie, it is no derogation from His omnipotence that He cannot. " Whatsoever God cannot do, only shows that the rest of His attributes and perfections are as essential to Him as His power, and as His power suffers no resistance, so the rest of His perfections admit no repugnance.

" Thus, God is *omnipotent*, and God alone. For if the power of all things beside God be the power of God, as derived from, and subordinate to Him, and His own power can be subordinate to none, none can be omnipotent but God."*

THE PROVIDENCE OF GOD.

9. This means the divine superintendence. The Providence of God is defined by St. Thomas : The reason of the order of things towards their end, as it exists in the divine mind. It is applied at the same time to the intellect as well as to the will of God. Order belongs to and proceeds from the intellect, and the end of things is intended by the will.

In a wide sense, Providence signifies the care which God has over all things ; whether this be viewed as His government of

---

*See an Analysis of Pearson on the Creed, Arts. & vi.

things, or the reason of all things as He intended it from eternity. Strictly speaking, however, Providence is distinguished from government, in the same way as cause and effect are distinguished from each other. Providence expresses the reason of order as it exists in the divine mind, and is sanctioned by the divine Will. The execution or carrying out of this ordination, by which things are superintended and guarded, is called government.

10. God disposes and governs all things by His providence. Thus the Wise Man speaks : *" Thy providence, O Father, governeth it* (a sailing vessel), *for Thou hast made a way even in the sea, and a most sure path amony the waves."** And in another place it is said of Wisdom, which is applied to divine providence : *" She reacheth from end to end mightly, and ordereth all things sweetly."†* And in Ecclesiastes,† speaking as to caution in words, it is enjoined not to speak against providence : *Say not before the angel there is no providence ; lest God be angry at thy words, and destroy all the works of thy hands.*

The providence of God is proved also from reason : God is an intelligent Being, therefore providence belongs to Him as an attribute ; because an intelligent being always ordains his actions, according to reason, towards some end. God also is the great and good Artificer of all things ; and, as such, He takes care of those things which He has made. St. Ambrose says : *Quis operator negligat operis sui curam ?*—" What workman would neglect the care of his own work ? "

Divine providence extends itself to all things. It is eternal and infinite, and therefore extends over everything, to the hairs of our heads, to the most minute animals, to the herbs of the fields. The Atheists, whose sentiments were refuted by Solomon, in the Book of Ecclesiastes ; and the Sadducees, who arose afterwards, denied this providence, and maintained that men are the only cause of their own happiness or misfortune, according to the good or evil use which they make of their liberty.

Democritus and Epicurus said that the world was made by chance. Others said, that incorruptible things only were guarded by providence, and that corruptible things were governed, not as individuals, but only as to species, because as such, namely, as to species, they were incorruptible. And, therefore, they have thought that Providence does not act in the moving of a leaf, or

---

*Wisdom xiv. 3.   †Wisdom viii. 1.   ‡Eccl. v. 6.

in the production of a worm. All such systems are false, inasmuch as they deny God's providence. God can take care of all things, and it is not unworthy of Him to do so ; and, no matter how insignificant and miserable the thing may be, it takes away nothing from the dignity of God to have it under His care ; on the contrary, it rather amplifies the idea of His greatness and dignity. In the Gospel we are told of our heavenly Father's care over the lilies of the fields and the birds of the air. This universal providence is apparent, from the order observed amongst the heavenly bodies and the other works of creation. The divine efficiency and power extend to all things, and, therefore, all things are subject to His providence.

11. Although this providence extends to all creatures, we must remember that God has special care over rational beings. Because His providence is according to the most perfect order, it is extended to things according to their nature and condition, and the condition of rational creatures is higher that that of others. Besides, rational beings are gifted with liberty, and therefore they need a special providence.

There is a common difficulty suggested against God's providence by the unthinking and the unhappy. They say, if God Who is all-wise, provides for everybody, how is it that the just are afflicted and the wicked are permitted to prosper? There are many answers to this difficulty. In the first place, it is not true that the just are, generally speaking, more unfortunate than the wicked. In the second place, God sometimes permits the good to be punished in this life, that they may be the better prepared for the next. Lastly we have to consider, that God lets no good go without its rewards, as He leaves no evil unpunished. The faults of the good are therefore punished by temporal evils here ; and the natural moral good acts of the wicked, as they are not to have a supernatural reward, are renumerated by temporal prosperity and temporal gifts. God reserves for the future the true rewards or punishments, according to the merits or demerits of our immortal souls.

SECTION 6 (ARTICLE I)

THE HOLY TRINITY.

1. The dogma of the Holy Trinity as expressed in the Athanasian Creed : what is meant by it ?—2. No clear idea can be formed of this Mystery, although we have some imperfect representations of it in creatures.—3. The most accurate representation of the Blessed Trinity is to be found in our own soul.—4. This Mystery is also ineffable; the example of St. Augustine.—5. It is the principal Mystery, and the foundation of the Christian faith.—6. We obtain the knowledge of this Mystery by revelation.—7. Proofs of the Holy Trinity taken from the Old Testament.—8. Proofs from the New Testament.—9. Proofs from Tradition.—10. This Mystery is not opposed to reason, but above it.—11. The knowledge which the Jews had in the Old Dispensation of this Mystery, and the reasons of its obscurity then.—12. The obligation of believing explicitly in the Holy Trinity in the New Law.—13. The Holy Trinity as the basis of all revealed religion, and the centre of all devotion.

AFTER considering God in His nature and in His attributes, we have to pass to the Mystery of the Holy Trinity, which is implicitly signified by the words, *The Father Almighty.* We have afterwards, in the Creed, explicit belief expressed in *God the Son*, and in *God the Holy Ghost*. Under each Article that expresses the Persons of the Blessed Trinity, we can consider what belongs to each Person, or what is attributed to each, and their relations to one another. Here, however, is the proper place to explain the faith of the Church as to the dogma of the Holy Trinity, and the considerations to be made regarding this Mystery.

1. We have this dogma distinctly expressed in the words of the Athanasian Creed : *Now, the Catholic faith is this, that we worship one God in Trinity, and Trinity in Unity. Neither confounding the Persons, nor dividing the substance. For there is one Person of the Father, another of the Son, another of the Holy Ghost. But the Godhead of the Father, and of the Son, and of the Holy Ghost is all one ; the glory equal, the majesty co-eternal,* &c.

The Mystery of the Trinity, therefore, means one and the same individual divine essence in three Persons really distinct—

the Father unbegotten, the Son begotten, and the Holy Ghost proceeding from the Father and the Son.

2. This is the dogma of the Holy Trinity; but, as to the idea we have to form of this Mystery, it is necessary to reflect, that it so far surpasses our understanding that no clear notion of it can be formed in this life. There are many representations of the Holy Trinity to be found in created things, but none of them perfect. Nevertheless, they are used to enable us to form some notion of this Mystery; thus, for example, the sun, which is at the same time fire, light, and heat; a plant is formed of root, stem, and branches. The symbolic triangle, or the mysterious union of three angles, presents an image of the Holy Trinity; and also the arithmetical sum $1 \times 1 \times 1 = 1$.

3. That figure or image which better than all others represents the Trinity, is to be found in our own soul, which is created to the image and likeness of God.

God is a pure act, a being entirely simple, the highest intelligent Being. Now, every intelligent being understands, and this act is called an act of intelligence (*intelligentia*). This act is either a *substance* or an *accidens*. There can be no *accidens* in God, therefore it is a *substance*. If a substance, it cannot be distinct from the divine substance or nature itself. Which *substance*, as understanding (*intelligens*), is called the Father; and as understood (*intellecta*), is called the Son; which are two of the Persons of the Holy Trinity distinct from each other, and one with the essence.

St. Thomas observes, that in every intelligent being there is a will; and we have seen that in God there is a Will, which is one and the same thing with the divine nature; the action of the Will is *love*, that is, the action of the Will of God *ad intra*. God, therefore, loves His own (*intelligentia*) act of intelligence, or the product of that act by which He understands. The act by which God loves is not distinct from Himself, or from His substance, and therefore it is God Himself; but inasmuch as it is the relation between the Person understanding (*intelligens*), and the Person understood (*intellecta*), the connexion, as I might say, between the Father and the Son, it is called the Holy Ghost, the third Person of the Holy Trinity, really distinct from the Persons of the Father and the Son, and one with them in essence. Thus, in the human soul, which is capable of understanding and of loving, we find that which represents, better than any other image, the Holy Trinity.

4. This Mystery, as it is above the capacity of our minds,

is also ineffable ; so that we cannot represent it by words ; and in this we need not be discouraged when we call to mind what happened to St. Augustine, as he was preparing himself to explain this Mystery to the people. It seemed to him that he was walking by the shore of a vast ocean, and was contemplating its mysterious and unfathomable depth. Suddenly, he seemed to see at his feet a little child amusing himself by boring a hole in the sand and pouring into it from a shell the water of the ocean. On being asked why he did this, the child replied that he was going to empty the ocean into that small hole. "But, how can that be?" said the holy Father. The child answered, " It is as easy for me to do this, as for you to undertake to explain the Mystery you are proposing to lay before your people. As well can this little hole contain the ocean, as the mind of man can take in the great mysteries of God." And St. Ambrose, the master of St. Augustine, exclaims, when speaking of this profound Mystery of the Blessed Trinity : "It is impossible to know this secret ; the mind fails, the voice is silent ; and not my voice only, but that of Angels. It is above the Powers, it is above the Angels, above the Cherubim and Seraphim : it passeth all understanding."[*]

And St. Bonaventure, speaking of the Blessed Trinity, says : " *Sed Mysterium illud curiose scrutari temeritas est, credere pietas est, nosse vita æterna est*"—"To scrutinize this Mystery out of curiosity is temerity ; to believe it, is piety ; to know it, is eternal life."

5. At the same time, we have to reflect that it is the principal Mystery, as it is the foundation of the whole Christian faith. "Take away this," says a learned Theologian,[†] " and there will be no Incarnation of the Word, no satisfaction of Christ, no Redemption of man, no effusion of the Holy Spirit, no giving of grace, no virtue or efficacy of Sacraments ; the whole work of salvation is destroyed."

6. We come to the knowledge of this mystery by revelation. With us there are two orders of knowledge ; one, the order of natural things; the other, the order of supernatural things. By the order of natural things we can ascend to the knowledge of the existence of God, His power, wisdom, &c. ; because natural things proceed from the power of God, inasmuch as He is one. But to the knowledge of the Trinity we cannot come, except by the means of the supernatural order of things, so that it may be said,

[*]De fide, lib. 1, c. 10. [†]Lieberman, Theol. Dog. lib. 1], p. 1. *De trinitate.*

that God descends to us by revelation, rather than that we ascend to God by reasoning. Therefore, for the proofs of this Mystery, we depend entirely on the words and revelation of God.

I may here subjoin a summary of the Scripture proofs of the Holy Trinity, taken from the Old and the New Testaments. This Mystery was only obscurely revealed in the Old, but clearly revealed in the New Testament.

7. From the Old Testament we take the following texts :—

(a) *"In the beginning God created heaven and earth . . . and the spirit of God moved over the waters."**

(b) *"And He said : Let us make man to our image and likeness."*†

(c) *"And he said : Behold Adam is become one of us, knowing good and evil.*‡*"*

(d) *"Come ye, let us go down and there confound their tongues."*§

(e) *"And the Lord rained upon Sodom and Gomorrha brimstone and fire from the Lord out of heaven."*‖

(f) *"May God, our God bless us ; may God bless us, and all the ends of the earth fear Him."***

(g) *"And they cried one to another, and said, Holy, holy, holy, the Lord God of hosts, all the earth is full of His glory."*††
 "What," says St. Ambrose, "could the three-fold repetition of sanctity under one name mean, but that the Father, the Son, and the Holy Ghost are one in holiness?"

8. From the New Testament, in which the Holy Trinity is clearly made known to us, we may give the following texts :—

(a) *"In the beginning was the Word, and the Word was with God, and the Word was God."*‡‡

(b) *"Going therefore, teach ye all nations ; baptizing them in the name of the Father, and of the Son, and of the Holy Ghost."*§§

(c) *"And the Angel answering said to her, The Holy Ghost shall come upon thee, and the power of the most High shall overshadow thee. And therefore also the Holy which shall be born of thee, shall be called the Son of God."*¶

---

* Gen. i. 1, 2.   † Ibid. verse 26.   ‡ Gen. iii. 22.
§ Ibid xi. 7.   ‖ Gen. xix. 24.   ** Ps. lxvi. 7-8.
†† Isa. vi. 8.   ‡‡ St. John i. 1. et seq.   §§ St. Matt. xxviii. 19.
¶ St. Luke i. 85.

(*d*)   "*In that same hour He* (Jesus) *rejoiced in the Holy Ghost, and said : I confess to Thee, O Father, Lord of heaven and earth.*"*

(*e*)   "*And I will ask the Father ; and He shall give you another Paraclete, that He may abide with you for ever.*"†

Finally, we have the explicit words of the first Epistle of St. John : "*And there are three who give testimony in heaven, the Father, the Word, and the Holy Ghost. And these three are one.*"‡

After enumerating the scriptural texts, in reference to the Blessed Trinity, I may refer to the divine tradition, which also proves to us this fundamental doctrine of religion.

9. The first document handed down by tradition is the form of Baptism used in the Church ever since our Saviour's time, and according to His commandment: "*Go ye and teach all nations,*" &c. Secondly, the public worship and adoration of the Blessed Trinity. This adoration, in ancient times, is witnessed in the writings of Justin, Irenaeus, and of the early Fathers of the Church. Justin Martyr, in his second apology for the Christians, says : " We worship and adore the Father, and He who comes from Him—the Son, and the Holy Ghost."

Then we have the doxology, or *Gloria Patri*, &c., handed down to us from the age of the Apostles ; and we have the threefold repetition of the Kyrie in the Mass, in honour of each of the divine Persons.

Finally, there is the argument from prescription. The dogma of the Holy Trinity was taught and believed in the Church, when the Sabellians were condemned in the third century ; the Arians in the fourth century ; the Socinians and others in the sixteenth century. It exists to-day as from the beginning—the same faith, and the same doctrine of the Church, as expressly declared in all our Creeds.

These are some of the proofs of this doctrine taken from the fountains of revelations, namely Scripture and tradition. As far as human reason is concerned, we must be satisfied to know that the Mystery of the Trinity is not against reason, but only above reason.

10. " Many truths which are known, and therefore are intelligible to more learned persons, are unintelligible to the less learned. And as no human mind is perfectly wise, and can understand everything, it follows that there is something unintelligible to every man. As God is greater than man, and as the

---

* St. Luke x. 21.   † St. John xxiv. 16.   ‡ 1 St. John v. 7.

idea of God outmeasures the mind of man, there is something in God which man cannot comprehend ; and so we expect to find Mystery in Him. St. Paul, therefore, says, that His judgments and ways are incomprehensible and unsearchable. A being who could be perfectly understood and measured by the mind of man, would not be God. For he would not be greater than man, inasmuch as the mind of man cannot measure what is greater than itself. But in the Mystery of the Trinity, nothing is taught that is *against* reason. Is it against reason (for this is the point on which it may appear that there is a contradiction) that the Father is God, the Son is God, and the Holy Ghost is God; and yet there is but one God, and not three Gods ? No. For what we believe is this, that the Father is God, and the Son is the *same* God, and the Holy Ghost is the *same* God ; and, therefore, all having the same Godhead, there are not three Gods, but only one God. Remember the principle that the Trinity is in the Persons, the Unity in the essence and Godhead. But must it be that, if there are three Persons, we cannot conceive anything else but three Gods? No, not at all ; unless you assume what is quite false—that substance and Person mean the same; which they don't mean. To show you this, I will only show you yourself. You have two substances, which form in you but one person. Your body is one substance, a material substance ; your soul is another distinct substance, a spiritual substance. Yet, you are but one person ; therefore it does not follow that there must be the same number of substances and Persons in God, as there are not the same number in yourself. You can understand this in yourself, perhaps ; you cannot understand it in God. You are not called upon to understand it, you are only called upon to believe it, *because there are three that give testimony in heaven.* Grant that God can understand Himself, as well as you can understand yourself, and you will admit that the Trinity is incomprehensible to you, but not to Him."*

11. The Jews of to-day deny that the Trinity of Persons has been revealed. In olden times, before the coming of Christ, the chief dogma of the Jews was that there is one God ; and as to their belief in the Holy Trinity, we have to distinguish them into three classes. 1st. The Prophets and the just of the Old Law. 2nd. The crowd or common people of the Jews. 3rd. The interpreters of the Law. All agree that the common multitude of the Jews had only a very confused knowledge, or,

*Lectures on Catholic Faith and Practice, by the Rev. J. N. Sweeney, O.S.B., Lec. xi.

perhaps, no knowledge at all, of the Holy Trinity. The Patriarchs and Prophets, and many of the just, had a knowledge of the Holy Trinity, according to the words of our Saviour : "*Many Prophets and just have desired to see what you have seen and have not seen.*"* Those who belonged to the third class, namely, the *Legisperiti*, or interpreters of the law, seem to have a middle place between the multitude and the Prophets. They knew this Mystery better than the people in general, as it was their duty to expound the Scriptures. And, as we have seen, the Trinity, at least obscurely, is made known in the Old Testament. They had not the same clear revelation of it as was imparted to the Patriarchs and Prophets.

The following reasons are assigned for the obscurity which surrounded this Mystery in the time of the Old Dispensation.

(a) That its open and clear declaration might be reserved to the Son, who was the *expected* of nations, and who was to fulfil all things.

(b) That the New Testament might be more excellent than the Old, in its more full and explicit revelations.

(c) That all danger of idolatry might be removed from the Jewish nation and people, who were so prone to this crime.

(d) The reason of St. Augustine : That gradually, and as it were insensibly, the weakness of men might be brought to the highest knowledge of things.

12. I have already explained, when treating of faith, that all Christians are obliged to know explicitly this Mystery, and to elicit an act of faith in it. This, according to many, is necessary as a *means* to salvation, though others hold, as a probable opinion, that it is not necessary as a *means*, but only by the *necessity of precept*, for salvation. But it is certain that, except in case of necessity, such as danger of death, one ignorant of this Mystery cannot lawfully be absolved in the Tribunal of Penance.

The Mystery of the Trinity is not a mere speculative doctrine, it is the basis of all revealed religion, and the centre of all our devotions.

(a) "It tells us of the Hidden Life of God ; and furnishes us with thoughts now, which will be the nourishment of our happiness hereafter. Well does the Church, in the Office of the Blessed Trinity, feel and express this, when she exclaims : ' We invoke Thee, we praise

*St. Matt. xiii.

Thee, we adore Thee, O Blessed Trinity! Our hope, our Salvation, and our Honour, O Blessed Trinity!'"

(b) "The Incarnation, which is the source of all grace and blessing to us, is inconceivable without the Trinity..."

(c) "The Church, which is the continuation of the Incarnation, is existing and ever working through this Mystery. Our dearest Saviour dwells so often upon the efficacy of the working of the Church, when it should have become perfected by *the Holy Ghost, whom the Father will send in my Name.* The work of the Church is to secure for us, and increase within us, that grace which links us to the Trinity ; for it makes us children of the Father, joint-heirs with the Son, and temples of the Holy Ghost."

(d) "In prayer, we frequently invoke the Trinity. Our Litanies begin and end with this invocation. Our Collects conclude with the assurance that we present all our petitions through Jesus Christ the Son, who with the Father and the Holy Ghost, liveth and reigneth one God for ever and ever. In the beginning and end of your prayers you sign yourself with the sign of the Cross, and profess your faith in the Name of the Father, and of the Son, and of the Holy Ghost. As you enter the Church, you take the holy water in the same Name. You end your Psalms and Hymns by singing Glory to the same three Divine Persons ; and, as again you leave the Church to enter once more into the distractions of the world, you go forth signing yourself in that Name, by which every good work is commenced and completed."*

(e) All the Sacraments of the Church are administered in the Name of the Holy Trinity, and, at length, when passing out of this world, the last words and prayers of the priest who attends us will be in the words of the Ritual : *Depart, Christian soul, out of this world, in the name of God the Father Almighty, who created thee ; in the name of Jesus Christ, the Son of the living God, who suffered for thee ; in the name of the Holy Ghost, who sanctified thee.*

---

*Rev. J. N. Sweeney's Lectures.

H

SECTION 7 (ARTICLE I.)

GOD THE FATHER: THE FIRST PERSON OF THE BLESSED TRINITY.

1. The three names proper to the First Person of the Holy Trinity : *Father, Principium* and *Unbegotten.*—2. The sense in which God is called our Father, and the sense in which He is called the Father of His only begotten Son.—3. The difference between the Divine Sonship, and that arising from human generation.

AFTER treating of the Trinity in general, we naturally come to consider separately the three divine Persons. Our belief in each one of them is expressed in different Articles of the Creed ; and in the first Article we express our explicit belief in God the Father : I believe in God the *Father* Almighty.

We have in this Section to reflect on the doctrine which we are taught concerning the First Person of the Blessed Trinity, and in what sense He is called the Father.

1. In the first place, there are three names proper to God the Father, viz., *Father, Unbegotten,* and *Principium*—beginning or origin. (a) He is the *principium,* because the other two Persons proceed from Him, and He does not proceed from any other ; and that is called the *principium,* or origin, from which another proceeds in whatsoever way.

Although the First Person is called in Latin *principium,* He is never called by the name *cause,* as applied to Him in contradistinction to the Son and to the Holy Ghost, because these two Divine Persons cannot be said to proceed from Him as from a cause, inasmuch as this would make them subordinate in nature to Him, whilst the three have one and the same divine nature. Besides, cause and effect are correlative in the sense that where there is a cause there is an effect, and the divine Persons cannot be called effects, because They are not made. (b) Then, *cause* is not given as the proper name to the first Person, lest heretics should take occasion from this to declare that the Son and the Holy Ghost are only creatures, they having God the Father as Their cause. God is, properly and strictly speaking, the cause of all creatures; but the Son and the Holy Ghost are not creatures, and, properly speaking, have no *cause* of their being, but a principle from which they proceed.

Father is a name proper to the first Person, because it distinguishes Him from the other Persons. The same may be said of *unbegotten*, because He is unbegotten Who is not from another, either by generation or in any other way.

The First Person is therefore called (*a*) a *principle* (or *principium*), without a principle or origin, because the two other Persons proceed from Him, and He proceeds from no other. (*b*) Unbegotten, because He is entirely and in every conceivable manner, unproducible. (*c*) The Father, because He has a Son. *Ipse invocabit me, Pater meus es tu.**

2. I wish to dwell more at length on this name *Father*. God is our Father, and He is the Father of His only-begotten Son. God is our Father,—

   (*a*)   On account of creation and conservation.
   (*b*)   On account of redemption.
   (*c*)   On account of adoption and regeneration by grace.
   (*d*)   On account of the glory and beatitude which His saints enjoy.

As our Father, therefore, He is entitled to our filial fear, honour, and obedience. It is after this manner Christ has taught us to pray to God, beginning with *Our Father*. As His children, we should have Christian patience under the sufferings that our Father sends to purify and chastise us. We ought to prove ourselves His children by loving one another, and especially our enemies. And, above all, act according to the admonition given in St. Luke's Gospel : *Be ye merciful as your heavenly Father is merciful.†*

But the most proper explanation of God's paternity is, that He is the Father of our Lord Jesus Christ. As we find one Person, in a most special manner, the Son of God, so we must look on God as, in a special manner, the Father of that Son.

The disparity between our filiation and that of Christ is very great, as He, being the true and proper Son of God, has the highest kind of filiation. There is one degree of filiation, or Sonship, founded on creation—the lowest, as belonging to all, good and bad ; another, higher, grounded on sanctification and adoption, belonging to the faithful in this life ; a third, above the rest, founded on the resurrection and eternal beatitude,

---

*Ps. lxxxviii.   †St. Luke vi. 36.

belonging to the Saints in heaven. And there is another, of a greater eminence, and far exceeding all these, which belongs to the true Son of God alone, Who, amongst all, has received the title of *His Own Son*,[*] and a testimony from heaven : *This is My beloved Son* ; [†] even in the presence of John the Baptist ; and of Moses and Elias (certainly sons of God by the other three degrees of filiation) ; and therefore He could call God in a real and true sense *His own Father* (πατέρα ἴδιον).[‡] And thus we come to the most singular and eminent paternal relation *unto the God and Father of our Lord Jesus Christ.*[§]

"God may in several ways be called the Father of Christ. (a) As He was begotten by the Holy Ghost of the Virgin Mary. (b) As He was sent by Him with special authority as the King of Israel. (c) As He was raised from the dead, and made heir of all things. (d) In the more eminent and special manner, as He ever was, and ever is, with God *and* God. And according to this Paternity, by generation totally divine, we believe in God as the Eternal Father of an Eternal Son. As always God, so always Father, and that in a far more proper manner than any creature."

3. "For (a) the condition of human generation, and of the relations thence arising, is so fluctuating that the same person, now a son, may become a father, and then cease to be either son or father, losing both relations by death ; whereas, in the Godhead these relations are fixed, the Father having never been a Son, the Son never becoming a Father. And (b) God hath begotten a Son of the same nature and essence with Himself, not only *specifically* but *individually*. If a man begetteth a son *in his own likeness, after his own image*, [||] *i.e.* of the same nature, of the same substance with himself, and thus obtaineth the name of father because of the similitude of *his* nature—with which similitude many accidental disparities may exist in the son— how much more proper is the name to God Himself, Who hath begotten a Son of a nature and essence, the perfect identity whereof admits not the least disparity."[**]

---

* Rom. viii. 32.   † St. Matt. iii. 17, & xvii. 5.   ‡ St. John v. 18.
§ 2 Cor. xi. 31. || Gen. v. 3.
** An Analysis of Pearson on the Creed. Art. 1.

SECTION 8. (ARTICLE I.)

THE CREATION OF THE WORLD.

1. God considered in His external works, that is, in the works of His creation.—2. Three questions in regard to the origin of the world.—3. Pantheism, its meaning, its most celebrated advocate.—4. The world is not and cannot be God.—5. Spinosa's definition of substance, and the sense in which it is false.—6. The opinion that the world was made by chance, or by a necessity of nature and its advocates.—7. The reasons why the world could not come into existence by chance, or the fortuitous combination of atoms.—8. The world is not the result of necessity.—9. The true doctrine of the origin of the world.—10. The world was not made from matter, eternal and unproduced.—11. God made the world out of nothing by creation.—12. The time of the world's creation: (a) The world is not from eternity, but created in time. (b) The question of the possibility of eternal creation.—13. The question as to the age of the world and the age of the human race.—14. Three opinions as to the age of the world.

IN the preceding Sections we have studied God, His nature, His attributes, and His own life. We have seen that He exists, that His nature is *self-existent* of itself; that His attributes comprehend all possible perfections, and that therefore He is an infinitely perfect Being: That, as Father, He has an only begotten Son, Who is eternal and equal to Him in all things; and that from the Father and the Son proceedeth the Holy Ghost as a third divine Person; and thus in the mystery of the Holy Trinity we have the Father, Son, and Holy Ghost, three distinct Persons, but one God having one and the same divine nature.

1. Now we come to consider God in His external action, that is to say, in the works which have effect distinct from Himself—His creation, of which we men are a part.

We express our faith on this point when we say in the words of the Apostles' Creed: *I believe in God ... Creator of heaven and earth.* And more fully in the words of the Nicene Creed: *Maker of heaven and earth, and of all things visible and invisible.*

2. The Catholic doctrine, as to the origin of the world, may be treated under three questions. (a) Whether the world is

God ; and what is to be thought of Pantheism?   (b) Whether the
world could be made by chance, or be the effect of natural
necessity?   (c) How and when did the world come into existence ?

3.   Whether the world is God, and what is to be thought of
Pantheism.

Pantheism is derived from two Greek words παυ—all, and θεος
—God.   It signifies that "God is all things," or "that God is the
whole universe," "never begotten, never to perish," as Pliny
says.   The most celebrated author of the system of Pantheism
was Spinosa, who was born in Amsterdam in the year 1632.   His
parents were Jews, and he was a Jew in his earlier years, but he
died an Atheist in the year 1677.   He taught, (a) that in the
nature of things there was only one substance, which of itself
and necessarily exists, which is God.   (b) That by the name of
substance, is to be understood a being that exists in itself, and is
conceived by itself.   (Id quod existit in se et per se concipitur.)

4.   A substance existing of necessity, and of its own nature,
would be indeed God ; but such a universal substance, embracing
all others in itself, does not exist ; and therefore we have to hold
against the Pantheists that the world is not, and cannot be, God.

This can be proved from the unity, the simplicity, and the
immutability of God ; and also from the fact that God must be a
Being of infinite intelligence.

God is *one*, and this the Pantheists themselves admit ; but
the world is not one, either in genus, or species, or in individuals,
therefore it cannot be God.

God is entirely *simple*.   No composition in Him.   The world
is not simple, but composed of parts, and has extension ; therefore the world is not God.

God is *immutable*, because He is all perfect ; but the world is
subject to various and continuous changes, as is evident from the
series of generations and corruptions which daily take place in it.

Lastly, God is an *intelligent* Being ; but the corporeal
world is material, and therefore non-intelligent ; therefore the
the world is not God, neither are all things in it God.

5.   Spinosa understood the definition of substance in a
wrong sense.   Substance is that which exists in itself, and is conceived by itself ; may be understood in a two-fold sense.   Its true
sense is when we understand existing *in itself* as not needing
another in which to inhere, as is the case in regard to *accidents*.
And in this sense no Pantheism can be deduced from the definition.   If by *existing in itself* we have to understand a being that
exists *of itself*, or *a self-existent being*, and that this is the nature

of a substance, then Spinosa and his definition are wrong; and his argument is begging the question; for a being that would exist *of itself* would certainly be God; but created substances do not exist *of themselves*, and therefore the definition is false in the sense of its application to all substances, or to any substance but God alone. The same explanation applies to the clause *per se concipitur—conceived by itself*.

We have to bear in mind that God contains in Himself all the perfections of His creatures; that He is intimately and substantially present in all things, and that nothing can be or act without His power and efficiency; for all things depend upon Him for their existence and their preservation.

6. Whether the world was made by chance or by necessity of nature?

There were some who said that the world was made, or put together rather, by a whole lot of minute particles of matter, which by chance and confusion formed various combinations, until, at last, they constituted the order which we see in things. The authors and supporters of such a system were Leucippus, Democritus, and Epicurus, and all those who denied the existence of a Supreme Being.

7. Against these, we say that the world could not exist by chance, or by the fortuitous combinations of particles of matter—

(a) Because that nature, which in many things always acts in the same way, cannot be the effect of chance or accident; but the course of nature, and of the world, and the bodies of the Universe, always act in the same way, according to physical and natural laws; therefore this cannot be the result of chance, which only takes place occasionally, and in a few things, and not after any rule or order.

(b) Order could not arise out of chance except by accident; but in the world we observe, even in those things that are contrary to each other, the most wonderful order and regularity; and these cannot be the effect of accident, as they are most certain and most constant.

(c) The particles of matter could not move themselves, as they are material; and motion is not essential to matter; nor, as the false system supposes, are they moved by God; He cannot in any case be the Author of disorder and confusion; therefore, they could not bring about the present world or the present natural order of things.

The disciple in Graveson's *Ecclesiastical History*,[*] is represented as answering this question. If any one could be so stupid as to assert, with the Epicureans, that this world is nothing else than a heap of small bodies, without life, without providence, without reason, but brought together by chance and blindly ; such an erring man would be at once refuted by the admirable structure of this world and its parts, and the most wise disposition or arrangement of all things in it. This cannot be attributed to the chance and rash accumulation of stupid and lifeless atoms ; and it can be only the work of the highest intelligence, which preordains all things according to order and knowledge.

8. As to the second part of the question, whether the world is the result of necessity, we have to note a few things.

That God made the world through a necessity of nature, was an opinion held by the Stoics of old. The same was held by Peter Abelard, and in more recent times by a J. B. Robinetus, who renewed the old error, and stated that the world was the necessary effect of the nature of God. Against this error, we assert that the world was made by God, not through any necessity, but by His free-will. This can be proved by many reasons.

(a) The world is not the result of chance as we have seen, therefore it is ordained to some end. But an agent who acts for an end, must act by intellect and will, and not by necessity ; God, therefore, by intellect and will created the world, and not by the necessity of nature.

(b) He who acts through necessity, cannot prescribe his own end or purpose, because he is determined to one end ; therefore that end must be determined by some other for him ; but it cannot be that God, who is the first Agent, should be determined or regulated by another. Therefore God does not act outside Himself through necessity.

(c) There are many things made by God, and many more possible things. Of the things that are possible, some He made, and some He has not made, according to the choice of His free-will, and not through any necessity. God, therefore, in creating the world, acted according to His own free choice and Will.

The opposite opinion is Pantheistic, as, in that supposition, the world would be necessary, and therefore God.

---

[*]Vet. Test.

9. After referring to the false systems, which have been invented to account for the origin of the world, we have now to state the true doctrine, namely, that the world received its existence from God.

To explain this, we have two things to consider : (a) the mode in which the world received its existence ; and (b) the time in which it was brought into existence.

The Manner or Mode of the World's Existence.

Here we have one more error to refute, the error of those who assert that God made the world out of pre-existing matter, and that it is not immediately from God, although He formed it. Some attribute this opinion to Plato. The Stoics held the theory of the eternity of matter; and the Manicheans admitted the theory of matter being eternal and unproduced.

10. The world was not made from matter, eternal and unproduced, because such matter would not depend upon God, or be subject to Him ; therefore He could not give it its form. As Lactantius says : " God does not need pre-existing matter in order to create, as He is omnipotent." St. Thomas teaches that matter eternal and unproduced is impossible. Such matter would have to be necessary, a pure act, immutable and most perfect. But none of these things can belong to matter, inasmuch as it is essentially subject to so many changes. Therefore, matter cannot be eternal and unproduced, but it must come from some other being who can produce it. It is not, however, against sound doctrine to hold that God made or formed the world out of matter first created by Himself.

11. God made the world out of nothing by creation. This is proved by the narrative given in the first Chapter of Genesis, which is, at the same time, the Theological and an historical argument for the creation of the world.

The same may be proved from reason. All things that are in the world have received existence from another, and not from themselves, and this other can be no one else but God. For, since those things that have not had existence from themselves, have their being by participation, they must have their cause in that Being who essentially exists. Therefore, all things have their existence from God, and are made out of nothing, because, as I have already shown, they are not produced from pre-existing matter ; and God alone is the only self-existent and essentially necessary Being ; therefore, all things are from Him, and depend upon Him for their existence.

The maxim, universally received, that nothing can be made out of nothing (*ex nihilo nihil fit*), has to be understood of corporeal generations, or with respect to natural and inferior agencies that cannot produce matter, and it was first framed in regard to the works of art and nature. Thus, in the works of art, no artificer can give any specimen of his art without materials ; and in the natural order of generation, we see plants proceed from seeds, fish from spawn, fowls from eggs. This could not have been so at first. The maxim then is true only in regard to the continuing of creatures, by successive generation, which could not have been begun or continued without a being antecedent to all such succession.

I may here note that there are two kinds of creation. (*a*) *Proper*—of things made out of nothing *immediately* ; such as immaterial substances, all angels and human souls, and the elemental bodies—as the earth, water and air, &c. (*b*) *Improper* —of things made *mediately*, that is, out of something formerly made out of nothing, as animals and vegetables ; and, in regard to the human body, we are told that God formed man of the dust of the earth.

THE TIME OF THE WORLD'S CREATION.

12. Three questions are to be examined with respect to the time of creation. (*a*) Whether the world was created actually in time, or from eternity. (*b*) Whether eternal creation is possible. (*c*) Is the age of the world known to us.

(*a*) Against the ancient Philosophers, Aristotle and Plato, and against materialists and naturalists in all ages, we have to hold that the world is not created from eternity, but produced in time. The world is not a necessary effect from God, but depends entirely on His free-will, and therefore it need not necessarily be eternal. The narrative of creation is given in the first Chapter of the book of Genesis : "*In the beginning God created heaven and earth.*" In Proverbs, it is said in regard to wisdom : "*The Lord possessed me in the beginning of His ways, before He made anything from the beginning.*"* And our divine Lord in His prayer to His Father, says : "*And now, glorify*

---

*Prov. viii. 22.

Thou me, O Father, with Thyself, with the glory which I had before the world was, with Thee."*

The doctrine, as to the fact of creation, is clearly defined in the Council of Lateran (*cap. firmiter*), in the words : " God, from the beginning, made out of nothing the creature, Angelical and worldly, spiritual and corporal, and then human composed of both." It is therefore to be held as of faith, that the world is not eternal, but produced or created in time. And its truth is proved also by the constant traditions both of Jews and Christians.

It cannot be urged against this teaching, that creation in time would be an argument against the immutability of God, because the creative action was always in God and one with His nature, but it was ordained to have its effect in time ; and, although it be true that there is an instant assignable before which God could not have made the world, yet we are assured by the inspired Word of God that whatsoever possibility of an eternal existence of the creature, by the free determination of God's will may be imagined, the world actually had a temporal beginning.

THE POSSIBILITY OF ETERNAL CREATION.

(b) This may seem to be an entirely Academic question, yet we must bear in mind that very many of the speculative questions of the Schools may be used for or against religion ; and, therefore, against the tendency of many modern works to undermine religious truth, it is important to know that our Christian teachers have forestalled all modern error, and that too on their own intellectual or scientific grounds.

For intelligence and reason, claimed by the opponents of Christianity, are the weapons to be used against them, and they must know that we fear not the use of such weapons ; therefore I have often introduced questions that appear to be purely speculative. Catholic Doctors are not agreed as to the possibility of the eternal creation of the world. Some, such as St. Thomas and Suarez, maintain that the world could have been created from eternity, had God so willed it ; although, actually, God willed to create it in time. This, they maintain, is repugnant neither on the part of God or on the part of the world, nor on the part of the creative action. Not on the part of God, for He always possesses the same eternal power and creative action ;

and it is not necessary that a cause should be in time or duration before its effect, provided it be by nature prior to it, as the sun in respect to its light. It is not repugnant on the part of the world, for, as creations, such as our souls, can last for ever, so they could be from eternity; nor would the world, even though it had always been, be called eternal in the same sense as eternity applies to God, namely, by essence, but only in its own duration *a parto ante*, as scholastics say, in the same way as some creatures are to exist for ever, and have therefore eternity *a parto post*, but not in the same way as God Himself. Nor is it repugnant on the part of the creative action, for creation can be in an instant, and does not depend upon time; and it is not necessary that a thing be *post nihil*—after nothing, but *ex nihil*—from or out of nothing.

Albertus Magnus, St. Bonaventure, Petavius, and other recent authors, maintain, on the contrary, that the world could not by any possibility be eternal, as this would imply a contradiction. They say,—

(a) That which is made must have the beginning of its duration; and, therefore, as the world was made by God, it must have a beginning of its duration.

(b) If the world were from eternity, we should attribute eternity to it; and eternity is proper to God, and belongs to Him alone.

(c) If the world had always been, there must be an infinite series of days in the past; and as what is passed is finished, so in this case the infinite would be passed over, which is impossible. Had there been an infinite series before to-day, we should never have seen to-day, the world would never have arrived at it. And even supposing that this day did arrive, other days would follow, and be added to the infinite; and an addition or increase superadded to that which is infinite, destroys at once the very notion of infinitude as we apprehend it.

Is the Age of the World Known?

13. This is the third question which we have to treat in connection with the creation of the world. In consulting the Sacred Scriptures on this point, we find given in them the chronology of the human race as comparatively recent; but as to the

chronology of the world itself, all that the Sacred Scriptures say is that "*In the beginning God created heaven and earth.*" There is great liberty of opinion given on the question of the age of the world, so that, as far as Holy Scripture is concerned, the world may have existed 1,000 or 1,000,000 years before man; and there may have been plants and animals in it as Geologists of our day suppose. The Church not only tolerates this opinion, but some of her eminent Doctors and Theologians openly teach it. We can, however, come to some definite knowledge as to the age of the human race, as computed by commentators from the Holy Scriptures. The age of the human race is nowhere in the Sacred Writings explicitly and accurately stated; but from various data and facts of Sacred History, by computation, we can calculate the number of years from Adam to Christ. That whole series of years may be divided into two parts: (a) from the creation of the world to the call of Abraham; and (b) from the call of Abraham till the coming of Christ. As to the last interval the difference of Chronologists is very slight; and we may say that they are substantially of one opinion, that the number of years in this period can be computed at 2,000.

As to the period from Adam to the call of Abraham there is a great difference of opinion amongst Chronologists. This diversity of opinion has arisen from different reading of the ancient versions of the Sacred Scriptures, and could have arisen, in part, from the manner of computation. The Genealogy from Adam to Noe, and from Noe to Abraham, is computed from the number of generations from father to son, viz. : *Adam lived a hundred and thirty years, and begot a son to his own image and likeness, and called his name Seth. And the days of Adam, after he begot Seth, were eight hundred years......And all the time that Adam lived came to nine hundred and thirty years,* and he died, &c., and so on to Abraham. Abraham, however, was seventy-five years when he received the call of God; and in this way, the number of years from Adam to the call of Abraham is counted. The more ancient versions of the Pentateuch, now extant, are the three known as the Hebrew, the Samaritan, and the Septuagint; and in these three we find a great difference in the enumeration of the years from Adam to Christ, and especially in the period from Adam to the call of Abraham; so that, in the whole period up to Christ, we find a difference of 1,500 years as to the age of the human race. We can, however, even with this difference taken into consideration, learn from Scripture and tradition that the age of the human race, from

Adam to Christ, does not exceed 6,000 years, and is not less than
4,000 years, and if we add to that 1,892 years, we can conclude
from data given in the Bible that the present age of the human
race is contained within the space of 6,000 and 8,000 years.

We have, however, to note (a) that this age of the human
race, is not determined by the Bible, but only made out by
calculations from it ; (b) that according to many modern writers,
some of them Catholics and men of great authority, the age of-
the human race, is not the same as the age of the world, or this
orb of the world.

14. As to the age of the world, or of this earth which we
inhabit, we have three opinions. The first opinion places an
indetermined period between the creation of heaven and earth,
and the work of the six days of creation. The second opinion
supposes each day of the six to represent an indefinite period of
time. The third opinion, which may be said to be the opinion
of the Fathers and of the older Theologians, except St. Augustine,
makes the age of the world correspond to the age of the human
race, and takes the six days of creation as six natural days of
24 hours each, formed as now by the earth turning on its axis.

Neither of the two opinions first stated have ever been
demonstrated with certainty up to the present, but neither of
them is against the text of Scripture. The text of the first
Chapter of Genesis admits of various interpretations. Recent
scientific investigations in Geology are much in favour of these
opinions. It appears certain that the Bible narrative admits of
an interpretation that the age of the world may have gone on for
an indefinite period before the creation of man, and this is all
that modern Catholic Geologists require.

I hope I may not be considered too antiquated if I say that
the old opinion may yet be regarded as being as well-founded as
either of the two others. The recent theories are not yet established with sufficient certitude to remove all doubts or suspicions that they may be altogether false. One thing is certain,
that we must not stretch the proofs of modern science too far,
and lead them beyond their object. The age of the world, like
the age of the human race, is an historical fact, and rests therefore more on Authority than on Geology. It is true that the
world would require many more years than what is ordinarily
given to grow, and to evolve geologically, in order to arrive at its
present state of rocks and strata, if it did grow or evolve ; but
that is just the question, and a question which can be settled by
no science with certainty unless it can first be known what the

world was like immediately on its creation, when it came from the hands of its Maker. This no one can know but God Himself, and those to whom He may reveal it. God acts in a uniform way in His ordinary Providence, and according to the laws of nature ; but very likely, in the first creation of things, the world, like Adam, was made by God in a perfect state, that is in its full and perfect magnitude.

And as no one would hold that Adam must be 21 years old on the day of his creation, because, according to the laws of the growth of children, so many years would be required to arrive at perfect manhood ; and it is commonly admitted that Adam did not grow in the ordinary way, but was created in his full stature ; so we may reasonably enough suppose that the world also may have come forth from the hands of God in its full state of formation, and this opinion may be reasonably held until supplanted by some more certain and better established one.

ARTICLE II

" And in Jesus Christ, His only Son, Our Lord."

" And in one Lord Jesus Christ, the only-begotten Son of God, *begotten of the Father before all ages, God of God, Light of Light, True God of True God, begotten, not made, consubstantial with the Father ; by Whom all things were made.*"

SECTION 1. (ARTICLE II.)

CHRIST'S NAME AND SONSHIP.

1. The additions made in this Second Article in the Nicene Creed.—2. Jesus is Our Lord's name, Christ is Our Lord's title.—3. The three great offices to which men were anointed : *Prophet, Priest, and King.* —4. Jesus Christ, the only-begotten Son of God.—5. The Divine Processions, their nature and division.—6. The Procession of the Son is called generation, and not the Procession of the Holy Ghost.— 7. What is meant by generation ; and why is the Procession of the Son called generation, and not the Procession of the Holy Ghost.—8. His eternal Sonship.

    1. WE may notice that great additions were made in the Nicene Creed. These additions were made as a declaration of the true faith against the heresy of Arius and his followers, who denied the Divinity of Christ.

    2. Jesus is our Lord's name. It is the Greek equivalent (Jehosua Ι'ησους) of the Hebrew Joshua (Jah or Jehovah, Hosea —Saviour) and means Jehovah, the Saviour ! *"Thou shalt call His name Jesus, for He shall save His people from their sins."**

---

* St. Matt. i. 21.

This name was given to our Lord at His Circumcision : *"And after eight days were accomplished, that the Child should be circumcised, His name was called Jesus, which was called by the Angel before He was conceived in the womb."* *

Christ is our Lord's title. It is the Greek equivalent of the Hebrew Messiah, and means *anointed*. To anoint ordinarily means to pour oil on the head.

3. Among the Jews, men were anointed to three great offices : Prophet, Priest, and King.

   (a) *Prophet.* Eliseus......*"thou shalt anoint to be prophet in thy room."*† This was the direction given by the Lord to Elias.

   (b) *Priest.* When Moses was consecrating Aaron to the priesthood, he poured oil upon his head, and *anointed and consecrated him.*‡

   (c) *King.* When David was anointed King ; *" Samuel took the horn of oil, and anointed him in the midst of his brethren ; and the Spirit of the Lord came upon David from that day forward."* ‖

These three offices were united in Jesus as the Christ.

   (a) *Prophet.* *"The Lord thy God will raise up to thee a* PROPHET *of thy nation and of thy brethren like unto me* (Moses) ; *Him thou shalt hear."*§

   (b) *Priest.* According to the words of St. Paul : *"Where the forerunner Jesus is entered for us, made a* HIGH-PRIEST *for ever according to the order of Melchizedech."*¶

   (c) *King.* In the words of the Angel addressed to the Blessed Virgin, at the time of the Incarnation : *"And the Lord shall give to Him the throne of David His father ; and He shall reign in the house of David for ever. And of His Kingdom there shall be no end."* **

Our Lord was anointed with the unction of the Holy Spirit at His Baptism, when the Spirit of God *descended like a dove and lighted upon Him.*

That Jesus was the Christ, He Himself distinctly told the woman of Samaria, when He said : *"I am He who am speaking with thee."*††

---

* St. Luke ii. 21.   † 3 Kings xix. 16.   ‡ Lev. viii. 12.
‖ 1 Kings xvi. 13.   § Deut. xviii. 15.   ¶ Heb. vi. 20.
    ** St. Luke i. 32, 33.   †† St. John iv. 26.

v

JESUS CHRIST HIS ONLY SON.   THE ONLY-BEGOTTEN SON OF GOD.

4. That Christ is the Son of God is clearly proved from many places of the Holy Scripture. Thus, Nathaniel answered and said, "*Rabbi, Thou art the Son of God, Thou art the King of Israel.*"[*] Martha expresses her faith in the words, "*Yea, Lord, I have believed that Thou art Christ the Son of the living God.*"[†] In the history of the Passion we read that the High-Priest said to our Saviour : "*I adjure Thee by the living God, that Thou tell us if Thou be the Christ the Son of God.*"[‡] St. Peter expresses the faith of the Apostles in the lifetime of our Lord when he says: "*Thou art Christ the Son of the living God.*"[§] And again : "*Lord, to whom shall we go ?   Thou hast the words of eternal life.   And we have believed and have known that Thou art the Christ the Son of God.*"[||]

Thus the Christ and the Son of God are always inseparable in Scriptural language, which clearly conveys to us the truth that Christ is the true Son of God.

Before speaking of Christ as man, which belongs more to the next Article of the Creed than to this, we have to consider how Christ is the Son of God, and the peculiarity of His generation.

To explain how Christ is the Son of God, involves the question of the Divine Processions and Relations.

THE DIVINE PROCESSIONS.

5. By *Procession*, we mean the coming forth or emanation of one thing from another.

Procession is two-fold (*a*) *ad intra* or *immanens*, that, whose term remains in the principle from which it proceeds, and does not go beyond it ; (*b*) *ad extra* or *transient*, which is that, whose term or effect goes outside the principle from which it proceeds ; thus our words, and the productions of nature, are examples of procession *ad extra*.

It is either *perfect* or *imperfect*. *Perfect*, when the term or that which proceeds subsists, and is the same as the subject from which it proceeds. *Imperfect*, when the term or effect either does not subsist, as in the example of the thoughts of the mind, or is not the same as its principle or fountain head, such

---

[*] St. John i. 49.   [†] St. John xi. 27.   [‡] St. Matt. xxvi. 63.
[§] Ibid xvi. 16.   [||] St. John vi. 69, 70.

as in created things; a son is not the same individual nature as his father.

In every procession we have three things to consider, namely, the *action*, the *principle*, and the *term*. The *principle* is that from which the *term* proceeds. The *action* is the very act of the principle which produces the term, it is the way to the *term*, and the *term* or result is that which is produced.

That there are Processions in God no one has denied, except those who have denied the Mystery of the Holy Trinity. It is also clear from the Sacred Scriptures, and from the definitions and declarations of the Councils of Nice and Constantinople.

The reason for this arises from the fact, that there are three Persons in God, really distinct in one and the same divine nature. And this cannot be unless there be Processions. There cannot be three Persons unless there be some opposition or difference between them by which one can be distinguished from another. But, in the divine Persons there can be no opposition,* except what is called *relative* opposition, and the *relations* are founded on the divine Processions, and therefore there must be Processions in God.

According to Scripture, and the Creeds of faith, there are two Processions (*ad intra*) in God. There are only three Persons—the Father unbegotten, the Son begotten, and the Holy Ghost proceeding. Therefore, there are two and only two Processions, namely, the Procession of the Son from the Father, and of the Holy Ghost from the Father and the Son. The reason of this is, because we have to admit Procession in God according to His internal actions, or the actions that remain in Himself, and these are two and two only—the act of the intellect, and the act of the will, virtually distinct from one another.

6. Now we have to consider the question of the Sonship; that is, that the Procession of the Son is called generation, and not the Procession of the Holy Ghost.

As we have explained, there are in God two Processions: the Procession of the Son from the intellect; and of the Holy Ghost from the Will. In regard to these, some things are of faith; and these I shall state before introducing those on which the opinions of Theologians differ.

It is of faith that the Second Person of the Blessed Trinity is the Son and the only begotten Son of God; and, therefore, it is

---

*Opposition is here used in its technical Theological sense.

of faith that the Procession of the Son is a *generation*, but the Procession of the Holy Ghost is not a generation.

Hence, it follows that the Son proceeds from the Father by generation; the Holy Spirit does not proceed by generation, but by simple procession from the Father and the Son.

This doctrine is proved from Scripture, for the reason that, in holy Scripture, the Second Person is called the Son, and said to be begotten, and the only begotten, whilst the Holy Ghost is never called Son, and never said to have been begotten, but simply *proceeding*, as is expressed in the Athanasian Creed: " *The Son is from the Father alone, not made, nor created, but begotten. The Holy Ghost from the Father and the Son, not made, nor created, but proceeding.*"

7. In further elucidation of this doctrine, it is necesssary to understand what is meant by generation.

Generation is two-fold, the generation of animate and inanimate things. The generation of inanimate, or not living things, is the change effected by bringing them from the state of non-existence into existence, or their production from nothing, the same as creation; or from something else, from which they are produced by some external agency. Amongst living things generation is defined: *Origo viventis a vivente conjuncto in similitudine naturæ specificæ* : "The origin or coming forth of a living being from another, in the similitude of its specific nature;" in other other words, generation means " a substantial production, by virtue of which the being produced is made like in nature to the being that produces it." Thus a man produces a man, a horse a horse, and so on, because those, by virtue of their production, are made in the same nature as their progenitors. Notice the words " by virtue of the production or the procession ;" because Eve proceeded, or was made, from the rib of Adam, and this, although it was the origin or substantial production of one living being from another in the likeness of nature, yet that similitude was not by virtue of the production, because any other species of creature might be produced from the rib of Adam in the same way : and it was not by virtue of her production that Eve was a human being, hence her procession was not a generation, and she was not a child of Adam.

The procession of the Word in the divine nature is a real generation. It is the procession of a living being from a living being, namely, from the divine intelligence, and joined or united with its principle ; for the action by which the Son proceeds does not proceed outside God, but remains in Him by the most intimate union. And He proceeds in the likeness of nature, because the concept of the intellect is the likeness of the thing understood, and existing in the same nature, because in God to be and to understand are one and the same thing.

As to the reason why the procession of the Son is called generation, and not the procession of the Holy Ghost, there are various opinions. St. Augustine assigns it as the reason, because the Son proceeds from *one*. No Son proceeds from *two* Fathers. Vasques and others say, that it is because the Son proceeds as the Image of the Father. Others, because the Son has from the Father a nature by which He can produce another, namely, the Holy Ghost, Who proceeds from the two. Lastly, the reason assigned by St. Thomas and his followers is, that the Son proceeds from the divine intellect, which of itself assimulates to itself that which it produces; and the Holy Ghost proceeds from the divine Will which does not assimulate by its *own act*, or make its object like to itself. Although the Holy Ghost is in all things equal to, and like to the Father and the Son, this likeness is by reason of the Divine Nature which is common to the Three, and not by reason of the Procession.

For the rest, let us be satisfied to confess with St. Gregory Nazianzen, the generation of the Son, as well the procession of the Holy Ghost, is rather to be honoured than investigated, as the Mystery is ineffable.

It is in this eternal generation of the Son that we express our faith when we say the Creed. He is the Son of God under many lesser titles; because He was conceived by the Holy Ghost; because sent by the Father; because of the resurrection as the first-born of the children of men; because of His actual possession of the inheritance of the Kingdom of heaven; but in a way above all these, in a way peculiar to Himself, and in a way in which no other Son can have any share or similitude, He is the *only-begotten* Son of God *by eternal generation*.

8. He was before John the Baptist according to the testimony of St. John himself: *" This is He of whom I spoke: He that shall come after Me is preferred before Me, because He was before Me."**

He was before Abraham, which speaks a longer time than John the Baptist: *"Jesus said to them: Amen, amen, I say to you, before Abraham was made I am.†*

Christ's existence extends to a far longer period according to

---

* St. John i. 15. † St. John viii. 58.

the words of St. Peter : *"Because Christ also died once for our sins, the Just for the unjust, that He might offer us to God, being put to death indeed in the flesh, but enlivened in the Spirit. In which also coming He preached to those spirits that were in prison. Which had been sometime incredulous when they waited for the patience of God in the days of Noe when the Ark was a-building."** From which it appears, that Christ certainly preached by His same divine spirit, by which He afterwards raised Himself from the dead, to the souls in Limbo in the days of Noe, and while the ark was being prepared.†

Finally, He existed at the beginning of the world, for He created it as the Scriptures tell us. Hence St. Paul in his Epistle to the Hebrews tells us, (God) *"in these days hath spoken to us by His Son, Whom He hath appointed heir of all things, by Whom also He made the world."*‡

There remain two other expressions in the Nicene Creed, which belong to the explanation of this Article of Faith : namely, *Consubstantial to the Father, and, By Whom all things were made.*

---

* 1 St. Peter iii. 19, 20.   † Pearson, Art. ii.   ‡ Heb. i. 2.

SECTION 2. (ARTICLE II.)

THE DIVINITY OF CHRIST.

1. The meaning of the word consubstantial.—2. The Son the Second Person is consubstantial with the Father.—3. Scriptural proofs of the Divinity of Christ: (a) To Him divine powers and rights are attributed. (b) To Him divine honours are to be given. (c) Christ affirmed His Divinity by His words. (d) The disciples and Jews understood the words of Christ as asserting His Divinity.—4. The Divinity of the *Word* ὄλόγος as proved from the first portion of the Gospel of St. John.

CONSUBSTANTIAL.

1. THIS word means having one and the same substance. It may be two-fold : (a) Individual consubstantiality, and (b) Specific consubstantiality. That is, it may mean one and the same individual ; or one and the same only in species.

Individual consubstantiality of the three Persons of the Holy Trinity is the Catholic doctrine. Merely consubstantiality in species would mean three Gods, the same as Peter, James, and John signify three men, although they have the same specific human nature. If the three divine Persons were one only in species, they could be said to have three individual natures and to be three Gods, which is Polytheism.

If the Son and the Holy Ghost be God, in the same way as the Father, there is in them only one and the same divine nature, one and the same individual divinity. Here we have to confine ourselves to the Son, the Second Person of the Trinity ; as we have our faith in the Holy Ghost expressed in another Article of the Creed.

THE PERSON OF THE SON IS CONSUBSTANTIAL WITH THE FATHER.

2. The proofs for this truth may be taken from the different places of the Sacred Scriptures, which prove at the same time the divinity of the Word and the divinity of Jesus Christ. The first regard the Word in Himself, and the second the Word incarnate

3. This truth is defined clearly in the Council of Nice, and expressed clearly in the words of the Creed. I shall here confine myself to the Gospel revelations concerning the divinity of Jesus Christ, and place the texts in the order in which they are given by the Abbé Moulin.*

(a) "*To Jesus Christ is attributed divine powers and rights.*" 1. "*Amen, amen, I say unto you......for what things soever He* (the Father) *doth, these the Son also doth in like manner.*"† 2. He recommends us to practice virtue in His name.‡ 3. He declares that He has the power to forgive sins.‖ 4. This power He exercises in His own Person, and communicates to His disciples.§ 5. He announces Himself as the Supreme Judge of the living and the dead.¶ 6. He disposes of the rewards, and the places of the Kingdom of heaven, as His own inheritance: "*The Son of man shall send his Angels, and shall gather together His elect from the four winds, from the uttermost part of the earth to the uttermost part of heaven.*° *And every one that hath left house, or brethren, or sisters, or father, or mother, or wife, or children, or lands, for My name's sake, shall receive a hundred-fold, and shall possess life everlasting.*"** "*He that eateth My flesh and drinketh My blood hath everlasting life ; and I will raise him up at the last day.*"‖‖

(b) To the same Jesus Christ is attributed divine honours. 1. "*That all men may honour the Son, as they honour the Father. He who honoureth not the Son, honoureth not the Father who hath sent Him.*"‡‡ 2. "*He that loveth father or mother more than Me is not worthy of Me ; and he that loveth son or daughter more than Me is not worthy of Me.*"†† 3. "*If any one love Me, he will keep My word, and My Father will love him, and We will come to him and make our abode with him.*"§§

Together with faith and love, Jesus Christ commands adoration. (a) This is proved from the example of the blind man in the Gospel, to whom Jesus said : "*Dost thou believe in the Son of God ? He answered and said, Who is he Lord, that I may believe*

---

* Demons. de la divinité du Catholicisme, 2 Partie. Cap. iv.
† St. John v. 19.   ‡ St. Matt. x. 32 et seq.   ‖ St. Luke v. 24.
§ St. John xx. 23.   ¶ St. Matt. xxv.   ° St. Mark xiii. 27.
** St. Matt. xix. 29.   ‖‖ St. John vi. 55.   ‡‡ St. John v. 23.
†† St. Matt. x. 37.   §§ St. John xiv. 23.

in Him? And Jesus said to him, Thou hast both seen Him, and it is He that talketh with thee. Then the blind man said, I believe Lord. And falling down, he adored Him."* The holy women and the disciples adored Christ also. And when St. Thomas threw himself at His feet exclaiming, " My Lord and my God !" Jesus Christ approved of it, and said to him, "Because thou hast seen, Thomas, thou hast believed ; blessed are they who have not seen and have believed."†

(c) From these revelations we see that Jesus Christ affirmed His divinity by His manner of acting. He affirmed it still more explicitly by His words. He declared Himself to be Christ the Son of God, equal to the Father, and one with Him and the Holy Spirit. 1. "I and the Father are one."‡ 2. "Though you will not believe Me, believe the works ; that you may know and believe that the Father is in me and I in the Father."‖ 3. "I am the light of the world."§ 4. "I am the way, the truth, and the life."° 5. "He that seeth Me, seeth the Father also."= 6. "All things which the Father hath are mine."** 7. "And no man hath ascended into heaven but He that descended from heaven, the Son of man who is in heaven." ††

(d) In these revelations on the part of Jesus Christ, we find clear formal statements of His divinity. The disciples and the Jews were not deceived. Both the one and the other understood that Jesus Christ, in calling Himself the Son of God, did not signify merely a just man, or a friend of God, but that He meant the Divine Word, the Second Person of the Blessed Trinity, the eternal and only-begotten Son of God, God the same as the Father and the Holy Ghost. Thus, (1) when He asked His Apostles, "But whom do you say that I am ? Simon Peter answered and said, Thou art Christ, the Son of the living God. And Jesus answering said unto him, "Blessed art thou, Simon Bar-Jona, because flesh and blood hath not revealed it to thee, but my Father who is in heaven."‡‡ (2) And "she (Martha) saith to Him, Yea, Lord, I have believed that Thou

---

* St. John ix. 35, 38.   † St. John xx. 29.   ‡ St. John x. 30.
‖ St. John x. 38.   § St. John viii. 12.   ° St. John xiv. 6.
= St. John xiv. 9.   ** St. John xvi. 13.   †† St. John iii. 13.
‡‡ St. Matt. xvi. 15, 17.

art Christ, the Son of the living God, who art come into the world."*

St. John commences his Gospel by proclaiming the divinity of Christ. *"In the beginning was the Word, and the Word was with God, and the Word was God."* Later on I shall explain his words more fully. Other Evangelists and Sacred writers are no less explicit in their statements. Holy David, before them, proclaimed the eternal generation of Christ in the bosom of the Father. And Isaias salutes Him as *"God the powerful, the Father of the world to come, the Prince of peace."*

The incredulous Jews understood the assertions of Jesus Christ regarding His divinity in the sense here explained. When Christ on one occasion asked them why they wished to stone Him. *"The Jews answered Him : For a good work we stone Thee not, but for blasphemy ; and because that Thou, being a man, makest Thyself God."†* And when on the day of His Passion Caiphas exclaimed : *"I adjure Thee by the living God tell us if Thou be Christ the Son of God !"* Jesus answered : *Tu dixisti. Thou hast said it ;* in other words, *I am.* And Pilate, when he said he could find no cause for the condemnation of Christ, the Jews answered him, *"We have a law, and according to the law He should die, because He made Himself the Son of God."‡*

Jesus Christ is therefore truly God. Friends and enemies listened to and heard this doctrine from Himself and from His Apostles, and for 1900 years the Christian world has believed in the divinity of Jesus Christ.

Jesus Christ, Who is truly God, is also called *Our Lord.*

The word Lord is that name of God which is expressed in the Hebrew by Jehovah (in Greek Κυριος). And this was distinctly applied to Christ by the Angels at His birth : "For this day is born to you a Saviour, Who is *Christ the Lord,* in the City of David."§ St. Thomas calls Him : *My Lord and my God.*

This is also the title of King or Ruler ; and so Christ is *"King of kings and Lord of lords. God hath subjected all under His feet, and hath made Him head over all the Church."‖* And in the Acts of the Apostles it is said, *"Therefore let all the house of Israel know most certainly, that God hath made both Lord and Christ, this same Jesus whom you have crucified."***

Christ therefore, the only-begotten Son of God, is our Lord, because He is the Lord of all things and of all persons, which

---

* St. John xi. 27.   † St. John x. 33.   ‡ St. John xix. 7.
§ St. Luke ii. 2.   ‖ Eph. i. 22.   ** Acts ii. 36.

He must be, Who, as God made all things, and to Whom all power is given as Man. He is our Lord, not only because we are created by Him, but also, as we shall see afterwards, because of His Redemption, and the manner in which He purchased our sanctification and salvation.

As a connecting link between this Article and the next, I may quote the first portion of the beginning of St. John's Gospel, which contains the dogmatic description of the Person of Jesus Christ under the name of *the Word* (ὁ Λόγος).

4. "*In the beginning was the Word, and the Word was with God, and the Word was God. The same was in the beginning with God. All things were made by Him ; and without Him was made nothing that was made. In Him was life, and the life was the light of men. And the light shineth in darkness, and the darkness did not comprehend it. There was a man sent from God whose name was John. This man came for a witness, to give testimony of the light, that all men might believe through Him. He was not the light, but was to give testimony of the light. That was the true light, which enlighteneth every man that cometh into this world. He was in the world, and the world was made by Him, and the world knew Him not. He came unto His own, and His own received Him not. But as many as received Him, He gave them power to be made the Sons of God, to them that believed in His name. Who are born, not of blood, nor of the will of the flesh, nor of the will of man, but of God. And the Word was made flesh, and dwelt among us (and we saw His glory as it were of the only-begotten of the Father) full of grace and truth.*"*

In this portion of the Gospel of St. John we have the doctrine concerning the Person of the Word clearly delivered. His eternity, personality, and divinity ; His relation to His creatures, and His life-giving Incarnation.

In the beginning was the Word. (ὁ Λόγος). Only St. John, of all the writers of the New Testament, makes use of this expression to signify the Person of Christ, although St. Paul, by the words (ὁ Λογος του Θεου) " *the Word of God is living and effectual*," signifies the hypostatic Word of God.

The attributes of the Word as signified in this chapter are :—

(a) *His Personality.* It is said that the Word was *with* God ; that all things were made by Him ; that He came unto His own ; that He gave them power to become the

---

sons of God; that He dwelt amongst us. It is identified with Jesus Christ, Who is certainly a Person.

(b) *His Eternity.* He was in the beginning; that is, before all time.

(c) *His distinction from the Father.* He was *with* God the Father.

(d) *His Divinity and consubstantiality* with the Father. *And the Word was God.*

(e) *His creative power.* Of all things that were made by Him, nothing is excepted from the creative power of the Word.

(f) *He was the light and the life of men.* That is, the essential and divine life in the Word, and its participation in created things by the natural life which they have received; and, more especially, it signifies the supernatural life of grace here, and of beatitude hereafter; because that life is called the light of men......which the darkness did not comprehend, and which gave them power to become the sons of God. He is called the Life, inasmuch as He is at the same time the efficient and meritorious cause of that life in us. That He was the light of men, follows from His being the life. He was the supernatural light by faith and revelation here, and by the vision of God in heaven, because to no man has that light ever come except (*intuitu meritorum Christi*) through Christ.

(g) *His divine and only-begotten Sonship. And the Word was made flesh,* &c. This reveals the great mystery, the manner in which the Word came unto His own. Made *flesh*, that is, made man according to a hebraism. The Evangelist uses flesh instead of man (*caro* instead of *homo*) against the false teachers of his day, who denied the humanity of Christ on the ground that the flesh came from an evil principle. *And dwelt among us.* That is, He lived and conversed with us men on earth in the flesh, and not only as a visible man, but as the only-begotten Son of God, *full of grace and truth.* The Word, by His superabundant communication of His gifts to His creatures, shows Him to us *full of grace,* inasmuch as every grace and gift in the supernatural order comes through the Word to us; and *full of truth,* inasmuch as He, the Divine Word, teaches us the way of salvation, and opens to us the secrets of the divinity both in time and eternity.

ARTICLE III.

APOSTLES' CREED.	NICENE CREED.
"Who was conceived by the Holy Ghost, born of the Virgin Mary."	"*Who for us men, and for our Salvation, came down from heaven,* and became incarnate of the Holy Ghost of the Virgin Mary, *and was made man.*"

SECTION 1. (ARTICLE III.)

THE INCARNATION.

1. The meaning of the Incarnation.—2. Jesus Christ is truly God.—3. Christ is really and truly man.—4. Christ has a true human body.—5. Christ, the Word of God, took to Himself a true human soul.—6. The Personal or Hypostatic union of the two natures in Christ, and in Christ there are these two natures, Divine and human.—7. There is only one Person in Christ; to wit, the Person of the Son of God.—8. Nestorius, his heresy, and its condemnation.—9. Eutyches, his heresy, and its condemnation.—10. The doctrine of one Person and two natures in Christ as expressed in the Creed of St. Athanasius.—11. The *Communicatio Idiomatum*; its meaning.—12. It is defined as a dogma of faith that the blessèd Virgin is the Mother of God.—13. The rules to be observed in speaking of Christ according to the *Communicatio Idiomatum*.

1. THIS Article asserts the doctrine of the INCARNATION.
This word means Christ taking upon Him our human nature. By it the Son of God became the Son of man. Remaining perfect God, He became perfect man *of a rational soul and a human body subsisting. And the Word was made flesh, and dwelt among us.*
In the preceding Article we have seen that Christ is truly God, and the proofs of His divinity are there given. We have now to establish His humanity, that He is true man as well as

true God. And for this purpose I must proceed with some further explanation of the mystery of the Incarnation before speaking of Christ's conception and nativity. The Incarnation means that God the Son, the second Person of the Blessed Trinity, became man.

He was God from eternity, and He became man in time, so that we believe Jesus Christ to be true God and true man. True God and true man means that Jesus Christ has two natures, the nature of God and the nature of man ; but these two natures are united in one divine Person, namely, the Person of God the Son. Hence, our Lord has only one Person ; for as the Athanasian Creed expresses it, " As the rational soul and the flesh is one man, so God and man is one Christ." Our Lord says : " *I and the Father are one ;*" and again, " *The Father is greater than I.*" In these texts the same Person *I* speaks of Himself both as God and as man.*

In this doctrine we have to include the (*a*) divine nature of Jesus, (*b*) the human nature of Christ, (*c*) the Personal union of the two natures in Christ, and (*d*) the oneness or unity of the Person of Jesus Christ. These four points may now be explained in order.

THE DIVINE NATURE OF CHRIST.

2. That Jesus Christ is truly God, consubstantial with the Father, that is one and the same substance with the Father, is fully explained in the preceding Article ; and from this it follows that Christ has the nature of God, and that He is one and the same eternal Being as God the Father. This is shown by His words, and by His works ; and for nineteen centuries Jesus Christ has been adored, loved, and obeyed as God by millions of human beings. A countless number of Martyrs have given their lives rather than deny Christ to be God. How can this faith, and this love, be explained if Christ be not God ? As well might we assert that the earth has been enlightened and heated without the sun to give it light and heat.†

THE HUMAN NATURE OF CHRIST.

3. Christ is really and truly man, as He is perfect God. He has a rational soul and a human body like us ; " *for,*" in the words of St Paul, " *By a man came death, and by a man the resur-*

---

* Companion to the Catechism.   † l'Abbé Moulin.

rection of the dead." From which we conclude that Christ was as much a man as the first Adam. He is, therefore, called the Son of man; and in man's nature He was promised from the beginning. To Eve it was said, *"And in thy seed."* Then to Abraham, next to David and his son, and thus we have the genealogy of Christ as given by St. Matthew. The Son of David, the Son of Abraham, &c., consequently of the same nature with them. And we, therefore, are His brethren, descending from the same father Adam : *" Wherefore it behoved Him in all things to be made like unto His brethren, that He might become a merciful and faithful High Priest before God, that He might be a propitiation for the sins of the people."**

4. As man consists of two parts, body and soul, so doth Christ. Christ's body is true and real, not a mere shadow or phantasm. It was an earthly body formed of the substance of Mary, His mother, and not a body brought down from heaven. He assumed a body, at His conception, of the Blessed Virgin. *"Therefore because the children are partakers of flesh and blood, He also Himself in like manner hath been partaker of the same, that through death He might destroy him who had the empire of death, that is to say the devil."*†

The verity of His body stands on the truth of His nativity; and the actions and sufferings of His life show the nature of His flesh. He was first born with *a body prepared for Him,* of the same appearance with those of other infants; He grew up by degrees, and *came eating and drinking,* and when He did so suffered hunger and thirst. Those executioners, *who ploughed upon His back and made long furrows,* the thorns which pricked His temples, the nails which penetrated His hands and feet, and the spear which pierced His side, testify the natural tenderness and reality of His flesh. And lest His miraculous fasting, and walking on the water, and His sudden standing in the midst of His disciples when the doors were shut, should raise an opinion that His body was not truly flesh, He confirmed first His own disciples (and all others after them) by His action as narrated in the Gospel: *"See My hands and My feet that it is I myself; handle and see; for a spirit hath not flesh and bone as you see Me to have."*‖ The reality of Christ's body is also confirmed by the words of St. John: *"Every spirit which confesseth that Jesus Christ is come in the flesh, is of God. And every spirit which dissolveth Jesus is not of God."*§

---

* Heb. ii. 17.　† Heb. ii. 14.　‖ St. Luke xxiv. 39.　§ Eph. iv. 2, 3.

Christ, who is both God and man, was as soon denied by unbelievers to be man as God. Simon Magus was the first to deny this, and after him a sect called the *Docetae*, who imagined that Christ was man only in appearance.*

That the Word took to Himself a true human body, and not a mere phantom-like appearance, is also proved by the words of St. John: *Et verbum caro factum est*—"*And the Word was made flesh*"; the Evangelist speaks of real and true flesh, and therefore a real and true body.

5. The Word took to Himself a human soul. "*Jesus increased in wisdom and age and grace before God and man.*"† Wisdom and grace belong not to the flesh, or the body, but to the soul; and God's wisdom or knowledge cannot increase.

As we read in St. John's Gospel, Christ said, "*I lay down My life for My sheep.*" And again: "*Therefore doth the Father love Me because I lay down My life that I may take it again.*" These words cannot be understood merely of the body, because in no place is the body called life or soul; nor can they be understood of the Divinity, which the Incarnate Word cannot lay down and take up again; therefore, they must be understood of some kind of soul. That soul was (*a*) sensitive because it was capable of sadness, dread, disgust, &c. "*He began to grow sorrowful and to be sad.*"‡ "*And He began to fear and to be heavy, and He saith to them, My soul is sorrowful even unto death.*"§ "*And there appeared to Him an Angel from heaven strengthening Him.*"‖ That soul was a rational soul according to the words: "*Jesus therefore, when He had taken the vinegar, said, It is consummated: and bowing His head, He gave up the ghost.*"** And those others: "*Father, if Thou wilt, remove this chalice from Me; but yet not My will but Thine be done.*"†† And again: "*And Jesus crying with a loud voice, said, Father, into Thy hands I commend My spirit. And saying this, He gave up the ghost.*"‡‡ As His death was the separation of His soul from His body, so did His life, as man, consist in the union of that soul with that body. This particular truth must be maintained against the false teachers, who, in olden times, taught that Christ assumed human flesh, but that the Word or His Divinity was to that body in place of an informing soul.

---

* Pearson, Analysis of Art. iii.   † St. Luke ii. 53.   ‡ St. Matt. xxvi. 37
§ St. Mark xiv. 33-34.   ‖ St. Luke xxii. 43.   ** St. John xix. 30.
†† St. Luke xxii. 42.   ‡‡ St. Luke xxiii. 46.

The Personal Union of the Two Natures in Christ.

6. The divine nature and the human nature are quite distinct in Christ. The one is not the other; neither is one changed into the other. Each has its own operations. The divine nature has its divine intelligence and divine will; and the human nature has its human intellect and human will. This doctrine is proved from the Scriptures, wherein Christ is very often said to be true God and true man ; and this could not be said unless Christ has a double nature, divine and human, distinct and unconfused.

This union is called hypostatic, that is to say, personal, because both the divine operations and the human operations in Jesus Christ belong to one and the same Person.

By this hypostatic union, neither is the form or nature of God changed, nor the form or nature of man, nor does any third or new production result from the connection of the two, for then Christ would be neither God nor man.

Although the two natures are distinct they are not separated, for, by the hypostatic union, the human nature is joined to the Word by a most intimate, real, and physical union. The Word unites the humanity to Itself immediately, and by Itself without any medium coming between them; because, as St. Thomas says, " *Immediate et per se terminat, complet et perficit humanam naturam.*"

In Christ there are, therefore, two natures, divine and human, distinct and unconfused. This clearly follows from the proofs of Christ's divinity, and His humanity.

One Person in Christ, and that Divine.

7. There is, however, only one Person in Christ, and that the Divine Person of the Son of God. In holy Scripture one and the same Christ is constantly brought before us as the Son of God and the Son of man. But Christ is not thus brought before us as God and man on account of the identity of the divine and human nature, as is clear, but on account of the identity of Person ; and, therefore, in Christ there is only one Person, and that the Divine, united in two natures, truly, really, and substantially.

The reason of this is that God truly became man, according to the express testimony of St. John and other inspired writers

K

above quoted. But God did not become man by the change of
the Divinity into flesh, or into human nature, or *vice versa*, nor
by a mere moral or accidental union with man; therefore by
what is known as the hypostatic or personal union. Not by the
change of the Divinity into humanity, for God's nature cannot
admit of such a change or transformation; not by a mere moral
or accidental union such as exists between two friends, because,
however close that union may be, it can never be said that one
is or becomes the other; and it can be said of the Divine Word
that He became flesh or man. Moreover, all the just are united
to God by this moral union, and the moral union of just souls
with God is common to the three Divine Persons, and not
proper in any singular or peculiar way to the second Person.

Far otherwise is the union of the Word with our nature,
for in consequence of this union the Word is said to be made
man; to have annihilated Himself; to have taken the form of a
servant, and therefore the union with human nature is physical,
personal, or hypostatic.

8. Nestorius, Patriarch of Constantinople, and his followers,
asserted that there were two persons in Christ, and this heresy
was condemned in the Council of Ephesus, the third General
Council of the Church, in 431.

9. Eutyches, the Superior of a Monastery in Constantinople,
and his followers, asserted that there was only one nature in
Christ. This heresy was condenmed in the Council of Chalcedon,
which is the fourth General Council, in the year 451.

10. And the Faith of the Church in regard to the doctrine
of one Person, and two natures in Christ is distinctly expressed
in the Creed of St. Athanasius, "*For the right faith is that we
believe and confess that our Lord Jesus Christ, the Son of God, is
God and man.*

"*God of the substance of the Father, begotten before the world;
and man, of the substance of His Mother, born in the world.*

"*Perfect God and perfect man : of a reasonable soul and
human flesh subsisting : equal to the Father as touching His Godhead, and inferior to the Father as touching His manhood.*

"*Who although He be God and man, yet He is not two, but
one Christ.*

"*One, not by reason of conversion of the God-head into flesh,
but by taking of the manhood into God. One altogether, not by
confusion of substance, but by unity of Person.*

"*For as the rational soul and flesh is one man, so God and
Man is one Christ.*"

COMMUNICATIO IDIOMATUM.

11. Literally this is the communication of idioms, and it means that the attributes and properties of the divine and human natures may be mutually predicated or asserted of each other; so that we can say, God is Man, and Man is God, in speaking of Christ, and also that God suffered and died for us upon the Cross.

Nestorius and those who denied the personal union of the two natures in Christ, denied the *Communicatio Idiomatum*, as this is founded on the hypostatic or personal union. Eutyches and those who confounded the two natures into one, erred in the *Communicatio Idiomatum* in various ways; and to this class the Ubiquists of more recent times may be said to belong. These held the real communication of the divine attributes to the human nature of Christ, so that, after the Incarnation, they held that His human nature was everywhere, together with the divine nature, and that it has immensity; while our faith tells us that Christ's human nature is only in heaven and in the Blessed Sacrament of the Altar.

It is of faith that in Christ the *Communicatio Idiomatum* is to be admitted. This is proved from Holy Scripture, which in many places ascribes divine attributes to man, and human attributes to God. Thus St. John says, "And the *Word was made flesh*." And St. Paul, in his Epistle to the Philippians and elsewhere, speaks of the Son of God being born of a woman, and of the Lord of Glory being crucified.

12. This was defined in the Council of Ephesus, when it declared it to be a truth of faith, that the Blessed Virgin is the Mother of God. All the arguments and reasons that prove Christ to be both God and man, serve also to prove this *Communication*. When two forms are found in one substance they can in the concrete be mutually predicated of each other, such as we can say, in speaking of a blazing fire, what is red is hot; and again, we can predicate of man the properties of either soul or body. He is tall or stout, intelligent, good or bad, as the case may be, all predicated of the one person, man. Thus, in what may be called an expository syllogism, it may be said, *Christ is Man, and Christ is God*; therefore *Man is God, and God is Man*.

It is also of faith, that there is no real communication of attributes, for all the gifts that human nature can have must be finite and created, and therefore distinct from the uncreated divine perfections of God.

The divine perfections cannot in reality be communicated to the humanity, because they are infinite, and because it is impossible to communicate one of them without communicating all the others. It is needless to say, that finite perfections, as they exist in creatures, are repugnant to God, because He can have nothing by participation, or nothing which is imperfect in any way.

In speaking, therefore, of Christ, it is necessary for the sake of accuracy and correct doctrine to remember :—

(a) It is of faith that one nature in Christ cannot be predicated of the other in the abstract—that is, we cannot say that the *humanity* is the *divinity*, because the two natures remain distinct and unconfused in Christ; and in the abstract, they signify two distinct natures, and one is not therefore the other in this sense.

(b) It follows from the preceding, and it is of faith, that the properties or perfectious of the divinity cannot either in the abstract or in the concrete be predicated of the humanity. For it is defined that the properties of both natures remain distinct and unconfused, and incommunicable to each other.

(c) For the same reason, and with the same certainty, we have to believe that the properties of the humanity can not either in the abstract, or in the concrete, be predicated of the divinity taken in the abstract.

(d) From these it follows that the divinity in the abstract cannot properly and formally be predicated of man ; nor can humanity and its properties in the abstract be predicated of God.*

13. I may lay down the following rules to be observed, in speaking of the God Man, according to the *Communicatio Idiomatum*.

Rule 1.—God and His attributes can be predicated of Christ and of man by a true and correct predication, *e.g.*, It is of faith that this man, viz., Christ, is God ; therefore He is omnipotent, eternal, omniscient, &c.

---

* Divinity and humanity are abstract terms, and signify the divine and human natures. *God* and *man* are concrete terms, and signify the Person who terminates both natures and unites them in Himself.

Rule 2.—Whatever is said essentially of God, and whatever is said essentially and personally of the Son of God, can be absolutely predicated of this man, Christ.

Rule 3.—Although the divine attributes can be simply and absolutely predicated of Christ, this cannot be done with limitation (reduplication) as to His humanity. Hence this proposition is not true. Christ, inasmuch as He is man, is God.

Rule 4.—Whatever is essentially said of man can be absolutely predicated of God, in the person of Christ.

Rule 5.—This predication, though made of God absolutely, would not be correct with the limitation or reduplication to the divinity, so that we could not say that God, as such, was born and died.

Rule 6.—There are some expressions that require a human or created person in order to be verified, and these cannot be predicated either of Christ, or of the Word, or of God, *e.g.*, *Pure man*.

From the above doctrine, and the fact that the human nature in Jesus Christ belongs to the Person of the Son of God, it follows :—

(a) That that nature is adorable by reason of the divine Person to whom it is united.

(b) That for the same reason the human operations of the Man God are of infinite value.

(c) That the Blessed Virgin Mary is the Mother of God. We adore the humanity in Jesus Christ, because it is the humanity of the Son of God. The operations or works of this humanity are of infinite value, because they are the operations or works of the Son of God, who is infinite. Mary is the Mother of God, because she is the Mother of Jesus Christ, who is God.

SECTION 2. (ARTICLE III.)

THE CONCEPTION OF CHRIST OR THE MANNER OF HIS INCARNATION.

1.—The Gospel narrative of the Conception or Incarnation of Christ.—2. An Angel announces the Mystery.—3. The doctrine of Mary's Virginity revealed; or proved from the definition of the Church and the explicit testimony of Holy Scripture, and from congruous or becoming reasons.—4. The detestable heresy of Helvidius and the reasons of its condemnation.—5. Three objections against the perpetual virginity of the Blessed Virgin answered.—6. Mary's question, and the answer given by the Angel: "*The Holy Ghost shall come upon thee,*" &c.—7. The threefold work which was accomplished in one and the same instant, in the Mystery of the Incarnation.—8. The action of Mary and of the Holy Ghost in the accomplishment of this Mystery.—9. At the instant the Blessed Virgin gave her consent in the words, "*Behold the handmaid of the Lord,*" &c.; the word became flesh and dwelt among us.—10. The Blessed Virgin, in the Conception of Christ, received a new and singular perfection of sanctity.

THE Incarnation means that God the Son took to Himself the nature of man, according to the words of St. John: "*The Word was made flesh, and dwelt among us.*"

We are told in the Creed how the Son of God took to Himself the flesh and nature of man. He was conceived by the Holy Ghost, born of the Virgin Mary.

He was conceived. "*When the fulness of time was come, God sent His Son, made of a woman.*" *

1. Now that woman was a virgin. "*For the Angel Gabriel was sent from God......to a virgin......whose name was Mary. And the Angel said to her, Thou shalt conceive in thy womb, and bear a Son......And Mary said, How shall this be done, because I know not man. The Angel answered, The Holy Ghost shall come upon thee, and the power of the Most High shall overshadow thee; and therefore the most holy one that shall be born of thee shall be called the Son of God.*"† Thus was accomplished the prophecy of Isaias, "*Behold a virgin shall be with child, and shall bear a Son.*"‖ As, originally, God by His Almighty power made the first man of the slime or dust of the earth,° so the Divine Spirit, by the same Almighty power, formed the body of the

---

* Gal. iv. 4.   † St. Luke i. 26-38.   ‖ St. Matt. i. 23.
°Gen. ii. 17

Saviour in the womb of the Virgin, and enabled her, contrary to the order of nature, to perform the office of a mother. "If," says St. Ambrose, bishop of Milan, "you will not believe this doctrine of the priests, believe at least the oracles of Christ—believe the sayings of the Angels—believe the Apostles' Creed, which the Roman Church possesses and preserves pure and unadulterated."*

In explanation of this Mystery, all that is required is to dwell upon the Gospel narrative.

2. God sent an Angel to announce this Mystery.

The Angel Gabriel was sent by the power and the authority of God. He belongs to the order of Archangels, as he was sent to announce great and wonderful things. As a bad Angel was the cause of the ruin of the human race, so a good Angel is now employed to announce the reparation of mankind.

This Angel's name was Gabriel, the fortitude or strength of God ; and he is supposed to watch over the wars and battles of men. The announcement of the Incarnation therefore belonged to his office, as by the advent of Christ the power of Satan was to be overcome, and victory obtained over that power in favour of the human race.

He was sent into a city of Galilee called Nazareth. It was there the Blessed Virgin lived at the time.

He was sent to a Virgin, who was espoused to a man whose name was Joseph.

3. Here we have the doctrine of Mary's virginity clearly revealed. It is a dogma of faith that the Mother of God was always a virgin, both before the conception, in the conception of Christ, and ever afterwards.

Many Councils of the Church define and suppose this, the Creeds of faith affirm it, and it is proclaimed by all the Fathers of the Church by unanimous consent. Thus, in the 3rd Canon of the Council of Lateran held under Martin I., it is said : "If any one refuse to confess according to the Holy Fathers, properly and according to the truth, that the Holy Mother of God, the immaculate Mary ever Virgin......did conceive without a human father, of the Holy Ghost the Word of God, who was born of the Father before all ages, and did bring forth or beget Him without corruption, her virginity after His birth remaining ever afterwards ; let him be condemned."

And Paul IV. in his constitution, Cum quorundum, A.D.

---

* St. Ambose apud Dr. Lingard. Catechism. Art. III.

1555, amongst other heresies enumerates the errors of those who assert, dogmatize or believe, *that our Lord Jesus Christ was not conceived according to the flesh, in the womb of the most blessed and ever Virgin Mary, of the Holy Ghost, but, as other men was conceived, of the seed of Joseph* .....*or that the same blessed Virgin Mary was not the true Mother of God, or that she did not always preserve her virginal integrity, before the conception and birth of Christ, in His conception and birth, and after His birth.*

This singular privilege of the Mother of God rests not only on tradition but on the explicit testimony of Holy Scripture.

According to the Prophets, it was certain that the Messiah was to be born of a Virgin : that He was to be born miraculously, and be the Son of a *woman*, not of a *man*. (a) "*The seed of the woman shall crush the serpent's head.*"* (b) According with this promise is the prediction of Jeremias. "*For the Lord hath created a new thing upon the earth*: A WOMAN SHALL COMPASS A MAN.†" The *new* thing is that creation which was wrought in a woman only, without a man. And when the Jews would force the phrase of *compassing* a man to anything else than a conception, they contradict the first part of the promise neither *new* as common to all men, nor *a creation* as an easy natural production. (c) Then, we have the words of the Prophet Isaias, "*Therefore the Lord Himself shall give you a sign ; Behold a virgin shall conceive and bear a son, and his name shall be called Emmanuel,*"‡ which, as St. Matthew adds,|| "*being interpreted, is God with us.*"

"It is evident that Mary, the Mother of Jesus, was a virgin when she bore Him, and when she brought forth her first-born Son, and she was a virgin when and after she was espoused to St. Joseph ; (a) the angel *Gabriel was sent from God to a virgin espoused*, &c. She was a virgin also after the angel's salutation. She asks, (b) "*How shall this be done, because I know not man?*" Also after her conception by the Holy Ghost ; (c) "*For when his mother Mary was espoused to Joseph, before they came together, she was found with child of the Holy Ghost.* (d) Also when she had brought forth she remained a virgin, according to St. Matthew's application of Isaias : *A virgin shall conceive and shall bring forth a son.*"

The congruous reasons, assigned by St. Thomas, for the perpetual virginity of the Mother of God may be arranged in the following manner :—

It was congruous and reasonable that Christ should be

---

* Gen. iii. 15.   † Jer. xxxi. 22.   ‡ Isa. vii. 14.   St. Matthew i. 23.

conceived of a virgin : (*a*) To preserve the dignity of God the Father, who sent our Saviour into the world. He was the natural and true Son of God, and, therefore, it was incongruous that He should have any other Father but God, or that the dignity of Father should be transferred to another. (*b*) This was becoming the Son who was sent. He is the *Word of God*. The word of the mind is conceived without any corruption of the heart. On the contrary, the corruption of the heart interferes with the perfect conception of the word. Therefore, because flesh was assumed by the Word of God in such a manner that it became His flesh, it was therefore conceived without the corruption of His mother. (*c*) It was becoming to the sacred humanity which Christ assumed ; because sin could not be found in that by which the sin of the world was to be removed or blotted out. He was not therefore conceived in that manner by which, according to the common law of God, original sin is propagated. (*d*) The end of the Incarnation required this manner of Christ's coming, namely, being conceived and born of a virgin. He came that men might be born again to God, not by the will of the flesh, nor the will of man, but of God, that is, by the power of God.

There are three reasons assigned for the preservation of Mary's virginity in the birth of Christ. (*a*) It became the Word of God to be thus born, because the Word is not only conceived without corruption, but it also proceeds from the heart without corruption ; and, therefore, it was becoming that the body of the Word of God should be born of the unsullied womb of a virgin. (*b*) The effects of the Incarnation required that the virginity of Mary should be preserved in the birth of Christ, inasmuch as He came to remove all our stains. (*c*) This was due to the Mother of God that she might suffer no diminution of her honour.

4. The error of Helvidius is to be utterly detested, namely, that the Mother of Christ lost her virginity after the birth of Christ, and had other children. (*a*) This would be derogatory to the perfection of Christ, for, as by His divine nature, He was the only-begotten Son of the Father, so, according to His human nature, He should be the only Son of His Mother. (*b*) This error does an injury to the Holy Ghost, whose Sanctuary was the virginal womb in which He formed the body of Christ, and hence this sanctuary was not to be profaned by any unworthy carnal contact. (*c*) It is derogatory to the dignity and sanctity of the Mother of God, because it would seem to show her as a most ungrateful soul in not being content with such a Son, and to suffer the loss of her virginity after its miraculous preservation,

in the conception and birth of Christ. (d) This would impute the greatest presumption and dishonour to St. Joseph, inasmuch as he was made aware by the message of an angel that Mary was of child by the Holy Ghost, and that He who was born of her should be called the Son of God.

For these reasons holy writers generally apply to her in the figurative sense the words of the Prophet, *This gate shall be shut, it shall not be opened, and no man shall pass through it, because the Lord, the God of Israel, hath entered in by it, and it shall be shut.**

5. Against the perpetual virginity of the Blessed Virgin three objections are commonly quoted.

(a) From St. Matthew's testimony,† Joseph knew not Mary *until* she had brought forth her first-born Son : they would infer that afterwards he knew her. But the *negation anteceding* "until" is no *affirmation following it.* Thus, in Genesis,‡ when God said to Jacob, "I will not leave thee until I have done that......," it follows not that when that was done He left him.

(b) From Christ being termed the *first-born* Son of Mary, they infer she must have had a *second*; but might as well conclude that wherever *there is one* there *must be two.* For in this particular the Scripture notion of priority *excludes* an *antecedent*, but *infers* not a *consequent. Sanctify unto me,* saith the Lord, *all the first-born.* This was a fixed law obliging immediately on the birth. A sacrilegious Jew might keep back this offering till a second offspring appeared, if the first-born had included a relation to a second. Our Saviour was brought to Jerusalem to be presented to the Lord according to the Law of the Lord : every male child that openeth *the womb shall be called holy to the Lord.*° From which, it is evident, that He was called the *first-born* of Mary in the sense of the law of Moses ; and, consequently, that title proves not the mother to have any other offspring.

The third objection is that we read in the Scripture of *the brethren* of Our Lord. *Is not this the carpenter's son ? Is not His mother called Mary, and His brethren James and Joseph,*

---

*   xliv. 2.   † St. Matthew i. 25
‡ Gen. xxviii. 15.   °   ii. 22, 23.

Simon and Jude? * and elsewhere Our Lord's *brethren* are spoken of.

There are two ways of accounting for these being called the brethren of Christ. (*a*) Joseph might possibly have had children before Mary was espoused to him ; and then, as he was *reputed* and called our Saviour's father, they might be accounted and called His brethren. So the ancient, especially the Greek, Fathers answer. (*b*) We need not assert that Joseph ever had any offspring, for the language of the Jews includes in the name of brethren the wider relations of consanguinity. *We are brethren,* said Abraham to Lot.† Jacob told Rachel that he was her father's brother, whereas he was his nephew.‡ The kindred of the Blessed Virgin might thus be called the brethren and sisters of her only Son. James, Joseph, Simon, and Jude were not the sons of Mary, the mother of Jesus, but the sons of Mary, the wife of Cleophas, who was a near relation to our Blessed Lady.¶

6. We have now to explain what is included in the conception by the Holy Ghost. The Blessed Virgin, hearing the announcement of the Angel Gabriel, was surprised, and conscious of her own virginity, naturally asked the question, *How shall this be done, because I know not man ?* The Angel then told her how this mystery was to take place without the loss of her virginity, in the words of the Evangelist : *The Holy Ghost shall come upon thee, and the power of the Most High shall overshadow thee : And therefore also the Holy which shall be born of thee shall be called the Son of God.* That is, the Holy Ghost shall descend from heaven, and impart that most happy fecundity without detriment to thy virginity : *and the power of the Most High,* &c. ; because this can only be effected by the special power of God, that a woman who is a virgin, should conceive and bring forth a Son. Both clauses of the sentence signify the same thing, namely, the supernatural operation of the Holy Ghost in this mystery. And as a consequence of the supernatural conception, the Angel adds : *And therefore the Holy which shall be born of thee shall be called the Son of God.* The *Holy,* that is *Holy* in His conception as well as in His birth; *holy* because the principle from which Christ comes is holy ; *holy* because conceived by the Holy Ghost ; *holy* because filled with sanctifying grace ; *holy* because He is sanctity itself ; and, therefore, that Son, on account of His eternal generation of the Father, will be called the Son of God.

---

* St. Matthew xiii. 55.   † Gen. xiii.   ‡ Gen. xxix. 12.
¶ See Analysis of Pearson on the Creed, Article iii, Section 3.

7. To understand this mystery better, it is necessary to remark that two works were performed in it at one and the same instant. The first belonged to the humanity. The body of Chris* had to be formed and organized out of the most pure blood of the Blessed Virgin, into which body the soul—which was immediately created by God alone—was infused and united. And this work, which in other human beings is effected by both parents, was effected in the Blessed Virgin by the power of the Holy Ghost, together with the concurrence of Mary in fulfilling the functions of a mother. The other work belongs to the *divinity* of Christ, and consists in this: that the humanity, in the very same moment it is constituted, is united to the divinity in the Person of the Word, or of the Son ; or, the Person of the Son is communicated or joined to the humanity in such a way that one and the same Person is in the two natures—Divine and human. And this is the work of the incarnation of the Son—a work of the greatest power, and effected by God without Mary's co-operation ; for as God alone, without man's co-operation, created the soul which informs the body, so God alone, without the work of the Virgin, unites the divine person of the Word to that human nature.

Hence, in the announcement of the Angel, both these operations are included, for both the generation, the conception and birth, are terminated not only in the nature but in the Person, and therefore the Angel concludes, *The Holy that is born of thee shall be called the Son of God.* This explanation suffices to determine the action of the Holy Ghost in the incarnation.

8. Mary being truly the Mother of Christ, there is no reason to deny her in respect of Him whatsoever is given to other mothers in relation to the fruit of their womb; and, therefore, as regards the action of the Holy Spirit, no more need be attributed to it than what is necessary to cause the Virgin to perform the actions of a mother.

"We acknowledge in the generation of Jesus Christ, that He was made of the substance of His mother, and according to this sense He was called the Son of David and of Abraham. But He was not made of *the substance* of the Holy Spirit, whose essence cannot be made. And, because the Holy Ghost did not beget Him by any communication of His essence, He is not the Father of Him, though He (Christ) was conceived by Him. Nor did the Holy Ghost form any part of Christ's flesh of any other substance than of the Blessed Virgin."*

---

* See Analysis of Pearson, Art. iii. Sec. 2.

Hence we have to reject the error of the Socinians, who will not acknowledge Christ the only-begotten Son of God, and who invented a strange conjunction in His nature, one part received from the Virgin, and consequently from David and from Abraham, by which He was the Son of man; another conjoined with it, framed by the Spirit, by which He was the Son of God.

Mary, believing the words of the Angel, and consenting to his promises, said: *Behold the handmaid of the Lord; be it done to me according to thy word.* These are words of the greatest humility and obedience. The Blessed Virgin offers herself to God ready and prepared to do His Will; as if she had said, I am the handmaid, He is the Lord, whose authority it behoves me to obey, who of His own omnipotent right can do with me what He wills.

9. And immediately that the Blessed Virgin signified her consent, *The Word became flesh, and dwelt among us.* It is commonly asserted by holy Writers that the Blessed Virgin conceived in her womb the Divine Word before the Angel went away. She certainly did not conceive before she gave her consent. The Word was certainly not incarnate when the Angel said, *Thou shalt call His name Jesus; The Holy Ghost shall come upon thee,* &c., as these words are spoken in the future tense. As soon, however, as she gave her consent, nothing more remained to be done but the accomplishment of the great act of the Incarnation. This conception was begun and accomplished at the same time. It was begun when the Angel was sent to Mary; and the Holy Ghost, who began the work then, immediately accomplished and perfected it when Mary's consent was given. Hence the pious Suarez concludes: "Let us congratulate, with holy and spiritual gladness, the Holy Virgin because of the many and great blessings which she has received, that she might be rendered worthy to be the Mother of God. Let us invoke her aid and intercession with confidence, for she is raised to such a height that she can with the greatest confidence intercede for us with her divine Son."*

We celebrate the Feast of the Annunciation on the 25th of March, nine months before Christmas, when we celebrate the feast of Christ's nativity.

As to the hour of the Annunciation we know nothing for certain, as the holy Fathers are silent on this point. We may, however, with the pious Suarez, form a conjecture that it was at the same hour as that in which Jesus was born, namely, mid-

---

*l. c. D. 9. S. 4.

night, so that He dwelt for nine entire months in the womb of His mother. And to this, as well as to the Nativity of Christ, we may apply or accommodate the words of Wisdom : *For while all things were in quiet silence, and the night was in the midst of her course, Thy Almighty Word leapt down from heaven from Thy royal throne, as a fierce conqueror, into the midst of the land of destruction.** It is more properly said that the Word came down from heaven by His Incarnation rather than by His Nativity.

Speaking of the time and moment in which, after the entire faith and consent of the Blessed Virgin, the Word was made flesh in her, it is not difficult to believe that her mind was in a way elevated so as to transcend the state of a *viator* or a way-farer in this world. And that she was able to see and understand this Mystery, and, therefore, God as He is in Himself and as united to our humanity. Learned authors teach that this privilege was granted to our Lady during her mortal life, and there was no more opportune time for the granting of this favour than the moment of the Incarnation. This is a pious and probable opinion, but uncertain.

10. It is, however, commonly asserted by Theologians that the Blessed Virgin, in her own conception, received her first sanctification without any merit or any sacramental grace, but by a special privilege ; so, in the conception of her Son, without any merit she received a singular perfection of sanctity by reason of the new and wonderful manner of the presence of the Word within her : *The Holy Ghost shall come upon thee,* &c.

When our Lady visited St. Elizabeth, by the presence of Christ, John Baptist was sanctified, and Elizabeth filled with grace ; it is therefore reasonable to suppose that the divine Word, on entering the womb of the Blessed Virgin, sanctified her in a new and special manner.

---

* Wisdom. xviii. 14. 15.

SECTION 3. (Article III.)

CHRIST BORN OF THE VIRGIN MARY.

1. The signification of the name Mary: and its application to the Blessed Virgin.—2. Mary's condition and the special title by which she is known.—3. The Immaculate Conception of the Blessed Virgin: its definition and meaning.—4. The Dogma of the Immaculate Conception proved from Scripture, by tradition, and by reason.—5. Mary's Maternity, or Mary's function in regard to the Conception and the Birth of Christ.—6. The divine Maternity considered physically.—7. The divine Maternity morally considered.—8. Mary intercedes for us in heaven; and the difference between her mediation and that of her Divine Son.—9. The sense in which she may be said to co-operate with Christ in the work of Redemption.—10. The title of Queen of heaven as applied to Mary.—11. The sense in which devotion to the Mother of God may be said to be a sign of salvation.—12. The special question in regard to those who wear the Scapular of the Blessed Virgin explained.

UNDER this portion of the Article we have to consider three things. (*a*) The Name of Mary. (*b*) Her condition. (*c*) Her action or function in regard to Christ, that is, her Maternity.

MARY'S NAME.

1. According to Ven. Bede, Mary in the Hebrew means *Stella Maris—Star of the Sea.* In Syriac it means *Lady.* It was a name imposed on our Lady by divine authority, as is supposed by many, in the same way as the name of Isaac was revealed to Abraham, and the name of John the Baptist was revealed to Zachary and Elizabeth. It was certainly blessed and sanctioned by heaven according to the revealed words of St. Luke: *And the name of the Virgin was Mary.* This name was common to many even in our Lord's time: Mary Magdalene, Mary of Cleophas, and Mary of Salome. And in the Old Testament we have special mention of *Miriam,* which is the same as Mary. She was the sister of Moses, and a prophetess. She was a type of the Blessed Virgin; because, as she was called to be one of those who brought the people of God out of the Egyptian bondage, so was this Mary to become the mother of that Saviour who hath wrought a redemption for us, of which that was but a type.

No surname is given in Holy Writ for the Blessed Virgin ; and, as St. Thomas says, she is usually mentioned in the Gospels with the surname signifying her dignity, which is the *Mother of God*, or *the Mother of Jesus. Mary the mother of Jesus was there. Is not this the carpenter's son ; and is not his mother called Mary* ?

This name has always been held in great veneration by the faithful ; and the Church has instituted a Feast for its celebration, on the Sunday within the octave of the Nativity of the Blessed Virgin.

Her Condition.

2. As special characters are given to special persons by which they are distinguished from others of the same name, thus, Jacob is called Israel ; Abraham, the friend of God ; so Mary is designated by the title or character of *the Virgin. Born of the Virgin Mary*, because, in the purity and quality of her virginity, she is above all others.

On the Virginity of the Blessed Virgin I have written in the preceding section ; and here I may confine myself to referring to some of her other perfections, which are closely connected with her virginal purity, and which remind us of her condition, by which she was made worthy to become the Mother of God.

3. It is of faith that the Blessed Virgin was preserved from original sin. This was defined by Pius IX. on the 10th of December, 1854, in the Solemn Constitution which begins *Ineffabilis Dei ;* in which it is declared that it is a truth revealed by God, and therefore to be firmly and constantly believed by all the faithful ; that the most Blessed Virgin from the moment of her conception was, by the special privilege of God and by virtue of the merits of Christ, preserved free from the stain of original sin.

The sense of this Decree may be made more clear by dividing it into the following two propositions :

(*a*) The Blessed Virgin in the first instant of her conception was preserved free from the stain of original sin.

(*b*) This was effected by a special grace and privilege of God, and by virtue of the merits of Jesus Christ.

In the first of these are included (*a*) immunity from everything which belongs to the nature, or involves the reason of original sin, namely, the stain of the sin, and the guilt and punishment. The whole (*ratio*) or nature of original sin consists in the guilt or stain, and the punishment attached to it. (b) Immunity from the effects and consequences of original sin, namely, from concupiscence and all inordinate desires and inclinations to sin. With this we may connect that which is included in the decree of the Council of Trent,* namely, that the Blessed Virgin was never guilty of any, even the least, venial sin during her whole life. (c) Immunity, in the first instant of her conception, in such a way as that she was *not* before she was holy. The words *in the first instant* exclude every distinction between before and after in this matter, and we have to conclude that her body was not before it was animated, and it was not animated before it was sanctified ; and her pure soul, like the soul of our first parents, came forth into existence free from, and unstained by, the sin of Adam.

In the second proposition are included, (a) that the Blessed Virgin was preserved free from sin, not as the condition of her nature, but by the special grace of God. (b) This was not according to the common law, but by special privilege. (c) This did not take place without reference to the merits of Christ, but by virtue of Christ's merits, so that Jesus is the meritorious cause of the Immaculate conception, and of the sanctification and salvation of His mother, as He is of all others.

This doctrine is founded on the authority of Scripture. No argument from Holy Writ can be assigned against it. Those texts that are cited in proof of the propagation of original sin do not affect Mary's privilege, and she is not included in the decree of the Council of Trent, which declares the doctrine of original sin.

4. One or two of the texts quoted in proof of the doctrine are, (a) *I will place enmity between thee and the woman, and thy seed and her seed. She shall crush thy head, and thou shalt lie in wait for her heel.*† These words were addressed to the serpent, or evil spirit, who tempted our first parents. The seed of the woman is Jesus, and the woman is Mary, who was never by sin under the power of Satan, but was always his adversary, in the same manner and sense as the fruit of her womb. (b) The Angelical Salutation calls her *full of grace, blessed amongst women.* (c) In the Apocalypse, ‡that woman clothed with the sun, and the moon under her feet, is interpreted of the Blessed Virgin, the Immaculate Mother of God ; and this is used especially as a type or figure of her Immaculate conception. (d) Many texts of the

---

* Sess. vi. c. 28. † Gen. iii. 15. ‡ Apoc. xii.

L

Old Testament, especially from the Books of Psalms, Wisdom, and the Canticle of Canticles, are applied to our Blessed Lady by the Fathers of the Church, all of which signify her Immaculate perfection. To these we may add the hymn or Antiphon, which the Church accommodates to Mary in the office of the Immaculate Conception : *Tota pulchra es Maria,* &c.

The same doctrine is proved by tradition, which we obtain from the eulogies of the Holy Fathers, and all the liturgies and hymns of the Church which proclaim our Lady's sanctity and purity. Finally, we have the voice of the Universal Church both teaching and believing, that is, both of pastors and people proclaiming and receiving this doctrine as a truth of faith, which was defined *ex cathedra* by the Head of the Universal Church. In the same Constitution in which this doctrine is defined, the following reasons are assigned : "It behoved that the Venerable mother to whom God the Father wished so to give His only Son, whom He had begotten equal to Himself, and whom He loved as Himself, that He might be naturally one and the same Son of God the Father, and of the Virgin ; and whom the Son selected to be substantially His mother ; and of whom the Holy Ghost wished and operated that through which the Son, from Whom He proceeded, should be conceived and born ; it behoved, I repeat, that such a mother should always shine forth with the splendour of the most perfect sanctity, and, being free from all stain of original sin, should have the most complete triumph over the ancient serpent."

HER MATERNITY.

5. That is Mary's function in regard to the conception and birth of Christ.

The word *born* of the Virgin Mary, signifies not only the nativity of Christ, but also the *conception* and *generation.* When the *conception* is attributed to the Holy Ghost, and the *nativity* to the Blessed Virgin, it is not to be understood as if the Spirit had conceived Him, but the Blessed Virgin by the operation of the Spirit.

Mary is therefore the mother of our Saviour (a) by *conception,* by which she conceived of her own substance the real substance of our Saviour. *A Virgin shall conceive.** *Thou shalt conceive in thy womb.*† He is termed also the fruit of her

---

*Isa. vii. 14.　　　　† St. Luke i. 31.

womb* by St. Elizabeth. (*b*) By *Nutrition* of our Saviour's body, after it was conceived, by the true substance of her own; by which she was found *with child of the Holy Ghost*. She is described as *great with child*, and thus pronounced happy : *Blessed is the womb that bore Thee* † (*c*) By *Parturition*, whereby Christ was properly born by a true nativity. As we read, Elizabeth's *fu l time came that she should be delivered, and she brought forth a son*; so is it said of Mary, *when the days were accomplished that she should bring forth a Son, and she brought forth her first-born Son*. We must therefore acknowledge the Blessed Virgin truly and properly the mother of our Saviour, because He that was born of her was the Son of God. She is defined by the Church as the *Deipara,* which in the Greek is Θεοτόκος, and means in English the Mother of God. She is frequently styled by the Evangelists the Mother of Jesus; and by St. Elizabeth the Mother of our Lord. ‡

6. The divine maternity may be considered *physically* and *morally*.

Physically considered, it signifies (*a*) That the Blessed Virgin truly and properly concurred in forming Christ's body. (*b*) That some of Mary's substance, of which the body of Christ was formed and constituted in the beginning, and afterwards nourished by her blood and milk, was hypostatically united to *the Word*. And as God is in all creatures by essence, by presence, and by power ; and, in the just by sanctifying grace, He is in Mary alone by communication of substance, inasmuch as the flesh and blood of Jesus and Mary are the same. It is by reason of this that He may be said to be our brother and our flesh. And, although the body of Christ is exalted by the glory of the Resurrection, and raised above all the heavens by the power of the Ascension, it remains always the same body that was formed in the womb of the Blessed Virgin. (*c*) Finally, by reason of the divine maternity, a real relation is established between the Mother and Christ the Man-God.

This divine maternity is the cause and foundation of all the other gifts that were bestowed upon the Blessed Virgin, from the moment of her Immaculate Conception until her exaltation in heaven over all the Angels and Saints. It is the first of Mary's perfections, and that from which, and on account of which, all her other perfections follow.

Hence, we can explain why the Evangelists give a rather

---

* Ibid, verse 42.   † St. Matt. xi. 27.
‡ St. Luke i. 43.   *See* Analysis of Pearson, Art. iii.

long account of St. John the Baptist, and of some of the Apostles, and seldom mention the Blessed Virgin. For it is enough, and contains all that can be said of her, when they write of her *de qua natus est Jesus.* This is her full and entire history. If God enriched His ministers and servants with the abundance of His graces, how much more would He raise up and perfect her whom He had chosen before all, and loved above all, as His spouse, and the Mother of His divine Son?

The dignity of the divine Maternity raises her above all the Saints, and, by reason of it, the honour which we give her is special and superior to that honour which we give to the Angels and Saints. Because we honour her, not only on account of the degree of sanctifying grace with which her soul was enriched, which is the species of honour called *dulia*, given to the Saints, but we honour her by reason of her Maternity, and, therefore, by a higher kind of honour than that which is paid to any other creature. This is called by St. Thomas and by Catholic authors in general *Hyperdulia.*

7. The divine Maternity considered *morally*, tells us the exalted dignity of the Mother of God. The dignity of the Mother of God is distinct from, and above any other dignity of a pure creature, because it belongs to the order of the hypostatic union. It is intrinsically connected with it. Hence, so great is this dignity, that it can be called in a certain sense, infinite. St. Thomas says : The humanity of Christ, by reason of its being united to God ; created Beatitude because this is the fruition of God ; and the Blessed Virgin, because she is the Mother of God, receive a certain infinite dignity from the infinite Good, Who is God ; and in this respect, nothing can be made better or greater than they, inasmuch as nothing can be better than God ; so there could not be a better or more exalted *mother* than the mother of God.

We may, then, from this doctrine conclude the Blessed Virgin is the Mother of God, therefore, she is more excellent than all the Angels, the Seraphim and Cherubim ; she is the Mother of God, therefore, she is most pure and most holy, so that under God there cannot be purer or holier. She is the Mother of God, therefore, whatever privilege is conceded to any of the blessed belongs also to her, that is, in the order of grace and glory, because in this she is raised above all others.

It remains that I explain another point which accounts for and shows the reason of our Catholic devotion to the Mother of God, that is, Mary's *power* and *intercession.*

8. It is certain that the Blessed Virgin prays and intercedes for us in heaven. If others intercede for us in heaven, as it is clear from the Sacred Scriptures that the Angels and Saints do, how much more is this true of her, who, in grace and favour with God, and in charity towards men, surpasses all others.

This intercession can in no way be to the injury of Christ, on the contrary, it will be to His greater glory. It is true that Christ is the *primary* Mediator between us and God, for there is no other mediator before Him ; He is a *necessary* mediator, because without Him there is no salvation ; He is a *universal* mediator, whom all the just, and even the Blessed Virgin need ; He is a mediator of *infinite power*, who has strength and efficacy in Himself, and from whom all other intercession receives its value or power. The Angels and Saints are in a certain way mediators, but through Christ, because with Him and by Him they intercede for us ; and in like manner, the Blessed Virgin asks in His name when she prays for us, and through Him obtains whatever she asks for. For whatever all men—and amongst them the Blessed Virgin—obtain from God, is obtained through the merits of Christ. Wherefore, her prayer and intercession is not offered for us in the sense that it is absolutely necessary, as if the prayers and merits of Christ were wanting in anything, or not sufficient for us, but because Christ so wills it that His merits may be applied to us in a manner convenient and pleasing to Him, and according to the order established by Him ; and this application of His merits, after the manner ordained by Him, conduces not only to our advantage, but to the honour of the Saints, and especially to the honour of Mary His Mother. Since the Blessed Virgin knows all that goes on here below, and knows also our necessities. she prays for us not only in general, but in particular. Her intercession is most efficacious. "I believe," says the pious and learned Suarez, "that the Blessed Virgin, in this power and efficacy, surpasses not only all the Saints taken singly, but the whole court of heaven." Hence, we may conclude that the Blessed Virgin is to be invoked and prayed to by us, which is of faith according to the common usage of the whole Church, and her constant tradition ; but she is to be invoked and prayed to before all the Saints ; because (a) her mediation, if not absolutely necessary, is of the *greatest utility*. She is our mediatrix immediately after Christ. Hence, we do not apply to any of the Saints to intercede with others of their number for us, because they are all in the same order ; but we can make them intercessors for us with our Lady as the Queen of heaven. (b) Because she is the most powerful mediatrix for us after Christ. We have in her a universal advocate, inasmuch as she can obtain all things from her Omnipotent Son. Wherefore holy Church invokes her in more venerable titles, calling her *our hope, our life, our comfort,* and *Mother of Mercy,* and also prays to her more frequently and more constantly than to the other Saints. There is no day in which She does not offer up public prayers to her in the divine office, and in the holy Sacrifice of the Mass. Three times a day, by the Angelus bell, She gives a signal that all the people may offer up a prayer to Mary; and She has dedicated to her, in each year, many Feast Days. (c) She is, after Christ, the most universal mediatrix, inasmuch as through her Christ bestows His favours upon His creatures; although this does not mean that we cannot obtain any grace unless we first pray to the Blessed Virgin. Even when we do not pray to her, she is present by her prayers and her assistance; and, as through her, we received Christ Himself, the Author of all grace, it is not unreasonable to suppose that He bestows in His ordinary providence, through her intercession, His graces upon His creatures.

9. The mediation of the Blessed Virgin in the work of redemption, is not only that of *intercession,* but also of *co-operation.* For she, in giving her consent to the message of the Angel, by a moral causality influenced the work of the redemption of the human race. Moreover, by ministering her substance to Christ our Redeemer, she nourished and preserved Him for us, and at length willingly offered Him up for us on the altar of the Cross; wherefore, as the Son loved us and delivered Himself for us, so the Mother loved us and delivered her Son for us. The Fathers, as they make a comparison between Adam and Christ, also make a comparison between Eve and Mary. As Adam was the cause of our perdition, Christ is the cause of our salvation. And as Eve co-operated in the prevarication of our first parent, so Mary co-operated in the work of redemption.

10. That we may fully understand Mary's power, we find it necessary to refer to one other of her titles, that of Queen of heaven, which all Christians have ever given to her. It is not an empty title, but it signifies that Mary has that special dominion in heaven, which properly belongs to a Queen. This dominion arises from the union and affinity that exists between God and the Blessed Virgin. Because Christ is King and Lord, the mother who brought Him forth, is Queen and Mistress. This dominion is similar to that which belongs to a wife or mother, by reason of their connection with a king. Although she has not

the supreme power of commanding, she has that which belongs to a queen above all other subjects; and thus a higher honour is due to her than to the other Saints. She alone, under Christ, occupies a place in heaven above all the Choirs of Angels and Saints, as is becoming the Mother of the King, and the Queen of all the heavenly inhabitants.

11. There is one other question that seems to require some explanation, namely, in what sense can it be asserted that devotion to the Blessed Virgin is a sign of salvation, and a mark of predestination? It is an error to state that it is impossible for a client of Mary to be lost, in the sense that every one who is devout to the Blessed Virgin will infallibly rise from sin, or infallibly persevere to the end in grace. To no one, no matter how devote to Mary, can such a promise be made without a special revelation from God. It is, however, true that devotion to Mary is of the greatest importance, and that there can be a strong hope entertained that no one who piously perseveres in her service, will miserably perish. And, according to the teaching of the Fathers, even holding as we do the uncertainty of predestination, we may admit some regular and likely signs of final perseverance; and one of these is a special devotion to the Blessed Virgin, inasmuch as Mary turns with affection to those who love her, and uses, in their behalf, her all-powerful intercession with her Son; and thus she acts towards her clients, and takes root in an honourable people, and *in electis Dei radices mittit.*

12. As to the special question, in regard to the certainty of the salvation of those who wear the Scapular, I must repeat that it is a dogma of faith, that no one here on earth can be certain of grace or predestination without a special revelation, which we have not received in the case of those who wear the Scapular. We may, however, admit piously the general revelation in favour of the salvation of such souls, if all other conditions, both general and particular, be observed. The general conditions are the fulfilment of the Commandments and all Christian duties. The particular conditions are those rules prescribed for the members of the Sodality. The wearing of the Scapular is then a sign of salvation and predestination, in the sense that it is an emblem or token of a special protection by the Blessed Virgin, by which the members of the Sodality may be enabled more securely to keep the Commandments, and more safely to obtain their eternal beatitude. No more than this is meant when it is said that wearing the Scapular is a sign of salvation, or a pledge of pre-

destination. Then, it will be said, that there is nothing very
extraordinary or special in it, if it is only a promise that the
members of the Sodality will be saved if they keep the Commandments, and piously live a good life, as all Christians who do
this can be saved without the Scapular or the aid of any Sodality.
Although this is quite true, we must, at the same time, remember
and conclude that we obtain a special privilege by being enrolled
in Mary's Scapular, inasmuch as this is a sacred badge and
pledge of her special protection, which she imparts to her clients,
to enable them to keep the Commandments, to live a holy life,
and to die well.   And this is the special virtue which we attribute
to the wearing of the Scapular, according to the promise made
by our Lady to St. Simon ; and which may be extended to all
those who have enrolled themselves in her congregations and
confraternities as Children of Mary.

SECTION 4. (ARTICLE III.)

BORN OF THE VIRGIN MARY.

1. Bethlehem, the birth-place of Christ.—2. The decree of Augustus that all the world should be enrolled.—3. Joseph and Mary went up from Nazareth to Bethlehem.—4. The date of the Christian era.—5. The birth of Christ in the stable at Bethlehem.—6. The vision of the Shepherds and their visit to the Babe of Bethlehem.—7. The Circumcision of Christ on the eighth day.

1. THE Feast of our Lord's Nativity is celebrated on the 25th of December. The Prophet Micheas, 700 years before, had prophesied that the Messiah would be born in Bethlehem, a small town of Judea, about six miles distant from Jerusalem.

The Emperor Augustus had ordered that a census should be made throughout the Roman Empire, and all the kingdoms allied to it. In consequence of this, Joseph and Mary came from Nazareth to Bethlehem, their native place, or the city of their family; as the Jews were obliged to have themselves enrolled in their native place.

The time had come when Mary was to bring forth to the world the Incarnate Word. As there was no room for the Holy Family in the Inn, they sought shelter in a cave which was used as a stable. The birth of the Son of God was as miraculous as His conception. Mary brought forth her only-begotten and first-born Son without pain or sorrow. He came forth from the womb of Mary as the rays from the fire, as the perfume from the flower, and in the same manner as He afterwards came forth from the tomb, without breaking the seal which closed it.

Mary, adoring the Infant Saviour, wrapped Him in swaddling clothes and laid Him in a manger; that same manger which is still preserved and venerated in Rome, in the Church of St. Mary Major.

The birth of our Saviour, according to the Roman martyrology, took place in the year 5199 after the creation of the world; 2015 after the birth of Abraham; 1302 after the consecration of King David. This was in the 752nd year after the foundation of Rome, and in the 36th year of the reign of the Emperor Augustus.

The account of the birth of Christ, and the circumstances attending it, are given in St. Luke's Gospel.* St. Luke narrates the generation of Christ according to the flesh, as St. John gives us His divine and eternal generation ; and hence the Gospels read in the Masses of Christmas Day are taken from these two Evangelists.

2. St. Luke begins the narrative of our Saviour's birth, from the going forth of the decree of Cæsar Augustus that *all the world should be enrolled.*

The proper name of this Emperor was Octavius or Octavianus. He was called Cæsar after Julius Cæsar, who had adopted him ; and Augustus, because in his reign the Roman Empire was enlarged, and became more illustrious and celebrated than it had ever been.† A decree went forth that the whole world should be enrolled. St. Luke mentions this decree in order to show the reason, and the occasion, that brought Mary and Joseph to Bethlehem at that particular time.

3. According to the decree every one had to be enrolled in his own city. *And Joseph also went up from Galilee, out of the city of Nazareth into Judea, to the city of David, which is called Bethlehem, because he was of the house and family of David : to be enrolled with Mary his espoused wife, who was with child.*‡

Bethlehem in Hebrew signifies a house of bread. Christ is the living bread that came down from heaven. It is a small town six miles from Jerusalem. It was the scene of the death of Rachel, of the story of Ruth, and of the early years of the life of David.

Thus was fulfilled the prophecy of Micheas : *And Thou, Bethelem Ephrata, art a little one among the thousands of Juda ; out of thee shall He come forth unto me that is to be the ruler of Israel ; and His going forth is from the beginning from the days of eternity.*§

---

* St. Luke ii. 1-14.

† Augustus ; *i.e. August* or honourable, as a compliment to his own greatness ; and from him the month *August* which was before called *Sextilis*, received its name. He was proclaimed Emperor of Rome B.C. 29 ; and died A.D. 14. He had received the name Cæsar from Julius Cæsar by adoption, and by that name were called three of the family of Augustus, afterwards the heirs of the Empire ; and finally the Emperors themselves.

‡ St. Luke ii. 4 5   § Mic. v. 2.

Joseph did not go alone, but was accompanied by Mary his espoused wife. It is uncertain whether her presence was obligatory or voluntary. But it is obvious that, at so trying a time, and after what she had suffered by reason of former suspicions, she would cling to the presence and protection of her husband. It is also probable that she saw in the providential circumstances a fulfilment of prophecy. St. Thomas holds that the place, and the time, and other circumstances of the Nativity, were revealed beforehand to Mary and Joseph, because they were the first to shew Christ reverence and obedience, and be prepared for His Nativity, and His appearance in this world.

4. "There is a reasonable certainty that our Lord was born B.C. 4 of our era; and it is probable that He was born, according to the unanimous tradition of the Christian Church, in the Winter. There is nothing to guide us as to the actual day of His birth. It was unknown to the ancient Christians. Some thought that it took place on May 20th, or April 20th. There is no trace of December 25th earlier than the fourth century, but it is accepted by SS. Athanasius, Jerome, Ambrose, and the universal Church."*

5. *And when the days were accomplished that she should be delivered.* That is, the ordinary time of pregnancy, the space of nine months, from the day of the Incarnation, which took place on the Feast of the Annunciation, the 25th of March. *She brought forth her first-born son, and wrapped him in swaddling clothes, and laid Him in the manger.* She brought Him forth without any pain, or sorrow, or stain; and she laid Him in the manger, the most suitable place to be found for Him in that stable wherein He was born.

The ox and the ass that are traditionally given in representations of the Nativity are mentioned in the apocryphal Gospel of St. Matthew, and they were suggested by the words of the prophet Isaias: *The ox knoweth his owner, and the ass his master's crib, but Israel hath not known Me, and My people hath not understood.*†

St. Ignatius of Loyola, in his meditation on the Nativity, represents our Lady on the journey carried by an ass, and Joseph driving the ox, that he might be able to pay the tribute imposed upon all the people by the edict of Cæsar after his arrival in Bethlehem; and St. Vincent of Leirns says, that Joseph brought with him an ass to carry his pregnant wife, and an ox to sell at

---

* Cambridge Bible for Schools. St. Luke, *in loc. cit.*   † Isaias i. 3.

Bethlehem, where there was a great concourse of people, and thus pay the expenses of his journey.

Christ hidden in humility and poverty is manifested and glorified by Angels sent to the Shepherds.

6. *And there were in the same country Shepherds.* These were Bethlehemites, natives of the little village Beth-zur. They were feeding their flocks in the fields from which David was called to be anointed King over Israel by the prophet Samuel. The sheep used for daily sacrifice, and the lambs to be offered at the Passover, were pastured in the fields of Bethlehem. The shepherds were the first to whom the new-born Saviour was revealed. These were keeping the *night watches over their flock;* which does not prove, as some have supposed, that the Nativity took place in Spring, for, in some pastures in Palestine, the shepherds to this day watch over their flocks by night in the Winter, that they may not be killed by wolves, or stolen by robbers. The nights were divided into four parts called watches.

And behold an Angel of the Lord stood by them, and the brightness *of the Lord shone round about them.* The Angel appeared to them in human form. The brightness of the Lord dispelled the darkness of the night, that they might understand the divine mission of the Angel. Naturally, at this unusual vision and divine manifestation, the shepherds were terrified until the Angel's message re-assured them. *Fear not.* There is no cause for fear, but cause for great joy, *for behold,* said the Angel, *I bring you tidings of great joy, that shall be to all the people.* Not only to the Jews, but to all the nations and people of the world. Christ is born to all, and, therefore, there is reason that they and all should rejoice; *For this day is born to you a Saviour, who is Christ the Lord, in the city of David.*[*]

Now, the Messiah so long promised, for so many ages expected, has come : Christ the Anointed One, the Lord of all the anointed prophets, kings, and priests. He is born in the city of David, thus fulfilling the promise made to David long before. The Angel continues his instructions to the shepherds : *And this shall be a sign unto you. You shall find the Infant wrapped in swaddling clothes, and laid in a manger.* You will find the Infant, Who is the Word that was in the beginning, by Whom all things were made, Who came unto His own, and the world knew Him not, and His own received Him not. But the heavenly Spirits celebrated the event : *And suddenly there was*

---

[*] St. Luke 4. 10, 11.

with the Angel a multitude of the heavenly army praising God, and saying, Glory to God in the highest, and on earth peace to men of good-will. These words are both assertive and optative. *Glory to God in the highest, i.e.,* all the heavens glorify and should glorify Him, because God the Father sent His Son into the world for the salvation of men. *And on earth peace,* that is, peace between men and God, to whom Christ came to reconcile them ; according to these words of St. Paul : *Because in Him it hath well pleased the Father that all fulness should dwell. And through Him to reconcile all things unto Himself, by making peace through the blood of the Cross, both as to the things that are on earth, and the things that are in heaven.*[*] Peace was announced on earth but to men of good will, to those, who, with a good will, should believe in this new-born Saviour, and embrace Him with love.

St. Luke continues the narrative, and gives an account of the advent of the Shepherds to the Infant Jesus, and their return from Him to their watching : *And it came to pass, after the angels departed from them into heaven, the shepherds said one to another, Let us go over to Bethlehem, and let us see this Word that has come to pass which the Lord hath shown to us. And they came with haste ; and they found Mary and Joseph, and the Infant lying in the manger. And seeing, they understood of the word that had been spoken to them concerning this child. And all that heard wondered ; and at those things that were told them by the shepherds. But Mary kept all these words, pondering them in her heart. And the shepherds returned glorifying and praising God for all things they had heard and seen, as it was told unto them.*[†]

Having heard the glad tidings of the Angel, the Shepherds [‡] immediately encouraged each other to undertake the journey, saying, *Let us go over to Bethlehem* ; and the reason assigned is, *that we may see the Word that has come to pass,* that we may see this new and wonderful thing which God has first revealed to us, and given us the sign by which we may recognise our born Messiah. "For, unless we who are invited and called by Angels go and see and adore Him who is born to us, and first revealed to us, we shall be ungrateful to God, to the Angels, and to Christ ; and enemies to ourselves by neglecting such a great favour and grace. It is certain, that the Angels who spoke externally to the

---

* Coloss. i. 20.   † St. Luke ii. 15-20.
‡ Tradition asserts that Matthias, the Apostle chosen in the place of Judas, was one of these Shepherds. That some of them became afterwards of the number of Christ's disciples is probable.

Shepherds, also spoke to them interiorly, and enlightened their minds to know that Christ was God and their Redeemer, and they were therefore moved to go to Him, to love and to adore Him. For this reason the Shepherds went immediately to the manger, and there, with all humility and reverence, adored Christ. There is no doubt but at that moment they were justified, and if justified before, they then received a great increase of justice and holiness.* The Shepherds came with haste, and seeing Mary and Joseph and the Infant lying in the manger, they knew the truth of all that the Angel had told them of the Child; and what they saw they announced to others; and all who heard wondered at these things which were told them by the Shepherds, so that these Shepherds became the first Christian preachers.

St. Luke adds that *Mary kept all these words, pondering them in her heart.* This brings us in thought again to Mary. She kept all these things, viz., Christ's conception, His birth, the visit of the Shepherds, pondering them in her heart. Thus she gives us a singular example of silence, of prudence and modesty. She did not at once proclaim them to the world, but kept them in her heart until the day came when she communicated them to the Apostles and Evangelists (and especially to St. Luke), and through them to the whole world.†

Having seen and worshipped the Infant Jesus they returned to their flocks, *glorifying and praising God for all the things they had heard and seen.*

7. On the 8th day after the Nativity, the divine Infant was circumcised according to the prescription of the law, and His name was called Jesus, which He was called by the Angel before He was conceived in the womb.

---

* Cornelius a Lap. in hoc loco.
† On another occasion we have, His mother kept all these sayings *in her heart.* This is one of our guarantees that they are true. Mary kept them in memory, and the Evangelist appeals to her memory for them. That he derived them from her lips is certain from his assertion that she stored all these particulars in her memory, and that is how he is able to give them. Baring Gould. *The Birth of Jesus: the Shepherds.*

ARTICLE IV.

APOSTLES' CREED.	NICENE CREED.
"Suffered under Pontius Pilate, was crucified, dead, and buried."	" Was crucified also for us under Pontius Pilate, He suffered and was buried."

THIS Article, although one, has several parts which we may divide into separate sections.

SECTION 1. (Article IV.)

SUFFERED UNDER PONTIUS PILATE.

1. The reason for the transition in the Creed from the Birth of Christ to His sufferings.—2. Pontius Pilate: the reason why his name is recorded in the Creed.—3. The promised Messiah was to suffer.—4. The sufferings of Christ were agreed upon by Him and the Father. They were revealed to the Prophets and delivered to the Church.— 5. The reason why the Messiah came in a state of suffering.—6. All the sufferings agreed upon, revealed to the Prophets, and delivered to the Church, were endured by Jesus of Nazareth.—7. The sufferings of Christ considered in His Person.—8. What Christ suffered for us in His human nature, (a) in His body, (b) in His soul.—9. The occasion and intensity of His sufferings.—10. Lessons to be learned from this Article.

THIS Article of our Creed is commemorated by the Church on Good Friday.

1. No notice is taken in the Creed of the years between our Lord's Birth and His Crucifixion, because our Lord took our nature that He might suffer and die for us ; He took our flesh in order that He might give that flesh for the life of the world. And, although He lived that He might set us an example of a holy life, that we might walk in His footsteps, yet the great object of the Incarnation was our redemption ; that He might die for our sins, and rise again to impart to us His risen life.

2. *Pontius Pilate.* His name is recorded in the Creed—
(a) To mark the time when our Saviour suffered.
(b) To remind us of the innocency of our Lord ; for Pilate said, *I find no fault in Him.*
(c) To account for the manner of His death ; for crucifixion was a Roman, not a Jewish, form of punishment.

Pontius Pilate was the Roman Procurator, or Governor, of Judæa, from A.D. 27-37. He was hated by the Jews on account of his tyrannical and unjust conduct, and they appealed to the Roman Emperor against him. Accordingly, Pilate was deposed and banished to Vienne in Gaul, where he is supposed to have committed suicide.*

THE PROMISED MESSIAH WAS TO SUFFER.

3. In this truth, both before and after His death, Christ instructed His Apostles *It is written of the Son of man that He must suffer many things and be despised.*† After His resurrection He enlightened the two disciples on the way to Emmaus on this very point : *Ought not Christ to have suffered these things and so to enter into His glory?* And again appearing to His disciples, *He opened their understandings that they might know the Scriptures. And He said to them : Thus it is written, and thus it behoved Christ to suffer, and to rise again from the dead on the third day.*‡

The 53rd Chapter of Isaias is a description of a suffering Messiah. *Who hath believed our report, and to whom is the arm of the Lord revealed? And He shall grow up as a tender plant before Him, and as a root out of a thirsty ground : there is no beauty in Him, nor comeliness ; and we have seen Him, and there was no sightliness in Him that we should be desirous of Him. Despised, and the most abject of men ; a man of sorrows, and acquainted with infirmity ; and His look was as it were hidden and despised, whereupon we esteemed Him not. Surely He hath borne our infirmities, and carried our sorrows : and we have thought of Him as it were a leper, and as one struck by God and afflicted. But He was wounded for our iniquities, He was bruised for our sins : the chastisement of our peace was upon Him; and by His bruises we are healed. All we like sheep have gone astray; every one hath turned aside into his own way ; and the Lord hath laid on Him the iniquity of us all. He was offered because it was His*

---

* Oxford and Cambridge Church Catechism. Art. iv.
† St. Mark ix. 12.   ‡ St. Luke xxiv. 26, 46.

own will, and He opened not His mouth; He shall be led as a sheep to the slaughter, and shall be dumb as a lamb before his shearer, and He shall not open His mouth. He was taken away from distress and from judgment; who shall declare His generation? Because He is cut off out of the land of the living: for the wickedness of my people have I struck Him. And He shall give the ungodly for His burial, and the rich for His death; because He hath done no iniquity, neither was there deceit in His mouth. And the Lord was pleased to bruise Him in infirmity; if He shall lay down His life for sin, He shall see a long lived seed, and the will of the Lord shall be prospered in His hand. Because His soul hath laboured, He shall see and be filled; by His knowledge shall this My servant justify many, and He shall bear their iniquities. Therefore will I distribute to Him very many; and He shall divide the spoils of the strong, because He hath delivered His soul unto death, and was reputed with the wicked; and He hath borne the sins of many, and hath prayed for the transgressors.*

The person here treated of was certainly the Messiah, as is confessed by the most ancient Jews, and manifest from the place itself. For no man's *soul* can be made an *offering for our sins* but our Saviour's; on no other man hath God *laid the iniquity of us all*: on no other could the *chastisement of our peace lie*; with *no stripes* but His could we be *healed......*It was He who *bore our griefs* and *carried our sorrows.*

Notwithstanding this clear prophecy, the Jews resolved to expect a Messiah only glorious, and invented another to suffer; but the Scriptures never mention any Messiah but the one the seed of the woman and the Son of David, who is the one Meditator, who suffered and died for our redemption.

4. These sufferings which the Messiah had to endure were agreed upon by Him and the Father according to the words of the Acts. *For of a truth there assembled together in this city, against the holy child Jesus, whom thou hast anointed, Herod and Pontius Pilate, with the Gentiles and the people of Israel, to do what thy hand and thy counsel decreed to be done.*† Christ accepted this Covenant as expressed in the words of the Psalmist: *Then said I, Lo, I come (in the volume of the book it is written of me) to do Thy will, O Lord.*

The *determined* sufferings were divinely revealed to the Prophets, and delivered to the Church in types, and acted in sacrifices. Hence, St. Paul could say, *But being aided by the*

---

* Isaiah liii.   † Acts iv. 27, 28.

M

help of God, I stand unto this day, witnessing both to small and great, saying no other things than those which the prophets and Moses did say should come to pass, that Christ should suffer.[*]

"The prophets said so in express terms; Moses said so in the ceremonies instituted by his ministry. When he caused the Passover to be slain, he said the Shiloh was the Lamb slain before the foundation of the world; when he commanded. the sacrifice for sin, he said, without blood-shedding there was no remission, and therefore the Son of God must die for the sins of men; when he appointed Aaron to go into the Holy of Holies on the day of Atonement, he said that Christ, our High Priest, should never enter the highest heavens to expiate for us but by His own blood."[†]

5. The reason or cause of the sufferings of the Messiah, and of His coming in a state of suffering, and shedding His blood for our redemption, may be accounted for by the very nature of the sacrifice which He came to offer.

"If mankind had never sinned; if we had been born into the world as innocent and as holy as Adam was before the fall, nothing less than sacrifice could have satisfied the debt we owe to God as to the Author of our being, the All-holy, Almighty, Eternal God. By the destruction of the offering, men showed that they owed all to God, and were as nothing in His sight. But the shedding of blood is something more. An unbloody sacrifice, for instance, a sacrifice of corn and wine, is such as an innocent creature might make to his Creator. But we were no longer in that blessed state; when Adam fell, we lost our innocence; when Adam sinned we became sinners; we all sinned in him, and, as sinners, became subject to death, the punishment of sin. A bloody sacrifice is therefore the offering of sinful creatures to their offended God. Our state was changed; before, we owed to God the homage of our being; now we owe to Him the additional penalty of death. Not only so, we had incurred a debt which nothing we had to give could satisfy. God was angry with us; we were guilty in His sight; we stood in need of forgiveness and reconciliation. How were they to be obtained? In His love and mercy God provided a remedy. At the very moment when He pronounced upon our first parents the sentence of punishment, He told them of a Deliverer to come, for Whose sake He would pardon them and their children. This Deliverer was none other than our Saviour Jesus Christ, the Second Person

---

[*] Acts xxvi. 22.   [†] Analysis of Pearson on the Creed, in loco.

of the adorable Trinity, who was to become man, and die for us."*

6. We have now to consider that all these sufferings that were agreed upon, that were revealed by the prophets as the sufferings of the true Messiah, were undergone by Jesus of Nazareth.

On the approach of His death, Christ said to His Apostles : *All things shall be accomplished which were written by the prophets concerning the Son of man.* † When He delivered to them the Blessed Sacrament He said, *The Son of man indeed goeth according to that which is determined.* ‡ After His resurrection He rebuked the two disciples, *O foolish and slow of heart to believe in all things which the prophets have spoken: ought not Christ to have suffered these things, and so to enter into His glory ?* § And after the Ascension St. Peter proclaimed before the Jews, who had received the prophecies, and saw Christ's sufferings : *Those things which God before had showed by the mouth of all the prophets that His Christ should suffer, He hath so fulfilled.* ‖

It seems scarcely necessary to give these proofs or details, but the Creed itself enters into details concerning the death of our Saviour, in refutation of the heresy of the Docetes and Fantastics, Sectarians of the first ages, who sprang up under the very eyes of the Apostles. These, more or less, denied the reality of the sufferings, death, and burial of Jesus Christ, and held that these events took place in appearance only. It is necessary also to be reminded of these details, that we may understand better how much our redemption cost, and how Christ merited and satisfied for us by His Passion and death.

We have now to consider how Christ suffered. He suffered (a) in His Person, and (b) in His human nature.

CHRIST SUFFERED IN HIS PERSON.

7. I here quote again at some length from Pearson's Analysis, as his words clearly contain my meaning : " On looking back at the Second Article, as connected with this through the third, we find the Person *here* stated to have suffered, *there* named Jesus, and described as the only Son of God: whom we have already shown to be truly called *only-begotten*, because from all eternity

---

* *Explanation of the Sacrifice of the Mass*, by a Priest. pp. 30, 31.
† St. Luke xviii. 31. ‡ St. Luke xxii. 22. § St. Luke xxiv. 25, 26.
‖ Acts iii. 18.

generated of the substance of the Father, therefore as the eternal Son, so also the eternal God. Wherefore, by the immediate coherence of the Articles......it plainly appears that the eternal Son of God, God of God, suffered under Pontius Pilate, was crucified, dead and buried. *The Princes of this world...crucified the Lord of Glory.** And God purchased His Church with His own blood.† That Person which was begotten of the Father before all worlds, and so was really *the Lord of glory*, and most truly God took on Him the nature of man, and in that nature, being still the *same Person* He was before, did suffer. When our Saviour fasted forty days, there was no other person hungry than the Son of God who made the world. When He sat down weary by the well, when He was buffetted and scourged, there was no other person thirsty, &c.......When He was crucified and died, there was no other person who gave up the ghost but the Son of Him, and so of the same nature with Him, *Who only hath immortality.*‡ The Person who suffered was *God the Son.*

The same author continues to explain how Christ suffered not in His divine, but in His human nature : " The divine nature is of infinite and eternal happiness, never to be disturbed by the least degree of infelicity. Wherefore, while we profess that the Son of God suffered for us, we must deny that the divine nature of our Saviour suffered. For since the divine nature of the Son is common to the Father and the Holy Ghost, if *that* had been the subject of His Passion, then must the Father and the Holy Ghost have suffered also. Wherefore, as we attribute the Passion to the Son alone, so must we attribute it to that nature which is His alone, *i.e.,* the human......The Son alone is man, and so capable of suffering. *Christ suffered for us in the flesh,* in the nature of man which He, the eternal Word, took upon Him. Thus the proper subject of our Saviour's Passion was that nature which He took from us. The conjunction with humanity could put no imperfection on the Divinity. We must not conceive the Divine nature capable of any diminution, must not imagine the essence of the Word subject to the sufferings of the flesh He took, nor yet harbour so groundless an estimation of the great mystery of the Incarnation as to make the properties of one nature mix in confusion with the other. These wild collections of the Arian and Apollinarian heretics the Church hath long silenced with the sound assertion that all the sufferings of our Saviour were subjected in His human nature."

---

* 1. Cor. ii. 8.   † Acts xx. 28.
‡ 1. Tim. vi. 16.   § I Peter iv. 1

By reason, however, of the *communication of idioms* as above explained, it can be rightly said that *God suffered, that God died for us and our salvation*, inasmuch as He who suffered and died for us was both God and man, and because the one Person of the Son of God had human nature, and in that human nature suffered and died, and was buried.

8. It now remains for us to consider what Christ suffered for us in His human nature.

Christ suffered before He suffered under Pontius Pilate. He suffered during His whole life. He was always the *Man of sorrows and acquainted with infirmity.* He suffered in the two elements or parts of His human nature. (*a*) In His body. (*b*) In His soul.

(*a*) In His sacred body our Blessed Lord suffered from :—
> *Hunger.* In the wilderness (St. Luke iv. 2) ; and at the fig-tree (St. Mark xi. 12).
> *Thirst.* At Sychar (St. John iv. 7) ; on the Cross (St. John xix. 28).
> *Want.* He had no money; worked a miracle to pay the tax (St. Matthew xvii. 24-27; Cf 2 Corinthians viii. 9).
> *Weariness.* When He sat by the well (St. John iv. 6) ; and fell asleep in the boat (St. Mark iv. 38).
> *Exposure.* Foxes had holes, and the birds of the air had nests, but He had not where on to lay His head (St. Matthew viii. 20 ; St. Luke xxi. 37).
> *All the bodily pains of His cruel death.* Head—the crown of thorns ; face—blows and spitting ; back—the scourging ; hands and feet—the nails.

(*b*) He suffered in His soul from :—
> *Temptations.* After the forty days' fast : *He himself hath suffered, being tempted.* He was in all things like us save sin (Hebrew ii. 18 ; iv. 15).
> *Contact with sin.* He *endureth such opposition from sinners against Himself* (Heb. xii. 3).
> *Contact with suffering.* He *took our infirmities, and bore our diseases* (St. Matt. viii. 17). He sighed and wept at the sight of sorrow and suffering (St. John xi. 33, 35 ; St. Luke xix. 41).
> *Unkindness* and *ingratitude.* One disciple betrayed Him (St. Luke xxii. 48) ; another denied Him (St. Luke xxii. 61) ; all forsook Him (St. Mark xiv. 50).*

---

* This arrangement of the sufferings is taken from the Manual of Catechising, in loco.

The bitterness and intensity of these sufferings we may learn from the words of the Evangelist : *He began to be sorrowful and to be sad.* The English does not express all that is contained, even in the Latin words, *Caepit pavere, tædere, contristari et maestus esse*—He began to fear, to grow weary, to be sorrowful and sad. Thus pressed down by the weight of His grief, and tormented by anxiety and affliction of spirit, He said to His disciples, *My soul is sorrowful even unto death.* The same dereliction and sorrow is conveyed in the words of His prayer to His heavenly Father, *Father, if it be possible, let this chalice pass from Me.* Finally His bitter anguish of soul caused Him to fall into an agony ; and *being in an agony, He prayed the longer ; and His sweat became as drops of blood trickling down upon the ground.*

THE OCCASION OF HIS SUFFERINGS.

9. Inasmuch as He came to satisfy for our sins and the sins of all mankind, God laid upon Him the iniquities of us all. And as we are obliged to be sorry for our particular sins, so was He grieved for the sins of us all. If then we look on the perfection of His knowledge, His understanding of all the sins of men—all the guilt, offence, ingratitude, contained in them ; His absolute conformity to the Will of God, love of Him, and zeal for His glory ; His exceeding love for the sons of men ; His knowledge that their sins were sufficient to bring on them eternal destruction ; His consideration of them whom He so loved as lying under the wrath of God, whom He so truly worshipped ; His own exceeding abhorrence of sin from the infinite graces diffused through His soul ; we cannot wonder at that His sorrow. If the true contrition of *one* sinner for his own iniquities, not all known to himself, cannot be performed without great bitterness of remorse, what bounds can we set to the anguish proceeding from a full apprehension of all the transgressions of so many sinners ? Add, moreover, the immediate hand of God pressing on Him at once all this load of all the sorrows which can befall any of the saints of God ; that He, being touched with the feeling of our infirmities, might be a merciful High-Priest, able and willing to succour them that are tempted.* Thus may we behold and see if there be any sorrow like unto that sorrow which was done unto Him, *wherewith the Lord afflicted Him in the day of His fierce anger.*†

---

* Heb. ii. 17, 18 ; iv. 15. † Lam. i. 12.

10. From this Article we may learn the following lessons :—

(a) The truth (reality) of Christ's human nature, without which He could not be man, or suffer, or redeem us.

(b) The redemption of the human race, and the reconciliation of men with God. By His suffering He made full satisfaction to the injured Majesty of God, and made an expiation, atonement, and propitiation for all our sins.

(c) He merited for us, and purchased the eternal happiness of heaven for His faithful here on earth. *Ought not Christ to suffer, and so to enter into His glory?* And doth He not by the same right confer that glory on us?

(d) That we may learn that we are to suffer, and how we are to suffer. There was a moral heresy, as well as a dogmatical heresy, in connection with the sufferings of our Redeemer. The dogmatical heresy is extinct, as I have already said, but the moral one still exists, and is likely to exist for ever among men. It consists in denying, openly or tacitly, the necessity of suffering, bearing our Cross, dying or descending into the grave. To deny the obligation imposed upon all Christians of suffering, of *crucifying their flesh with its vices and concupiscences, of putting on the new man who, according to God, is created in justice and holiness of truth,*[*] is to renew the disedifying errors of those who abolished abstinence, fasting, and all works painful to the flesh, as injurious to the merits of Christ, and as a useless interference with Christian liberty.

"If God spared not His natural Son, how shall He spare His adopted sons, best known to be His children because chastised? As surely as if Christ be risen, we shall also rise ; so if Christ hath suffered, we must expect to suffer. And He alone hath also left us an absolutely perfect pattern to direct us in our sufferings ; even He who taught us in all our afflictions the exercise of admirable humility, perfect patience, and absolute submission to the will of God."[†]

---

[*] Ephes. iv. 22, 24,   [†] Analysis of the Creed, Pearson.

SECTION 2 (ARTICLE IV.)

THE PASSION OF CHRIST.

1. The types of Christ crucified.—2. The Crucifixion foretold by the Prophets.—3. The chief sufferings of Christ.—4. The Agony and Sweat of Blood.—5. The Betrayal, which includes (a) the traitor's kiss; (b) the arrest; (c) Malchus.—6. The Jewish or Ecclesiastical trial of Jesus.—7. Jesus before Annas.—8. The first trial before Caiphas.—9. St. Peter's denial.—10. The derision of Jesus. 11.—The third Jewish trial, or the second trial before Caiphas.—12. The remorse and despair of Judas.

THE Crucifixion of the Messiah was represented by Types and Figures in the Old Law, and foretold by prophecies.
1. The Types of Christ crucified were:—
(a) *Isaac.* The only son, offered up by his father, bore the wood on which he was offered, as Jesus, the only-begotten Son of God, given by His Father for the ransom of mankind, bore His Cross to the place of Crucifixion.
(b) *The Brazen Serpent. And as Moses lifted up the serpent in the desert, so must the Son of Man be lifted up · that whosoever believeth in Him may not perish; but may have life everlasting.**
(c) *The Paschal Lamb.* Not a bone of which was to be broken, plainly typified the Lamb of God who taketh away the sins of the world.
2. The crucifixion was foretold in prophecies:—
They shall look upon Me whom they have pierced. (Zach. xii. 10).
They gave Me also gall for my food, and in My thirst they gave Me vinegar to drink. (Psalms lxviii. 22).
They divided My garments amongst them, and upon my vesture they cast lots. (St. Matt. xxvii. 35; Ps. xxi. 19).
It is easy to show how all these prophecies were fulfilled in the Passion and Crucifixion of Christ.
It will be well to give a short account of the events of the

---

* St. John iii. 14, 15.

Passion that led up to the crucifixion, in explanation of the answer to the question : What were the chief sufferings of Christ ?

3. The chief sufferings of Christ were, *first*, His agony and His sweat of blood in the garden ; *secondly*, His being scourged at the pillar, and crowned with thorns ; and *thirdly*, His carrying the cross, His crucifixion, and His death between two thieves. The sufferings of our Lord make up what is called the Passion of Christ.

Let us consider these sufferings one by one.

4. *His agony and sweat of blood*, to which may be added the betrayal of Judas.

After the last supper, and the institution of the blessed Eucharist, *Jesus went forth with His disciples over the brook Cedron, where there was a garden, into which He entered with His disciples.* *

This brook Cedron is called also the ravine of Kedron, or of the Cedars. Its name is derived, according to some, from the black-green colour of the cedar trees that once grew there ; and according to others, from the dark colour of its water and the gloom of the valley itself. It is a winter torrent, and even in winter there is very little water in the Cedron. Across this brook David passed in his flight from His rebellious son Absalom.

Our Saviour descended this valley or ravine, crossed the brook, and ascended up the green slope beyond it into the Mount of Olives, where there was a garden or orchard, or an enclosed piece of ground. This garden was called Gethsemani, which means oil-press. Olive trees abound there, and mark the traditional site of the agony, and of the betrayal.

Jesus, leaving eight of His disciples to sleep under the trees, withdrew into the interior of the garden with Peter, James, and John. These three had witnessed His transfiguration, and they were now to witness the sufferings of His sacred heart. He said to them, *My soul is sorrowful even unto death*, and He told them : *Watch and pray that ye enter not into temptation.* He then withdrew from them about a stone's throw, probably farther, into the shadow of the ancient olive trees, that He might pass His darkest hour alone.

Here He offered His threefold prayer to His Father, saying, *Father if it be possible let this chalice pass from me, nevertheless not my will but thine be done.* After repeating this prayer three times, He came each time to His disciples, and found them

---

* St. John xviii. 1.

asleep. During three long hours He suffered in His soul all the torments of death; the deepest sorrow for all the sins of the world, so much so, that He fell into an agony, and His sweat became as drops of blood flowing down upon the ground.

His agony was not the mere shrinking from death and pain, which even inferior natures can overcome, but the mysterious burden of the world's guilt, the shrinking of a sinless being from the depths of satanic hate and horror through which He was to pass. And *His sweat became as drops of blood.* Such a thing as a " bloody sweat " seems not to be wholly unknown under abnormal pathological circumstances. The blood of Abel cried to heaven for vengeance; but this blood, speaking better than that of Abel, cries to heaven for mercy and forgiveness. St. Luke does not, however, use the term *bloody sweat*, but says that the dense sweat of agony fell from Him as drops of blood do from a wound.

An Angel from heaven appeared to comfort Him; as an angel came to Him after His temptation.

THE BETRAYAL.

5. This includes the *traitor's kiss; the Arrest; Malchus.*

And Judas who betrayed Him knew the place, for Jesus often went thither to pray. He came therefore with a band of soldiers, composed of Levitical guards and Roman soldiers, who, at this time were sent to Jerusalem to prevent a tumult or uproar amongst the thousands of pilgrims assembled to keep the Passover. The band elsewhere is called a cohort, which means the tenth part of a legion. The soldiers of the Jews were under their general, and the cohort, or part of a cohort, from the Fort Antonio, were under a Roman tribune. They brought with them lanterns and torches, which was the ordinary equipment for night duty, which, as it would appear, the Paschal moon would not render useless; besides, to their minds it was probable that dark woods or buildings would have to be searched.

(a) And he that was called Judas, one of the twelve, *went before them, and drew near to Jesus for to kiss Him. And Jesus said to him, Judas, dost thou betray the Son of man with a kiss?* [*] Judas had before given them a sign, saying, He whom I shall kiss that is He. He exclaimed, *Hail Rabbi!* and he kissed Him with the

---

* St. Luke xxii. 47.

words, "peace to Thee"; but received no "peace to thee" in reply. Overacting his part, he not only kissed his Lord, but kissed Him fervently (deosculatus est).

(b) *The Arrest.* As soon as Judas had kissed our Lord he fell back with the crowd of soldiers and others. Then Jesus went forth and said to them, *Whom seek ye?* Jesus went forth from the shade into the light, and from the circle of His disciples and the interior of the garden, to meet death.

They answered Him, *Jesus of Nazareth,* or the Nazarene —a comtemptuous expression. *Jesus saith to them, I am He...*

The "*He*" is not expressed in the Greek version; and *I am,* to Jewish ears, was the name of Jehovah. Judas, if not the chief priests, must have noticed the significant words. There is nothing in the narrative to show that either the whole company were miraculously blinded, or that Judas in particular was blinded or paralysed.

As soon therefore as He said to them, I am He, they went backwards and fell to the ground. Whether this was in mockery and derision, or the strange effect of guilt meeting with absolute innocence, or a supernatural effect wrought by Christ, is a question which we have not the means of determining. The result proved, both to the disciples and His foes, that His surrender was entirely voluntary. Once before, the majesty of His words had overwhelmed those who had come to arrest Him;* and it would have been so now had not He willed to be taken. He asked them again, *Whom seek ye?* Their first onset had been baffled; He Himself therefore gives them another opening; and they repeat the terms of their warrant that they have been sent to arrest Jesus of Nazareth. Then our Saviour answered: *I have told you that I am He. If therefore you seek Me let these go their way: This is your hour and the power of darkness.*

(c) *Malchus.* (MT) *Then they came up and laid hands on Jesus and held Him. And behold, one of them that were with Jesus* (Simon Peter, as St. John tells us) *stretching forth his hand, drew out his sword, and striking the servant of the High Priest* (whose name was Malchus), *cut off his ear* (his right ear). (L) *But Jesus answering, said, "Suffer ye thus far."* And

---

* St. John vii. 46.

when He had touched his ear He healed it. (MT) *Then Jesus saith to Peter, Put up again thy sword into its place ; for all that take the sword shall perish with the sword.* (J) *The chalice which My Father shall give Me, shall I not drink it?* (MT) *Thinkest thou that I cannot ask My Father, and He will give me presently twelve legions of angels ? How then shall the Scriptures be fulfilled, that so it must be done.*

Then turning to the chief Priests, who had evidently kept in the background till all possible danger was over, Jesus said to them : (MT) *You are come out as it were to a robber, with swords and clubs to apprehend Me. I sat daily with you, teaching in the Temple, and you laid not hands on Me. Now all this was done that the Scriptures of the prophets might be fulfilled.* Thus He reproaches them for their cowardice and secrecy, as if He had said, "If I had really done wrong, how is it that ye did not arrest Me in the Temple?" Then the disciples, all leaving Him, fled. Then the band, and the tribune, *and the servants of the Jews, took Jesus and bound Him.*

THE JEWISH OR ECCLESIASTICAL TRIAL OF CHRIST.

6. Before Christ was handed over to Pontius Pilate, the Roman governor, He was condemned by the Jewish Sanhedrin, and by the Jewish people. We may subjoin the order of the events of this portion of the Passion.

(a) From the garden of Gethsemane Jesus was taken to Annas ; thence, after brief questioning,[*]

(b) To Caiphas, either in another part of the sacerdotal palace, or to a residence of his own, where some members of the Sanhedrin had hastily met; and the first irregular trial of Jesus took place at night.[†]

(c) Early in the morning a *second* and formal trial was held by the Sanhedrin. This is related by St. Luke, and is mentioned by SS. Matthew and Mark.

(d) The trial before Pontius Pilate, consisting of two parts (1) a preliminary examination for which there is a technical legal phrase in St. Luke.[§] (2) A final trial and sentence to death.

---

[*] St. John xviii. 19-23.   [†] SS. Matthew, Mark, and Luke.
[§] St. Luke xxiii. 14.

(e) The remission to Herod between the two Roman trials (1) and (2) recorded only by St. Luke.

The question is sometimes asked, Was the trial of Jesus fair and legal according to the rules of Jewish law? The answer must be that the proceedings against Jesus violated both (a) the spirit, and (b) the express rules of Hebrew jurisprudence, the general tendency of which was to extreme clemency.

(a) The Talmud says: "The Sanhedrin is to save not to
. destroy life." No man could be condemned in his absence, or without a majority of two to one; the penalty for procuring false witnesses was death; the condemned was not to be executed on the day of his trial. This clemency was violated in the trial of Jesus Christ.

(b) But even the ordinary legal rules were disregarded in the following particulars :—(1) The examination by Annas without witnesses. (2) The trial by night. (3) The sentence on the first day of trial. (4) The trial of a Capital charge on the day before the Sabbath. (5) The suborning of witnesses. (6) The direct interrogation by the High Priest.*

JESUS BEFORE ANNAS.

7. Whether Annas was ' Chief' of the priests, or president, or vice-president of the Sanhedrin, we have no information ; certainly he was one of the most influential members of the hierarchy, as is shown by his securing the high-priesthood for no less than five of his sons, as well as for his son-in-law Caiphas, after he had been deposed himself. He held office A.D. 7-14, his son Eleazar, A.D. 16 ; Joseph Caiphas, A.D. 18-36 ; after him four sons of Annas held the office, the last of whom, another Annas, A.D. 82, put to death St. James the first bishop of Jerusalem.

The high-priests at this time were often mere nominees of the civil power, and were changed with a rapidity that must have scandalized serious Jews. He was father-in-law to Caiphas, and therefore Caiphas would be sure to respect the results of a preliminary examination conducted by him. Possibly the chief priests thought that Annas was a safer man than Caiphas, and, the father-in-law having taken the lead they wanted, the high-priest would be compelled to follow. This examination before Annas is given us by St. John only, who tacitly corrects the

---

* See Cambridge Bible for Schools.

impression that the examination before Caiphas was the only one.*

According to St. John's narrative three things happened in the house of Annas : (a) St. Peter denies our Lord the first time. (b) Christ is interrogated concerning His disciples and His doctrine. (c) He receives a blow on the face from the servant of the high-priest.

THE FIRST TRIAL BEFORE CAIPHAS.

8. Annas had simply tried to entangle Jesus by insidious questions. The course of the trial before Caiphas was different. The priests on that occasion sought false witnesses, but their false witnesses contradicted each other in their attempt to prove that He had threatened to destroy the Temple. Since Jesus kept silence, Caiphas rose in the midst of the assembly and adjured Him by the living God to say whether He was *the Christ the Son of God*. So adjured, Christ answered in the affirmative ; and ｜ n Caiphas rent his garments and appealed to the assembly, who, most illegally, by setting aside the need of any further witnesses, shouted aloud that He was a man guilty of death, that is, deserving of capital punishment. The high-priest rent his garments and said, He blasphemeth. The Sanhedrin do not pass sentence of death on Him, but merely re-affirm their foregone conclusion, and endeavour to have sentence passed and judgment executed by the Procurator.

Two other particular sufferings of that night remain to be mentioned, namely, (a) St. Peter's denial. (b) The derision of Christ.

ST. PETER'S DENIAL.

9. Peter followed afar off to see the end. This was an unwise exposure of himself to temptation. His admission into the courtyard of the High-Priest's house was due to the influence of St. John. They had kindled a fire in the midst of the courtyard, as the spring nights at Jerusalem are often cold, and the soldiers and officials were seated at the fire. Peter sat down amongst the servants of the High-Priest ; in the midst of a group of men who had just been engaged in the arrest of his Lord.

A certain maid, probably the portress, who had been meanwhile relieved, and who, after a fixed gaze, recognised Peter as

---

* Cambridge Bible for Schools, St. John.

the man whom she had admitted, exclaimed, *This man was also with Him.* (This account is given by St. Luke. The accounts given by the Evangelists of these denials of St. Peter are various, but not contrary.) St. Peter answered and denied our Lord the first time with the words : *Woman I know Him not*; or, *I know not the Man.*

After a little while. The trial before the sacerdotal Committee naturally took some time, and they were awaiting the result. St. Peter, after the first denial before them all, probably hoped to shake off this dangerous curiosity ; and, perhaps, as his guilt was brought more home to him by the crowing of the cock the first time, stole back out of the light of the brazier, where he had been sitting with the servants, to the gate or vestibule. Of his second denial St. John says, *They said to him* ; and as the portress was sure to have gossipped about him to the girl who relieved her at her post, the second denial was due to his being pointed out by the second maid to the group of idlers who were hanging about the doors, one of whom was prominent in pressing the charge against him. And Peter again denied, saying, *Man, I am not.* Showing his displeasure by his manner.

About the space of an hour after this—to St. Peter it must must have been one of the most terrible hours of his life—the charge was made a third time against him. Here again the main charge was prominently made by *one*, a kinsman of Malchus, who had seen Peter in the garden, and was known to St. John from his acquaintance with the High-Priest's household. But others came up and joined in it, and they added, for *even thy speech betrayeth thee.* Peter was discovered by his use of. the Galilean dialect. The Galileans were unable to pronounce the gutturals distinctly, and they lisped, pronouncing *sh* like *th.* Peter then denied again, and began to curse and to swear that he knew not the Man, and immediately the cock crew. It crew for the second time, verifying the words of Christ uttered in warning to St. Peter : *Before the cock crow twice thou shalt deny Me thrice.*

St. Luke then tells us our Lord turned and looked on Peter. Jesus must have looked on His erring Apostle either from the chamber in which He was being tried, or else at the moment when the trial was over, and He was being led across the court-yard amid the coarse insults of the servants. And *Peter went out and wept bitterly.* He went out into the night, and to meet the morning dawn, and *wept*, not merely shed tears, but wept aloud, and continued weeping.

. St. John gives both the prophecy and its fulfilment concerning St. Peter's fall, •to prove our Saviour's foreknowledge of it; and it is to be noticed in St. John's account, that he mentions most what may lessen the fault of his brother Apostle: that servants and officers were about him; that in the second case he was pressed by more than one; and that on the last occasion a kinsman of Malchus was among the accusers, which may greatly have increased Peter's terror. Moreover, this instance of human frailty in one so exalted, is given us with fourfold emphasis, that none may presume and none dispair.

THE DERISION.

10. Jesus, after He was declared a blasphemer, and one guilty of death by the Sanhedrin, is left in the hands of the soldiers; and St. Luke tells us how they treat Him. *And the men that held Jesus mocked Him and smote Him. And when they had blindfolded Him they struck him on the face, and asked Him saying, Prophecy who is it that struck Thee. And, blaspheming, many other things they said against Him.* No less than five forms of beating are referred to by the Evangelists in describing this pathetic scene.

THE THIRD JEWISH TRIAL, OR THE SECOND TRIAL BEFORE CAIPHAS.

11. *As soon as it was day.* The oral law decided that the Sanhedrin could only meet by daylight. *The ancients of the people, the chief priests and the scribes, came together.* Here we have the three constituent parts of the Sanhedrin. The Sanhedrin was the successor of the Great Synagogue which ended with Simon the Just. "*Where* they met is uncertain. It was either in the Paved Hall or Hall of Squares, or in the Temple Synagogue, a chamber which abutted on the middle *wall of partition*; or in the shops or booths founded by the house of Hanan to sell doves, etc., for the temple."*

They brought Him into their Council, namely, the Sanhedrin. Formerly this tribunal gloried in its justice and mildness, but it was now an extremely degenerated body, and unworthy of its earlier traditions. The Jewish authorities had lost the power of inflicting death, they could only pass sentence of excommunication, and hand over to the secular power.

* Cambridge Bible for Schools, St. Luke.

They ask our Saviour: *Art Thou the Christ ?* Jesus: *If I tell you you will not believe ; and if I also ask* YOU *you will not answer me nor let me go. Hereafter shall the Son of man sit on the right hand of the power af God. Then said they all : Art Thou the Son of God ? Who said : You say that I am. And they said, what need we any further testimony, for we ourselves have heard it from His own mouth. And the whole multitude rising up, led Him to Pilate.*

12. Here follows the account of the remorse and horrible end of Judas, given by St. Matthew.

How that Judas, seeing that He was condemned, repented himself. His repentance was not one that brought about a change of heart or life, but merely remorse or regret. *He returned the thirty pieces of silver for which he sold our Lord, and cast them down in the temple, and went and hanged himself with a halter.*

But the chief-priests, having taken the pieces of silver, said, It is not lawful to put them into the corbona (the treasury) *because it is the price of blood. And after they had consulted together they bought with them the potter's field, to be a burying place for strangers. For this cause that field was called haceldama, that is, the field of blood, even to this day.*

SECTION 3. (ARTICLE IV.)

THE PASSION OF CHRIST.—*Continued.*

1. The first trial of Jesus before Pilate.—2. The trial before Herod.—3 The second trial of Christ before Pilate.—4. Barabbas.—5. The message of Pilate's wife.—6. The choice of the people between Jesus and Barabbas.—7. The scourging.—8. The crowning with thorns: (*a*) the scarlet cloak, (*b*) the crown of thorns, (*c*) the reed.—9. The Ecce Homo.—10. Jesus is sentenced to death.

THE FIRST TRIAL BEFORE PILATE.

1. *Then they led Jesus from Caiphas to the Governor's Hall,* and it was morning. This hall of judgment was at Pilate's house or palace, the official residence of the Procurator. It is probable that Pilate occupied a part of the fortress of Antonio. It was early in the morning. A Roman court might be held directly after sunrise ; and as Pilate had probably been informed that an important case was to be brought before him, delay in which might cause serious disturbance, there is nothing improbable in his being ready to open his court between 4.0 and 5.0 a.m.

The chief Priests and the accusing Jews would not enter the hall that they might not be defiled. Pilate, because they would not enter, went out to them, and, true to the Roman sense of justice, refused to confirm the sentence of the Sanhedrin, and determined to try the case himself. He asked them : *What accusation bring you against this man ?* They bring three distinct charges against Christ, which, being political, Pilate must hear. (*a*) Perverting the nation. (*b*) Forbidding tribute to Cæsar. (*c*) Saying that He Himself is Christ, a King.

Pilate, on hearing their accusation, returns to the hall where Jesus was, and addressing himself to our Lord, asked Him, *Art Thou the King of the Jews?* The answer of Jesus, and His explanation to Pilate of the Kingdom of God, are given at length in St. John's Gospel* : *Jesus answered, sayest thou this of thyself or have others told it thee of Me ?* Pilate answered, *Am I a Jew ?* (Is it likely that I, a Roman governor, have any interest in these

---

* St. John xviii. 33—37.

Jewish questions). *Thy own nation and the chief Priests have delivered Thee up to me. What hast Thou done ?* (What didst Thou do to make Thy own people turn against Thee ?) *Jesus answered, My Kingdom is not of this world ; if My Kingdom were of this world, My servants would certainly strive that I should not be delivered up to the Jews ; but now My kingdom is not from hence. Pilate therefore said to Him, Art Thou a King then ? Jesus answered, Thou sayest that I am a King ; for this was I born, and for this came I into the world that I should give testimony of the truth. Every one who is of the truth, heareth My voice. Pilate saith to Him, What is truth ? And when he said this he went out again to the Jews, and said to them, I find no cause in Him.* When, therefore, Pilate came out again to the Jews he had Jesus with him. *And he said to the chief Priests and the multitude, I find no cause in Him.* That is, I find no crime in this case for which this man should be put to death.

The Jews hearing this outside the hall, began more and more to accuse Jesus. Pilate, who was with Jesus on the platform of the hall, again asked him, saying, (M) *Answerest Thou nothing ? Behold in how many things they accuse Thee. But Jesus still answered nothing, so that Pilate wondered.* (L) *But they were more earnest, saying, He stirreth up the people, teaching throughout all Judea, beginning from Galilee to this place. But Pilate, hearing Galilee, asked if the man were of Galilee. And when he understood that He was of Herod's jurisdiction, he sent Him away to Herod, who was also himself at Jerusalem in these days.*

THE TRIAL BEFORE HEROD.

2. St. Luke alone gives this interesting incident of the Passion. He seems to have had special information about Herod's Court. Pilate's object may have been (*a*) to get rid of the responsibility—or at least to divide it—by ascertaining Herod's opinion ; (*b*) to do a cheap act of courtesy, which might soothe the irritation which Herod, as well as the Jews, felt against him.

Herod, as well as Pilate, was at Jerusalem at this time, although the former lived usually at Tiberias, and Pilate at Cæsarea. During the immense assemblage of the Jewish feasts, the two rulers had come to Jerusalem, Pilate to maintain order, Herod to gain popularity among his subjects by a decent semblance of conformity to the national religion. At Jerusalem Herod occupied the old palace of the Asmonæan princes.

Herod hoped to see our Lord perform some miracle. He asked Him many questions, but Christ answered him nothing. No; a murderer of the Prophets, who was living in open and flagrant incest, and who had no higher motive than mean curiosity, deserved no answer. Our Lord used of Herod the only purely contemptuous word which He is ever recorded to have uttered.*

The Jews vehemently accused our Lord before Herod. They were bent on securing their purpose, and, perhaps, feared that Herod's well-known weakness and superstition might rob them of their prey; especially as he was much less afraid of them than Pilate, having strong influence in Rome.

And Herod with his army (*i.e.,* his soldiers) *set Him at nought, and mocked, putting on Him a white garment* (probably a *white* festal garment), *and sent Him back to Pilate.* This involved a second acquittal of our Lord from every political charge brought against Him. Had He in any way been guilty of either (*a*) perverting the people; (*b*) forbidding tribute to be paid to Cæsar; or (*c*) claiming to be a King; it would have been Herod's duty, and still more, his interest, to punish Him. His dismissal of the case was a deliberate avowal of His innocence.

And Herod and Pilate were made friends that same day, for before they were enemies to one another. This is the first type of Judaism and Heathenism leagued together to crush Christianity.†

THE SECOND TRIAL OF CHRIST BEFORE PILATE.

8. After Christ was brought back to Pilate, he, the governor, made a formal speech to the chief Priests and the people.

(L) *You have presented unto me this man as one that perverteth the people, and behold, I, having examined Him before you can find no cause in this man in these things wherein you accuse Him; no, nor Herod either. For I sent you to Him, and behold nothing worthy of death is done to Him. I will chastise Him, therefore, and release Him.*

"Now was the golden opportunity which Pilate should have seized, in order to do what he knew to be right; and he was really anxious to do it, because the meek majesty of the Lord had made a deep impression upon him, and because, even while seated on the throne, he was shaken by a presentiment of warning conveyed to him by the dream of his wife. But men live

---

* St. Luke xiii. 32.
† See Cambridge Bible for Schools. St. Luke.

under the coercion of their own past acts, and Pilate, by his cruelty and greed, had so bitterly offended the inhabitants of every province of Judea, that he dared not do anything more to provoke the accusation which he knew to be hanging over his head. He declares that he has found no fault in Him. Pilate's word is a direct contradiction of that of the high Priest. The *I* is emphatic. You bring a charge, *I*, after a public examination, find it to be baseless. *I will therefore chastise Him.* This was the point at which Pilate began to yield to the fatal vacillation which soon passed into guilt, and made it afterwards impossible or Him to escape. He had just declared the prisoner absolutely nnocent. To subject Him, therefore, to the horrible punish-. ment of scourging merely to gratify the pride of the Jews, and to humble Him in their eyes, was an act of disgraceful illegality, which he must have felt to be most unworthy of the high Roman sense of justice. The guilty dread which made Pilate a weak man, made him also the unconscious fulfiller of prophecy."* †

After this follows the narrative of three events. (*a*) The proposition to release one of the prisoners on the occasion (of the Passover) ; and Pilate asked them, *Whom will ye that I release unto you* : *Barabbus or Jesus, who is called the Christ?* (*b*) The message of Pilate's wife. (*c*) Barabbas preferred to Jesus.

4. It was a custom to release a prisoner on the occasion of this Festival of the Passover. No trace of this custom is found in the Talmud. But the release of prisoners was usual at certain festivals at Rome, and at Athens ; during the Panathenaic festival prisoners enjoyed temporary liberty. It is not, therefore, improbable that Herod the Great, who certainly familiarised the Jews with other usages of Greece and Rome, introduced this custom, and that the Roman governor, finding the custom established, and gratifying to the Jews, in accordance with Roman practice, retained the observance of it.

Barabbas or Bar-Abbas, son of Abba (father), son of a (distinguished) father. At this stage of the trial Barabbas may have been led out, and the choice offered them between Jesus Bar-Abbas, and Jesus, who is called Christ, as they stood on the pavement side by side.

St. John adds : *Now Barabbas was a robber.* There is a tragic impressiveness in this brief remark. The *robber* is the bandit, or brigand, who is more dangerous to persons than to property, and sometimes combines something of chivalry with

---

* Isaiah liii. 3.   † Cambridge Bible for Schools. St. Luke.

his violence. In the case of Barabbas, we know, from St
Mark and St. Luke, that he had been guilty of insurrection and
consequent bloodshed rather than of stealing ; and this was very
likely the case also with the two robbers crucified with Jesus.
Thus, by a strange irony of fate, the hierarchy obtain the release
of a man guilty of the very political crime with which they
charged Christ—sedition. The people, no doubt, had some
sympathy with the insurrectionary movement of Barabbas, and
on this the priests worked.

THE MESSAGE OF PILATE'S WIFE.

5. Pilate was sitting on the tribunal to ascertain the popular
decision. At this point he was interrupted by his wife's messengers.
The message she sent to Him was : *Have thou nothing to do with
that just man, for I have suffered many things in a dream because
of Him.* This dream of Pilate's wife is recorded by St. Matthew
only. Claudia Procula, or Procla, was the woman's name, and
according to Cornelius a Lapide she is venerated as a Saint
amongst the Greeks. It is most probable that this vision came
from God, to proclaim the innocence of Christ before the unjust
sentence of His condemnation is pronounced.

THE CHOICE OF THE PEOPLE.

6. While Pilate was engaged with the messengers, the chief
Priests employed themselves in persuading the people to demand
Barabbas rather than Christ. When the messengers had left,
Pilate said to them (L) *Whether will you of the two to be released
unto you ?* But the *whole multitude cried out* : *Away with this
man, and release unto us Barabbas. Pilate said to them* : (MR)
*What will you then that I do to the King of the Jews? But they
cried out, Crucify Him. And Pilate saith unto them. Why, what
evil hath He done ?* (L) *I find no cause of death in Him ; I will
chastise Him therefore, and let Him go.* (MT) *But they cried out
the more, saying, Let Him be crucified.*

There is no further question of a show of legality or justice ;
the traditional clemency is quite forgotten ; the fanatical crowd,
pressing round the doors of the Prætorium, which they cannot
enter, join with excited gesticulation in one loud and furious cry
for the blood of Jesus.

Pilate, seeing that he gained no advantage, but excited more
the multitude, (MT) *taking water, he washed his hands before the*

*people, saying, I am innocent of the blood of this just man, you look
to it. And the whole people answering, said, His blood be upon us
and upon our children.* In washing his hands Pilate followed a
Jewish custom which all would understand. The terrible cry of
the Jews : *His blood be upon us and upon our children* is peculiar
to St. Matthew. St. Peter finds as the sole excuse for his fellow-
countrymen, *I wot that through ignorance ye did it as did also
your rulers.** The prayer of Jesus on the Cross for His murderers
was meant for these as well as for the Roman soldiers. All
these things took place outside the Prætorium ; we come now to
consider what happened inside the Prætorium, namely, the
scourging and mockery by the soldiers.

THE SCOURGING.

7. " Because the attempt to release Him in honour of the
Feast had failed, Pilate now tries whether the severe and degrading
punishment of scourging will not satisfy the Jews. In Pilate's
hands the boasted justice of Roman law ends in the policy:
What evil did He do ? I find no cause of death in Him : I will
therefore chastise Him and let Him go. Scourging was part of
Roman capital punishment ; and had we only the two first Gospels
we might suppose that the scourging was inflicted immediately
before Crucifixion ; but this is not stated, and St. John, combined
with St. Luke, makes it clear that scourging was inflicted as a
separate punishment, in the hope that it would suffice. The
supposition of a second scourging as part of the execution is
unnecessary and improbable. Pilate, sick of the bloody work,
and angry at being forced to commit a judicial murder, would
not have allowed it ; and it may be doubted whether any human
frame could have survived a Roman scourging twice in one day.
One infliction was sometimes fatal.†

" We can only obtain from all the four Evangelists, and
especially from St. John, a full conception of the earnestness
with which Pilate strove to escape from the necessity of what he
felt to be a needless crime. If he was not, as Tertullian says,
jam pro conscientia sua Christianus, he was evidently impressed,
and the difficulty of doing right must have come upon him as
a terrible Nemesis for his past sins. It is noteworthy that he
took step after step to secure the acquittal of Jesus. (*a*) He
emphatically and publicly announced His perfect innocence.

---

* Acts iii. 17.   † Cambridge Bible for Schools. St. John.

(*b*) He sent Him to Herod. (*c*) He made an offer to release Him as a boon. (*d*) He tried to make scourging take the place of crucifixion. (*e*) He appealed to compassion. St. John shows still more clearly how, in successive stages of the trial, he sets aside (*a*) the vague general charge of being an evil-doer; (*b*) of being in any seditious sense a King; (*c*) of any guilt in His religious claims. He only yields at last through fear, which makes him release a man guilty of the *very* crime for which he delivers Jesus to a slaves's death. The fact that Pilate's patron, Sejanus, had probably by this time fallen, and that Tiberius was executing all connected with him, may have enhanced Pilate's fears. He knew that an accusation of High Treason (under the *Lex Majestatis*) was generally fatal."

The Crown of Thorns; and Jesus Mocked by the Roman Soldiers.

8. Herod and his troops had set an example which the Roman soldiers were ready enough to follow. Pilate countenanced the brutality as aiding his own plan of satisfying Jewish hatred with something less than death. The soldiers had inflicted the scourging, for Pilate, being only Procurator, would have had no lictors. St. Matthew narrates this incident as well as St. John. *Then the soldiers of the Governor, taking Jesus into the hall, gathered together unto Him the whole band. And stripping Him, they put a scarlet cloak about Him, and platting a crown of thorns they put it upon His head, and a reed in His right hand. And bowing the knee before Him, they mocked Him, saying: Hail, King of the Jews. And spitting upon Him they took the reed and struck His head."*

The hall, into which they led our Lord, was the Prætorium, a part of the residence of the Governor.

    (*a*)   *The scarlet cloak.* St. Mark calls it *purple*. Purple, with the ancients, was a vague term for bright, rich colour, and would be used of crimson as well as of violet. The robe was a military *chlamys*, or *paludamentum*. One of Pilate's cast-off cloaks. The garment in which Herod had mocked Jesus was white. The scourging and mockery were very possibly visible to the Jews.

    (*b*)   *The Crown of Thorns.* The context seems to show that this was in mockery of a royal crown rather than the victor's wreath. The plant is supposed to be of a thorny *nâbk* with flexible branches and leaves like ivy, abundant in the Jordan valley and round about Jerusalem.

(c) *The Reed in the Right Hand* was in mockery of the sceptre of a king. *The Hail King of the Jews*: like the Procurator, the soldiers mock the Jews as well as their victim.

THE *Ecce Homo*, AND THE LAST SCENE OF THE TRIAL BEFORE PILATE.

9. This took place outside the Prætorium, and it includes Pilate's appeal—*Behold the man;* and the Jews' rejoinder, *He made Himself the Son of God.* I here subjoin St. John's narrative, that needs no note or comment: *Pilate took Jesus, and went forth again, and saith to them: Behold, I bring him forth unto you, that you may know that I find no cause in Him. (Jesus, therefore, came forth wearing the crown of thorns and the purple garments.) And he saith to them,* BEHOLD THE MAN. *When the chief priests, therefore, and the servants had seen Him, they cried out, saying, Crucify—crucify Him! Pilate saith to them: Take Him you and crucify Him, for I find no cause in Him. The Jews answered him: We have a law, and according to the law He ought to die, because He made Himself the Son of God.*

When Pilate therefore had heard this saying, he feared the more. And he entered into the hall again, and said to Jesus, Whence art thou? But Jesus gave him no answer. Pilate therefore saith to Him: Speakest Thou not to me? Knowest Thou not that I have power to crucify Thee, and I have power to release Thee. Jesus answered: Thou shouldst not have any power against Me, unless it were given to thee from above; therefore, he that hath delivered Me to thee hath the greater sin. And from henceforth Pilate sought to release Him. But the Jews cried out, saying: If thou release this man, thou art not Cæsar's friend. For whosoever maketh himself King, speaketh against Cæsar.

Pilate, hearing these words, feared lest he should be accused of enmity and perfidy towards Cæsar; and, on the other hand, he was unwilling to condemn Christ, Who had said that He was a King, but that His kingdom was not of this world. Doubtful, therefore, and hesitating, *he brought Jesus forth, and sat down in the judgment seat, in the place which is called Lithostrotos, and in Hebrew Gabbatha.* Literally, this means stone-paved. Josephus

says that the Temple mount, on part of which the fortress of
Antonio stood, was covered with a tesselated pavement. It was,
we may conclude, from its having a Hebrew name, a fixed spot,
and not the portable mosaic work which Roman generals sometimes carried about with them.

AND IT WAS THE PARASCEVE OF THE PASCH, ABOUT THE SIXTH HOUR.

10. Pilate, wishing to try a last experiment, pointing to
Jesus, Whom he brought out with him, with his finger, and
prompted by divine inspiration according to some of the Fathers
of the Church, *he saith to the Jews : Behold your King. But they
cried out : Away with Him ! away with Him ! Crucify Him.
Pilate saith to them, Shall I crucify your King ? The chief priests
answered, We have no King but Cæsar.* Sooner than acknowledge
that Jesus is the Messiah, the chief priests proclaim that a heathen
emperor is their king. And their baseness is at once followed by
Pilate's ; sooner than meet a dangerous charge, he condemns the
innocent to death. *Then, therefore, he delivered Him to them to be
crucified. And they took Jesus, and led Him away.* St. Luke
says that *Pilate gave sentence that it should be as they required.**
The two technical formulæ for the sentence of death would be—
to the prisoner, *Ibis ad crucem* (Thou shalt go to the cross) ; to
the attendant soldiers, *I miles expedi crucem* (Go, soldiers, get
ready the Cross).

---

* xxiii. 24.

SECTION 4. (ARTICLE IV.)

THE CRUCIFIXION AND DEATH OF CHRIST.

1. The carrying of the Cross—(a) the Cross itself; (b) Simon of Cyrene; (c) the veil of Veronica; (d) the women of Jerusalem.—2. Calvary. —3. The Vinegar and Gall.—4. The fastening Him to the Cross.—5. The title on the Cross.—6. The parting of His garments and the seamless garment.—7. Christ is mocked on the Cross.—8. The last words of Christ from the Cross.—9. The friends of Jesus who stood round the Cross.--10. The darkness.—11. The words, *Eli, Eli, lama Sabacthani*: My God, my God, why hast Thou forsaken Me.—12. The fifth word, *I thirst.*—13. The sixth word, *Consummatum est*: It is finished.—14. Christ dies.

UNDER this head we have to consider (a) The carrying of the Cross. (b) The Crucifixion and the three hours' agony. (c) The death, and the events that followed immediately on the death of Christ.

THE CARRYING OF THE CROSS, OR JESUS LED FORTH TO CRUCIFIXION.

1. The Jews having, by clamour and threats, obtained the condemnation of Christ (J) *took Jesus and led Him forth, that is,* from the tribunal to the prætorium, where (MT) *they took off the cloak from Him, and put on Him His own garments, and led Him away to crucify Him.* (J) *And bearing His own Cross, He went forth to that place which is called Calvary, but in Hebrew Golgotha, where they crucified Him.* (MT) *And going out* (of the city) *they found a man of Cyrene, named Simon, coming out of the country,* (M) *the father of Alexander and Rufus:* (MT) *him they forced to take up the Cross.* (L) *And they laid the Cross on him to carry after Jesus. And there followed Him a great multitude of people, and of women, who bewailed and lamented Him. But Jesus, turning to them, said, Daughters of Jerusalem, weep not over Me, but weep for yourselves and your children. For, behold, the days will come wherein they will say, Blessed are the barren, and the wombs that have not borne, and the paps that have not given suck. Then*

*shall they begin to say to the mountains, Fall upon us ; and to the
hills, Cover us. For if in the green wood they do these things,
what shall be done in the dry?* And there were also two malefactors
led with Him to be put to death.
It was about nine o'clock in the morning when Jesus was
condemned to death. St. John tells us, it was the Friday of
the Passover ; it was about the sixth hour.
Pilate delivered Him unto them to be crucified. And they
took Jesus, and led Him away. The eternal Son is given by
the Father, comes to His own inheritance, and His own people
received Him not. The Incarnate Son is given up by Pilate to
His own people, and they receive Him to crucify Him. The
glorified Son will come again to His own people to receive them
unto Himself.

*And bearing His own Cross he went forth to that place called Cal-
vary, and in Hebrew, Golgotha.* Christ, on taking the Cross, may be
represented in the words of the hymn of the Church, as saying
in salutation of that Cross : *Salve, crux pretiosa, diu desiderata,
sollicite amata, sine intermissione quaesita, et aliquando cupienti
animo praeparata.*

(*a*)   The Cross on which our Saviour suffered was such as
is usually shown in pictures, the crux *immissa* †, or
Latin Cross, as distinguished from the crux *commissa*
T, or the crux *decussata* X, the form of the Cross on
which St. Andrew suffered. The length of the Cross
was fifteen feet, and the transverse beam was seven
or eight feet long. A projecting rest was fastened to it
to support the feet of the sufferer when nailed to the
Cross. The following particulars of what happened
on the way to Calvary are mentioned by the Evangelists. A man of Cyrene helped to carry the Cross ; a
great company of people, and of women, followed
Christ ; His touching address to the women of
Jerusalem ; the last warning of the coming sorrows ;
the leading of two malefactors with Him. Tradition
hands down to us two other events ; namely, the
meeting with His Blessed Mother, and St. Veronica
wipes His face with a veil or towel. As Mary was
present on Calvary when Christ was crucified, the
tradition is well founded that tells us of her meeting
her divine Son on the way to Calvary.
The following was the first remarkable incident which is
recorded in connection with the carrying of the Cross.

(b) *Simon of Cyrene.* This man is said to be coming out of the country, and that he was the father of Alexander and Rufus. It has been thought that the fact of his coming out of the country implies that Simon was returning from work, and hence that it cannot be the actual day of the Feast. Simon was probably coming into the city for the Feast, like so many others. Some infer that Simon was already an adherent of Christ, and it is said that he may have been one of those Men of Cyrene who preached, afterwards, the *word* to the Greeks when others preached to the Jews only.

Cyrene was a city in north-eastern Africa, famous for the beauty of its position. A large colony of Jews had settled there, as in other African and Egyptian cities, to avoid the oppression of the Syrian Kings. He was forced or compelled to carry the Cross. It is not certain whether they made Simon carry the entire Cross or merely part of the burden. From this, various Gnostic Sects devised the fable that Simon was executed by mistake for Jesus; a fable which, through Apocryphical legends, has found its way into the Koran.

(c) The tradition as to the veil of St. Veronica is, that this holy woman, moved with love and compassion towards Jesus suffering under the weight of His Cross, made her way through the crowd and soldiers, and wiped the perspiration and dust from His face with a veil or towel; and, as a reward or acknowledgment of this service, Jesus imprinted on the veil the image of His sacred countenance. The real name of this woman was Bernice, but after this event she was called Veronica, which means literally a true image.

(d) In the meantime the other women of Jerusalem had assembled and wept for Him, that is, they were bewailing and beating their breasts in compassion for Him.

Jesus addressed to them the only words recorded between His condemnation and His Crucifixion. He calls them daughters of Jerusalem, and therefore these wailing women were not His former Galilean followers. He tells them to weep (a) *for themselves*; for some of them at least would survive till the terrible days of the siege of Jerusalem; (b) *for their children*, reminding them of the terrible imprecation of the Jews themselves: *His*

blood be upon us and upon our children. Then His warning words
continue, *Blessed are the barren;* which words received their
most painful illustration in the incident of the siege, which had
long been foretold in prophecy, that women were driven even to
kill and eat their own children. The "Blessed" showed an
awful reversal of the proper blessedness of motherhood.
They will cry *to the mountains, Fall upon us.* Hundreds of
Jews at the end of the siege hid themselves in subterranean
recesses; and no less than two thousand were killed by being
buried under the ruins of these hiding places. We cannot fail to
see in these events something of what St. John calls the *wrath
of the Lamb.*[*] Even a terrible destruction is entreated as a relief
from yet more horrible calamities. *For if in the green wood they
do these things, what shall be done in the dry?* This proverb can
only mean either, (*a*) If they act thus cruelly and shamefully
while the tree of their natural life is green, what horrors of crime
shall mark the period of its blighting? or, (*b*) If they act thus
to *Me,* the Innocent and the Holy, what shall be the fate of these,
the guilty and false? For the historical fulfilment, in the horrors
of a massacre so great as to weary the very soldiers, *see* Josephus.
B. J. vi. 44.

The two other malefactors conducted with Christ to the
place of Crucifixion were, perhaps, followers of the released
Barabbas. They were robbers, or brigands, and are called thieves
in our translation of the Testament.

CALVARY.

2. The place of public execution appears to have been
situated north-west of the city. It was outside the gate,
and yet nigh unto the city. Calvary is no where in the Scripture
called a hill; and it was certainly not, in any sense, a steep or
lofty hill. The only grounds for speaking of it as a hill are (*a*)
tradition and (*b*) the name. Golgotha, according to some, in
the Hebrew means a hill, or is derived from a hill; or, according
to others, it is derived from the Hebrew word which signifies
death. Calvary is the Latin form for Golgotha, and means a
skull. The name has led to the legend about Adam's body being
buried there, and his skull lying at the foot of the Cross, which
is so often introduced into pictures. The name is also thought
to be derived from the shape and appearance of the hillock or
mound on which the crosses were reared.

---

[*] Apoc. vi. 6.

3. Before nailing Him to the Cross they offered Him vinegar, mingled with gall or myrrh, to drink. The potion was a stupefying draught given to criminals to deaden the sense of pain. Jesus refuses this alleviation of His sufferings.

4. The Lamb of God, Who is then offering Himself in Sacrifice, is extended on the Cross. His hands and feet are fastened to it by nails. The Cross is raised and planted in the ground with Jesus hanging upon it crucified, and with Him are crucified two thieves, one on the left and the other on the right hand side, and Jesus in the midst. The Crucifixion took place about mid-day, which St. Mark calls the third hour and St. John the sixth, according to the different mode of reckoning which they each followed or adopted. The hour of Crucifixion is commonly admitted to be noon, or twelve o'clock.

THE TITLE ON THE CROSS.

5. It was common to put on the Cross the name and crime of the person executed, after making him carry it round his neck to the place of execution. St. John tells us that Pilate wrote the title himself, and, according to the same Evangelist, the writing was JESUS OF NAZARETH, THE KING OF THE JEWS. The other three give the inscription thus :—(St. Matthew) THIS IS JESUS, THE KING OF THE JEWS. (St. Mark) THE KING OF THE JEWS. (St. Luke) THIS IS THE KING OF THE JEWS.

The writing was in *Hebrew*, in *Greek*, and in *Latin*, the three representative languages of the world at that time ; the languages of religion, of empire, and of intellect. Thus did they proclaim among the heathen that the Lord is King, or that the Lord reigned from a tree.*

The chief Priests of the Jews objected to His being called *the King of the Jews*, Pilate answered them, *What I have written I have written*. His answer illustrates the mixture of obstinacy and relentlessness, which Philo says was characteristic of him. His own interests are not at stake, so he will have his way; when he had anything to fear or to gain he could be supple enough. A shrewd, practical man of the world, with all a Roman official's contemptuous impartiality, and all the disbelief in truth and disinterestedness which the age had taught him, he seems to have been one of the many whose self-interest is stronger than their convictions, and who can walk uprightly when to do so is easy, but fail in the presence of danger and difficulty.†

---

* Ps. xcvi. 10.   † Cambridge Bible for Schools. St. John.

The Parting of His Garments, and Casting Lots for His Coat.

6. The garment which they divided was the loose, outer garment, or toga, with the girdle and fastenings. This was large enough to be worth dividing, and they divide it into four parts, corresponding to the quarternion of soldiers in charge of the prisoner. As a rule, the prisoner has to be guarded and kept alive, so that four quarternions mount guard in turn, one for each turn. The clothes of executed criminals were the perquisite of the soldiers on duty.

The Seamless Garment.

This was the inner garment, or coat; it fitted somewhat close to the body, reaching from the neck to the knees or ankles. In our Saviour's case it was without a seam, and Josephus tells us that that of the High Priest was seamless, whereas, in other cases, this garment was commonly made of two pieces. For this tunic the soldiers cast lots, thus verifying the words of prophecy : *They parted My garments amongst them, and upon My vesture they cast lots.*

Christ is Mocked by Words of Blasphemy and Hatred.

7. *If Thou be the Son of God, come down from the Cross, and then we will believe in Thee. He saved others, Himself He cannot save. Vah ! Thou that destroyest the Temple of God, and in three days rebuildest it, save Thy own self.*

Christ our Lord, who is the Master and Teacher of all, speaks from His Cross, and by His words teaches the whole world.

6. The Words of Jesus from the Cross are :—

(a) The prayer for the murderers, *Father, forgive them for they know not what they do.* (St. Luke xxiii. 34.)

(b) The promise to the penitent. *Amen, I say to thee, this day shalt thou be with Me in Paradise.* (St. Luke xxiii. 43.)

(c) The commendation to His Mother and St. John : *Woman, behold thy Son. (Son), behold thy mother.* (St. John xix. 26.)

(d) *Eli, Eli, lama sabacthani?* that is, *My God! My God! why hast Thou forsaken me?* (St. Matthew xxvii. 46; St. Mark xv. 34.)

(e) The sole expression of human agony : *I thirst.* (St. John xix. 28.)

(f) *It is consummated*; or, *It is finished.* (St. John xix. 30.)

(g) *Father, into Thy hands I commend My spirit.* (St. Luke xxiii. 46.)

Thus His words from the Cross refer to His enemies, to penitents, to His mother and disciple, to the agony of His soul, to the anguish of His body, to His work, and to His heavenly Father.

9. The friends of Christ who stood by the Cross, as mentioned by St. John, were His mother, and His Mother's sister Mary, of (the wife of) Cleophas, and Mary Magdalene, and the disciple whom Jesus loved.

The Greek, like the English, leaves us in doubt whether we have two women or one in His mother's sister, and Mary of Cleophas ; whether, altogether, there are four women or three. The former is much the more probable alternative. (a) It avoids the very improbable supposition of two sisters having the same name. (b) St. John is fond of parallel expressions, " His mother and His mother's sister," Mary of Cleophas, and Mary Magdalene are two pairs set one against the other. (c) St. Mark mentions Mary Magdalene, Mary the mother of James the Less, and Salome. Mary Magdalene is common to both narratives, Mary the mother of James the Less is the same as Mary of Cleophas ; the natural inference is that Salome is the same as His mother's sister. If this is correct (d) St. John's silence about the name of *His mother's sister* is explained. She was his own mother, and he is habitually reserved about all connected with himself. He never mentions his own name, nor his brother's, nor that of the Blessed Virgin.

THE DARKNESS.

10. Now there was darkness on the face of the earth from the sixth to the ninth hour, that is, from twelve to three o'clock in the afternoon. This darkness was not that of an eclipse, for it was the time of the Paschal full moon, but a miraculous darkness, symbolic of that solemn hour, and veiling the agonies of the Son of Man. when human soul and body alike were enduring

o

the extremity of anguish and suffering for sin. It is not certain that the darkness was universal, that is, over the whole world; although Origen and St. Jerome appeal to two heathen historians —Phlegon and Thallus—for a proof of this. During the three hours' darkness no incident is recorded, but we can trace a deepening sense of remorse and horror in the crowd.

11. And about the ninth hour Jesus cried with a loud voice, *Eli, Eli, lama sabacthani.* These are the Armaic words exactly as they were pronounced by Jesus. Their translation, " My God ! My God !" is also given, and the repetition gives a deeply pathetic force to the expressions. It is an expression of utter loneliness and desolation, the depths of which it is not for men to fathom. It is going beyond Scripture to say that a sense of God's wrath extorted that cry ; for to the last breath He was the well-beloved of the Father ; and the repeated My God ! My God ! is a witness even then to His confidence in His Father's love. This was the fourth word from the Cross.

12. The fifth—*I thirst.* At this moment *they putting a sponge full of vinegar about hyssop, put it to His mouth.* The hyssop probably was the reed used to reach His mouth. The *hyssopus* of St. John is the same as the *arundo* of St. Matthew, and the *calamus* of St. Mark. The vinegar was near the place of execution ; it served the soldiers as a cooling drink when mixed with water, but it would increase the sufferings of Christ at that moment. Christ had refused the stupefying draught before His Crucifixion, as it would have clouded His faculties. He accepts the drink now offered Him, which will revive His faculties for the effort of a willing surrender of His life.

13. When Jesus had received the vinegar He said, *Consummatum est : It is finished.* Just as the thirst was there before He expressed it, so the consciousness that His work was finished was there before He declared it. The Messiah's work of redemption was accomplished; His Father's commandment had been obeyed; types and prophecies had been fulfilled; His life had been lived, and His teaching completed; His last earthly tie was severed, and the end had come. The final *wages of sin* alone remained to be paid.

His Death.

14. (L) *Then Jesus, crying with a loud voice, said : Father, into Thy hands I commend My spirit.* (J) *And bowing His head He gave up the Ghost.*

Two of the Evangelists mark with special clearness that the death of the Messiah was entirely voluntary. St. Matthew says, *Yielded up the Ghost.* St. John, *He gave up the Ghost.* St. Luke and St. Mark have the same manner of expression: *He gave up the Ghost.* None of the four say He died; and St. Luke more clearly shews that the surrender of His life was a willing one by the words: *Father, into Thy hands I commend My spirit.* No one taketh it from Me, but I lay it down of Myself. It was the one thing which Christ claimed to do of *Himself.* St. John omits the loud voice which all the Synoptists give as immediately preceding Christ's death. It proved that His end was voluntary, and not the necessary result of exhaustion.

"Dead then our Saviour was upon the Cross; and, being a truly and properly mortal man, He underwent a true and proper death in the same manner as we die. Now, since we are properly said to die when we cease to live, since life consists in the union to the body of the soul, whence flow motion, sensation, and whatsoever vital perfection we have; death can be nothing else but the solution of that vital union, or the actual separation of the soul united before to the body. When, therefore, we read that Christ our Saviour died, we must conceive it a true and proper death, consequently that His body was bereft of His soul, and of all vital influence from the same.

"That the unspotted soul of Christ was thus actually separated from His body, that His body from that soul's separation was bereft of natural life, appears moreover by His own resignation: *Father, into Thy hands I commend My spirit*; and by the Evangelist's expression, *Having said thus, He gave up the Ghost.......* So the eternal Son of God did properly and truly die on the Cross.

"To declare in what the nature and condition of the death of a Person so totally singular peculiarly consisted, we have to remember that there were two different substantial unions in Christ: one of the parts of His human nature to each other, the other of His natures human and Divine. (*a*) The union of the parts of His human nature was (as already shown) dissolved on the Cross, and as far then as Humanity consists in that union, so far the Humanity of Christ on His death did cease to be; but (*b*) the *union* of the *natures* remained still as to the parts, nor was the soul or body separated from the divinity, but still subsisted as before, by the subsistence of the Second Person of the Trinity.

"The truth of this assertion appears from the language of

this very Creed, according to which the same Person (*i e.*, the eternal Son of God as before proved) Who was *conceived, born,* and *suffered,* also was *buried* in respect of His body, and descended into hell in respect of His soul; so that neither His body, nor His blood, nor His soul, had lost their hypostatical union with the Word.

"Again, as God redeemed us by His own blood, so hath it been the constant language of the Church that God died for us; which cannot be true except the soul and body, in the instant of separation, were united to the Deity.

"Indeed, since God never substracts His grace from any without their abuse of it......we cannot imagine the grace of union to be taken from Christ, Who never offended, and that too in the highest act of His obedience."*

*Analysis of the Creed.   Pearson.

SECTION 5 (ARTICLE IV).

WHAT HAPPENED AT THE DEATH OF CHRIST: HIS BURIAL.

1. The veil of the Temple.—2. The earthquake.—3. The Centurion.—
4. The taking down from the Cross; (a) the breaking of the legs of the
two robbers; (b) the opened side, and the blood and water.—5. The
question as to the physical cause of the death of Christ.—6. St. John's
final testimony to Christ.—7. Joseph of Aramathea and Nicodemus.
—8. The Body of Jesus is taken down from the Cross.—9. The
Burial of Christ.—10. The lessons inculcated by our belief in
Christ's Burial.

THE events that followed the Crucifixion and death were—
(a) The veil of the Temple rent. (b) The earthquake. (c) The
Saints arise. (d) The remorse of the Centurion and the spectators. (e) The watching of the women.

THE VEIL OF THE TEMPLE.

1. *And behold the veil of the Temple was rent in two from
the top even to the bottom.* The veil meant, is that which separated the Holy of Holies from the Holy Place: the *inner* veil,
which was very heavy and splendid with embroidery. The
obvious significance of the portent was the departure of the
Sheckinah or Presence of God from His own now deserted
Temple. This particular event is (naturally) not mentioned by
the Jews, but we may have a reference to it in the various omens
of coming wrath which they say occurred *forty years* before the
destruction of the Temple.

The rending of the veil signifies that henceforth there is
free access for man to God the Father through Jesus Christ.

2. *The earthquake,* and the other particular incidents, are
thus mentioned by St. Matthew: *And the rocks were rent. And
the graves were opened: and many bodies of the saints that had
slept arose, and coming out of the tombs after His resurrection
came into the holy city and appeared to many.*

Now the Centurion and they that were with him watching Jesus, having seen the earthquake, and the things that were done, were sore afraid, saying, Indeed, this man was the Son of God.

3. The Centurion was in command of the guard of soldiers who watched the Crucifixion. St. Luke, as well as St. Matthew, mentions this incident. *Now the centurion seeing what was done, glorified God, saying : Indeed, this was a just man. And all the multitude of them that were come together to that sight, and saw the things that were done, returned, striking their breasts.*

The remark that He was *a just man* might have been drawn forth by the silent majesty and holiness of the Sufferer. After the earthquake he added : *Indeed this man was the Son of God.* The Centurion had twice heard our Lord pray to His Father, and he, like Pilate, had been overpowered by the awful dread that He was something more than man. And all the people returned, smiting their breasts. The people had not acted spontaneously in this matter of the Crucifixion, but had been goaded on by the Priests.

And all His acquaintance, and the women that had followed Him from Galilee, stood afar off beholding these things.

There is, perhaps, in the *afar off* a sad allusion to the words of the Psalmist : *They that were near me stood afar off.**

THE TAKING DOWN FROM THE CROSS, AND THE BURIAL.

4. After the death of Jesus the Jews brought their petition to Pilate that the bodies should not remain on the Cross on the Sabbath ; they besought him that their legs might be broken, and that they might be taken away. The Jews here, as elsewhere, show themselves to be among those who *strain at a gnat and swallow a camel.* In the midst of deliberate judicial murder they are scrupulous about the ceremonial observances. Even after the death of our Lord they continue their relentless hostility. They do not know whether any of the three sufferers are dead or not; their request shows that—in order to save the Sabbath, and, perhaps, also to inflict still further suffering—they ask Pilate for this terrible addition to the punishment of Crucifixion.

(a) The breaking of the legs, or the *crurifragium*, like crucifixion, was a punishment commonly reserved for slaves. The two were sometimes combined as here. Lactantius says : His executioners did not think it

---

necessary to break His bones, *as was their prevailing custom*; which seems to imply that to Jewish crucifixions this horror was commonly added, perhaps, to hasten death. For even without a Sabbath to make matters more urgent, corpses ought to be removed before night-fall; * whereas the Roman custom was to leave them to putrefy on the cross, like our obsolete custom of hanging in chains.

The soldiers, therefore, came in consequence of the fresh order from Pilate which the Jews would bring. And they broke the legs of the two thieves, and when they came to Jesus they saw that He was dead, and they did not break His legs ; (b) *but one of the soldiers, with a spear, opened His side, and immediately there came out blood and water.*

He opened His side to make sure that He was dead.

The blood and water are symbolical. Blood symbolizes the work of redemption which had just been completed by His death; and water symbolizes the birth from above, with its cleansing from sin, which was the result of His death, and is the means by which we appropriate it, or by which His satisfactions are applied to our souls. From the pierced heart of Jesus a stream of blood and water flows, from which the Sacraments draw their value ; and, as St. Ambrose remarks, from which the Church herself came forth. The redemption of mankind was already achieved, the formation of the New Covenant was already established, and Jesus had said that all things were accomplished. But there were still a few drops of blood gathered in His heart. These He also gives. He gives all that He has for the love of us, according to His words : *If a man give all the substance of his house for love he shall regard it as nothing.*†

5. There has been much discussion as to the *physical* cause of Christ's death; and those who investigate this try to frame an hypothesis which will at the same time account for the effusion of blood and water. Two or three such hypotheses have been put forward ; but it may be doubted whether they are not altogether out of place. It has been seen how the Evangelists insist on the fact that our Lord's death was a voluntary surrender of life, not a result forced upon Him. Of course it may be that the voluntariness consisted in welcoming causes which must prove fatal. But it is more simple to believe that He delivered up His life before natural causes became fatal. No one, either

---

* Deut. xxi, 23. † Cant. viii. 7.

Jew or Roman, took it from Him by any means whatever : *He lays it down of Himself.* And if we decline to investigate the physical cause of the Lord's death, we need not ask for a physical explanation of what is recorded here. St. John assures us that he saw it with his own eyes, and he records it that we may believe ; *i.e.,* he regards it as a sign that the corpse was no ordinary one, but a body that even in death was Divine.

6. *And he that saw it hath given testimony, and his testimony is true. And he knoweth that he saith truth, that you may also believe.* It may be asked, Why does St. John attest thus earnestly the trustworthiness of his narrative on this particular point? Four reasons may be assigned. This incident proved (*a*) the reality of Christ's *humanity* against Docetic views ; and these verses, therefore, are conclusive evidence against the theory that the fourth Gospel is the work of a Docetic Gnostic. (*b*) The reality of Christ's *divinity*, against Ebionite views : while His human form was no mere phantom, but flesh and blood, yet He was not therefore a mere man, but the *Son of God.* (*c*) The reality of Christ's death, and therefore of His *Resurrection*, against Jewish insinuations of trickery. (*d*) The clear and unexpected fulfilment of two Messianic prophecies. *For these things were done that the Scripture might be fulfilled* : YOU SHALL NOT BREAK A BONE OF HIM. *And again another Scripture saith* : THEY SHALL LOOK ON HIM WHOM THEY PIERCED.

Joseph of Aramathea, Nicodemus. The taking down from the Cross, and the Entombment.

Mention is made by the Evangelists of two remarkable men, who saw to the last offices or duties towards the body of Christ after His death. These were Joseph of Aramathea and Nicodemus.

7. *Joseph of Aramathea* was a rich man, a member of the Sanhedrin, a good and just man, *who had not consented to the counsel and deed of them.* It is remarkable that Joseph is the only Sanhedrist of whom this exception is recorded. Like Simon and Anna, he waited for the Kingdom of God, and had become a disciple of Christ.

Nicodemus. He was also a member of the Sanhedrin. He was the same that came to Jesus at night, and whom our Lord addressed as a *Master in Israel*, and to whom He said, *Unless a man be born again of water and the Holy Ghost, he cannot enter into the Kingdom of Heaven.** His acquaintance with Joseph of

---

* St. John iii. 10.

Aramathea is thus explained. They were both members of the Sanhedrin, and, in secret, disciples of Christ. It would seem that Joseph's unusual courage at this time had inspired Nicodemus also. We are not told whether Nicodemus had consented or no to the counsel or deed of the Jews in condemning Christ to death.

Joseph went unto Pilate, and begged the body of Jesus. This was a bold, and might even have proved to be a perilous, request. Pilate seems to have granted the request without delay, and without any bribe. He was surprised to hear of the rapid death of Jesus, and at all he heard from the centurion as to the details of that death. St. Matthew tells us that *Pilate commanded the body to be delivered,* after having ascertained that Jesus was dead. Usually, those who suffered crucifixion lingered for days upon the Cross. By Roman law the corpse of a crucified person was not buried except by express permission of the Emperor. A concession was made in favour of the Jews, whose law did not permit a man to hang all night upon a tree.* "The readiness of Pilate to grant Joseph's request is quite in accordance with his anxiety to release Jesus, and his displeasure against the Jews. If Joseph had not made this request, the body of Jesus would have been placed in one of the common burying grounds appointed by the Council."†

Nicodemus had brought *a mixture of myrrh and aloes, about a hundred pound weight* for the burial rites. Myrrh and aloes are both aromatic substances, and the purpose of this large quantity was probably to cover the body entirely. The hundred pound weight would be 1200 ounces. It is a rich man's proof of devotion, and possibly of remorse for a timidity in the past which now seemed irremediable ; his courage had come too late.

8. *They took down the Body of Jesus, and bound it in linen cloths with the spices, as the manner of the Jews is to bury.*

The clothes seem to refer to the bandages which kept the whole together, and there was, as well as these bandages, the large linen winding sheet which Joseph had brought. The manner of the Jews as regards the embalming of bodies was different from that of the Egyptians. These, in all cases, removed part of the intestines, and steeped the body in nitre.

9. *Now there was in the place where He was crucified a garden, and in the garden a new sepulchre, wherein no man yet had been laid. There, therefore, because of the parascene of the Jews, they laid Jesus, because the sepulchre was nigh at hand.*

---

* Deut. xxi. 23. † Lightfoot, H, Heb.

The garden probably belonged to Joseph, and St. Matthew tells us that the sepulchre was his. As to the sepulchre, St. Matthew states that it was new, and St. Luke that no one had ever yet been laid in it, and it was hewn in a rock. The mouth of these rocky tombs was closed with a large stone, called by the Jews *Gólal*, which could only be rolled there by the labour of several men. Joseph and Nicodemus, with the aid of some others, rolled a great stone to the door of the monument, and then went away.

10. "The belief in Christ's burial teaches us: (a) the truth both of Christ's Death and Resurrection. Pilate required to be satisfied that our Saviour was dead before he would give his body to be interred. That we might believe Christ truly risen from the dead, we must be as sure that He died, of which we can have no greater assurance than this, that His body was delivered by His enemies from the Cross, and laid by His disciples in the tomb. (b) To work within us a correspondence with His burial. *We are buried with Him in Baptism,** buried with Him by Baptism into death, that, like as Christ was raised up from the dead by the glory of the Father, we also may walk in the newness of life, according to the words of St. Paul : *For we are buried together with Him by baptism into death; that, as Christ is arisen from the dead by the glory of the Father, so we also may walk in newness of life.*† (c) That we might for ever learn what honour is fit to be given and received at our Christian funerals. When Christianity began to increase, the Greek and Roman custom of burning the bodies of the dead ceased ; and after a few Emperors had received baptism, there was not a body burnt in the Roman Empire. For the first Christians wholly abstained from burning bodies, and followed the example of our Saviour's funeral, making use of precious ointments for the dead, which they refused while they lived. The description of the persons who interred Christ, and the enumeration of their virtues, and the everlasting commendation of her who broke the box of precious ointment for His burial, have been thought sufficient grounds for the decent sepulture of Christians ; as natural reason teaches us to give some kind of respect to the dead bodies of men in reference to the souls which before inhabited them, so much the more the followers of our Saviour, looking on our bodies as living temples of the Holy Ghost, and bought by Christ to be one day made like unto His glorious body, thought them not to be neglected after death, but carefully to be laid up in the ward-

---

*Coll. ii. 12.   †Rom. vi. 4.

robe of the grave, with such due respect as might become the honour of the dead and the comfort of the living.   And thus this decent custom, by God's providence, proved very effectual in the conversion of the heathen."*

*Pearson's Analysis.

ARTICLE V.

APOSTLES' CREED.	NICENE CREED.
"He descended into hell; the third day He rose again from the dead."	"And the third day He rose again according to the Scriptures."

SECTION 1. (ARTICLE V.)

1. When the "Descent of Christ into hell" was introduced into the Creed.
—2. The meaning of this part of the Article.—3. The meaning of the words—Hell, Gehenna, Hades, and Paradise, in the Jewish sense.—4. The purpose of Christ's descent into Limbo.—5. Dr. Lingard's notes on the descent of Christ into Limbo.—6. The Resurrection of Christ on Easter Sunday; why called Easter.—7. The meaning of a Resurrection.—8. Christ truly and properly rose from the dead.—9. The Resurrection of Christ attested; (a) By His various apparitions; (b) By His enemies; (c) By Angels.—10. What Christ effected by His Resurrection.—11. The Resurrection, the greatest of Christ's miracles.

THIS Article contains two parts; namely, the *Descent of Christ into hell*, and *His Resurrection*.

1. THE former part is not to be found in the oldest Creeds. It first occurs in the Creed of the Church of Aquileia about 400 A.D. After that it came into the Creed of all the Churches, and has been acknowledged ever since as part of the Apostles' Creed. Although not expressed in the Creed, the doctrine which it contains always belonged to the Creed of Faith, and was professed ever since the days of the Apostles, according to the words of St. Peter : * speaking of Christ (*Who*) *being put to death indeed in the flesh, but enlivened in the spirit. In which also coming He preached to those that were in prison;* and those others of the Acts referring to the prophecy of David concerning our Lord : *Because Thou wilt not leave my soul in hell, nor suffer Thy Holy One to see corruption.*†

2. This part of the Article signifies that as soon as Christ

---

* 1 Peter iii. 19.   † Acts ii. 27.

died on the Cross His soul descended into hell, or the lower place (*descendit ad inferos*), to that place which we call *Limbo*. It was there that the souls of the just were detained, expecting the day of redemption, when heaven would be opened to them. The soul of Christ, at the same moment, without doubt, manifested its power in hell proper, and in purgatory; in hell proper, to convict the demons and the lost souls of their malice and incredulity; in purgatory, to console the suffering souls therein detained, and to announce the time of their speedy release, and their admission into heaven.

It was, however, only in the abode of the just that He appeared substantially present, and where it is probable His soul remained as long as His body remained in the tomb. There His soul, remaining united to the Divine Word, manifested its glory to the innumerable souls, from that of Adam to the good Thief, who were ready to enter their beatitude, or the enjoyment of the beatific vision. There Christ conversed with them, and preached to them, and gave them the joyful assurance that very soon they would accompany Him in His glorious Ascension into heaven.

3. The word *Hell* is derived from the Anglo-Saxon *helan* —to hide, and, therefore, according to its etymology, means the *hidden place : the abode of departed spirits.*

There are two words in the Greek Testament translated into the English word *hell.*

(a) Gehenna, signifying the hell of torments; taking this signification from the Valley of Hinnom, where human sacrifices were offered to the idol god, Moloch : *And whosoever shall say, Thou fool, shall be in danger of hell fire (gehenna.)** And again : *Than having two eyes to be cast into hell fire (gehenna)*† *where their worm dieth not, and the fire is not extinguished.*

(b) *Hades*, or the place of departed spirits, called in the Hebrew *Sheol*. *And the rich man died, and was buried in hell (Hades) ; and lifting up his eyes when he was in torments, he saw Abraham afar off, and Lazarus in his bosom.*‡

Paradise was the Jewish name for that part of Hades inhabited by the spirits of the just. It was also known by the Jews under the names of :—

(a) The Garden of Eden.

---

* St. Matthew v. 22.   † St. Mark ix. 27, 28.   ‡ St. Luke xvi. 22, 23.

(b) Under the throne of Glory.
(c) Abraham's bosom.

To us it is known as Limbo : the place of rest, where the souls of the just, who died before Christ, were detained. Not purgatory itself, nor the hell of torments, but the place of the just souls from the first ; namely, the soul of Abel to the soul of the Good Thief.

4. The purpose of Christ's descent into Limbo was :—

(a) That He might proclaim these glad tidings of His victory ; and, so Peter tells us, that He preached, or rather made proclamation, unto the spirits that were in prison.

(b) That, by the virtue of His descent, He might liberate the soul of the saints from that state in which they were detained, and translate them to the far more glorious state of beatitude in His heavenly Kingdom. Not that Christ merited by His descent, for our redemption by way of merit and satisfaction was effected on the Cross.

5. Dr. Lingard gives the following notes on the descent of Christ into hell, and the purpose of that descent :

" At the present day, usage has confined the name of *hell* and its representatives in the dead languages, to the habitation of the wicked after death ; but in former times it was employed in a wider sense, for the abode and state of all departed souls, whether they were in suffering, or punishment, or not. Now Jesus, in consequence of His having taken the nature of man, was *tempted and tried in all things according to His likeness to us without sin.*[*] He died as we die ; His body was deposited in the grave like the bodies of other men ; and His soul, like those of others, descended to the general abode of departed souls. This is plainly indicated by St Peter when, applying the words of the Psalmist to the Resurrection of our Saviour, he says: *God did not leave His soul in hell*—the abode of souls—*nor suffer His holy one to see corruption* ; [†] that is, suffer His body to moulder away in the grave.

"Heaven was not open to man till after the resurrection and ascention of Jesus. The disobedience of Adam had closed heaven against all his posterity ; it was thrown open to man by the obedience of Christ *who took away the sins of the world,*[‡] and

---

* Hebrew iv. 15.   † Acts ii. 27.   ‡ St. John i. 29.

was a propitiation for the sins of the whole world.* Hence it was the doctrine of the ancient Church that the souls of the patriarchs, prophets, and of good men, were detained in some other abode till Christ had paid their ransom by His death ; and then, *ascending up on high, He led captivity captive, and gave gifts unto men* ;† that is, He delivered the captives from confinement, and allotted to them their respective portions in heaven.

"We are told that Christ preached the gospel, that is, the doctrine of redemption through His death, whilst He was in Limbo. There is a remarkable passage in the first Epistle of St. Peter‡ which appears to refer to this subject. *Being indeed put to death in the flesh, but quickened in the spirit, in which moreover He went and preached to the spirits in prison, who once had been incredulous, when the patience of God waited in the days of Noah.* There can be no doubt that the Apostle alludes to some historical fact of ancient times, well known to those to whom he directed his Epistle, but which has been permitted to fall into oblivion. But whatever that fact may have been, we may fairly draw from his words the following inferences : (a) That the spirits in question were the souls of men who had lived in the days of Noah. (b) That through disobedience and obstinacy they had not profited by some benefit, offered to them by *the patience of God.* (c) That they were on that account detained in confinement, and suffering punishment ; which is plainly indicated by the word prison coupled with their incredulity. (d) That to them the spirit or soul of Christ went, and ministered some kind of instruction, for He is said to have *preached to them.* (e) That this happened when He had been *put to death in the flesh, but was quickened in the spirit,* evidently between His death and resurrection.

"But what was the instruction which He preached to them ? We may discover it in another passage of the same Epistle following the former. After mentioning the judgment of the living and the dead, the sacred writer adds : *for this end was the gospel preached to the dead, that having been judged according to man in the flesh, they might be saved according to God in the spirit.*‖ Now, though there may be some doubt with respect to the correct rendering and meaning of this passage, there can be none with respect to the fact, so plainly stated, of the *gospel* having been preached to the *dead,* and preached to them to the end that they

---

* 1 St. John ii. 2. † Eph. ii. 8.
‡ 1 St. Peter iii. 18-20. ‖ 1 St. Peter iv. 6.

might be saved. But when was it preached to the dead? On no other occasion, as far as we know, than that when our blessed Lord went and *preached to the spirits in prison.* Hence it is reasonable to infer that redemption through His death was the doctrine which He announced to them, the sum of what is meant by the *gospel* or good tidings."

In other words, Christ descended into Limbo, to bring the souls there imprisoned the glad news that the price of their redemption had beed paid—that He for Whom they had so ardently longed, was now come to deliver them—in fine to comfort them and set them free.

THE THIRD DAY HE ROSE AGAIN FROM THE DEAD.

6. The Resurrection is commemorated by the Church on Easter Sunday. The Spring was called Easter by our ancestors from the prevalence of easterly winds at that season. Hence, because the feast of the Resurrection was the principal festival during the Spring, that feast was called Easter Sunday; in the same manner as, according to Bede, they had, whilst they were idolaters, applied the same epithet to a feast kept at that time in honour of one of their false deities.*

We have first to consider what is the meaning of a true resurrection and its essential characters.

7. A resurrection means *a substantial change, by which what was before and was corrupted* (or destroyed) *is reproduced the same thing again.* (*a*) *A change*; not a second or a new creation, as if a man or angel were annihilated, and made again out of nothing (*b*) *A substantial* change; not an *accidental* alteration as from sickness to health. (*c*) A change of what *was* before and *was corrupted*; (1) things *incorruptible* cannot be reproduced; and (2) of things *corruptible, some* such as the forms of inanimate bodies, and all irrational souls, *when corrupted* cease to be; consequently, even if such were reproduced out of the same matter, there would not be a restitution of the *same individual*, only of the *same species*, by another individual. But when a rational soul is separated from its body, which is the corruption of a man, that soul still exists, and is capable of reunion with the body; and if these two be again united by an essential and vital union, from which life necessarily flows, then the *same man* lives who lived before, and consequently this reunion is a perfect and proper resurrection from death to life.†

---

* Lingard's Catechism.   † Pearson, Analysis *in loco.*

8. Christ truly and properly rose from the dead in this sense; as is certain from the fact (a) that our Saviour possessed a real body after His Resurrection, as proved by His own words: *Handle Me and see, for a spirit hath not flesh and bones as ye see that I have.** (b) It was the same body which He had on earth, and which had been nailed to the Cross. *Look at my hands and My feet, for it is I myself; and as He said this He showed them His hands and His feet.*† (c) This body was animated with *a human soul*, for He *conversed with His Apostles, and interpreted the passages respecting the Messiah in the whole Scripture.*‡ (d) That soul was the same which animated His body before death: for He adds: *these are the words which I spoke to you whilst I was with you.* It was then the same body and the same soul. It was the same soul that remained always united to the Divinity, and testified that Divinity after the Resurrection by the miracle of catching the fishes; by breathing on the Apostles the Holy Ghost; by ascending into heaven; and thus showing, since the Divinity never was so united to any human soul but only in that Person, that this was the same soul with which He lived and wrought all the miracles before.

He rose again : God raised Him up on the third day, and openly, not unto all the people, but unto witnesses chosen beforehand of God, unto us who did eat and drink with Him after His resurrection ‖

9. The Resurrection from the dead of Christ is attested :—
(a) *By His appearance to His Apostles and Disciples.*
1. To His Blessed Mother according to tradition, and for many congruous reasons.
2. To Mary Magdalene, who at first took Him for the gardener. (St. John xx. 11-18.)
3. To the ministering women, whom He bade tell His disciples to go into Galilee, where they should see Him. (St. Matthew xxviii. 9, 10.)
4. To the two disciples journeying to Emmaus, to whom He was revealed in the breaking of bread. (St. Luke xxiv. 13-33.)
5. To St. Peter : The Lord is risen indeed, and hath appeared to Simon. (St. Luke xxiv. 34.)
6. To the ten Apostles (Thomas being absent). (St. Luke xxiv. 36-48; St. John xx. 24.)

---

* St. Luke xxiv. 39.   † Ibid, verses 39, 40.
‡ Ibid., verse 27.   ‖ Acts x. 40, 41.

P

The above six appearances all occurred on the day of His Resurrection.

7. To the eleven Apostles, when Thomas was present. (St. John xx. 26-29.)

9. To the seven Apostles fishing in the Lake of Galilee. The second miraculous draught of fishes. (St. John xxi. 1-14.)

9. To the eleven Apostles, and probably the 500 brethren in Galilee, on the appointed mountain when He gave the great Commission. (St. Matthew xxviii. 16-18.) *After that, He was seen of above five hundred brethren at once.* (1 Cor. xv. 6.)

10. To James : *After that, He was seen of James.* (1 Cor. xv. 7.)

11. To the Apostles at the Ascension. (St. Luke xxiv. 50.)

(b) *By His enemies. Behold some of the guards came into the city, and told the chief priests all things that had been done.* (St. Matthew xxviii. 11.)

(c) *By the Angels; who said unto the women when they visited the tomb : Why seek you the living with the dead ? He is not here, but is risen.*

10. *Christ by His Resurrection—*

(a) *Fulfilled Prophecy. Thou wilt not leave My soul in hell (Hades) ; nor wilt Thou give Thy holy one to see corruption.* (Psalms xv. 10.)

(b) *Justified His own predictions, viz., That they should kill Him, and the third day He should rise again.* (St. Matthew xxviii. 22.)

(c) *Gave the clearest proof of His Godhead. Who was predestined the Son of God in power, according to the spirit of sanctification by the Resurrection of our Lord Jesus Christ from the dead.* (Romans i. 4.)

(d) *Gave us the sign of the acceptance of the Sacrifice He offered on the Cross. Who was delivered up for our sins, and rose again for our justification.* (Romans iv. 25.)

(e) *Gave us an earnest and pledge of our Resurrection. But now Christ is risen from the dead ; the first fruits of them that sleep. For by man came death, and by a man the resurrection of the dead. And as in Adam all die, so also in Christ all shall be made alive.* (1 Cor. xv. 20-22.)

THE THIRD DAY.

"Christ was buried on Friday, and was thus in the tomb part of that day, the whole of Saturday (the Jewish Sabbath), and part of Sunday (the first day in the week). Thus He rose on the third day of His burial. Christ foretold this by the sign of the prophet Jonas. *For as Jonas was in the whale's belly three days and three nights, so shall the Son of Man be in the heart of the earth three days and three nights.**

"This is in keeping with the method of expressing time by the Jews, who were accustomed to speak of any part of the day as a whole day."†

11. The Resurrection is the greatest of Christ's miracles. It is a miracle of *His power*, for He rose of Himself; a miracle of *His goodness*, for His Resurrection is a pledge of the glorious resurrection of those who believe in Him; a miracle of *His wisdom*, for it is as it were the corner stone of Christianity; it is the fact of the Resurrection on which our faith, our hope, our worship, and our history rest, according to the words of St. Paul: *And if Christ be not risen again, then is our preaching vain, and your faith is also vain.*‡

This miracle has, therefore, been the object of the attacks of all unbelievers, who very well understand that if the fact of the Resurrection be once admitted, they cannot deny the divine Mission, and the Divinity of Jesus Christ.

The Apostles, according to these, were imposters, or were under a hallucination, as M. Renan expresses it. Either of these suppositions would argue the most extraordinary miracle that ever the world heard of. Even in the supposition that the Apostles were deceived, or wished to deceive others by such an incredible invention, could not the enemies of Christ easily have confounded their folly by exhuming the body of Christ and exposing it to the people? But they say the Apostles had taken it away and hidden it. Admitting this incredible hypothesis; how could a small band of poor and illiterate men convince themselves of this falsehood so as to lay down their lives by martyrdom for its truth; cause myriads of men to believe in it, and found upon this fact a religion so worthy of the respect and love of mankind, that it will last to the end of time?

---

* St. Matthew xii. 40.   † Gill's Church Catechism, *in loco.*
‡ Cor. xv. 14.

SECTION 2 (ARTICLE V).

THE HISTORY OF THE RESURRECTION.

1. The time of the Resurrection.—2. The conduct of the guards.—3. The earthquake, and the apparition of Angels, and apparent discrepancies accounted for.—4. Mary Magdalene and two other holy women come to the tomb.—5. The two Apostles, Peter and John, run to the tomb. —6. The apparition to Mary Magdalene.—7. Explanation of the words, *Touch me not.*—8. The other holy women go to the tomb and find not Jesus, but two Angels appear to them.—9. His apparition to the holy women.—10. The soldiers are bribed.—11. Other apparitions of Christ : (*a*) To Peter ; (*b*) to the disciples going to Emmaus ; (*c*) to the Apostles assembled together, Thomas being absent ; (*d*) to the Apostles eight days after, Thomas being present ; (*e*) to the seven on the sea of Tiberias ; (*f*) the apparitions mentioned by St. Paul to as many as 500 assembled together.—12. The Apostles could not have been deceived as to the fact of the Resurrection.—13. The Qualities of the resuscitated Body of Christ.—14. The Wounds of His Passion retained in His glorified Body.— 15. The effects of Christ's Resurrection.

1. On the third day after His death, which was the first day of the week (our Sunday), early in the morning, Jesus, by an act of His divine omnipotence, reunited His soul to His body, and came forth alive from the tomb, without displacing the stone that closed up the door of the Sepulchre. This was at the rising of the sun, or, properly, when the sun had risen. Although St. John says, *while it was yet dark*, it would appear that he refers to the time that Mary Magdalene set out to come to the Sepulchre, though the sun began to rise before she and the others reached it.

2. The guards did not see Him rise or go forth from the tomb ; but the earth trembled at the same moment. An Angel of the Lord descended from heaven, and removed the stone from the door of the Sepulchre, and sat upon it. And the face of the Angel shone as lightning, and his garments were white as snow. Struck with fear, the guards became insensible and as it were dead ; as soon as they recovered they went into the city, and recounted to the chief-priests all that had happened to them whilst they kept watch at the tomb.

3. The earthquake is peculiar to St. Matthew in the account

of the Resurrection. He tells us *there was a great earthquake at that moment.* St. Matthew says: *The Angel of the Lord descended from heaven.* St. Luke: *Two men stood by them in shining garments.* St. John mentions: *Two angels in white, sitting.*

To reconcile these statements as to the Angels, let it suffice once for all to say that there must have been thousand of Angels about, and that now one was seen and again two, and sitting or standing as the apparition appeared to them, and that therefore it is useless to attempt to shew any discrepancy in the accounts which the Evangelists give of these angelical manifestations.*

St. Matthew tells us that the Angel *rolled back the stone from the door and sat upon it.* All four Gospels note the displacement of the stone; St. Mark alone notes the placing of it, and St. Matthew the sealing.

For fear of this Angel, whose countenance was as lightning, whose raiment white as snow, it is no wonder that *the keepers did shake, and became as dead men.*

4. In the meantime, Mary Magdalene and two other holy women were directing their course towards the sepulchre, bringing with them the spices and aromatics which they had prepared for the anointing of His body. As they were ignorant of the presence of the guard, and of the sealing of the stone, they said among themselves on their journey: *Who will remove the stone from the door of the sepulchre?* On their arrival, however, they found the sepulchre open. Magdalene ran in haste to tell Peter and John. *They have taken away,* she said, *the Lord out of the tomb, and we know not where they have laid Him.*

5. The two Apostles ran and ascertained the fact. St. John outran Peter and arrived first, but St. Peter was the first to enter the sepulchre, and saw the place where the body of Jesus was laid, and on the right the napkin that covered His head. St. John followed him into the tomb, and ascertained that the body of Jesus was not there, and then both Apostles returned to Jerusalem, and apparently did not then remember that Jesus had predicted His Resurrection. *For as yet they knew not the*

---

* On the mention, omission, and numbers of these Angels, Van Oosterzee quotes a very striking remark from Lessing — "Cold discrepancy-mongers, do ye not see that the Evangelists do not count the Angels? ... There were millions of them. They appeared not always one and the same, not always the same two; sometimes this one appeared, sometimes that; sometimes on this place, sometimes on that; sometimes alone, sometimes in company; sometimes they said this, sometimes they said that."

*Scripture, that He must rise again from the dead.** St. John notes the careful arrangement of the grave-cloths, when he tells us that when St. Peter entered the tomb, he saw the linen cloths lying ; and the napkin that had been about His head, not lying with the linen cloths, but apart, wrapped up into one place. This careful arrangement of the grave-cloths proved that the body had not been taken away in haste as by a foe, and friends would scarcely have removed them at all ; and it is evident, that the empty and orderly tomb made a deep and lasting impression upon this Apostle's mind.

6. When the two Apostles had departed, *Mary stood at the sepulchre, without, weeping. Now, as she was weeping, she stooped down and looked into the sepulchre, and she saw two angels in white, sitting, one at the head, and one at the feet, where the body of Jesus had been laid. They say to her, Woman, why weepest thou ? She saith to them, Because they have taken away my Lord ; and I know not where they have laid Him.* Mary Magdalene had returned to the sepulchre, after the hurrying Apostles, and she stood there by it after they had gone away. Her words, *They have taken away my Lord, and I know not where they have laid Him,* represent her relationship with Christ, and her loss as personal, and the burden of her thoughts since she first saw that the stone had been removed. "The extreme simplicity of the narrative reflects something of the solemn majesty of the scene."†

At this moment a man appeared to her, and said to her, as the Angel had said : *Woman ; why weepest thou? whom seekest thou ? She, thinking that it was the gardener, said to him ; Sir, if thou hast taken Him hence, tell me where thou hast laid Him, and I will take Him away.*

It was Jesus, and He said to her : *Mary !* At the sound of His voice she knew Him at once and cried out : *Rabboni !* (which is to say Master), and at the same time she threw herself at His feet, and Jesus said to her : *Do not touch Me, for I am not yet ascended to My Father ; but go to My brethren, and say to them : I ascend to My Father and to your Father, to My God and to your God.* Mary made haste and went and told the sad and disheartened disciples : *I have seen the Lord, and these things He said to me.*

7. The passage *Touch me not, &c.,* "is one of well-known difficulty. At first sight the reason given for refraining from touching would seem to be more suitable to a permission to

---

* St. John xx. 9.   † Westcot *in loco.*

touch. It is perhaps needless to enquire whether the *for* reiers to the whole of what follows, or only to the first sentence : *I am not yet ascended to the father* ? In either case the meaning would be, that the Ascension has not yet taken place, although it soon will, whereas Mary's action assumes that it has taken place. If *for* refers to the first clause only, then the emphasis is thrown on Mary's mistake ; if *for* refers to the whole of what is said, then the emphasis is thrown on the promise that what Mary craves shall be granted in a higher way to both her and others very soon. The translation *touch me not* is inadequate and gives a false impression. The verb (*haptesthai*) does not mean to touch and handle with a view to seeing whether His body was real ; this Christ not only allowed but enjoined;* rather it means *to hold on to* and *cling to*. Moreover it is the present (not aorist) imperative, and the full meaning will therefore be : *Do·not continue holding Me*, or simply : *Hold Me not*. The old and often interrupted earthly intercourse is over ; the new and continuous intercourse with the Ascended Lord has not yet begun ; but that Presence will be granted soon, and there will be no need of straining eyes and clinging hands to realize it."†

8. In the meantime the other women who had followed Jesus from Galilee had arrived at the sepulchre, the sun being now rising, and going in they found not the body of the Lord Jesus. And as they were astonished in their mind at this, behold, two men stood by them in shining apparel. And as they were afraid and bowed down their countenance towards the ground, they said unto them : *Why seek you the living with the dead? He is not here, but is risen. Remember how He spoke unto you when He was yet in Galilee,* &c.‡ *And going quickly tell ye His disciples (and Peter) that He is risen ; and, behold, He will go before you into Galilee ; there you shall see Him. Lo, I have foretold it to you.*§

The women *found not the body*, and even advanced sceptics admit this circumstance as indisputable, nor has one of them been able to invent the most remotely plausible explanation of the fact by natural causes.

" It is hardly possible for us even to conceive the overwhelming joy that the conviction of this truth must have brought to these holy women, whose recollection of the divine words and looks, and love-inspiring sweetness of character, would be quick-

---

* St. Luke xxiv. 39. † Cambridge Bible for Schools, St. John.
‡ St. Luke. § St. Matt.

ened by the painful watching, and the passionate sorrow for their seeming loss."*

They were instructed to go and tell the disciples; and St. Mark makes special mention of Peter. He more than the rest would be longing for the Lord's return. St. Peter's fall was probably known, and also his deep repentance : he is still the chief of the Apostels, and as such the first to be consulted.

9. The Magdalene, Joanna, Mary the mother of James, joined the other holy women, and were going to bring the great news of all they had seen and heard to the Apostles. On the way Jesus appeared to them and saluted them. They kissed His feet and adored Him. *Then Jesus said to them : Fear not. Go, tell my brethren, that they go into Galilce, there they shall see Me.†

Jesus had already appeared to Mary Magdalene alone. We must suppose that she was now joined by the other Mary, and perhaps by Salome, Joanna and others ; and whilst these were going to announce the great news to the rest of the disciples (Peter and John already knew), the Lord Jesus met them. His words of salutation were : *All hail.* Literally, *rejoice* ; the Greek salutation, both on meeting and parting. He called his disciples His *brethren*, as being Himself a man, and their kinsman according to man's nature. Now that Christ had clearly manifested the power of the godhead, there was special need of reminding His disciples that He was still man, and that they were brethren. Mary Magdalene and the holy women recounted to the Apostles all that they had seen and heard, but St. Luke tells us that these were incredulous. *Their words seemed to them idle tales, and they believed them not.* This persistent incredulity on the part of the Apostles was permitted by God, that their testimony afterwards might have greater force and authority.

10. The chief priests paid attention to what the soldiers, who guarded the sepulchre, narrated to them. St. Matthew tells us how the Roman guards were bribed. *And they* (the chief priests) *being assembled together with the ancients, taking counsel, gave a great sum of money to the soldiers, saying : Say you His disciple' came by night, and stole Him away, when we were asleep. And if the governor shall hear of this we will persuade him and secure you. So they, taking the money, did as they were taught : and this word was spread abroad among the Jews even unto this day.‡

---

* Cambridge Bible for Schools. St. Matt.   † St. Matt. xxviii. 10.
‡ St. Matt. xxviii. 13-15.

The penalty for their sleeping would be death. They received evidently many pieces of silver as a bribe, and the soldiers might readily believe that Pilate was open to the same inducement, which persuaded them. St. Matthew found it specially necessary in his day to narrate the true facts of the case.

11. The first Apostle to whom our Saviour appeared on the day of His Resurrection was (a) St. Peter ; (b) on the evening of the same day He manifested Himself to the two disciples going to Emmaus, who at last recognised Him in the breaking of bread. His apparition to the disciples at Emmaus is narrated by St. Luke alone. These two disciples were not Apostles, one was called Cleophas, of whom we know nothing, unless he was the same as Alphaeus. The other is unknown, and no conjecture can be made concerning him. It is not probable that it was St. Luke himself. The town of Emmaus was distant from Jerusalem sixty furlongs, that is 6½ miles. The disciples did not know Jesus ; neither did Mary Magdalene at first recognise Him, nor the disciples on the lake, which served only to indicate that after the Resurrection the Body of our Lord was a glorified Body, of which the conditions transcended those of ordinary mortality ; as He could take different forms from that which He had worn when on earth.

(c) When all the Apostles, with the exception of Thomas Didymus, were that night assembled in the Cenacle, the doors being closed, Jesus appeared in their midst, and said to them : Peace be to you; it is I, fear not. But they being troubled and frightened supposed that they saw a spirit. *And He said to them : why are you troubled, and why do thoughts arise in your hearts? See My hands and feet, that it is I Myself; handle, and see ; for a spirit hath not flesh and bones, as you see Me to have. And when He had said this, He showed them His hands and His feet. But while they yet believed not, and wondered for joy, He said : Have you here any thing to eat? And they offered Him a piece of a broiled fish, and a honey-comb. And when He had eaten before them, taking the remains, He gave them to them, &c.*

This is one of the most remarkable apparances of the Risen Christ. His intercourse with them on this occasion consisted of a greeting, a reproach and consolation (St. Luke xxiv. 36-38. ; St. Mark xvi. 14.) ; a demonstration of the reality of His person (St. Luke xxiv. 39-43 ; St. John xx. 20.) ; an opening of their understandings (St. Luke xxiv. 44-46) ; an appointment of the Apostles to the ministries of remission and forgiveness (St. Luke xxiv. 47-48 ; St. John xix. 21-23) ; a promise of the Holy Spirit, for the fulfilment of which they were to wait in Jerusalem. (St. Luke xxiv. 49). At the close of this great scene He once more pronounced the benediction of peace, and breathed on them with the words: *Receive ye the Holy Ghost. Whose sins you shall forgive they are forgiven; and whose sins you shall retain, they are retained.* (St. John xx.)

As soon as Thomas, who is called Didymus, joined the company of the other Apostles, they said to Him: We have seen the Lord. But he said to them: *Except I shall see in His hands the prints of the nails, and put my finger into the place of the nails, and put my hands into His side, I will not believe.* The test which Thomas selects has various points of contact with the surroundings. The wounds had been the cause of all his melancholy sadness since the Crucifixion; it is they that must reassure him. The print of them would prove beyond all doubt that it was indeed His Lord that had returned to him. Moreover, the ten had no doubt told him of their own terror and hesitation, and how Jesus had invited them to handle and see, in order to convince themselves. This would suggest a similar proof to Thomas.

(*d*). After eight days Jesus appeared again under similar circumstances to the Apostles, Thomas being this time present. Jesus said to him: *Put in thy finger hither, and see My hands, and bring hither thy hand and put it into My side; and be not faithless, but believing. Thomas answered and said to Him: My Lord and my God. Jesus saith to him: Because thou hast seen Me, Thomas, thou hast believed; blessed are they that have not seen and have believed.*

This happened eight days after the Resurrection, that is eight days including both extremes, according to the Jewish method. This was therefore the Sunday following Easter Sunday. We are not to understand that the disciples had not met together during the interval, but that there is no appearance of Jesus to record. The first step is here taken towards establishing Sunday as 'the Lord's day' as the Christian weekly festival. The Passover is over, so that the meeting of the disciples has nothing to do with that.

(*e*). There is one other manifestation of Jesus recorded, namely His manifestation to the seven Apostles, when they had gone out fishing on the Sea of Tiberias, when Christ caused the miraculous draught of fishes to be taken, and when He gave St. Peter the Commission to feed His sheep and His lambs, by which He conferred upon him and his successors the power over the whole flock of Christ, both pastors and people. On that occasion He also predicted St. Peter's death.

(*f*). Jesus appeared also on many other occasions before
His Ascension that are not recorded, and St. Paul mentions that
He appeared at one time to as many as five hundred assembled
together.

12. The Apostles therefore could not be deceived as to the
fact of the Resurrection, and it was not possible for them to invent and propagate the falsehood, had the Body of our Lord been
taken away, as the chief priests sought to persuade the people,
through bribing the guards. How, it may be asked, could the
Apostles, by such a trick or lie, convert the world and establish
the Christian religion with all its divine characters or marks?
Jesus therefore is risen from the dead, and as we have just seen
in the foregoing narrative, He rose again on the third day *according to the Scriptures*; words added by the Council of Constantinople to the Creed, because the absolute necessity of the mystery
of the Resurrection is taught in such an emphatic manner by the
Apostle when he says : *If Christ be not risen again, then is our
preaching vain, and your faith is also vain, for you are yet in your
sins.** And St. Augustin, speaking of this Article, says : " It is of
little moment to believe that Christ died ; this the Pagans, Jews,
and all the wicked believe ; in a word, all believe that Christ
died ; but that He rose again from the dead is the belief of the
Christian, and this we deem of great moment."

Before concluding the instruction on the mystery of the Resurrection, it may be useful to give a short explanation of the
qualities of the Body of Christ after the Resurrection, and the
effects of His Resurrection.

THE QUALITIES OF THE RESUSCITATED BODY OF CHRIST.

13. In going forth from the tomb, the Body of Christ possessed four glorious qualities, which are called—*brightness, incorruptibility, agility, and subtilty. (a) Brightness or clearness.* That
is to say, the Body of Christ had in a high degree transparency
with a shining brightness like the light ef the sun, the splendour
of which was seen in His apparitions.

(*b*) *Incorruptibility.* That is to say, the Body of Christ
was unalterable, impervious to suffering or pain, and
immortal.

(*c*). *Agility.* That is to say, the Body of Christ could move

* 1 Cor. xv. 14-17.

from place to place with the rapidity of light, or the quickness of thought.

(d) *Subtilty*. That is to say, the Body of Christ could penetrate other bodies without experiencing any resistance whatever. Thus it came out of the sealed tomb, and stood in the midst of the Apostles, the doors being shut.

The glorified Body of Christ was of incomparable beauty. It had a grace and majesty of which nothing in this world can give an idea.

14. Jesus wished to retain in His glorified Body the wounds of His Passion. This He did (a) to convince His Apostles of the truth of His Resurrection; (b) for His own glory, in as much as these wounds are as rays of light that add to the beauty and the glory of His humanity in heaven; (c) that He may continually show them to His Father in supplication for us and our salvation. These are the Wounds by which He redeemed us; (d) that He may confound the wicked on the last day, those who will not seek a place of rest in those Sacred Wounds which their crimes have opened.

The Effects of the Resurrection.

15. The Resurrection is the foundation of our faith, the model of our spiritual life, and the cause of our future resurrection.

(a) Among all the religions of the world none but the Christian can say: The wicked put to death my Founder, but He came forth from the tomb as He had predicted. He was therefore God, and all that He taught is true. It also shows that faith in Jesus Christ and in His Church is so certain and reasonable, since it is proved by a fact of history, which no one can doubt or deny.

(b) Jesus Christ died for our sins, but He died only once. Being risen from the dead He no more dies, but lives for God and in God. This also a Christian ought to do. By Baptism he has been buried with Christ in His death, in as much as he dies to sin. From that he should rise and live a life truly divine in conformity with Jesus Christ risen from the dead. If he should lose the grace of Baptism, that may be restored by penance, so that the stains of sin may be removed, and he may continually die to sin, and live to God in Christ Jesus our Lord.

(o)   Jesus Christ, the Word Incarnate, arose in His own flesh. By this He has communicated to all flesh the privilege of resurrection. *As Jesus*, says St. Paul, *rose from the dead, we also will arise with Him and as He rose from the dead.*

" From the resurrection of Christ, therefore, we should derive two important lessons of instruction : the one, that after we have washed away the stains of sin we should begin to live a new life, distinguished by integrity, innocence, holiness, modesty, justice, beneficence and humility ; the other, that we should so persevere in that newness of life, as never more, with the divine assistance, to stray from the path of virtue on which we have entered.

" Nor do the words of the Apostle prove only that the resurrection of Christ is proposed as the model of our resurrection : they also declare that it gives us power to rise again ; and imparts to us strength and courage to persevere in holiness and righteousness, and in the observance of the Commandments of God."*

---

* Catechism of Council of Trent.

ARTICLE VI.

" He ascended into heaven, and sitteth at the right hand of God, the Father Almighty."

" He ascended into heaven, and sitteth at the right hand of the Father."

1. The Ascension forty days after the Resurrection.—2. The term of forty days a remarkable scriptural period, and Christ's work during that period.—3. The Ascension represented in figures and foretold by the Prophets.—4. The circumstances of the Ascension as to time, place, and persons present—5. His last blessing.—6. The apparition of Angels and their words.—7. Those who accompanied Christ in His ascension.—8. What is meant by Heaven.—9. The reasons of Christ's Ascension.—10. The second part of the Article : sitteth at the right hand of God the Father Almighty, explained.

1. IN commemoration of the Ascension, the Church celebrates Ascension Day, which occurs on the fortieth day after Easter.

" He ascended into Heaven forty days after His Resurrection, and in the presence of His Apostles, as related by St. Luke. The difference between the Resurrection and the Ascension is very noticeable. No witnesses were needed to the Resurrection, because Christ's appearances afterwards showed that He had risen. But when He ascended, when it was of the utmost importance that men should be assured that He had really gone up to heaven, then, in the presence of many witnesses He ascended into heaven as if it were the natural close of His divine life on earth."*

After His Resurrection, Jesus remained forty days on the earth, appearing to His disciples and speaking to them of the Kingdom of God. By the Kingdom of God it is necessary to understand, in the first place, the Kingdom of heaven, into which

He was soon to enter for the joy and glory of those who would believe on Him. The Kingdom of God also signifies the *Church militant* on earth, of which, after Christ, the Apostles were the founders. He had to instruct them in all that concerned that Church, the administration of the Sacraments, the government of the Church, its mission, the persecutions which it would have to undergo, and the triumphs it should gain through His assistance, and according to His promise. *Behold I am with you all days, even to the consummation of the world.*

2. The term of *forty days* is a remarkable scriptural period :—
(a) The flood was forty days upon the earth. (Gen. vii. 17.)
(b) Moses was with Jehovah on Mount Sinai forty days. (Deut. ix. 19.)
(c) Elias went in the strength of that meat forty days and forty nights unto Horeb, the Mount of God. (1 Kings xix. 8.)

The term of forty days occurs three times in the life of Christ.
(a) Between His Birth and Presentation in the Temple. (St. Luke ii. 22.)
(b) Christ fasted forty days in the desert.
(c) The period between His Resurrection and His ascension into heaven.

During this period our Lord expounded the Scriptures, and instructed His Apostles in all that concerned His Church—or the Kingdom of God—and He gave them His last commission : *Go and teach all nations, baptizing them in the Name of the Father, and of the Son, and of the Holy Ghost.**

3. The Ascension was represented in figures, and foretold by the prophets, and also by our Divine Saviour Himself.

The High Priest under the Law, an express type of the Messiah, when making the typical atonement representing the propitiation made by Christ for the sins of the world, was to enter himself, alone, and only once in the year, into the Holy of Holies, thereby showing *that the High Priest of good things to come, by a greater . . . tabernacle . . . was to enter into the Holy place, having obtained eternal redemption for us.*† " The Jews all believed that the tabernacle signified this world, and the Holy of Holies the highest heavens ; wherefore as the High Priest, having slain the Sacrifice, passed with the blood thereof through the rest of the tabernacle into the Holy of Holies, so the Messiah, here offering

---

*St. Matt. xxviii. 19.   †Heb. ix. 11, 12.

Himself, and slain, was to pass through the courts of this world below, and with His blood to enter the highest heavens."*

The Ascension was declared prophetically by the Psalmist. *Thou hast ascended on high, Thou hast led captivity captive ; Thou hast received gifts for men.*† And it was foretold by our Lord Himself : *I ascend unto My Father, and your Father, and to My God and your God.*‡

The account of the Ascension is given in St. Mark's Gospel (xvi. 14-20), St. Luke's (xxiv. 50-52), and in the Acts of the Apostles (i. 7-12). From these sources we learn the following particulars and circumstances, as to the *time, place, persons,* and the manner of His Ascension.

4. Our Lord's Ascension took place, as I have said, on the fortieth day after His Resurrection, the fifth day of the week (or Thursday) which, according to a probable opinion, fell on the 25th of May. The disciples had all assembled from Galilee at Jerusalem, and when they were gathered together in the Cenacle or Supper Room, where Christ had eaten with them the last Supper, and instituted the Blessed Sacrament, He appears in their midst. After He had eaten, and conversed in a loving manner with them, especially concerning the coming of the Holy Ghost, about one o'clock in the day, He went forth with His Apostles, and other disciples also, to the number of about 120, and He led them to Mount Olivet (which was the scene of His Agony) in the direction of the town of Bethany; or probably He led them round by Bethany, where they would be joined by the Magdalene, her sister, and Lazarus. We may reflect on the last colloquies between Jesus and His Blessed Mother on this occasion, and also on the last embraces and farewell between the Lord and His disciples, although no mention is made of them in the Holy Scripture.

5. The traditional scene of the Ascension is the central summit of the Mount of Olives (*Jebel-el-Tur*). Having arrived at the place, our Saviour, with upraised hands, blessed them, namely the Blessed Virgin and the Apostles, invoking many favours and graces to be bestowed upon them, and using probably words similar to those used on a former occasion : *That they may be one, as thou, Father, in Me and I in Thee : that they also may be one in Us : that the world may believe that Thou hast sent Me.*§ He raised His hands either in the form of a Cross extended

---

*Pearson. Analysis.   †Psalm lxviii. 18.
‡St. John xx. 17.   § St. John xvii. 81.

towards heaven as Moses did; or He made the sign of the Cross over them, after the manner in which the blessings of the Church have been imparted ever since.

Whilst He blessed, and as they were looking at Him, He was raised up from the earth towards heaven; and as the disciples still continued gazing in wonder at the mysterious Ascension, a cloud, glorious and resplendent, received Him out of their sight; and, whilst enveloping Christ with its heavenly brightness and splendour, it showed forth to all the spectators the majesty of the triumphal entrance of Christ into His heavenly Kingdom.

6. And whilst they were beholding Him going up to heaven, *behold two men stood by them in white garments. Who also said*: *Ye men of Galilee, why stand you looking up to heaven? This Jesus who is taken up from you into heaven shall so come as you have seen Him going into heaven.* These are called men, but they are evidently angels: the expressions *clothed in white* (St. John xx. 12), *two men in shining garments* (St. Luke xxiv. 4.), *a man in bright clothing* (Acts x. 30), was the jewish manner of signifying Angels, or heavenly messengers.

7. Those who accompanied our Lord in His Ascension, were all the just who were in the Limbo of the Fathers, and those who in Purgatory had finished the period of their temporal punishment. Some have thought that the bodies of the Saints that had arisen at the Resurrection of Christ, being clothed with their glorified qualities, were also in that heavenly company according to the words of the Psalmist : *Ascending on high He led captivity captive.* As to the Angels, there is no doubt but they all came forth to meet Christ in His Ascension, to receive Him and to conduct Him above all the heavens to the right hand of the Father. Of Christ as the King of Angels it is written : *Adore Him, all ye His Angels.** And again : *Lift up your gates, O ye princes, and be ye lifted up, O eternal gates : and the King of glory shall enter in.*†

As to what is meant by heaven, we must remember that the name may be taken in various senses. The clouds are called the *clouds of heaven*, but that heaven is the *first*, and our Saviour certainly went higher than that, and ascended at least as far as St. Paul, who was caught up into the third heaven. It means therefore the highest heaven, that far off land where God manifests His glory. It means that Christ in His Sacred humanity, body and soul, ascended to that place where the Majesty of God

---

* Ps. xcvi. 7.   † Ps. xxiii. 7.

O

is most resplendent, that the flesh of our flesh is above all the Angels at the right hand of God the Father: it means that whatsoever heaven there is higher than all the rest called heavens, into that place did He ascend in His humanity, where in the splendour of *His Deity* He was before He took our human nature upon Him.

Some modern scientific men originated an objection in regard to the Ascension on the ground of the conditions of the Solar system. If He ascends out of this world He is above to some, He is below to others, and how can He be stationary and we ever moving? To all this we have only to answer, that He is exalted into the sphere of the Deity. He is now in a condition far above the condition of our space, and whatever region of the earth people live in, they can look up towards that far off heavenly home above them, that really existing place in which Christ's Sacred Humanity resides, which is known as the *Heaven of Heavens.*

9. The reasons why Christ thus ascended into heaven are:— (*a*) In order to confirm His doctrine and to prove that it is a heavenly doctrine. (*b*) That He might open the gates closed by Adam's sin. (*c*) That He might shew that His Kingdom was not an earthly or temporal, but a heavenly one; according to His own words: *My kingdom is not of this world.* (*d*) That with His glorified Body He might occupy His own proper throne of glory. Heaven is the proper dwelling place for a glorified body. (*e*) That He might rejoice the Angels by His appearance and adorn heaven by His glory: *for the Lamb is the lamp thereof.** (*f*) That He might send the Holy Ghost, and continually plead our cause with the Father through His five Sacred Wounds. (*g*) That from His throne in heaven He may rule and direct His Church and the whole world.

Dr. Lingard says in his note on the Ascension of Christ: "With His ascent into heaven our Saviour closed His earthly pilgrimage, He ascended before the eyes of His disciples: and this visible ascent was calculated, 1st, not only to confirm them in the belief of His Mission, but to disabuse their minds of the notion that His was an earthly Kingdom, a notion which they had cherished to that very moment. 2nd, To show that the place which He was going to prepare for His faithful servants (*that where He was they also might be*) was not on earth but in heaven; and 3rd, to lay a firm foundation for our hopes; since we now must

---

*Apoc. xxi. 23.

know, *that we have for our advocate with the Father*, one *Who ever liveth to make intercession for us.** And that as God hath quickened us together with Christ, *and hath raised us up together*, so He will make us *sit together in heavenly places in Christ Jesus.†*

10. The second part of the Article: *Sitteth at the right hand of God the Father Almighty.* This does not mean that God the Father has hands. He is a spirit—but that Christ, in His human nature, is raised to a seat in heaven above all created beings.

Sitteth—remaineth. This word does not signify our Lord's posture of Body, for St. Stephen declared he saw Christ *standing* on the right hand of God. By *sitting* is signified the occupation or continuance in a permanent state. It signifies also that our Saviour, after His great work here on earth of our redemption, enjoys an immutable rest in eternal beatitude : that He is there as King and Judge, King of kings, and Judge of the living and the dead ; and as a King He is seated on His throne, and as Judge on the tribunal of Justice.

The right hand of God. This is also a metaphorical expression which signifies the place of highest honour, power and glory in heaven. *And the Lord Jesus after he had spoken to them was taken up into heaven, and sitteth at the right hand of God.‡* And St. Peter says of Christ : *Who is gone into heaven, and is on the right hand of God.§* And this is also the fulfilment of the prophetic words of David : *The Lord said unto my Lord, sit thou at my right hand, until I make thy enemies thy footstool.***

At the right hand of His Father, Christ is in heaven our Advocate and Mediator. We are not to think of Him there as though His sitting at the right hand of the Father implies a state of inactive rest. In the highest heavens He exercises the two-fold functions of Priest and King : *King* according to the words : *This man offering one sacrifice for sins, for ever sitteth on the right hand of God. From henceforth expecting* (waiting) *until His enemies be made His footstool.††* *Priest.* If any man sin, we have an advocate with the Father, Jesus Christ the Just ; and He is the propitiation for our sins.‡‡* And St. Paul says, that *Christ Jesus : Who is on the right hand of God, who also maketh intercession for us.§§*

---

*Heb. vii. 25. †Eph. ii. 6. ‡St. Mark xvi. 19.
§1 St. Peter iii. 22. ** Psalm cx. ††Heb. x. 12, 13.
‡‡1 St. John ii. 1, 2. §§Rom. viii. 34.

ARTICLE VII.

APOSTLES' CREED.	NICENE CREED.
"From thence He shall come to judge the living and the dead."	"And He shall come again with glory to judge the living and the dead; *of Whose Kingdom there shall be no end.*"

1. Christ shall come again. — 2. The manner of His second coming. —
3. The purpose of His coming, and proofs of the future judgment.—
4. Those who are to be judged the *Living* and the *Dead.*—5. Those things that are to fall under judgment. — 6. The final sentence and description of the last judgment.—7. The execution of the sentence.—
8. The particular judgment at the death of each one.—9. Some of the signs that are to precede the General Judgment :— (a) the falling off from the faith.—(b) Satan let loose on the earth.—(c) The Antichristian empire.—(d) Antechrist.—(e) Enoch and Elias will return to earth.—(f) The Church will be victorious.—(g) The Sign of the Son of Man will be seen in the heavens.—(h) Christ will be seen coming in the clouds of heaven.

THE Church commemorates this hope of the second coming of Christ by the Season of Advent.

This Article contains four assertions :

(1). That Christ shall come again.

(2). That He shall come from heaven.

(3). That the purpose of His coming is to judge.

(4). That the persons whom He shall judge are all men, whether dead before His coming, or then alive.

CHRIST WHO IS GONE FROM US SHALL COME AGAIN.

1. (1) This the Angel testified : *This Jesus Who is taken up from you into heaven shall so come as you have seen Him going into heaven.** (b) This Christ promised : *And if I shall go, and prepare a place for you; I will come again, and will take you to Myself.*†

---

* Acts i. 11.   † St. John xiv. 3.

This Coming of Christ is represented under various images

(a) The Master returning to His household. (St. Matt. xxiv. 45-51.)

(b) The Nobleman returning from a long journey. Parable of the Pounds. (St. Luke xix. 12-23.)

(c) The Bridegroom returning or coming for His Bride. Parable of the Ten Virgins. (St. Matt. xxv. 1-13.)

(2). He shall come from heaven, *from thence,* that is from the highest heaven; where, having thither ascended, He now sitteth on the right hand of God, shall Christ come hereafter to judge both the living and the dead.

2. THE MANNER OF THE SECOND COMING OF CHRIST SHALL BE:

(a) *In the same body:* This same Jesus Who is taken up from you into heaven shall so come as you have seen Him going into heaven.*

(b) *His coming will be sudden and unexpected.* We know not the day nor the hour. *He shall come as a thief in the night; watch ye, therefore, because you know not the day nor the hour.* (St. Matt. xxv. 13.)

(c) *His coming will be glorious and terrible* according to the words:— *Hereafter you shall see the Son of Man sitting on the right hand of the power of God, and coming in the clouds of heaven.* (St. Matt. xxvi. 64.)
And when the Son of Man shall come in His majesty, and all the Angels with Him, then shall He sit upon the seat of His majesty. (St. Matt. xxv. 31.)

(d) *He shall come accompanied by angelic hosts.* For the Lord Himself shall come down from heaven with commandment, and with the voice of an Archangel, and with the trumpet of God: and the dead who are in Christ shall first rise. *Then we who are alive, who are left, shall be taken up together with them in the clouds to meet Christ,* &c. (1 Thess. iv. 16.)

3. THE PURPOSE OF CHRIST'S COMING IS TO JUDGE.

(3). That there is a judgment to come is one of the dogmas of our faith which is demonstrated by the testimony of conscience, and may be demonstrated from the supreme dominion of God over us and all His creatures.

"There is in the soul of man a conscience which gives testimony to this truth. The antecedent or directive conscience tells us what to do. The subsequent or reflective conscience warns us as to what we have to receive. Looking back on the actions we have done, it either approves or condemns them; and if it did no more it would only prove a judgment in this life, and every man his own judge. But because it also, in reference to our good actions, creates in us a complecency, confidence, &c., and in reference to our evil actions accuses us and breeds in us fearful expectation, &c., and all this apart from anything to be enjoyed or suffered in this life; therefore it is not so much a judge as a witness, bound over to testify for or against us at some judgment to be passed on us after this life. For all men are a law unto themselves ...... their conscience also bearing witness, and their thoughts the meanwhile accusing or excusing one another in the day when God shall judge the secrets of hearts."*

This can also, as I have said, be demonstrated from God's dominion and His providence over all His creatures: God is a just and righteous Lord, and therefore in the end He will manifest that justice. To us, as the affairs of the present world are ordered, the justice of things does not now appear: rewards do not correspond to virtues, nor punishments to the sins of men, therefore there must be a judgment to come in which God will show a perfect demonstration of His justice, and to which every man shall in his heart bear an undeniable witness.

The divine words also persuade us of this truth: *It is appointed unto men once to die, and after death judgment*—the one is as certain as the other. The testimonies of the Law and the Prophets, the predictions of Christ and His Apostles, are so many and so well-known that they need not be repeated. There is nothing more certain in the Word of God, no doctrine more clear, than that of *eternal judgment.*†

Dr. Lingard, speaking of the judgment at the last day, says:

"When all the objects which God had in view in the creation of man shall have been fully accomplished, then will our blessed Lord put an end to the present order of things on our earth, and at the same time will satisfactorily solve the apparent anomalies in the ways of divine Providence, by summoning the whole human race before Him in judgment, and alloting to each individual according to his previous conduct in this world, an everlasting inheritance of weal or woe in another. *For God hath appointed a*

---

* 1 Rom. ii, 14-16. Pearson's Analysis *in loco.*   † Heb. vi. 2.

*day in which He will judge the world in righteousness by that man
whom He hath appointed, whom He hath raised from the dead.* To
whom the Father hath given authority to execute judgment because
He is the Son of Man.†* So that Christ in His sacred humanity
will be the judge of the living and the dead."

4. THOSE WHO ARE TO BE JUDGED ARE THE LIVING AND THE DEAD.

(4). This is not limited to the interpretation as referring
only to all who are dead before Christ's coming, or then alive :
because all are to die first ; and even those alive up to that day of
General Judgment will, by some means or other, have to depart
this life, their souls must be separated from their bodies by death
before the judgment.

By the *living* is therefore meant the just, who leave this
world in a state of grace, that is to say, alive with the divine
principle of charity which causes us to love God about all things,
and our neighbour as ourselves. By the *dead* is meant those who
appear before God in sin or devoid of charity. They are dead to
the spiritual life of grace : as it is written, *He who loves not
abideth in death.*‡ Our divine Lord gives us to understand the
same thing, when in His anticipated account of the General
Judgment He mentions works of charity alone : *I was hungry, I
was thirsty, &c., and you gave Me to eat, to drink, &c. Come,
ye blessed of My Father, &c. I was hungry, I was thirsty, &c., and
you gave Me not to eat and drink, &c. Go, ye cursed, &c.*

5. This judgment will be according to men's works, extending to

(a) *Our thoughts. Therefore judge not before the time ; until
the Lord come, who both will bring to light the hidden
things of darkness, and will make manifest the counsels
of the heart ; and then shall every man have praise from
God.* (1 Cor. iv. 51.)

(b) *Our words. But I say unto you that every idle word that
man shall speak, they shall render an account for it in
the day of judgment.* (St. Matt. xii. 36.)

(c) *Deeds. And they were judged every one according to their
works.* (Apoc. xx. 13.) *For we must all be manifested
before the judgment seat of Christ, that every one may*

---

receive the proper things of the body, according as he hath done, whether it be good or evil. (2 Cor. v. 10.)

THE SENTENCE WHICH WILL BE FINAL.

6. We have a description of the last Judgment, given by St Mathew, in the simile of the sheep and goats, in which he also gives us the last sentence referred to already.

And when the Son of man shall come in His majesty, and all the angels with Him, then shall He sit on the seat of His majesty. And all nations shall be gathered together before Him, and He shall separate them one from another, as the shepherd separateth the sheep from the goats. And He shall set the sheep on His right hand, but the goats on His left. Then shall the King say to them that shall be on His right hand : Come, ye blessed of My Father, possess you the Kingdom prepared for you from the foundation of the world. For I was hungry, and you gave Me to eat ; I was thirsty, and you gave Me to drink ; I was a stranger, and you took Me in : Naked, and you covered Me ; sick, and you visited Me ; I was in prison, and you came to Me. Then shall the just answer Him, saying : Lord, when did we see Thee hungry, and fed Thee ; thirsty, and gave Thee drink ? And when did we see Thee a stranger, and took Thee in ? or naked, and covered Thee ? Or when did we see Thee sick and in prison, and came to Thee ? And the King answering shall say to them : Amen, I say to you, as long as you did it to one of these My least brethren you did it to Me. Then He shall say to them also that shall be on His left hand : Depart from Me, ye cursed, into everlasting fire which was prepared for the devil and his angels. For I was hungry, and you gave Me not to eat ; I was thirsty, and you gave Me not to drink. I was a stranger, and you took Me not in ; naked, and you covered Me not ; sick and in prison, and you did not visit Me. Then they also shall answer Him, saying : Lord, when did we see Thee hungry or thirsty, or a stranger, or naked, or sick, or in prison, and did not minister to Thee ? Then He shall answer them saying : Amen, I say to you, as long as you did it not to one of these least ones, neither did you do it to Me. And these shall go into everlasting punishment ; but the just into life everlasting.*

St. John also in the Apocalypse gives us a description of the last judgment : *And I saw a great white throne, and one sitting on it, from whose face the earth and heaven fled away, and there was*

---

* St. Matt. xxv. 31-46.

no place found for them. And I saw the dead, great and small, standing in the presence of the throne, and the books were opened; and another book was opened which is the book of life; and the dead were judged by those things that were written in the books, according to their works. And the sea gave up the dead that were in it, and death and hell gave up their dead that were in them. And they were judged, everyone according to their works. And hell and death were cast into the pool of fire. This is the second death. And whosoever was not written in the book of life was cast into the pool of fire.

From the above description we can form some idea of the judiciary process of the last judgment.

(a). There is described a throne of judicature on which the Son of Man shall appear as judge. *In the regeneration the Son of Man shall sit on the throne of His majesty.*†

(b). There is to be a personal appearance of all men before that judgment seat. *I saw the dead standing before the throne of God. All nations shall be gathered before Him.*

(c). The thoughts, words and actions of all men, thus brought before Christ's judgment seat, shall appear. *He will bring to light the hidden things of darkness.* To this end the books were opened, and *the dead were judged out of those things that were written in the books according to their works.*

(d). According to their thoughts, words and actions, a final sentence will be passed on all men. Here note the two sentences side by side, and the correspondence between them :—

SENTENCE OF THE JUST.	SENTENCE OF THE WICKED.
Come, ye blessed of My Father, possess the Kingdom prepared for you from the foundation of the world.	*Depart from Me, ye cursed, into everlasting fire, prepared for the devil and his angels.*

Observe that the words *ye blessed of My Father* in contrast to *ye cursed. Of My Father* is not added to the curse, as it is to the blessing, because the blessing comes from God, the curse is brought by the sinner himself. Observe also the words *Kingdom prepared* for you, as addressed to the just, and the fire *prepared,* not for men, but for the devil and his angels : for though men were not, or were not sinners, that fire would still burn for the devil and his angels.

---

* Apoc. xx. 11-15.   † St. Matt. xix. 28.

THE EXECUTION OF THE SENTENCE.

7. *And these shall go into everlasting punishment, but the just into life eternal.*

And hence the Nicene Creed adds the words: *Of Whose Kingdom there shall be no end.* This is to refute those who taught that after the judgment Jesus would return to the bosom of His Father, and cease to have a distinct human (personal) existence.*

Besides the general judgment, we must know that in this Article of the Creed we also profess our faith in the particular judgment. The Christian Religion teaches that two judgments await us : the *particular* judgment, which will decide the fate of each individual the moment he quits this life ; and the *general* judgment, which will take place at the end of the world.

It is of faith that all who die in a state of mortal sin are immediately condemned to everlasting torments ; and on the other hand, it is of faith that the just, who die in God's grace, and who have nothing to atone for in Purgatory, are immediately after death received into eternal beatitude ; therefore there must be the judgment for each soul as soon as it leaves the body. No punishment can be justly inflicted, and no reward granted, before judgment, and as God is most just, the particular judgment must therefore precede the granting of rewards or punishments. Hence it takes place the very moment that the soul leaves the body. Besides, there is no reason for the delay of this judgment or for deferring the sentence. God being *omnipotent, omniscient* and most merciful and just, does not require any period of time to examine the cause or to execute the sentence. And on the part of the soul, when once it has passed out of this life it ceases to merit or to demerit. It has reached the end of its way, of the weary journey of life, and were it to remain a hundred or a thousand years in that other state, it would have no more thoughts, words or actions, that could fall under judgment, or for which it would be either rewarded or punished.

8. Every one is judged in particular at his death, according to the words : *It is appointed for men once to die, and after that the judgment.*†

Some have pretended that the souls of the departed remain in the deep sleep of death, in a state of utter insensibility till the

---

* The Parables illustrating the Second Advent of Christ and the Judgment are :— 1. The ten Virgins (St. Matt. xxv. 1-13.)—2. The Talents (St. Matt. xxv. 14-30.)—3. The Pounds (St. Luke xix. 12-27).

† Heb. ix. 27.

day of resurrection. But this is irreconcilable with the promise of our Saviour to the thief who confessed Him on the Cross, that he should be with Him that day in paradice (St. Luke xxiii. 43.); and with the early expressed wish of St. Paul *to depart and be with Christ* (Phil. 1. 23.); and with the universal belief of the ancient Christian writers, which must have been derived from the Apostles.

Hence we admit a particular judgment of each individual on the separation of the soul from the body. The steward must render an account of his stewardship, when he can be steward no longer: and to such judgment should be referred those passages of Scripture which teach that after *death cometh judgment*: *that we must all stand before the judgment seat of Christ, and must every one render an account of himself to God.*

We know that this judgment takes place at the moment of death, but our Saviour has never revealed the time of His Second Advent, or the Day of general Judgment. He has only given signs by which we can know when the end of time approaches.

9. Amongst these signs we may enumerate the following:—

(a) There will be a great falling off from the faith: and it will be as in the days of Noe. Men will seek for pleasure and riches. They will not receive the truth which will save them; God, says St. Paul, will leave them to the spirit of error, that is, through their own fault He will withhold His efficacious graces from them.

(b) Satan, the father of lies, will be let loose upon the earth: and multiply all his wiles and deceits to seduce men and to cause them to sin.

(c) There will be formed a formidable anti-Christian empire composed of men of whom the continental Freemasons are an image.

(d) At the head of this Empire will be Antichrist, the most impious and perverse man that the world has ever seen; whom St. Paul calls a man of sin, the son of perdition. Aided by diabolical forces he will proceed so far as to make himself pass for God, and to be adored. Those who refuse will be massacred, and the blood of martyrs will again flow in torrents. Satan in appearance will imitate so well the divine power as to seduce if possible even the elect. In the midst of this terrible confusion God will not abandon His faithful people. The heroes and defenders of the faith will perform greater wonders than those of Antichrist.

(e) Enoch and Elias, who have been taken out of this world without dying, will return in those latter days and sustain the Church in the last terrible conflict. The first, representing the primitive religion, the second the Mosaic religion, and both uniting to bear testimony to the divinity of Jesus Christ. Enoch will preach repentance to the nations. Elias will bring back the Jews to the true faith. The Conversion of the Jewish people is given by St. Paul as a sign of the end of the world.

(f) The church will be victorious, and will enjoy her triumph for some time ; the good will live united to Christ, and preparing themselves for His coming ; the wicked will continue to deceive themselves, to indulge their passions, and to give way to a false security.

(g) When all of a sudden, as the lightning comes forth from the East, and reaches even to the West, will be seen the Sign of the Son of Man in the heavens. The trumpet of the judgment will sound and be heard from pole to pole ; all the dead, from Adam to the last man, will rise, the bodies of the just glorious and bright as stars, those of the wicked dark and hideous to behold.

(h) Then Jesus Christ will appear in the clouds surrounded by all His angels, and preceded by a large brilliant Cross. The just risen from the dead will raise themselves in the air, and advance to meet Him. They will be separated from the wicked as the sheep from the goats.

Then will take place the judgment of the living and the dead, that is, the good and the bad.

In this judgment the Apostles will be the companions and assistants of our Lord. The Angels and demons will be there as witnesses : the first will receive an increase of joy at the salvation of those men whom they helped to practice virtue : the latter will have their anguish redoubled at the condemnation of those whom they have led into sin.

When the judgment is over, the Sovereign Judge will pronounce sentence in the manner already described, and the execution of the sentence will follow immediately.

After which this earth will be purified and renovated, *and there will be a new heaven and a new earth, in which justice shall dwell.*

ARTICLE VIII.

APOSTLES' CREED.	NICENE CREED.
" I believe in the Holy Ghost."	" And I believe in the Holy Ghost, *the Lord and Lifegiver, Who proceedeth from the Father and the Son, Who together with the Father and the Son is adored and glorified, Who spoke by the Prophets.*"

SECTION 1. (Article VIII.)

1. When this mystery is commemorated. The meaning of the words *Penticost*; *Holy Ghost.*—2. The Holy Ghost is a Person and not a mere virtue or power of God.—3. The objections of the Socinians to the Personality of the Holy Ghost answered.—4. The Holy Ghost is God and Lord, that is, consubstantial with the Father and the Son.— 5. He is the Lifegiver.—6. The Procession of the Holy Ghost: proofs of the Procession of the Holy Ghost from the Father and the Son.— 7. The addition of the *Filioque* to the Nicene Creed.—8. The reason why He is called the Third Person.

1. THE Church commemorates the descent of the Holy Ghost on Whit Sunday, the Feast of Pentecost, that is, forty days after Easter, and ten days after Our Blessed Redeemer ascended into heaven.

The word Holy Ghost is applied to the Third Person of the Blessed Trinity. *Holy* because He sanctifies or makes holy: *Ghost* or Spirit from the Anglo-Saxon *Gast*, which signifies *spirit* or *breath* as opposed to *body*. Hence the expression, *our ghostly father*, that is, *our spiritual father*.

Analysing, or rather dividing, the Article as expressed in the Nicene Creed, we have the following propositions :—

(*a*). The Holy Ghost is a Person.
(*b*). The Holy Ghost is the Lord, or God.
(*c*). He is the Life-giver.
(*d*). He proceedeth from the Father and the Son.
(*e*). He spoke by the Prophets.

Let us examine each of these propositions separately.

2. The Holy Ghost is a Person and not a mere virtue or perfection of God.

(a) *I will send HIM unto you.* (St. John xvi. 7.)

(b) He is called by our Lord the Comforter, that is, the strengthener or supporter. *But the Comforter Who is the Holy Ghost.* (St. John xiv. 26.)

(c) He is said *to come* to men : *If I go not away, the Paraclete, or Comforter, will not come to you.* (St. John xvi. 7.)

(d) He is said to speak to men, and to bid men do things. *The Holy Ghost said to them, separate Me Barnabas and Saul for the work whereunto I have taken them.* (Acts xiii. 2.)

(e) He is said to give gifts to men. *To one is given by the Spirit the word of wisdom,* &c. (1 Cor. xii. 8.)

(f) He is said to intercede for men : *For the Spirit Himself asketh for us with unspeakable groanings.* (Rom. viii. 26.)

(g) He is said to love men : *I beseech you therefore, brethren, through our Lord Jesus Christ, and by the charity of the Holy Ghost, that you help me in your prayers for me with God.* (Rom. xv. 30.)

(h) He can be grieved : *And grieve not the Holy Spirit, whereby you are sealed unto the day of redemption.* (Eph. iv. 30.)

From all these it is evident that Scripture expressions attributed Personality to the Holy Ghost.

3. The Socinians who deny the Personality of the Holy Ghost bring against the doctrine two objections.

First, they say, that it is ordinary in Scripture to find personal expressions given to things that are not persons ; as, for example, Charity is said to be long-suffering, Charity is kind and humble, &c. These actions are attributed to Charity, because the person who has that virtue is kind and humble, &c. ; and in the same way personal actions are attributed to the Holy Ghost, Who is no Person but a virtue, a power or efficacy of God the Father of our Lord Jesus Christ : because God the Father performs those actions by that virtue in Himself which is called the Holy Ghost.

To this we may answer, that many of the personal actions attributed in Scripture to the Holy Ghost cannot be ascribed to God the Father or to the Son : Thus *the Spirit maketh inter-*

cession. When the Paraclete is come, Whom I will send unto you from the Father. When He the Spirit of truth is come, He will guide you into all truth; for He shall not speak of Himself, but whatsoever He shall hear that shall He speak. Therefore that Person sent by the Father to men, and sent by the Son also, is not a power, but one Who is to speak and teach them all truth; and by no figure of speech can such personal actions be attributed to a mere virtue or efficacy.

Secondly, they say that there are attributes or expressions in Scripture of the Holy Ghost which cannot belong to a Person as such; that the Spirit is given, that it is given sometimes in measure and sometimes without measure, that men drink of it; that it is doubled and distributed.

To this we answer, that the Holy Ghost is given by God to those who obey Him, and that a person can be given: *e.g.*, *Unto us a Son is given*: God so loved the world as to give, or send His only-begotten Son. The other expressions refer to the operations or effects of the Spirit, Who is the cause of them. And since to that Spirit, or the cause, those attributes are given which can agree to nothing but a Person, we conclude, against the Socinians and Jews, that the Holy Ghost is not a quality but a Person.

4. The Holy Ghost is God and Lord, that is, consubstantial with the Father and the Son: and therefore together with the Father and the Son is adored and glorified.

(*a*) The Father eternal, the Son eternal, the Holy *Ghost eternal.* (Athan. Creed.)

(*b*) *He is omniscient*, that is, knoweth all things: For *the Spirit searcheth all things, yea, the deep things of God......So the things also that are of God no man knoweth, but the Spirit of God.* (1 Cor. ii. 10, 11.)

(*c*) *He is associated with God* in the act of creation. *The Spirit of God moved upon the face of the waters.* (Gen. i. 2.)

(*d*) *To sin against Him is to sin against God.* Ananias, in lying to the Holy Ghost, is declared to have lied to God. (Acts v. 3, 4.)

(*e*) *In His name we are baptized: Go ye therefore and teach all nations, baptizing them in the name of the Father and of the Son, and of the Holy Ghost.* (St. Matt. xxviii. 19.)

(*f*) He is called God and Lord. (Acts v. 3. *et seq.*) Thus the Angels *cried out: Holy, Holy, Holy, the Lord God of hosts, all the earth is full of Thy glory.* (Isa. vi. 3.)

The Holy, Holy, Holy, signifies the three Persons, Father, Son, and Holy Ghost, in one God. Hence the Nicene Creed calls Him *the Lord*.

5. HE IS ALSO THE LIFE-GIVER.

(a) He gives natural life. (1) He helped in the work of creation. *The Spirit of the Lord moved upon the face of the waters.* (Gen. 1. 2.) (2) *He raises* the dead. *He that raised up Jesus Christ from the dead shall quicken also your mortal bodies, because of His Spirit that dwelleth in you.* (Rom. viii. 11.)

(b) He gives spiritual life. (1) *Unless a man be born again of water and the Holy Ghost he cannot enter into the Kingdom of heaven.* (St. John iii. 5.) (2) *Receive ye the Holy Ghost ; whose sins you shall forgive they are forgiven, and whose sins you shall retain they are retained.**

We have already instructed on the plurality and consubstantiality of Persons in the Blessed Trinity, when treating on the Mystery of the Holy Trinity in the first Article of the Creed, to which place I refer the reader.

Here we have to refer to the special doctrine concerning—

THE PROCESSION OF THE HOLY GHOST.

6. The Greek Schismatics bring two well-known accusations against the Catholic Church. (a) That She teaches that the Holy Ghost proceeds from the Son as well as from the Father. (b) That She has added to the Creed of faith of Constantinople the words *Filioque*.

Hence we have to examine two questions which affect the Catholic teaching in regard to the Holy Ghost.

1st. *His Procession from the Son.* His Procession from the Father is admitted by all who believe in the Trinity according to the words of St. John : *But, the Paraclete, the Holy Ghost, Whom the Father will send in My name, He will teach you all things,* &c. (xiv. 26.) We have therefore only to prove His Procession from the Son against the Greek Schismatics, or rather heretics, for such they are by the very fact of denying the Procession of the Holy Ghost from the Son.

There are three Scriptural proofs of the Procession of the

---

* This summary of proofs, common in every manual, is put down according to the arrangement of Gill's Church Catechism.

Holy Ghost from the Son. (a) That He, the Holy Ghost, receives of the Son. (b) That the Son sends Him. (c) That He is called the Spirit of the Son.

(a) When one of the divine Persons receives of another, He may be said to proceed from that other; because, in the Divine Persons, one cannot receive from the other except something substantial and by a substantial act, which is no other than *Procession*. And in the Gospel of St. John it is said, *He* (the Holy Ghost) *shall glorify Me; because He shall receive of Mine, and shall show it to you.**

In His prayer to His Father Christ says : *All Mine are Thine, and Thine are Mine.*† These words mean that whatever the Father has, that the Son also has, unless where the *relative opposition* intervenes. The Father has the *vis spirandi*, or that from which the Holy Ghost proceeds, therefore the Son also has that same power, in as much as no *relative opposition* exists between that power in the Father and the Son.

(b) The Son sends the Holy Ghost : *Whom I shall send from the Father.* But the Holy Ghost is not sent by the Son as from a superior, by command; or from a more wise person, by counsel ; therefore He can be said to be sent in no other way but by reason of His procession from the Son.

(c) In the same manner the Holy Ghost is called the Spirit of the Son, as He is called the Spirit of the Father. *And the* SPIRIT *of Jesus suffered them not.* (Acts. xvi. 7.) *Now if any man have not the Spirit of Christ he is none of us.* (Rom. viii. 9.) *And because you are sons; God hath sent that Spirit of His Son into your hearts.* (Gal. iv. 6.)

Therefore the Holy Ghost proceeds from the Son in the same way that He proceeds from the Father.

The Procession of the Holy Ghost from the Son was expressly declared and defined in the IV. Council of Lateran, under Innocent III.; the II. Council of Lyons, under Gregory X.; and also in the Council of Florence.

The Procession of the Holy Ghost from the Son necessarily follows from the doctrine of the Trinity. One Person could not be consubstantial with another unless he proceeded from Him, as it is by Procession that the relationship exists between the Divine Persons : that is, that by which they are consubstantial with each other, and yet distinct persons.

Again, if the Holy Ghost did not proceed from the Son, He

---

* St. John xvi. 14.   † St. John xvii. 10.

could not be distinguished from Him ; because the distinction of
Persons is founded on relations when relative opposition is established between them, such as between *Paternity* and *Filiation,
Active* and *Passive Spiration* ; and there would be no relative
opposition unless one have the relation of principle, or fountain,
or that from which Procession originates, to the other.

The Scotists do not admit this reason, although the Council
of Florence uses it against the Greeks.

We need not enter further into this difficult discussion more
than by quoting the definition of faith as given by the Council of
Florence : " We define that the Holy Ghost proceeds eternally
from the Father and the Son, as from one sole principle, and by
one and the same Spiration." (*Spiratio.*)

The second accusation brought against the Church by the
Greeks is that She added the words *Filioque* (*and from the Son*) to
the Creed.

7. The words *Filioque*—*and from the Son*—are not found in
the Nicene Creed, though they have been adopted by the Catholic
Church. Their use was one of the causes that gave rise to the
great schism between the East and the West (A.D. 1053) ; the
Eastern or Greek Church refusing to use an expression which had
not been sanctioned by a General Council. The Greek Schismatics still refuse to use the expression *and from the Son.*

The Church, rightly and wisely, has added these words to
the Creed of Constantinople. She has a perfect right to make an
addition of the kind to the Creed whenever she judges it necessary
to do so for illustrating a truth of faith, or for vindicating the
truth against new errors. She has done this in the Nicene Creed,
and in the Creed of Pope Pius IV. And this addition was
necessary in order to guard against the false interpretation given
by the Greeks to the words *Who proceedeth from the Father*, as,
from the omission of the word *Filioque*, they asserted the heresy
that the Holy Ghost did not proceed from the Son, which is
against faith. Wherefore the Council of Florence declared this
addition legitimate in its definition of faith, to which all the
Greeks, as well as the Latins, subscribed. " *Definimus ajunt
Patres explicationem illo-um verborum, Filioque, veritatis declar-
an ae gratiâ, et immenente tunc necessitate licite ac rationabiliter
symbolo fuisse appositam.*"

"We define that the explanation by the words Filioque, for
the sake of declaring the truth, and in the urgent necessity of the
time, was wisely and rightly added to the Creed."

We have proved the Procession of the Holy Ghost from the

Son, and in the words of St. Gregory Nazianzen: *Si ita credendum cur non ita dicendum.*

The General Council of Nice had only : *I believe in the Holy Ghost.* The General Council of Constantinople, against Macedonius, who made the Holy Ghost a created power, added *The Lord and Life-giver who proceedeth from the Father.* The words *Filioque, and from the Son,* were afterwards added by the Western Church, and adopted by Greeks and Latins in the definition of the Council of Florence.

The Holy Ghost is therefore a Person, He is consubstantial with the Father and the Son, and one God with them; He is a distinct Person from the Father and the Son, and proceeds from them as from one principle.

8. He is the Third Person of the Blessed Trinity, and it may be well to give a word of explanation of the order *first, second,* and *third,* as applied to the three Divine Persons.

" As there is a number of Persons in the Trinity, by which the Persons are neither more nor less than three, so is there also an order by which, of these Persons, the Father is the first, the Son the second, and the Holy Ghost the third ; an order not arbitrary but necessary. The Godhead was communicated from the Father to the Son, and not from the Son to the Father, eternally indeed, therefore admitting no priority of time ; yet must there be acknowledged a priority of order, by which the Father, not the Son, is first ; and the Son, not the Father, second. Again the same Godhead was communicated by the Father and the Son to the Holy Ghost ; eternally, therefore admitting no priority of time, yet that order must be observed, so that the Spirit receiving the Godhead from the Father, the first Person, cannot be the first ;— from the Son, the second, cannot be the second ; therefore must be the third. Both the number and order are signified by the Apostle : *There are three that give testimony in heaven, the Father, the Word, and the Holy Ghost, and these three are one.** And the same number is sufficiently declared, and the order expressly mentioned in the baptismal institution.

" The Holy Ghost, the third Person, Who proceeds from the Father and the Son, is the most high and eternal God, of the same nature, attributes, and operations with the Father and the Son, as receiving the same essence from the Father and the Son by proceeding from them both."†

---

* 1 St. John v. 7.   † Analysis of the Creed. Pearson.

SECTION 2. (ARTICLE VIII.

THE COMING OF THE HOLY GHOST AND HIS OFFICE.

1. The Office attributed to the Holy Ghost by the words: *Who spoke by the Prophets.*—2. Mission understood as applied to the Divine Persons,—3. The Father or First Person cannot be said to be sent.—4. The Son and the Holy Ghost are sent (a) By an invisible mission; (b) By a visible mission.—5. *Pentecost.* (a) The injunction given to the Apostles; (b) The upper room where they awaited the coming of the Holy Ghost; (c) The names of the Apostles assembled there; (d) Their manner of preparation; (e) The significance of the mention of the holy women and Mary the Mother of Jesus.—6. The description of the descent of the Holy Ghost. (a) The sound from heaven; (b) The parted tongues as it were of fire; (c) Those who received the gifts of the Holy Ghost; (d) Divers tongues.—7. Dr. Lingard's Notes on this Mystery.—8. The Mission of the Holy Ghost in the Church,—9. The Seven Gifts of the Holy Ghost.—10. The Twelve Fruits of the Holy Ghost.—11. The *gratiae gratis datae* (or graces gratuitously given) of the Holy Ghost.

1. IN the Nicene Creed it is said of the Holy Ghost, as designating His Office : *Who spoke by the Prophets.*

Let us understand first, that no prophecy of Scripture is made by private interpretation. For prophecy came not by the will of man at any time; but holy men of God spoke, inspired by the Holy Ghost.

It may be useful for the purpose of understanding better this lesson to give some explanation of the meaning of the Mission of the Divine Persons : as we are familiar with the expressions, the *Internal Mission of the Holy Ghost,* and the *External (Temporal) Mission of the Holy Ghost.*[*]

2. Mission as it applies to a divine Person imports on the one side the origin of the Person sent from the Person sending; and on the other, a new way or manner of existing in something else. And as two of the Divine Persons originate one from another, and begin to exist in a new way in some creature, the term Mission can be applied to them. Hence we have expressions such as the following : *As the living Father hath sent me. I am not alone, but I and the Father Who sent me. When the Paraclete shall come,*

---

[*] Titles of Cardinal Manning's two books.

Whom I shall send from the Father, the Spirit of truth. And if I go I shall send Him to you.

The Mission, or giving, as applied to the Divine Persons is only verified, or applied, in time : because the Mission, or sending, implies that the Divine Person is now in that creature to whom he is sent, and is possessed by that creature to whom he is given. And the existence in a new way of a Divine Person in any creature, and His being received and possessed by that creature, are always something temporal, or that must take place in time : thus *when the plentitude of time came God sent His Son.*

The invisible Mission of a divine Person is explained by sanctifying grace in the soul. It is in this manner, and by this means, that a divine Person exists in a new manner in a creature ; because it is by the effect which he produces in the creature through his operation ; and no effect brings the divine Person in a new manner into the souls of His creatures here on earth, except sanctifying grace.

3. The Father, or first Person of the Most Holy Trinity, cannot be said to be sent—because Mission in the divine Persons involves procession by origin ; and the Father in no way proceeds, or has His origin, from another ; according to the words of the Creed of St. Athanasius : "The Father is made of no one, neither created, nor begotten. The Son is from the Father alone, not made, nor created, but begotten. The Holy Ghost is from the Father and the Son, not made, nor created, nor begotten, but proceeding."

4. The Son and the Holy Ghost are sent (*a*) by an *invisible* Mission. The Mission of a divine Person, as I have said, signifies two things, viz :— a new mode of existence and of dwelling in a creature, and origin from another divine Person. And in the Son and the Holy Ghost we find both these things : their origin, as in the Mystery of the Trinity, and their indwelling in creatures by sanctifying grace, according to the words of St. John : *If any one love Me, he will keep My word, and My Father will love him, and We will come to him, and will make Our abode with him.**

The invisible Mission of the divine Persons takes place in all souls who are participators of grace, and who are living in the state of love and friendship with God.

(*b*) The divine Persons are also sent *visibly*, because it is becoming that the invisible Mission of the divine Persons be made

---

* St. John xiv. 23.

manifest externally to men, for thus they are led by visible signs to acknowledge and to receive the invisible things of God.

The Incarnation and the mysteries of the life, sufferings, death, resurrection, and ascension of Christ, tell us of His earthly and visible Mission to men in order to effect their redemption, and to lead them to their sanctification and salvation. The Holy Ghost also descended in visible forms. This He did at the Baptism of Christ in a form of a dove.* In the form of a luminous cloud at the Transfiguration.† And in the form of tongues of fire on the day of Pentecost.‡

Pentecost. The greatest manifestation of the Holy Ghost was given fifty days after the Resurrection of our Lord; the day on which the Jews celebrated their Penticost in memory of the promulgation of the Law on Mount Sinai.

On ascending into heaven Jesus told His disciples not to depart from Jerusalem, but to expect or await there the promise of the Father; according to the words of St. Luke: *And I send the promise of My Father upon you; but stay you in the city till you be endued with power from on high.*|| *You shall receive* (He said) *the power of the Holy Ghost coming upon you; and you shall be witnesses unto Me in Jerusalem, and in all Judea and Samaria, and even to the uttermost part of the earth.*§

   (a).   The injunction not to depart from Jerusalem is only given by St. Luke. It was important that they should keep together until the Holy Ghost was given. It would thus be made more manifest that, though hereafter scattered abroad, their inspiration was supplied from one common source. To the Jews, to whom the Apostles were first to preach, this would appeal, because their own prophet had said: *Out of Zion shall go forth the law, and the word of the Lord from Jerusalem.***

On the day of the Ascension, the Apostles and disciples returned to the upper room, in Jerusalem, where they prepared themselves for the coming and reception of the Holy Ghost.

Then they returned to Jerusalem, from the Mount that is called Olivet, which is nigh Jerusalem, within a Sabbath day's journey. And when they were come in they went up into an upper room, where abode Peter and John, James and Andrew, Philip and Thomas, Bartholemew and Matthew, James and Alpheus, and Simon Zelotes,

---

* St. Matt. iii.　　　† St. Matt. xvii.　　　‡ Acts ii.
|| St. Luke xxiv. 49.　　§ Acts i. 8.　　　** Isa ii. 3.

and Jude the brother of James. All these were persevering with one mind in prayer, with the women, and Mary the mother of Jesus, and with His brethren.*

(b) The upper room is probably the same as that mentioned by St. Mark (xiv. 15), and St. Luke (xxii. 12), which was used by our Lord and His disciples for the Passover feast. The same as that in which He instituted the Blessed Eucharist, and appeared to His Apostles after His Resurrection. It was some large room in Jerusalem, which could be spared by the owners, and which was let or lent to the followers and disciples of our Saviour. It is related that, when the Emperor Adrian came to Jerusalem, he found the whole city utterly destroyed, and the Temple of God laid waste, excepting a few small houses, and a Church of God, diminutive in size, which was erected, as he (the Emperor) asserts, on the return of the disciples after the Saviour's Ascension from Mount Olivet, in the district of Zion. We have it also on the authority of Nicephorus, that St. Helena, the mother of Constantine, there raised a magnificent temple, the vestibule of which was on the very site of the house into whose upper room the Holy Ghost descended.

It is probable that the eleven Apostles were the tenants of that room, to which the disciples resorted for conference and communion.

(c) The names of the Apostles are given, though they had been already recorded in the Gospel.† Perhaps because it seemed fitting that the names of those who are now to be the leaders of the new teaching should be recited at the outset, that each one may be known to have taken his share in the labours ; and also, as all the twelve had fled before the Crucifixion, this enumeration of them, as again at their posts, may show that there had been in all of them, except Judas, only weakness of the flesh, and not unwillingness of the Spirit.

"It may be noticed that, whereas in the list of Apostles given in St. Luke's Gospel, the name of Andrew stands second in the first group of four, and next after Peter, in this repeated list Andrew is placed fourth. History gives no reason for this change ;

---

* Acts i. 12-14.   † St. Luke vi. 14.

but we see in the Gospels, when important events occurred in Christ's ministry, such as the raising of the daughter of Jairus, the Transfiguration, and the Agony in Gethsemane, that the three disciples chosen to be present with Jesus are Peter, James and John, but not Andrew. Whatever may have been the reason for such an omission, the fact may, in some degree, explain the altered position of Andrew's name in the list of the twelve."*

(d). These all continued in prayer with the women, and Mary the Mother of Jesus. Prayer was the most fitting preparation for the gift they were expecting.

They prayed with one accord for the descent of the Holy Ghost. For although He was promised, and promised absolutely, nevertheless when God gives a promise, no matter how distinct, no matter how seemingly absolute, it still lies upon us that we should pray for its fulfilment earnestly and continuously, till we receive it. Thus Daniel *knew by books* that the time was come for the restoration of Israel, but instead of waiting for that restoration with folded arms, he *set his face unto the Lord to seek it by prayer and supplication, with fasting.*†

(e) The women here mentioned were some of those who during the lifetime of Jesus had ministered to Him of their substance, and had been at the Cross, and at His grave. The frequent mention of these and other women in the course of Christ's ministry is a noteworthy feature of the Gospel story, and bespeaks more consideration shown by Him for women than was usual among His nation or with other great teachers.

Almost all commentators notice the presence of the women as being one especial mark of the new state of things. In the Temple, God's house of prayer, which was soon to be destroyed, the women prayed apart; here in the new and better house of prayer they prayed as part of the Church, as on an equality with men. We may notice also the circumstances or conditions that accompanied the prayers of that assembly, because they remind us of the conditions on which God hears our prayers; namely, *unanimity*, that is united in charity; *perseverance ;* and with *Mary, the Mother of Jesus.*

Mary, the Mother of Jesus, would naturally remain with St. John, to whose care she had been confided by Jesus at the Crucifixion. This is the last mention made of her in the New Testament, and thus the Scripture leaves her on her knees in

---

* Camb. Bible for Schools Acts. *In loco.*　　　† Dan. ix. 2, 3.

prayer and intercession for us, her children. She is mentioned apart from the other women as having a more deep interest in all that concerns Jesus than the rest had ; and her position, her action and power in the Church, were designed by God Himself.

The only other remarkable event mentioned in connection with the ten days spent by the Apostles in prayer, awaiting the coming of the Holy Ghost, was the election of the Apostle Matthias in the place of Judas Iscariot.

6. On the tenth day, about 9 o'clock in the morning it is supposed, *there came suddenly a sound from heaven, as of a mighty rushing wind coming, and it filled the whole house where they were sitting. And there appeared to them parted tongues as it were of fire, and it sat upon every one of them. And they were all filled with the Holy Ghost, and they began to speak in divers tongues, according as the Holy Ghost gave them to speak.**

This was the *Day of Pentecost,* which was the second of the three great Jewish feasts. The Passover being the first, and the third the feast of Tabernacles. Penticost is the Greek name of the feast, derived from *Pentecostes* — fiftieth ; because it was kept on the fiftieth day after the Passover-Sabbath. The counting of the fifty days began from the end of the 16th Nisan, which happened in the year in which our Lord was crucified on a Saturday ; the fiftieth day from it would fall on a Sunday. This feast was also, as I have said above, the celebration or commemoration of the giving of the Law from Sinai, and so was peculiarly fitted to be the day of the promulgation of the new and better law of faith and grace.

When they were all together in one place; that place was not one of the chambers of the Temple, as some have supposed, as they would not be allowed to occupy one of them on account of their connection with Jesus. St. Cyril, Bishop of Jerusalem, preaching in Jerusalem, speaks of the Holy Ghost : "Who on the day of Pentecost descended on the Apos 'es in the form of fiery tongues, here in Jerusalem, in the upper Church of the Apostles."

    (a) The verb used to express the *sound from heaven,* announcing the coming of the Holy Ghost, is used by St. Peter, of the voice which came from heaven at the Transfiguration ; also of the gift of prophecy, and the motion of the prophets by the Holy Ghost. It is to be remembered that there was no violent storm ; in all probability perfect stillness of the air ; and yet there

---

* Acts ii. 2 *et seq.*

suddenly came an awful sound as of a spirit passing ; the violence of the sound representing the energy, the irresistible force of the Spirit, which, as the hurricane, carries all before it.

(b)   *The parted tongues as it were of fire,* need not be understood of real fire.   The appearance is not called *fire,* but only compared to fire.   The idea conveyed by the description is that flame-like tongues were distributing themselves throughout the assembly, and the result is expressed by what follows : *and it sat upon each one of them.*

Just as the sound of wind was not occasioned by an actual wind, but came from heaven, so these tongues were not any natural fire, much less electricity, but a supernatural light, the outward and visible sign of the presence of the Spirit, just as was the dove upon the head of our Lord.   The intention of the writer is to describe something far more persistent than meteoric light, or flashes of electricity.   The sound which is heard fills the house, and the flames rest for some time on the heads of the disciples.

The verse here referred to describes a great miracle, and its simplicity of statement marks it as the record of one who felt that no additional words could make the matter other than one which passed the human understanding.

And they were all filled with the Holy Ghost, and they began to speak with divers tongues as the Holy Ghost gave them to speak. St. Chrysostom supposes that these *all* are the hundred and twenty, and not only the twelve Apostles.

(c)   Cornelius a Lapide extends the gifts of the Holy Ghost, then bestowed to the hundred and twenty there assembled, and especially to our Blessed Lady.   This would not make them all Apostles or priests, for it was not then, but before, that the Apostles were ordained priests, and consecrated bishops ; and even by admitting that all who were present did then receive the gifts of the Holy Ghost, no argument could be drawn therefrom contrary to the Apostolic succession, or the position assigned by our Lord to His twelve Apostles. The Spirit at Pentecost was not given as the power of *order,* or of jurisdiction, or of office, but by the diffusion of the gifts of the Holy Ghost, especially those gifts known as the graces *gratis datae,* which are bestowed primarily for the good of others, and the propagation and confirmation of the faith. These gifts are enumerated by St. Paul in his first epistle to the Corinthians.* However this may be, it seems that it was the Apostles only who spoke in divers tongues, as the people, when they heard the several languages spoken, exclaimed: *Are not all these who speak Galileans ?*

(d). This gift was a power given to them for spreading the Gospel. The Lord had said to the twelve: *Go ye and teach all nations. Go ye into the world, and preach the Gospel to every creature.* " How were they, ignorant Galileans, the most of them we must suppose in mature life, to learn the languages of the nations? We cannot suppose that such a commission, couched in such general terms, really meant nothing but : 'Go ye to those who speak Syriac and to those who speak Greek,' but unless a miracle was performed it would amount to this. In all probability they only knew sufficient Greek for the purposes of trade or necessary intercourse upon matters which strangers would have in common. But for such a miracle they would have been utterly unable to speak an intelligible word respecting salvation, or grace, or resurrection, or eternal life, to any poor uneducated Arab or Egyptian, or Mesopotamian or Persian ; *i.e.*, to any man of the bordering nations.

" Unless there had been some such miracle, sceptics might have, with good reason, drawn attention to the extraordinary anomaly that persons totally without linguistic training or leisure for it, were sent to all nations, as if they knew all languages."-

Thus was fulfilled the promise of our Lord, to send the Para clete or the Comforter.

I here subjoin Dr. Lingard's Notes on this Mystery.

7. *" The Comforter. I will ask the Father, and He will give to you another comforter, that He may abide with you for ever, the spirit of truth.*‡ Now the Apostles were not to remain in the world for ever, but only for a few years. Hence we infer that this promise of the Spirit of truth was made not to them only, but also to those *who should believe in Him through their word* :§ that is, the Church unto the end of time in conformity with the

---

* Ch. xii. † Acts of Apostles. By M. F. Sadler, *in loco.*
‡ St. John xiv. 16. § St. John xvii. 20.

prediction of the prophet Isaias : *My spirit that is in thee, and My words that I have put into thy mouth, shall not depart out of thy mouth, nor out of the mouth of thy seed, nor out of the mouth of thy seed's seed, saith the Lord, from henceforth and for ever.*[*]

"*Tongues of fire.* The Holy Ghost descended on our Saviour in the form of a dove, a fit emblem of that peace, that reconciliation between God and man which Christ was about to accomplish by His death. The same Holy Spirit descended on the disciples in the visible form of fire, an emblem of that supernatural change which He was about to work in their hearts by the purification of their feelings and aspirations from the dross and feculence of sensual notions and affections. *I am come*, said our Lord, *to send fire upon the earth, and what do I will but that it be kindled.*[†] *He*, says the Baptist, *shall baptize you with the Holy Ghost and with fire.*

"The chief work attributed to the Holy Ghost is the foundation of the Church.

"*Foundation.* It was on the feast of Pentecost, immediately after the descend of the Holy Ghost, that the Christian faith was for the first time announced to the world. The Apostles, as long as our Saviour remained upon earth, seem to have been incapable of understanding His doctrine : *I have yet*, He said, *many things to say unto you, but ye cannot bear them now. Howbeit, when He, the Spirit of truth is come, He shall teach you all truth.*[‡] At the appointed time that Spirit came ; the minds of the Apostles were instantly opened to the knowledge of the truth, and from that moment they acted as the authorized and infallible teachers of religious doctrine. *They were all filled with the Holy Ghost, and began to speak with divers tongues, according as the Holy Ghost gave them to speak.*

"Then Peter, *being filled with the Holy Ghost*, spoke to the people ; and the men who, during three years, had closed their ears to the discourses, their eyes to the miracles of Jesus, were now *pricked in their hearts, and said unto Peter and the rest of the Apostles : Men and brethren, what shall we do ? And the same day there were added unto them about three thousand souls.*[§]

Thus by the Holy Spirit, through the ministry of the Apostles, was laid the foundation of the Christian Church, first in Jerusalem, and afterwards in the different countries which they visited : *And the wall of that city had twelve foundations, and in them the twelve names of the twelve Apostles of the Lamb*[°]

---

* Isa. lix 21.   † St. Luke xii. 40.   ‡ St. John xvi. 12.
§ Acts ii. 37-41.   ° Apoc. xxi. 14.

"*The preservation of the Church.* This follows from the promise of our Saviour already noticed. For if the Spirit of truth is to be with the Church for ever, the consequence of His presence must be to preserve it from doctrinal error."

THE MISSION OF THE HOLY GHOST IN THE CHURCH.

8. Before the coming of Christ, the Holy Ghost spoke by the prophets, and inspired the sacred writings. From the commencement of the world He was the life of the society of the children of God. On the day of Pentecost He became the living principle which animates and directs the Church which Christ came to found. He was with that Church in the beginning by *revelation*, or the manifestation of things unknown or future ; by *inspiration*, moving the Sacred writers to write, and telling them what to write, and saving them from error in the act of writing ; and all along He remains with her by His special *assistance*, by which she is infallible in her teaching in all matters of faith and morals. And He remains with her for ever, according to the promise of our Saviour, to keep her invincible in the midst of her enemies, and fruitful in good works and in saints.

The Holy Ghost also works in the life of each particular soul as in the life of the Christian Community. Hence He is called the *Spirit that vivifies.* He lives in the souls of the just, and vivifies by His grace.

With sanctifying grace the Holy Ghost communicates His gifts so that souls may more easily, and more perfectly, act according to His movements and inspirations.

9. The gifts of the Holy Ghost are seven : *Wisdom, Understanding, Counsel, Fortitude, Knowledge, Piety,* and *the Fear of the Lord* according to the words of the Prophet Isaias. *The spirit of wisdom and understanding, the spirit of counsel and fortitude, the spirit of knowledge and of Godliness. And he shall be filled with the spirit of the fear of the Lord.*[*]

Wisdom. To choose the one thing needful ; that is to love the things of God, such as prayer, the Word of the Lord, and the Sacraments.

Understanding. To know how to attain the one thing needful. It is a gift which manifests to us, with clearness, the secret mysteries of religion, as far as our souls are capable of receiving it.

Counsel. The habit of seeking guidance from God. It is also

---

* Isa. xi. 23.

a gift which makes us know what we should do, or avoid, especially in cases of doubt and difficulty.

Fortitude. Which means strength to follow where He, the Spirit, shall lead us. It is a gift which enables us to gain the victory over ourselves, the devil, and the world, and to triumph over all evil.

Knowledge. That we may learn to know God: this gift teaches us to judge rightly of all things, and delivers us from illusions and prejudices dangerous to our salvation.

Piety. That knowing God we may become like Him. It is a gift that makes us love God with a filial affection, and inspires us with sentiments of affection towards those who are near to God, His Angels, and Saints, and the poor, who are specially dear to God.

The fear of the Lord; meaning reverence and adoration. This is a gift that inspires a horror for sin, because it offends God, and renders us amenable to the punishment of divine justice. The beginning of wisdom is the fear of the Lord.

These seven gifts of the Holy Spirit are symbolized by the seven lamps of the golden candlesticks, seen by Zacharias.* And the seven lamps of fire, burning before the throne (which are the seven spirits of God) seen by St. John.†

10. The seven gifts produce in the souls of the just twelve principle fruits, which St. Paul enumerates as the fruits of the Holy Spirit; namely, *Charity, Joy, Peace, Patience, Benignity, Goodness, Longanimity, Faith, Mildness, Modesty, Continency and Chastity.*‡ These precious fruits are virtues and graces which the Divine Spirit causes to spring up in our hearts.

"Longanimity means long-suffering for Christ's sake, or a disposition to endure long under trials and difficulties. Benignity means the goodness of heart which disposes us to relieve the wants of others, and to bear with, and compassionate their weaknesses ; and continency means the restraint which a person imposes upon his desires and passions. According to St. Anselm, *continency* is in struggling—in *combat, chastity* in peace . . . continency is chastity militant, and exercised by temptation."§

Besides these seven interior gifts, common to the souls of the just, there are seven other gifts of the Holy Spirit, which are called *gratis datae—gratuitously given.* These are only communicated to a small number of persons, in exceptional cases, and for the sanctification of others.

---

* Zac. iv. 2.   † Apoc. iv. 5.   ‡ Gal. v. 22, 23.
§ Companion to the Catechism.

11. These are the gifts of *Prophecy, of Miracles, of Healing, of Banishing Devils, the gift of Tongues, and of Tears,* according to the words of St. Paul: *And the manifestation of the Spirit is given to every man unto profit. To one indeed, by the Spirit, is given the word of wisdom; and to another the word of knowledge according to the same Spirit; to another faith, in the same Spirit; to another the grace of healing in one Spirit; to another the working of miracles; to another prophecy; to another the discerning of spirits; to another diverse kinds of tongues; to another the interpretation of speeches. But all these things one and the same Spirit worketh, dividing to every one according as He will.* *

---

* 1 Cor. xii. 7, *et seq.*

ARTICLE IX.

APOSTLES' CREED.	NICENE CREED.
" The Holy Catholic Church, the Communion of Saints."	" And (I believe) One, Holy, Catholic and Apostolic Church."

CHAPTER I.

SECTION 1. (ARTICLE IX.)

THE INSTITUTION OR ESTABLISHMENT OF THE CHURCH.

1. The meaning of the word Church : and what is included in its general meaning.—2. The Church *militant* defined.—3. The institution of the Church and its first Apostles, with St. Peter at their head.—4. The Church to last for all time.—5. The Church *teaching* (*docens*) and the Church *believing* (*credens* or *discens*).—6. Christ instituted or founded the Church.—7. The Church compared to a human being with body and soul.—8. The Church considered as to its soul.—Who are in the soul of the Church ?—9. The Church considered as to its body, and who are they that belong to the body of the Church. The question as to (a) Occult heretics ; (b) Infants and those not baptized ; (c) Catechumens ; (d) Apostates ; (e) The children of heretics ; (f) Those excommunicated.—10. The Church a necessary society.—11. The meaning of the proposition : "Out of the Church there is no salvation," and its truth.—12. The distinction between fundamental and non-fundamental Articles of Faith cannot be admitted in the Protestant sense.

1. OUR Lord Jesus Christ has founded on earth a universal Society which is called His Church. The Greek word Εκκλησία, used by the Apostles, signified a *calling forth* in its origin, and by usage came to signify a congregation of men or a company assembled. Our English word *Church* is derived from the Greek Κυριος = Lord, Οἰκια = house. The Lord's house, and may be applied to the building or the congregation. The meaning of the word is that given in the Catechism : namely, "the union of the faithful under one head."

According to this definition it embraces the saints in heaven, the souls in purgatory, and the faithful upon earth ; and on this account, and according to this general acceptation of the word, we have the Church in its threefold states, *i.e.*, *Triumphant* in heaven, *Suffering* in purgatory, and *Militant* upon earth.

It is of the Church in this last state or condition that we now treat : that is the Church of the faithful on earth.

2. This Church may be defined : " The congregation of all the faithful, who, being baptized, profess the same faith, partake of the same sacraments, and are governed by their lawful pastors, under one visible head on earth."* Or, in fewer words, the true Church is " the congregation of the faithful who profess the true faith and acknowledge the authority of the Pope."

3. Christ founded or instituted the Church. Before leaving this world He appointed over His flock visible heads, who should be their doctors, their pontiffs, and their legislators. Their *doctors* to teach and instruct them ; their *pontiffs* as intermediaries between them and God, through whom, as instruments, the sacraments were to be administered, and the life of grace communicated ; *legislators*, to direct them by laws to their eternal destiny.

The first chiefs or heads of the Church were the Apostles. Jesus Christ gave them power to teach as doctors : *Go, teach all nations, that they may learn and guard all that I have commanded.* He gave them the power to sanctify souls as pontiffs : *Baptize all nations ; whose sins you shall forgive they are forgiven.* He gave them the power to make laws as legislators : *Whatsoever you shall bind upon earth shall be bound also in heaven.* To bind here must be understood to oblige by a law to do or to omit something.

To the end that He might give to His Church the unity of monarchy, Jesus Christ placed at the head of the Apostles one of themselves, Simon, son of Jona, and to him He gave the new name of Peter. He made him the visible head of the whole Church, and conferred on him the supreme power to teach and to govern.

This is the import of the words addressed by our Lord to St. Peter. *Thou art Peter, and upon this rock I will build my Church : To thee will I give the keys of the kingdom of heaven ; whatsoever thou shalt bind upon earth, shall be bound also in heaven ; and whatsoever thou shalt loose upon earth, shall be loosed also in heaven ; confirm thy brethren* (in the truth). *Feed my lambs, feed my sheep* (that is to say the faithful and their pastors).

4 As the Church of Jesus Christ was instituted to subsist for all time, the doctrinal and legislative power conferred on St. Peter and the Apostles was not to die or expire with them, because

---

* Maynooth Catechism.

8

it was not for them but for the Church that Christ instituted it. It must therefore reside in their successors.

Now the successors of St. Peter are the Roman Pontiffs, and the successors of the Apostles are the bishops appointed by the Supreme Head of the Church, over different provinces or dioceses. The successor of St. Peter, namely the Roman Pontiff, or the Pope, possesses ecclesiastical authority, principally and absolutely; and the bishops, the successors of the Apostles, possess it in conjunction with, and dependance on the Pope.

5. The Church, as embracing the Roman Pontiff, and the bishops, represents ecclesiastical authority, or the Church teaching; but it embraces also the simple priests and the body of the faithful, that is the Christian society which is subject to the bishops, and above all, to the Pope, who is the vicar of Christ on earth.

Hence we have the distinction between the Church *teaching* (docens) and the Church (discens or credens), *learning* or *believing*. The former is constituted by the Pastors, with the Roman Pontiff at their head; the latter is made up of all the faithful who live under the authority of their lawful Pastors.

6. Christ instituted, or founded, a Church of the kind here defined and explained. This proposition may be proved from the Scripture as shown in the following texts:

*Thou art Peter, and upon this rock I will build my Church, and the gates of hell shall not prevail against it.** And the same Evangelist, St. Matthew, speaking of fraternal correction, says: *And if he* (thy brother) *will not hear them, tell the Church. And if he will not hear the Church, let him be to thee as the heathen and the publican.*†

The same is proved from the words of St. John's Gospel, where Christ speaks of Himself as the Good Shepherd, and expresses His will that there may be *one fold and one shepherd.*‡

It is also proved by tradition; for in all the Creeds of faith we have the words: *I believe in the Holy Catholic Church*; and the very existence in every age of that Church, which takes its name from Christ, is a proof of its divine origin.

It is also clear to reason that a Church was required for the preservation of the Christian religion, and the salvation of the faithful. He who wishes the end must wish the means necessary for obtaining that end. Christ certainly wished that His, the Christian religion, should always be preserved, or last in the world,

---

* St. Matt. xvi. 18.   † St. Matt. xviii. 17.   ‡ St. John x. 16.

and that the faithful should have the means of salvation. And the end for which He founded the Church was for the conservation of the Christian religion, and the salvation of men.

What kind of Church did Christ institute?

7. Christ instituted His Church after the model of a human individual, as He wished it to be a society, and as it were, a moral person. And as a human being is made up of body and soul, so the Church is made up of *body* and *soul*.

This division of the Church into *body* and *soul* is very ancient, most useful and necessary, in order to discern who belong to the Church, and of those who belong to her, to know whether they are in the *body* only, or in the *soul* of the Church.

THE CHURCH CONSIDERED AS TO ITS SOUL.

8. Sanctifying grace, faith, hope, and charity, with the gifts annexed to them, are those things which constitute, or place us, in *the soul* of the Church.

The Church, considered as to its *soul*, may be defined : "the society of those who are called to the faith of Christ, and who are united to Christ by supernatural gifts and graces." According to this, strictly speaking, all and only the just belong to the soul of the Church, those, namely, who are endowed with sanctifying grace. Since, however, faith is the foundation of all justification, sinners who retain faith may be said to belong in a certain sense, and in an imperfect way, to the *soul* of the Church. Inasmuch as they still retain faith and hope, they have in their souls the seeds of the supernatural life, by which, through God's assistance, they recover the grace and charity which they have lost.

From this it follows :—(*a*) That not all the elect, or predestined, are actually in the soul of the Church ; for it may be that many of the elect are at the present moment without grace, and even without the gift of faith, as was St. Paul before his conversion. (*b*) That not all who are in the soul of the Church are elect or predestined, because many of those who are now just may become sinners ; and many who are now heretics and sinners, were once faithful and just. (*c*) That those belong to the soul of the Church, who, although outside her body, are nevertheless adorned with those graces by which they are made just and acceptable in the sight of God : as for example, Catechumens who are inflamed by the charity of God ; also material heretics and schismatics, who are in invincible ignorance, and who are otherwise obedient to the law of God, and possess their souls in grace and charity.

THE CHURCH AS TO THE BODY.

9. The Church, as to its body, is the society of those who profess the true faith of Christ ; whether they be just or sinners. The true Church of Christ, as to its *body* therefore, may be defined : " The society of the baptized united in the profession of the same Christian faith, in the participation of the same Sacraments, under the one head Jesus Christ, and His vicar upon earth."

(a)   All and only those belong to the body of the Church who are admitted into it by Baptism, and who have not been separated from it by heresy or schism or excommunication : all those, and only those, are to be considered members of the Church's body, who are not infidels, (that is, unbaptized), catechumens, public heretics, schismatics or excommunicated.

(b)   The question as to whether occult heretics may be said to belong to the body of the Church is disputed among Theologians.

Heretics are those who fall away from the faith by denying some Catholic dogma, and pertinaciously adhere to a perverse opinion. They are either *public* or *occult*, *external*, or *internal* only. Schismatics are those who separate themselves from Catholic Unity and obedience to the Holy See.

The question in dispute concerns occult heretics and not merely internal heretics : Some deny that these belong to the body of the Church. (1) Because the Church is the society or congregation of the faithful, and occult heretics cannot be said to be amongst the faithful. (2) The Church is a body having not only external union but internal union of its members amongst themselves and with the head ; but occult heretics cannot be said to have any internal union either amongst themselves or with the head of the Church, which is Christ Jesus ; for faith is the first bond of union, and the foundation of all *external* as well as *internal* union.

To make this matter clearer, let it be understood that by the Church, as to its body, is meant a society of Christian men who are united by the profession of the same faith, and the participation of the same Sacraments under legitimate Pastors, whose Primate in honour and jurisdiction is the Roman Pontiff. The body or visible part of the Church is made up of these. Hence it follows—(1) That infidels, or non-baptized persons, are not in, or do not belong to, the body of the Church, because they have not the character of Baptism, that Sacrament which is called by the Council of Trent—the *Janua Eccleciae*, or *door of the Church.* *

(c). Catechumens do not belong to the body of the Church, but they may be said to belong to the soul, inasmuch as they have the desire of Baptism—*Baptismus in voto*, and at the same time possess the Theological virtues of faith, hope and charity.

(d). Apostates, whether heretics or schismatics, when they are *public*, are certainly cut off, or cut themselves off, from the body of the Church. When they are *occult*, then the question is the same as occult heretics, disputed ; although many grave authors hold that they do not belong to the body of the Church for the reasons given above, many others hold that they do ; and that occult heretics not only internal, but also external, are members of the Church, although dead members. Others again, whilst admitting that internal heretics are members of the body of the Church, deny it of all external heretics. We may say in conclusion, and in reconciliation of all the various opinions—(1) It is certain that occult heretics do not belong to the soul of the Church, for they have lost their faith. (2) They do not belong to the body of the Church in the same way as the faithful, even though they be sinners : and in regard to those occult heretics who are regarded by all as faithful Catholics, we can say that they belong to the Church by *external appearance only*.

(e). The children of heretics, that is of parents who belong to an heretical sect, are members of the Church if they are validly baptized, and they remain such, at least until they come to the use of reason, but after they reach the age in which they become capable of the sin of heresy and schism, and if they remain in invincible ignorance, and are only material heretics or schismatics, it is doubtful whether they have to be considered members of the Church or not.

(f). As to the question of those who are excommunicated, it is not certain whether they are entirely cut off from

* Trid. Sess. 14. c. 2.

the Church so as not to be numbered as her members. It is certain that the Church has the power of expelling from her communion not only heretics and schismatics, but also other great sinners, but whether it is her intention to cut off entirely those who are excommunicated is doubtful.

It is more probable that the excommunicated, who are what are called *tolerated*, and *not to be avoided*, remain members of the Church. In the case of the *non-tolerated*, and those to be avoided, the words, or terms, in which the sentence of excommunication is inflicted, have to be examined, and the case has to be judged according to the sentence, whether it be or be not a total separation of communion with the body of the Church.

We have now a second proposition as to the constitution or foundation of the Church to explain, namely :—

10. Christ instituted His Church as a necessary Society. This means that all are bound to belong to the Church and to enter her fold.

This is proved clearly from the following texts of Holy Scripture :—

(a) In St. Matthew and St. Luke the kingdom of heaven, that is the Church, is compared to a King who made a marriage feast for his son ; and when those who were invited were unwilling to come, the master of the house, being angry, said that *none of those men that were invited shall taste of my supper.*[*]

(b) *And he said to them* (the Apostles) *go ye into the whole world, and preach the Gospel to every creature. He that believeth and is baptized shall be saved*; *but he that believeth not shall be condemned.*[†]

(c) *And if he will not hear the Church, let him be to thee as the heathen and the publican.*[‡]

The reason of all this is that the Church is one with Christ. She is His spouse, His mystical body as St. Paul tells us. It is through her that He is always visible, always speaking, and always acting in the world. It is through her that He continues to instruct men, that He causes them to live a life of grace, and leads them to their eternal happiness. He has founded her, that through her He may apply to mankind the fruits of His Redemption to the end of time.

11. Hence it follows that the following proposition is true.

---

* St. Matt. xxii. St. Luke xiv.   † St. Mark xvi. 15.   ‡ St. Matt. xviii. 17.

Out of the Church there is no salvation. "No one," says St. Augustine, "can be saved who has not Christ for his head, and no one can have Christ for his head who does not belong to His body, which is the Church."

The sense of the proposition is that no one who *through his own fault* dies out of the Church will obtain salvation. The words *through his own fault* must be here inserted, because no adult, especially of those who have received baptism, will be deprived of salvation except through his own fault. Who will deny the proposition as thus understood? It says no more than this: those who die in mortal sin will not obtain salvation; for those who through their own fault die out of the Church, die in a state of mortal sin, and those who die in that state will certainly eternally perish.

The inspired writings exclude from salvation those who refuse to receive the true Christian doctrine, and to enter the Church. It is in this sense St. Paul speaks when he says: *And though we, or an angel from heaven, preach a Gospel to you, besides that which we have preached to you, let him be anathema. If anyone preach to you a Gospel besides that which you have received, let him be anathema.*[*] And again in his epistle to Titus he says: *A man that is a heretic after the first and second admonition, avoid. Knowing that he, that is such a one, is subverted, and sinneth, being condemned by his own judgment.*[†]

It is clear also from the 10th chapter of the Gospel of St. John, where our Saviour speaks of himself as the Good Shepherd, that the fold which He rules and directs is one in the sense that all the sheep or pastors who belong to it hear His voice, follow it and fly from the voice of the hireling; and those who hear not the Church, hear not the voice of its Chief Pastor, neither do they follow it and turn away from the voice of the hireling. He says: *I am the good Shepherd; and I know mine and mine know me, ... And other sheep I have that are not of this fold; these also I must bring, and they shall hear my voice, and there shall be one fold and one shepherd.*[‡]

Let no one regard this as a hard and intolerant doctrine. God wishes the salvation of all men. The ordinary means which He has established for their salvation is the Church. He commands them to hear the Church, which is the chief work of His power, His wisdom, and His love, for mankind. It is therefore just that those who voluntarily, and through their own fault,

---

[*] Gal. i. 9.   [†] 1 Titus iii. 10, 11.   [‡] St. John x. 14, 16.

refuse to hear the Church, should be excluded from the inheritance of the children of God.

12. In connection with this doctrine we have to bear in mind that the distinction between *fundamental* and *non-fundamental* Articles of faith cannot be admitted in the Protestant sense. According to that teaching it would follow that there are many dogmas of religious doctrine revealed or inspired by God, which can be denied without danger to salvation; and there are others so necessary that no one is allowed to be ignorant of them, much less to reject them without risking his eternal salvation.

It is however repugnant to religion, and insulting to the divine authority, to admit such a distinction between the Articles of faith which belong to the same divine revelation or inspiration. Hence the doctors of the Church teach that any one who denies one Article of faith cannot have divine faith in any of the others; because when the formal object or motive of faith ceases, faith itself vanishes. And he who denies one Article of faith loses the formal object or motive of faith, which is the authority of God and His veracity. If he disbelieves that authority in one, he cannot retain it as the sole motive of his faith in other dogmas; for the one he denies, as well as those he holds, rests on the same authority; namely, that it is inspired by God, and proposed by the Church as His revealed word. If the formal object or motive of faith ceases, the faith itself ceases, as no virtue can be without its formal object.

In regard to this distinction of Articles *fundamental* and *non-fundamental* in the sense of Protestants it may be added :— (a) That such a system can nowhere be found, and has no authority in the Sacred Scriptures, which Protestants regard as the one and only rule of faith. (b) They do not agree, and they will never be able to agree amongst themselves as to which Articles are *fundamental*, and which are not.

SECTION 2. (ARTICLE IX.)

THE VISIBILITY OF THE CHURCH AND HER PERPETUITY.

1 Visibility in itself, and as applied to a *society* in its *material* and *formal* sense. —2. What we are to understand by the visibility of the Church. —3. The visibility of the Church proved from Scripture. — 4. Protestant theories in regard to the visibility of the Church. — 5. The Church's perpetuity : its meaning and truth.

THERE are two properties that belong essentially to the Church, and follow from her very constitution, that it may be well to refer to before treating of the Notes of the Church : that is, the *visibility* and the *perpetuity* of the Church.

VISIBILITY MAY BE EITHER MATERIAL OR FORMAL.

1. *Material visibility* is that which we see in a thing, when we attend only to its corporeal aspect. In this sense a man, as to his body, is visible.

Formal visibility is when the external signs, or that which is seen by the eye, conveys to the mind the invisible or interior qualities of a thing. Thus man regarded as a rational animal is an example of what is meant by *formal visibility*.

A Society is said to be visible in a material sense, when it is made up of men assembled together in a congregation, without attending to the object or ends that binds them together in one body. They may be either Theologians, or Philosophers, or Mathematicians, or members of any other body, but the material visibility does not tell us what they are, but simply regards them as men gathered together. The *formal visibility* of a society is that by which we regard it, not merely as an assembly of men, but an assembly of men united together for some specific object; thus we have a military society, lawyers' society, clerical society, &c.

2. When we speak of the visibility of the Church, we have to understand that it is not only visible in the *material* sense, that is, a society of men who are visible to their fellow-creatures, but in a *formal* sense, that is. that she can be seen as the society

of the faithful, and that she manifests conspicuously the characters of her divinity.

The question therefore to which we have to attend regards not only the *material* visibility of the Church, but the *formal* visibility, that is, her visibility as the true Church of Christ.

The Church is visible in this two-fold sense. Her material visibility is self-evident, because she is composed of men here on earth. Speaking of her formal visibility we say, a society, that it may be *visible*, should manifest or show such signs or properties as that it may be known to be that particular and individual society, and distinct from all others : *ex. gr.*: The societies of doctors, of soldiers, of lawyers, are not formally visible unless they show distinct and visible signs, as do the armies of different countries, of France, Spain, and England for example.   Thus in the matter of the Church ; if one Church should manifest itself to the world by such signs that she may be discerned, not only as some Christian Church, but as a singular and individual Church, absolutely distinct from all others, then it is understood as this individual and particular Church which all can know and see if they wish.   If there be any notes or marks which prove the Church to which they belong to be not only some Christian Church, but the one true Church of Christ, then such a Church is *formally* visible, inasmuch as she can be discerned from all others as the one true, Christian Church.

3.   That the Church is visible in this sense may be proved from the following texts of Holy Scripture.

(a)   Our Saviour, in His sermon on the Mount, speaking to His Apostles, said : *You are the light of the world. A city seated on a mountain cannot be hid.* *   Therefore that Church which He was to found was not to be less conspicuous than a city on the top of a mountain, and therefore no less visible.

(b)   Christ teaching that incorrigible sinners should be denounced to the Church, says : *But if thy brother shall offend against thee, go, and rebuke him between thee and him alone . . . . . and if he will not hear them, tell the Church. And if he will not hear the Church, let him be to thee as the heathen and the publican.†* That tribunal should be visible before which delinquents are to be accused, and which is to pronounce a definite sentence upon their conduct.

---

* St. Matt. v. 14.   † St. Matt. xviii. 15. *et seq.*

(c) St. Paul, in his first epistle to the Corinthians, writes : *For I think that God hath set forth us Apostles ; the last, as it were, men appointed to death ; we are made a spectacle to the world, and to Angels, and to men.*[*]

We must therefore confess that Church as visible of which the Son of God said : *tell the Church,* and the Apostles wrote : *we are made a spectacle, &c.* How could that be called a spectacle which cannot be seen? That opinion, therefore, which would deny the visibility of the Church contradicts not only the Scripture, but denies all the testimony of antiquity, destroys all judgment, and would only introduce unceasing anarchy and confusion.

From the above doctrine and arguments we may conclude how false and erroneous are all the Protestant theories concerning the visibility of the Church.

4. These theories may be reduced to the following three :—

(a) The opinion of those who affirm that the Church is entirely and essentially invisible.

(b) The opinion of those who pretend that there is a double Church, one visible and the other invisible.

(c) The opinion of some others, who admit that the Church, by its divine ordination was visible, but not so essentially and indefectibly as to prevent it, in course of time, from becoming obscure, and finally so obscure as to be almost invisible.

5. To the visibility may be united the perpetuity of the Church. On this point I shall only say a few words here, as I shall have to advert to it again when treating of the indefectibility of the Church.

The visible Church of Christ is perpetual, or to last till the end of time. This may be proved in the first place from the Apostles' Creed, which Christians will continue to say to the end of the world. *I believe in the Holy Catholic Church.* This profession of faith will never be false, and a time will never come when men can cease to believe in it.

It is of the Church of Christ the prophet Isaias speaks when he says : *And in the last days the mountain of the house of the Lord shall be prepared on the top of the mountains, and it shall be exalted above the hills, and all nations shall flow into it.*[†] St. Jerome understands these words of the Church of Christ.

The perpetuity of the Church may be proved also from the promises which Christ made to her. *Behold I am with you all*

---

[*] 1 Cor. iv. 9.   [†] Isa. ii. 2.

days, even to the consummation of the world. Where one or two are gathered together in My name, there am I in their midst. And from the commission given to the Apostles : *Go and teach all nations.*

It follows also from the fact that the Church is founded as a necessary society, out of which there is no salvation, in the sense above explained.

SECTION III. (ARTICLE IX.).

THE NOTES OR MARKS OF THE TRUE CHURCH.

1. The meaning of a Note or Mark of the Church, and its conditions.—2. The true Church of Christ must have some Notes or Marks.—3. The four Notes of the Church—*Unity, Sanctity, Catholicity*, and *Apostolicity*, —4. These four have the conditions required for a true Note of the Church—5. Unity, a true Note of the Church, and the reasons why the Church must be *one*, and the sense in which she is *one*.—6. Sanctity, a true Note of the Church, and the sense in which the Church is holy.—7. Catholicity as a Note of the Church (*a*) as to place, (*b*) as to time, (*c*) as to doctrine.—8. Apostolicity as a Note of the Church.—9. These four Notes flow from the original constitution of the Church, and each has the characters of a true and distinctive sign.—10. *Positive and Negative Notes*—their meaning.—11. The manner in which the Notes of the Church are applied as *negative* and *positive*.—12. Neither the *preaching of the pure Word of God*, or the *administration of the Sacraments*, can be called a Note of the Church.

1. A NOTE, or Mark, of the Church, may be defined as an external manifestation of an invisible property, divinely implanted in the Church. A note in general of anything is that which can lead us to the knowledge of that thing.

That something may be regarded as a Note of the Church, two conditions are required.

(*a*) It ought to adhere in such a way to the Church that it cannot be taken from it; or that she cannot lose it, that is, it should belong to her very nature and constitution, and be planted in her by Christ.

(*b*) It should possess all the qualities of a true sign. As to the first condition ; namely, it should belong to the original and essential constitution of the Church, and flow from her very nature ; because it should designate the true Church, and if it is other than a property fow ng from, and essentially belonging to the very natu e of the Church, it would not point to the true Chu ch but to some other. It would be just as apt to point to a false Church as to the true. Hence this condition is absolutely required for a Note of the Church.

As to the second condition; namely, a Note should have all the qualities of a *distinctive sign*. A sign is that which leads us to the knowledge of something else, as in the Sacraments. And the reason why a Note of the Church should have all the qualities of a distinctive sign is, because notes which have not these qualities, or characters, are common, and if common they cannot distinguish one society from another; therefore the Notes of the Church, because they are to distinguish the true Church from all others, should possess the qualities, or characters, of a distinctive sign.

The Notes of the Church must therefore be (*a*) more known than the thing signified. (*b*) They must be proper to that thing, and not common to others; (*c*) they must be obvious.

2. The true Church of Christ must have some Notes by which she can be distinguished, and known as distinct, from all false sects, and by which, as a society, she may be made clearly visible to all. All are obliged to believe the Church, and to belong to her under penalty of perdition; and unless the Church should possess such Notes by which she may be known from all false sects, men could not find her out, or believe in her, or enter her fold. Hence she must possess Notes or Marks. As in natural things the essences are not known by themselves immediately, but by certain external properties which are essential to them, and distinguish them from other things; in like manner in supernatural things, such as is the true Church, their essences are not seen or known immediately; but through certain external properties that make them known to us. Therefore it is necessary that the Church should have Notes of this kind.

3. Four Notes of the Church are enumerated in the Nicene Creed, namely *Unity, Sanctity, Catholicity*, and *Apostolicity*.

Unity consists in this, that all hold the same doctrine, join in the same worship, and live under the same government or authority. Or in the words of the Catechism: "That all her members agree in one Faith, have all the same Sacrifice and Sacraments, and are all united under one Head."

Sanctity considered as a Note involves two things: (*a*) She should have all those means which can produce, conserve, and perfect sanctity in her members. (*b*) She should in every age, and at all times, produce, and show forth, the fruits of sanctity; that is, it is required that she teach a holy doctrine, offer to all the means of holiness, and be distinguished by the eminent holiness of her children.

Catholicity may be considered under the threefold aspect as to *doctrine, place, and time.* (*a*) As to *doctrine*, that she teach all those things which belong to the doctrine of Christ. (*b*) As to *place*, that there be nothing in her which would impede her propagation throughout the world, and that she be widely spread throughout all nations. (*c*) As to *time*, that from her very institution, she never fails, or is interrupted so as to cease even for a short time. *Catholic* or *universal* means that she subsist in all ages, teach all nations, and be the one Ark of salvation for all.

Apostolicity consists in this, (*a*) that she have her origin from the Apostles after Christ, (*b*) that she profess the same doctrine which they professed and taught, (*c*) and that she have the succession of her pastors in an uninterrupted course from the Apostles. That is, that she hold and teach the doctrines and traditions of the Apostles, and through the unbroken succession of her Pastors, that she derive her orders, and her mission, from them.

4. The four Notes here enumerated have all the conditions required for the true Notes of the Church. (*a*) They flow from her original and immutable nature and constitution. (*b*) They have all the qualities of a true and distinctive sign.

5. First, as to the Note of *Unity.* This belongs to the original constitution of the Church, as may be proved by the inspired words of St. Paul. Exhorting the faithful to unity, he says : *Careful to keep the unity of the Spirit in the bond of peace. One body and one Spirit ; as you are called in one hope of your calling. One Lord, one faith, one baptism. One God and Father of all, who is above all, and through all, and in us all.* In this text the Apostle enumerates those things in which the Christian Church is one. The *unity of society, one body ; unity of external worship, one baptism ; internal unity, one Spirit ; one hope of your calling, one faith.* The same Apostle, writing to the Corinthians, says : *For as the body is one, and hath many members ; and all the members of the body, whereas they are many yet are one body, so also is Christ. For in one Spirit were we all baptized into one body, whether Jews or Gentiles, whether bond or free ; and in one Spirit we have all been made to drink.†*

Christ, in speaking of the Church which He intended to found, never refers to it in the plural number, but always in the singular, calling it His flock, His sheep-fold, and one over which the one Pastor presides. His Kingdom—His Church : from which it follows that Christ instituted only one Church, and that His

---

* Eph. iv. 8., *et seq.*   † 1 Cor. xii. 12, 13.

Church can be only one ; therefore unity belongs to the Church's original nature and constitution.

This must also appear from the reason that the Church is the society of those who profess the Christian religion ; but religion is one, and can only be one, therefore that society which professes the true religion must be one.

That the Church is the society of those who profess the Christian religion is certain from its definition. It is certain, also, that Christ brought and taught only one religion to men. All religions that call themselves Christian, although they differ in many points from one another, yet they all propose their doctrine as that delivered by Christ, therefore we must say that the Christian Religion proposes contradictory truths, which we cannot say of divine revelation ; or there is only one of all these bodies professing Christianity, which contains, and teaches the entire, genuine, and pure doctrine of Christ ; therefore that body, or Church, must be one, because the Church is nothing else but faith, and the Christian religion as it lives, and is, as it were, individualised in the faithful believing.

This unity extends itself to doctrine, to faith, to authority, to the whole religion. Religion, as we know, comprises two things, the true knowledge and worship of God as made known to us by divine revelation. The principle upon which unity of faith and communion depends, is that of *authority*, for without authority all men could not be brought to the profession of, or to agreement in, one faith, and those who might be led away by false doctrine could not be recalled to the true faith. The same may be said of unity of communion, for considering the nature and condition of human beings, they could not all be kept in one congregation or society without some centre of authority to which all should be bound to submit.

Without extending our arguments further, we may now sum up the preceding reasons which prove that the Note of Unity flows from the original constitution of the Church.

UNITY.

1st. In the profession of the same doctrine.

2nd. In the communion or participation of the same Sacraments and rites which necessarily belong to the worship of God.

3rd. In unity of body ; or of all the members under one head, the result of one government and authority, by which the people are united to their pastors, and the pastors united with the one Head of the Church, who is the Vicar of Christ on earth.

The Note of Unity is, therefore, inseparable from the Church of Christ. It has all the characters of a true sign, for where it is, it becomes apparent to all. It manifests the Church to the whole world by the profession of the same faith, by the same worship and Sacraments, and the same ecclesiastical rule, or government.

SANCTITY AS A NOTE OF THE CHURCH.

6. The Note of Sanctity flows, or is derived, from the original constitution and nature of the Church. This may be proved from several heads.

(a) Christ, the founder of the Church, is the fountain of Sanctity.

(b) The doctrine of the Church is holy because it is the doctrine of the true religion.

(c) The worship of the Church is holy because it is the true worship of God.

(d) The Sacraments of the Church are holy because they are instituted by Christ, as the means, or channels, of divine grace, by which men are sanctified. The Church is holy in all these things by reason of her divine institution.

This may be shown from the consideration of the end for which the Church was instituted.

The Church, as a perfect society, should have the means of attaining its end; but the end of the Church is the conservation of religion, and the salvation of men; therefore the Church should have all the means that are necessary for the attainment of this two-fold end. But the Church which has not the Note of Sanctity will not have the means of sanctity, or the means that are required for the conservation of religion, and the salvation of men. Therefore the Church of Christ, by its very institution and end, must be holy or have the Note of Sanctity.

The Church must have the means of sanctity, because she is instituted by Christ to procure the salvation of men, and she should therefore produce her effect and make saints, otherwise men could say that she has failed in the end, or purpose, for which God destined her, which would be an impious assertion. For, to what purpose would she have the means of sanctity if these means were not applied; and to what purpose would they be applied if no result were derived from their application? Hence

T

the Church must be holy in the full sense above explained ; that is, that she teach a holy doctrine, that she offer to all the means of holiness, and that she be distinguished by the eminent holiness of her children.

It appears also very clearly from Holy Scripture that the Church should have the Note, or character, of Sanctity.

(a) In the Scripture the Church is called the *body* of Christ, the *spouse* of Christ, the *tabernacle of God with men*, the *house* of God, the *temple* of God.*

(b) Christ wished His Church to produce the fruits of sanctity, and to make men holy. To this end He instituted the Sacrament of Baptism, according to the words : *but you are washed, but you are sanctified, but you are justified in the name of our Lord Jesus Christ, and the Spirit of God.*† The same may be said of the Holy Eucharist. *Let a man prove himself that he may so eat of this bread, and drink of this chalice*, &c. It was for this purpose He gave to His Church the power of forgiving sins through the Sacrament of Penance, and that He instituted the other Sacraments ; and finally, the whole constitution of His Church is ordained for the same end, according to the words of St. Paul : *And he* (Christ) *gave some Apostles and some prophets, and other some evangelists, and other some pastors and doctors, for the perfecting of the saints, for the work of the ministry, for the edifying of the body of Christ.*‡

We may here note that some may be perfect members of the Church, those who belong to her soul and to her body; and that there may be some imperfect members, who may not have the life of grace, but who are externally united among themselves, and with the living members by the profession of the same faith, and that they may receive the same Sacraments ; although these are not to be reckoned as living members of the Church, they may be numbered as in the body of the Church, and belonging to the faithful ; for men may be called faithful and Christians, not from the virtue of charity only, but also from faith, and the profession of faith.

Sanctity is, at the same time, a property and a Note of the Church. As a property it may be viewed in many aspects. The

---

* Colos. i. 24. Ephes. i. 22, 23 ; ii. 19, *et seq.*, *et* Chap. v.
† 1 Cor. vi. 11.   ‡ Eph. iv. 11 12.

Church is holy (a) in its Author, (b) in its essence or constitution, (c) in its end, (d) in its means, (e) in its Head, Jesus Christ, (f) in its members. As a Note, it may be viewed only in its body and members, and is made manifest (a) in the worship and exemplary lives of the saints; and (b) by miracles and other divine manifestations of the Spirit of God that works in her and in her members.

CATHOLICITY AS A NOTE OF THE CHURCH.

7. Catholicity is a true Note of the Church because it has all the conditions that are required for the *notes* as above specified.

Christ wished His Church to be *Catholic* or *Universal*.

(a) *As to place: He said to them* (the Apostles), *Go ye into the whole world and preach the gospel to every creature.*[*]

(b) *As to time or duration: Behold I am with you all days even to the consummation of the world.*[†]

(c) *As to doctrine: Going therefore, teach ye all nations. . . . teaching them to observe all things whatsoever I have commanded you.*[‡]

If the Church did not contain all the doctrine of religion it would be imperfect; and the Church cannot be said to be imperfect, because it has for its Author and Founder Christ our Lord.

The Church was instituted to preserve the Christian religion in its integrity, and how could that be maintained in its integrity, if the Church does not retain and teach all the doctrines that belong to it.

Again we may advert to the doctrine that out of the Church there is no salvation. And as God wishes all men to be saved, and to come to the knowledge of the truth, He thereby wished all men to become members of the Church, and therefore He made that Church Catholic, or Universal, into which He wished all men to enter.

Moreover, the Church was instituted for the preservation of religion; and as Christ wished his religion to be perpetual, or to last to the end of time; so He instituted His Church Catholic as to time and duration, to last to the end of the world. And thus will be verified the words spoken of our Saviour at the time of the Incarnation. *And he shall reign in the house of Jacob for ever:*[§] and thus we may praise His Name in the words of Daniel

---

[*] St. Mark xvi. 15. [†] St. Matthew xxviii. 20. [‡] Ibid. xix. 20. [§] St. Luke i. 32.

the prophet : *Blessed be the name of the Lord from eternity and for evermore ; for wisdom and fortitude are His ;** and to the Church as Catholic the parable of the mustard seed is applied. *The Kingdom of God. . . . . is like a grain of mustard seed, which a man took and cast into his garden, and it grew and became a great tree, and the birds of the air lodged in the branches thereof.*† This Note, with that of Sanctity, is the one mentioned, and which is always professed in the Apostles' Creed : *I believe in the Holy Catholic Church.* Hence St. Ignatius Martyr has said : *Ubi Christus est ibi est Ecclesia Catholica*—Where Christ is there the Catholic Church is.

APOSTOLICITY, A NOTE OF THE CHURCH.

8. Apostolicity of origin, of doctrine, and of succession, necessarily flows from the original nature and constitution of the Church ; for Christ built His Church on the foundation of the Apostles ; to the Apostles He gave immediately the power of teaching, of ministering and of ruling, and from them the true Church of Christ derives its origin, and the lawful order and succession of its pastors.

9. I have shown that all these four Notes must belong to the very nature and constitution of the Church, and flow from her original institution ; it only remains that I point out that these four have the characters or qualities of true and distinctive signs. They are (1st) more known than the thing signified by them ; for they are at once apparent and fall under our eyes. What can be more easily known than the form of public government, the succession of pastors, the extent and duration of a society? And what can be better known than what all the members of a society publicly profess and publicly acknowledge.

(2nd). They are proper or special to that which they signify, for as I have repeatedly said, they belong to the nature and primary constitution of the Church, and there is no other society outside the Church to which they belong.

(3rd). They are obvious ; for they consist in external things, which can either be seen by the eyes, or promulgated to all ; or can be learned without much laborious research from the public acts and monuments of history.

POSITIVE AND NEGATIVE NOTES.

10. Before treating of the application of the Notes of the Church, it will be necessary to introduce another distinction as

---

* Dan. ii. 20.   † St. Luke xiii. 19.

to the Notes of the Church, and to explain it and also to notice the Protestant theory of the Church's Notes. Notes are either *positive* or *negative*.

A positive note is that which directly indicates the thing signified, that is, it tells us that it is such a thing.

A negative note does not tell us that it is such a thing; but that it may be. When we have a negative note, it does not follow from it that a thing is such as is indicated, but where a negative note is absent or wanting, it follows that the thing is not that which we seek; *ex. gr.:* A good life is a *positive* note of a pure heart because the heart of that man is certainly pure whose life is good. On the other hand, external modesty is a *negative* note of a pure heart; it signifies that the heart may be pure but not that it is so: but if external modesty is wanting, it is a sign that the heart is not pure. To discover and distinguish the true Church, *negative* notes are not sufficient, but positive notes are required.

11. All agree in the following three points:—

(1). The four Notes above enumerated are true Notes of the Church, because (a) they are proper to the true Church, and do not belong to any sect or other Christian Society. (b) They are more easily known than the Church itself, as they lead to her knowledge. (c) They are manifest, not only to those who are of the household of faith, but even to those outside her fold.

(2). All the four taken together certainly amount to a *positive note.*

(3). Each one taken separately amounts to a *negative note.*

It may be asked whether each of the four taken separately amounts to a *positive note ?* To which I may answer by the following four statements:

(1). It is certain that *Unity* as it exists in the Catholic Church is a *positive note.*

(2). *Sanctity* as it exists in the Catholic Church is, without doubt, a *positive note.*

(3). *Formal Catholicity,* that is Catholicity considered not only as to pure extension, but as to the extension of men as forming one sacred commonwealth, or one Church throughout the whole world, is a *positive note.*

(4). *Apostolicity,* inasmuch as it points out one Church to be the very Church of the Apostles, continued and unchanged, is a *positive note.*

12. Protestants assign two Notes of the Church, namely, *the preaching of the pure Word of God, and the administration of*

the Sacraments, but neither of these things can be called Notes of the true Church.

The *preaching of the pure Word of God* cannot be a Note of the Church, because you have to find out the Church itself before you can know whether the preaching is that of the pure Word of God or not. The knowledge as to whether the preaching is the pure Word or not must be obtained either from the Scripture, or from private judgment, or from the authority of the Church ; but this knowledge cannot be obtained from the Scripture without the definition of the Church ; nor from each one's private judgment, as is self-evident ; therefore it can only be obtained from the Church ; and therefore, before one can know where the preaching of the true Word is to be found, he must find the Church.

The preaching of the *pure Word* cannot be a Note of the Church, because all sects who propound contradictory doctrines and preach them vigorously, claim for themselves by the same right and title the preaching of the *pure Word* ; therefore such preaching cannot point to the true Church.

The *administration of the Sacraments* is not a Note of the Church—First, because the Sacraments are contained in the pure or genuine Word of God ; and, secondly, because neither the Sacraments themselves nor their administration can be known until we know or find out the true Church.

SECTION 4. (ARTICLE IX).

THE APPLICATION OF THE NOTES TO THE CATHOLIC CHURCH.

1. The Catholic Church is one; (a) in *government*; (b) in *faith*; (c) in *worship.*—2. The Sanctity of the Catholic Church. The meaning of sanctity, its division, its degrees.—3. The Catholic Church is holy (a) in her doctrine; (b) in the means of holiness which she possesses; (c) in the fruits of sanctity within her.—4. Catholicity applied to the Church. The meaning of the word *Roman* Catholic, the signification of the word Catholic, and the various kinds of Catholicity. —5. The sense in which the true Church is Catholic. —6. The Apostolicity of the Catholic Church. (a) She has her origin and doctrine from the Apostles. (b) She has the succession of Pastors uninterrupted from their time.—7. She has the succession (a) of Orders and (b) of Jurisdiction.—8. Summary. (a) The Roman Catholic Church possesses the Note of Unity. (b) She possesses the Note of Sanctity. (c) Of Catholicity, and (d) of Apostolicity.—9. False Churches wanting (a) in Unity; (b) in Sanctity; (c) in Catholicity, and (d) in Apostolicity.

THE UNITY OF THE CATHOLIC CHURCH.

1. THE Catholic Church is one in *government*, in *faith*, and in *worship*.

(a) *One in government.* All Catholics hold the Supremacy of the Roman Pontiff as a dogma of faith; all his commands and laws are received with obedience and reverence by the pastors and the faithful, which shows the Church's Unity under one Supreme Head, and in subjection to his authority.

(b) *One in faith.* All who are in the Church are bound to submit to her definitions; so that any one who would deny a definition of the Church in matters of faith or morals, would thereby cut himself off from her communion; and it has never happened in the history of the Church, that a man who denied even one dogma of faith was regarded by the Church or her members otherwise than as a heretic, and one who had separated himself from the communion of the faithful.

(c) *One in Worship.* All Catholics acknowledge and receive the same Sacraments, and believe in and assist at the one Sacrifice of the Holy Mass.

This Unity in the threefold respect here mentioned is granted even by her adversaries to the Catholic Church, and it is the unity signified by the definition of the IV. Council of Lateran (cap. finiter), "*Una est Fidelium universalis Ecclesia extra quam nullus omnino salvatur.*" *The universal Church is one out of which no one can be saved.*

SANCTITY OF THE CATHOLIC CHURCH.

2. Sanctity in general signifies that something is clean and pure before God, that is pleasing to God.

In a twofold way a thing may be called holy. First, if it be consecrated to God by a certain form of consecration or benediction, as, for example, a chalice, a church, a priest. Secondly, a thing is called holy which of itself, or by reason of its end, conduces to the sanctification of men, such as good works, the Sacraments, &c. Here we speak of sanctity in this second sense.

Personal sanctity consists in immunity or freedom from sin, which in the present state has always and essentially connected with it, sanctifying grace.

There are three grades of this sanctity.

(1). The lowest degree is that sanctity by which a man keeps himself free from mortal sin, but is not solicitous about advancing in perfection, or avoiding venial sins.

(2). The second degree is that in which a man not only avoids grave sins, but endeavours to avoid all venial sins, and tends towards perfection.

(3). The third degree is the heroic sanctity of the saints.

3. The Catholic Church is holy, not only in her Author and Founder, Jesus Christ; not only in her end, but also in her doctrine ; in the *means of sanctity which she possesses ;* and in *the fruits of sanctity which she produces.*

(a) In her *doctrine.* Doctrine is holy, not only inasmuch as it is true, but inasmuch as it leads to sanctification. The doctrine of the Catholic Church is both *speculative* and *practical.* The *speculative* proposes or teaches dogmas, the *practical* delivers precepts. The *speculative doctrine* is holy because it teaches all the truths revealed by God, and which concern God, and the eternal salvation of men. The *practical doctrine* is holy, because the moral precepts taught and inculcated by the Catholic Church are those which God Himself has delivered; and, besides these, she exhorts her children to practice and observe not only the precepts, but also the evangelical counsels.

(*b*) *The means of Sanctity.* The Catholic Church is holy in the means of sanctity which she possesses, and of which her children can avail themselves. These means are proper and special to the Catholic Church, and amongst them I may particularise the following :

(1). All the *Sacraments* of the New Law.

(2). The most efficacious means of sacramental confession, and that frequent.

(3). The mortification of the body, fasts, prayers, and penances.

The Catholic Church continually exhorts her children to the practices of virtues, especially the virtues of humility and chastity.

(4) The sanctity of the people depends in great measure on the goodness of the Clergy, according to the words of the Prophet : *And I will give you pastors according to My own heart, and they shall feed you with knowledge and doctrine.** The clergy and priests of the Catholic Church show their goodness amongst other things, especially in this one respect, that in all kinds of dangers, of persecutions and of maladies, they have never forsaken or neglected their people.

(*c*). *The fruit of sanctity* in the Catholic Church. It may be said (1) that the greater part of the Church may claim sanctity in its first and lowest degree; for it may be fairly supposed that most Catholics keep their souls free from grievous sins ; and those who fail to possess this first grade of sanctity have only to blame their own malice and negligence, and not the Church, which offers them so many means of sanctity, if only they will accept and use them. (2) Many in the Catholic Church are holy in the second degree ; all those, namely, who desire perfection and tend towards it. and who have consecrated their lives to the service of God, especially in Convents and Monasteries and Religious Houses, throughout the

---

* Jer. iii. 15.

whole world, and in every age of the Church. (3) In the histories and lives of the saints we have the examples of innumerable men and women who practised virtue and possessed sanctity in an heroic degree. These saints were members of the Catholic Church, and examples of this kind make her illustrious not only in every age, but in every generation, and in every year, in the lives and virtues of her children. Miracles are also the fruits of sanctity, and these are always to be found in the Catholic Church and in her alone.

THE CATHOLICITY OF THE CHURCH.

4. It may be asked, what is the meaning of the word *Roman Catholic* ? It means a Catholic in communion with the See of Rome. We do not adopt that name, although we glory in our communion with the See of Rome, although we may be English or Irish in nationality. We do not adopt the name, because it implies what we cannot admit, that a man may be a Catholic without being in communion with the centre of Catholic Unity, the See of Rome.

" There is nothing offensive in the appellation *Roman* Catholic, as in other names with which we are frequently honoured. If then we refuse to adopt it, the reason is, because it imports what is irreconcileable with our principles, that churches which have separated from the ancient Catholic Church may still have a right to the title of Catholic."*

Catholicity may be defined : — "The wide spread diffusion of the Church throughout the world, together with a large and conspicuous multitude of members."

Catholicity may be either (*juris*) that is of right, or (*facti*) that is of fact, actual existence. The Catholicity of *fact* is the actual extension of the Church. Catholicity of *right* may again be divided into two.

(*a*). It is the power or faculty, divine and efficacious in the Church, to make and to keep itself Catholic. This kind of Catholicity is the same as the Church's indefectibility of which I shall treat later.

(*b*) It is the power or faculty in the Catholic Church of converting non-Catholics to the true faith.

Catholicity of fact is either *simultaneous* or *continuous*.

---

* Dr. Lingard's Catechism.

Simultaneous Catholicity would be if the Church should all at once and at the same time occupy all parts of the world. Catholicity would be *continuous* or *successive* when by degrees, and not all at once, it should spread itself throughout the world.

Catholicity *of fact* is again either *physical* or *moral*. *Physical* is when all the parts of the world are occupied. *Moral* when many and the principal parts of the world are occupied.

5. (*a*) The Church is not Catholic by what is called at the same time *physical* and *simultaneous.*

(*b*) She is Catholic by Catholicity *moral* and *continuous.*

(*c*) Before the end of the world the Gospel will be preached successively to all nations and peoples, so that there will be no nation or people on the face of the earth that will not have had at some time or other the Gospel preached to it. This is the common opinion of the Fathers and Theologians.

(*d*) It is certain that the true Church, amongst all others calling themselves Church, excels and is conspicuous for its Catholicity, not only in its successive growth, but its simultaneous propagation and its permanent state.

(*e*) The Church is Catholic by Catholicity of right, as to its first kind, which will be shown when speaking of her infallibility; and that she is Catholic as to its second species, is known to all from the whole history of the Church, the propagation of the faith, and daily experience.

The Church is Catholic by reason of her doctrine, because she holds all truths, condemns all errors, and teaches none.

Finally she is Catholic in such a manner that she and she alone was always known as Catholic; she and she alone is called, and will be called, Catholic, and known as Catholic by all, for in the past all the efforts of sects have never been able to cause themselves to be designated or known by this name.

THE APOSTOLICITY OF THE CATHOLIC CHURCH.

6. The Catholic Church is Apostolic, because (*a*) she has had her origin and her doctrine from the Apostles; (*b*) because she has the succession of her pastors uninterrupted from them.

As to her origin from the Apostles, it is acknowledged by all, even her worst adversaries, that the Catholic Church is the Church of the first ages, which all confess was Apostolic. This

fact is evident, as nothing can be better known than the novelty
of heretics and of all heresies, and the antiquity of the Catholic
Church. No one can state or point out any time in which the
Church ceased to be Apostolic.

As to her doctrine ; her doctrine, like her origin, is that of
the Apostles. It is the one same Catholic doctrine. Adversaries
have never been able to prove any change of faith up to the
present day, and no change can be discovered if the doctrine of
the Apostolic and ancient times be compared with the doctrine
of the Church at the present time.

7. She is Apostolic as to succession. The succession of
pastors comes down in an uninterrupted course from the Apostles.
(a) She has the succession of Orders. All acknowledge this who
in any sense admit the Sacrament and the power of Orders ;
because, if they deny this succession, they cannot regard their own
Orders as valid, inasmuch as they have received them from no
other than the Catholic Church. (b) She has the succession as
to jurisdiction. That Church has the succession of jurisdiction which has never fallen away from the Church
founded by the Apostles, and such is the Roman Catholic
Church. There is no fact of history more certain than the
succession of Pontiffs, from St. Peter to Leo. XIII.

The Roman Catholic Church has therefore the three conditions required for *Apostolicity.* She holds and teaches the
doctrine of the Apostles. She has her Orders from the Apostles,
and her Mission from the Apostles. Her doctrine is Apostolic,
as is evident from the Creeds of faith, the Sacraments, and the
Holy Sacrifice of the Mass. Her Orders are Apostolic, as they
have come down in a continuous and unbroken succession of
Bishops and Pastors from St. Peter, to whom our Lord committed
the care of His faithful, to the present Pontiff, and the Bishops
of the Catholic Church throughout the world. Her Mission is
from them because she alone is governed by the lawful successors
of the Apostles, and teaches, as I have already written, the
doctrine of the Apostles.

8. The four characters or marks of the Church which prove
her divinity are to be found in the Roman Catholic Church and
in her alone ; and, therefore, she alone is the true Church. As
too much importance or prominence cannot be given to this truth,
I wish to sum up all that refers to this doctrine as stated and
explained by the Abbe A. R. Moulin*

---

* Exposition Elementaire de la Doctrine Catholique.

(a) The Roman Catholic Church possesses the *Note of Unity*, for all her Children profess the same Creed, acknowledge the same commandments of God and of the Church, receive the same Sacraments, and obey the same Supreme Head, who is the Pope. She has no variety or contradictions in her faith. She believes to-day the same as she has always believed in past ages. The dogmas which have been added to her Creed, as for example, in our time, that of the *Immaculate Conception*, and *the infallibility of the Pope*, are no new dogmas, they are taken from the Sacred Scripture and tradition, and brought to light and proclaimed at the proper and opportune moment as the inspired truth of God.

(b) The Roman Catholic Church is *holy*, for (1) in her dogmas, in her moral precepts, in her worship, in her discipline, all is pure and irreproachable, all is of such a nature as is calculated to remove evil and wickedness, and to promote the most exalted virtue. (2) As a fact, the Roman Catholic Church has transformed the world in a moral and religious point of view, in making her honour virtue, and holding up before her so many heroic examples of sanctity. She has exercised the greatest influence in the world in making men better and happier. She alone produces heroes of holiness to whom we pay honour and respect. (3) She alone has converted to the faith the barbarians of the Middle Ages, and in our day, as well as in past ages, converts the morals and lives of idolatrous nations, and plants in their midst the Cross and the spirit of Jesus Christ. Miracles without number are worked within her fold from the time of the Apostles up to the present day. All these wonders show clearly that the Roman Church is assisted by the Holy Spirit. The enemies of the Church, in attacking her sanctity, continually refer to the scandals and disorders that history lays to the charge of the clergy and the Catholic faithful; because a minister of religion, or a member of some religious congregation, now and then has been unfaithful to his duty, or a scandal to his brethren; these take occasion therefrom to blame the entire Church, and to hold her up to the public indignation. To all such accusations we answer

(1) that exaggeration and calumny form a great part of these accusations; (2) that the Church is the first to condemn and repress such scandals, and far from allowing vices she punishes them by the most stringent laws; (3) that it is not from her doctrine that evil arises, as is the case with the theories and false doctrine of her accusers; but from the abuse of liberty and infidelity to grace; (4) that it is the height of injustice to blame the entire Church for the crimes and vices of a small number; to pass over in silence all that is good in the Church, and only publish that which is evil; (5) that as the Church has not succumbed in the midst of abuses, disorders and profanations, which she has suppressed with such wonderful power and fortitude, is one of the strongest proofs of her divine institution, and that God does not cease to be with her and to protect her.

(c) The Roman Catholic Church possesses *Catholicity*, for since the day of Pentecost, when three thousand people, representing the several countries of the world, were converted by St. Peter, she has always had subjects and faithful children in every part of the world. She surpasses in her numbers all sects dissenting from her, taken together; She adapts herself to all countries and to all forms of government, and well deserves the name *Catholic*, which even her worst enemies are forced to call her.

The Roman Catholic Church possesses *Apostolicity*, for the 260 Popes, who have succeeded each other in the See of Rome, are the successors of the Apostle St. Peter, and all the other Episcopal Sees have been founded either by the other Apostles in union with St. Peter, or by the Roman Pontiffs, the successors of the Apostles. The Mission, which the Roman Catholic Church exercises, has therefore been derived from Jesus Christ through His Apostles.

The Roman Catholic Church, having all these marks, which Jesus Christ has given to and planted in His Church, is the true Church, and out of her there is no salvation.

9. Before concluding this instruction, I wish to say a few words about *false churches*. We see a number of heretical and schismatical sects, who have separated themselves from the Church. They are false, because they have not the notes or marks of the Church founded by Jesus Christ.

(a) They have no *unity*. The Greek Schism is divided into about a dozen independent sects without any authority to judge as a last resource in matters of doctrine and discipline. In Russia they are settled by the will of the Czar; in the Musselman States matters of religious difficulty are referred for final settlement to the Turkish government.

Protestantism from its very beginning was split up into innumerable sects disagreeing from one another; afterwards it became more or less subject to the civil power, like the Greek sects. The freedom of private opinion, the liberty left to each one to form his belief from the reading of the Bible, were principles calculated to cause divisions and variations, and prevent any kind of unity in Protestant faith and doctrine. "The devil is in amongst us", said Luther, "and soon we shall have as many religions as there are heads." Out of this anarchy has arisen a great force of infidelity and incredulity in all matters of religion.

(b) There is in all separate sects an absence of *sanctity*. The authors of the Greek Schism, Photius in the ninth century, and Michael Cerularius in the eleventh century, had no other motive in their separation than blind ambition and the desire of power. The leaders and founders of protestantism : Luther, Calvin, Zwinglius, &c., were notorious for their vices. The historian Cobbett says of them, that there was only one point of doctrine on which they agreed, namely, the inutility of good works, and their lives prove how sincerely true they were to this principle.

Amongst the Greek Schismatics the Clergy are badly prepared for their functions, they live in a state of abjection and contempt; they receive no consideration or respect from the people, and they can neither spread nor fulfil the Gospel teaching.

Amongst Protestants the most efficacious means of sanctification have disappeared : abstinence, fasting, mortifications, religious vows, devotion to the Blessed Virgin and to the Saints, confession, communion, &c.

Neither the Greek Schism or Protestantism have done anything for civilisation; they rather obstructed it than promoted it. The first has been the instrument of despotism in the East ; the second covered Europe with blood and ruins in the sixteenth century, and has been ever since the helper and instrument of the freemasons, who are the authors of most of the disorders and revolutions of the last two centuries.

In fine, neither Protestants nor Greek Schismatics have shown that the action of the Holy Spirit is with them. They have given no examples of heroic virtue, no saints, no pure constant and invincible zeal for the propagation of the faith, such as is shown by the example and martyrdom of so many Catholic missioners, and they have never been able to obtain the sanction of a miracle for their work and their doctrine.

(c) There is an absence of *Catholicity* in the separated sects. The Greek Church is contained within the confines of a part of the East, principally in Greece, Russia, and Turkey. As to Protestantism, each of the principal sects is more or less circumscribed within the limits of one determined place or country, the Lutherans in Germany, the Calvinists in Geneva and France, the Anglicans in England. All are national and none Catholic.

(d) There is an absence of *Apostolicity* amongst them. These are separated from the Pope, who is the heir of St. Peter, the chief of the Apostles; they have a purely human, and in no sense an Apostolic, origin. Their ministers have no lawful mission, and they cannot say that they have been sent by Jesus Christ to teach and baptise all nations.

Heretics and Schismatics are, therefore, out of the ordinary way of salvation, but those amongst them who are in invincible ignorance of the truth, and practice sincerely the Christian religion as well as they know it, may, with God's grace, obtain salvation.

The same observation may apply also to infidels who have lived in invincible ignorance of Christianity, provided they know and believe those things that are necessary—*necessitate medii*—for salvation.

SECTION 5. (ARTICLE IX.)

THE PROPERTIES OF THE CHURCH.

1. The other chief properties of the Church.—2. The Indefectibility of the Church, and the sense in which she is indefectible.—3. The errors of heretics in regard to the Indefectibility of the Church.—The Infallibility of the Church.—5. The three propositions of faith in regard to the Infallibility of the Church.—6. Proofs of the Church's *Indefectibility* and *Infallibility.*—7. Further proofs of the Infallibility of the Church.—8. The object of Infallibility and the dogmas to which it extends.—9. The Subject of Infallibility.

1. BESIDES the four Notes or marks, the Church has many other properties inherent in and essential to her. The principal of these are *indefectibility* in being or existence ; *infallibility* in teaching ; and *authority* or power in ruling or governing. These three properties or attributes are denied by all non-Catholic sects, because otherwise they could not account for their existence, or assign any plausible reason for not belonging to the one true Church. We have now to explain separately these properties or attributes.

INDEFECTIBILITY.

2. This is a property by which the Church cannot fail; it is that by which she cannot either lose or have diminished any of her divine qualities or gifts even for a short time.

The doctrine of the indefectibility of the Church may be comprised in the following propositions :—

(a) The whole Church is *indefectible.*
(b) One part of the Church, namely, the Apostolic See, is *indefectible.*
(c) The particular Church of this or that particular diocese, or this or that particular nation, may fail and fall away.

Perpetuity is included in *indefectibility.* Although, rigorously speaking, unless God had ordained otherwise, the Church could

U

be *perpetual*, without being in all respects *indefectible*; as a man remains the same human being even to death, although he fails in many respects, both in soul and body. *Perpetuity* imports continuation without interruption, but indefectibility imports duration and immutability as well.

Indefectibility means more than *infallibility*. *Infallibility* extends only to those things which concern the Church's teaching in matters of faith and morals, but it does not imply that she is to continue always, or to the end of the world, but that as long as she exists, she cannot err in these matters.

3. Heretics, in regard to the indefectibility of the Church, err on two points.

(1) As to the possibility of defection.

(2) As to the fact of defection.

They have held various opinions as to the possibility of defection.

(a) Some have held that the whole Church can fail entirely for a time.

(b) Some say the *visible* Church can fail, but not the *invisible* Church, as if these were two distinct Churches.

(c) Others affirm that, although the Church cannot fail entirely, she can do so in part, at least for a time, and even always by losing this or that attribute or perfection, or retaining it, but maimed and vitiated.

As to the fact of defection. All heretics of every sect hold that the Church has, in some way or other, failed; otherwise, as I have said, they cannot assign any reason for their separation from her; but as to the time of her defection, they are not agreed. On this point there are two extreme opinions. The first dates the defection of the Church from the Council of Constance, in the year 1414. The second holds that defection began in the very time of the Apostles; in their time, they say, and in every age since, the Church was affected by a number of errors. This latter opinion is held by a great number of recent Protestant writers, such as Goode, Whately, and some Puseyites, as Palmer.

Against all these errors, Catholics hold the indefectibility of the Church, as above explained, and the proofs of it, and of her infallibility, may be said to be the same; and I shall therefore prove both at the same time, after I explain the nature and meaning of Infallibility.

THE INFALLIBILITY OF THE CHURCH.

4. *Infallibility* means the gift of not erring. It may be called *inerrancy*.

Inerrancy may be either of *right* (*juris*), or in *fact* (*facti*). *Inerrancy in fact* may be found in one who, although he can err, does not actually do so. *Inerrancy of right* is that which signifies that one not only holds and teaches the truth, but that it is impossible for him to do otherwise, that is, that one not only does not actually err, but that he cannot err; this inerrancy is called *infallibility*.

Infallibility, as it is the gift of inerrancy, which God has imparted to the Church, is either *passive* or *active*.

Passive infallibility is the gift of inerrancy, which is imparted to the Church, believing (*ecclesia credens*) so that it may never, even in the least matter, believe or profess error in anything appertaining to faith.

Active infallibility is that which is imparted to the body of Pastors or Bishops, in which must be included the Chief Pastor of all. It means infallibility in teaching.

5. The following three propositions are to be believed by Catholic faith :—

(*a*) The whole Church, or the universal Church, is infallible in believing, and in the profession of faith, so that it cannot happen that all the faithful should ever believe or profess a doctrine contrary to faith.

(*b*) The body of Pastors in which is comprehended the Sovereign Pontiff, either assembled in Council or dispersed throughout the world, is infallible in teaching.

(*c*) The Sovereign, or Roman Pontiff, speaking *ex Cathedra*, is infallible in teaching.

Active infallibility, or infallibility in doctrine only, may be defined : " A special providence or assistance of God, by which the Church, in teaching or defining, is preserved from all error."

For this gift we do not require that special inspiration which moved the Sacred Writers in giving us the books of Scripture. Nor is immunity from error required in matters that do not belong to doctrine ; and it need not be extended to the reasons and explanations which accompany a definition, only to that which is the defined doctrine ; and the positive motion or action of God, such as is granted in inspiration, is not required for the gift of infallibility.

That divine assistance suffices which preserves from error. But we must admit not only a *negative* assistance in the Church, but also that when it would be needed, and as it would be needed, God would give a *positive* assistance, but not in such a way as that it could be called inspiration, in the same way as the Scriptures, and divine tradition are inspired.

We may now assert the proposition, and assign the proofs which are given in support of the doctrine explained in this Section.

6. The Church is *indefectible* and *infallible*. Both parts of this proposition are so closely connected that the reasons for one prove the other; we may, however, for the sake of order, take them separately.

The Church is indefectible. This may be proved—

(a) From the promises of Christ. He promised (1) that the gates of hell would not prevail against her.* (2) That He would be with her all days, even to the consummation of the world, &c.† From which we may conclude that, should the Church fail, the promises of Christ would not be fulfilled. The gates of hell would prevail, and Christ would cease to be with His Church. Therefore, the Church cannot be said to fail, but must be indefectible.

(b) The properties and attributes which are essential to the Church, and flow from her original constitution, cannot fail, or the Church cannot lose them, or suffer them to be impaired. For if in any of them she did fail, or if any of them should be wanting in time, then she should cease to be that Church which was founded by Christ. For Christ founded His Church, that in all times and places she could supply men with the due means of salvation; and, therefore, she ought always to be, and to be capable of being deemed, the true Church of Christ, which would not be the case were she at any time to fail even in part, or lose any of her essential attributes. Men might then be deceived, as they would not be able to recognise any longer that which is the true Church established by Christ on earth. They would, therefore, be destitute of those means which would guide men in that affair which is the most excellent and necessary of all,

---

* St. Matt. xvi.   † Ibid. xviii. See also St. Matt. xii. 26; Ephes. iv. 16.

namely, in the knowledge of the true religion. And all this would be at variance with the end, which Christ had in view in establishing His Church.

Against the fact of her defection, we can say that the present state of the Catholic Church, after so many ages, is an incontrovertible argument that she possesses the prerogative of *indefectibility.* "The Church," says St. Augustine, "will not be conquered, nor eradicated, nor will she yield to any temptation or trial until the end of the world comes."[*]

THE CHURCH IS INFALLIBLE IN THE DOCTRINE OF FAITH AND MORALS.

7. The arguments which prove the *indefectibility* are equally forcible for the *infallibility* of the Church. But besides these, there are many other arguments from Scripture and the Fathers, which prove the Church's infallibility.

The Scripture proofs may be taken both from the Old and New Testament. In the Old Testament, Isaias speaks of the joyful flourishing of Christ's Kingdom, and that in His Church shall be a holy and secure way.[†] In the New Testament we have, in the Gospel of St. Matthew, the commission given to the Apostles : Going, therefore, teach all nations, baptizing them in the name of the Father, and of the Son, and of the Holy Ghost. *Teaching them to observe all things whatsoever I have commanded you ; and, behold, I am with you all days, even to the consummation of the world.*[‡] And in the Gospel of St. John, in His last discourse to His Apostles, Christ often speaks in terms which clearly signify the infallible guidance of the Holy Spirit : *And I will ask the Father, and he shall give you another Paraclete, that he may abide with you for ever ;*[§] and again : *But the Paraclete, the Holy Ghost, whom the Father will send in my name, he will teach you all things, and bring all things to your mind, whatsoever I shall have said to you.*[||]

---

[*] Enarratio in Plms. ix. n. 6.

[†] *And a path and a way shall be there, and it shall be called the holy way : the unclean shall not pass over it, and this shall be unto you a straight way, so that fools shall not err therein.* (Isa. xxxv. 8).

He that heareth you heareth me, and he that despiseth you despiseth me, and he that despiseth me despiseth him that sent me. (St. Luke x. 16).

If he hear not the Church, let him be to thee as the heathen and the publican. (St. Matthew xviii.). And in the Epis. to Timothy, St. Paul calls the *Church, the pillar and the ground of the truth.*

[‡] St. Matt. xxviii. 19, 20.   [§] St. John xiv. 16.   [||] Ibid. v. 26.

It is evident from the Scriptures (a) that Christ wished
Christian doctrine to be preserved pure and free from error as
long as His Church should last, namely to the end of time.
(b) He wished this doctrine to be preserved pure and free from
error in His whole Church. Christ, wishing this, provided and
gave the means necessary to preserve His doctrine in its purity
and integrity. And considering (a) the nature and the number
of the Christian dogmas, (b) the Catholicity of the Church,
(c) the infirmity and malice of men, (d) their strong proclivities
to sects, &c.; considering all these things, it is certain that the
Christian doctrine could not be protected and preserved pure and
free from error in this world without the special providence and
assistance of God, which we call the gift of infallibility.

God established His Church that she should always be one
in faith; therefore that she should be incorruptible in the teaching
of that faith. If she could err in teaching, she might propose
what is false and erroneous to be believed, and in this case she
could no longer be one in her faith; because she would be teaching truth and falsehood. The connection between the truth and
the unity of the Church is expressly declared in St. Paul's words —
one Lord, one faith. And He gave some apostles, and some prophets,
and other some evangelists, and other some pastors and doctors......
that henceforth we be no more children tossed to and fro, and carried about with every wind of doctrine by the wickedness of men, by
cunning craftiness, by which they lie in wait to deceive.*

THE OBJECT OF INFALLIBILITY.

8.   The object of passive infallibility is the doctrine believed.
The object of active infallibility is the *dogmas of faith*. This
infallibility extends to the following heads:

(a)   In defining that something is revealed.
(b)   In defining that something is not revealed even though
it be a sacred or supernatural truth; as for example,
the number of the elect, the day of judgment, &c.
(c)   In defining that something is not revealed in *that sense*
in which it is not, or that a truth pertains in no way
to sacred doctrine or revelation.
(d)   In defining something to be directly opposed to a revealed truth, and therefore heretical.
(e)   In defining something to be indirectly opposed to revealed truth.

---

* Ephes. iv. 11, 14.

(*f*) In defining that the deposit of faith is preserved pure and entire, so that the dogmas transmitted to the Church by Christ and His apostles have been preserved, and will always be preserved, and that none of them ever have been or ever will be lost.*

THE SUBJECT OF INFALLIBILITY.

9. By the *subject* of *infallibility* I mean that in which the gift or prerogative resides, or in other words, those to whom it has been promised and given.

The subject of *passive infallibility* is the universal Church taken as a whole.

The subject of *active infallibility* is—(*a*) The body of Pastors, that is of Bishops (in which the Sovereign Pontiff is included), either dispersed or assembled in Council. (*b*) The Sovereign Pontiff, when he defines *ex cathedra*.

The Church is at the same time the *witness* of doctrine, its *judge*, and *teacher*, which three words signify the same thing under different aspects. The Church is the *witness*, inasmuch as she defines that some doctrine, *v.g.*, that of the Immaculate Conception is a dogma of faith. She is a *judge*, inasmuch as she settles controversies; that is amongst different opinions and teachings, she judges and defines what is true and to be held, and what is false and to be rejected. She is the *teacher* in her daily ministry, by which, through her living voice, she instructs the faithful in all things, and directs them in the safe doctrine of morals, as it were leading them by the hand in the way of salvation.

---

*Apud. Murray de Ecole. D. xi. Sect. 1.

SECTION 6. (ARTICLE IX.)

DOGMATIC AND MORAL FACTS.

In connection with the authority and infallibility of the Church we have to deal with *dogmatic* and *moral* facts, inasmuch as these are closely connected with revealed doctrine. The faithful may easily be deceived in regard to the Church's authority in these matters, and to save them from any surprise or mistake I think it must be useful to give an explanation of some of these facts and the Church's authority in regard to them.

1. *A dogmatic fact* is a *fact* that is so closely connected with a dogma of faith, that its knowledge is necessary in order to teach the dogma or to preserve it pure and entire.

A moral fact is that which is so closely connected with morals that the knowledge of it is necessary in order to teach the principles of morals, or to preserve from error the morals of the faithful.

A fact may be closely connected with a dogma of faith and with morals at the same time, and then it is both a dogmatic and a moral fact. Dogmatic facts may be revealed or not revealed. If revealed they are the object of divine faith, and like all other revealed truths fall under the object of the Church's infallible teaching.

2. I here subjoin the chief dogmatic, moral, and mixed facts.

(a) Whether this or that Pope, *v.g.*, Leo XIII., is the true Sovereign Pontiff.

(b) Whether this or that Council, *v.g.*, the Council of Trent, was Ecumenical or not.

(c)   Whether certain dogmas are expressed correctly and
      more accurately by certain words and expressions
      than by others, such as the Divinity of the Son by
      consubstantial, and the manner of the real presence in
      the Blessed Sacrament by *transubstantiation*, or
      whether other words are incorrect.

(d)   Whether this or that book contains sound or unsound
      doctrine. The same may be said of part of a book or
      manuscript, or of things done, for instance, at a General
      Council.

(e)   Whether this or that system of education, whether for
      the clergy or laity, is good or bad, safe or dangerous.

(f)   Whether this or that Society, say the Society of the
      Freemasons, is good or bad in itself, whether it is safe
      or dangerous either intrinsically or extrinsically.

(g)   Whether those canonized by the Church are truly Saints.

(h)   Whether this or that Religious Order is good and useful
      in the Church.

To illustrate the authority of the Church in these matters,
out of the above facts I select one or two on which in particular
to write.

8.   Let us take the dogmatic fact of the approbation and
condemnation of books. The Catholic doctrine teaches that the
Church has, by divine right, authority not only to approve
particular propositions, and reject others as they may be in
accordance with or contrary to faith and morals, but also that
she can approve whole books, or any other writings, as containing
true and sound doctrine, or condemn them as containing false
and depraved doctrine.

All agree as to the Church's authority in regard to approving
or condemning singular or particular propositions. But the
question was raised by the Jansenists as to the authority of the
Church of condemning a whole book, on account of the false or
wrong doctrine contained in it; or the right of the Church to
attribute to any particular book a depraved doctrine as really
signified and contained in it.

About a book and its sense, the question may be as to the
mere fact only, or the *dogmatic fact*.

(a)   Whether the book, to which the title *Augustinus* is
      given, was really written by Jansenius.

(b)   Whether the condemned propositions are contained in
      it in so many words; it suffices that they be contained
      in it as to their sense.

(c) Whether the author of the book really held in his own mind the condemned doctrine or not. As to these matters of pure simple fact, the Church does not judge. But as to the dogmatic fact itself, there are two questions to be attended to. (1) The question of *right*, or rather the question of doctrine, as to whether it is sound or not. (2) The question of fact whether, namely, this doctrine is contained in this book, or that it is really contained in that book is the *dogmatic fact*. Hence the Church, in defining that the five famous propositions of Jansenius are heretical, determines the question of right, and defines a dogma; and in defining that these propositions are contained in the book of Jansenius, she defines a dogmatic fact, and in this her judgment is infallible.

I may here note that a proposition may be condemned either (*ut jacet*) as it is in itself, or in the sense intended by the author. In the sense intended by the author, does not mean that the author had that sense really in his mind when expressing the proposition, but that it is elicited from his words.

4. Now the Church has the right and the office of preserving and protecting for the faithful the purity and integrity of faith and morals, and this authority would be vain and useless unless she were able to state whether the doctrine of books were sound or not, and to condemn the books themselves. And we must, therefore, hold that the Church has, by divine right, the authority to define that a false and dangerous doctrine is contained in a particular book.

The Church has always, from the very beginning, vindicated to herself this right, as divinely imparted to her; and she would not have arrogated to herself, in the manner she has done, such a right, unless she really possessed it. We may, therefore, state that the Church, in defining that dogmatic fact, is infallible.

(a) If the Church were fallible in such a sentence, it might happen that she would condemn a book as heretical and scandalous which contained only sound and pure doctrine, and by this very act she would fail in her office of keeping the faith safe. This she would do in a three-fold respect, (1) by defining an erroneous doctrine to be contained where alone Catholic doctrine is to be found; (2) by turning away the faithful from pastures as pernicious, which, in reality, are healthy and salubrious; (3) by teaching error to the faithful.

(b) This may be proved from the words of Clement XI., to the following effect, in his Constitution *vineam Domini Sabaoth*. " That every occasion of error may in the future be removed, and that all the children of the Catholic Church may hear the Church not only by silence, for the impious *in tenebris conticiscunt*, but by interior submission, which is the true obedience of an orthodox man ; let them learn that we decree and declare by this our Constitution to be always in force, that the submission which is due to the designated Apostolic Constitution is by no means satisfied by obsequious silence. . . . ." This Constitution has reference to the condemnation of the five famous propositions of Jansenius, as contained in the book entitled Augustinus, as the Jansenists had endeavoured by every means in their power to evade the condemnation of the Church, and as a last resort, claimed the right to remain silent as to the Church's condemnation, without acknowledging her right, or the justice of her sentence, or accepting it in their minds. This the Constitution of Clement XI. declares to be insufficient for the obedience due to the authority and teaching of the Church.

(c) The Jansenists themselves admitted that the Church is infallible in defining a book or any writing to be Catholic and free from error, as the Council of Trent defined concerning the Vulgate version of the Sacred Scripture and the Canon of the Mass. Therefore, the Church can declare the doctrine of a book to be heretical. There is a parity between the two.

(d) Finally the Church has always exercised this right, as is manifest from her public acts. The Council of Nice condemned the Thalium of Arius, the Council of Ephesus and Chalcedon condemned the writings of Nestorius, &c.

All this doctrine applies to the propositions and books condemned by Apostolic authority from time to time, a summary of which may be found in the Syllabus of Pius. IX.

After treating of one dogmatic fact, I may take a moral fact in illustration of the authority of the Church in regard to these moral facts, as well as the dogmatic ones.

THE CANONIZATION OF THE SAINTS.

5. Canonization is the public testimony of the Church of the true sanctity and the glory of a departed soul.

A person is called a Saint who is properly canonized, that is, one who, by the Sovereign Pontiff, is inscribed in the number and catalogue of the Saints, publicly, solemnly, and canonically, and declared and defined to be a Saint, and as such to be regarded by all the faithful of Christ.

A person is called *blessed*, that is beatified, who, by special concession of the Sovereign Pontiff, may be venerated as being in heaven by public veneration in some Province, or in some Religious Order or Orders, or in some particular place or country.

The following are the differences between Canonization and Beatification :—

In Canonization. (a) A person is declared to be a Saint. (b) That he is to be regarded as such by the whole Church. (c) That he may be venerated by public honour in the whole Church. (d) The sentence of Canonization is final and definitive, and the cause is finished by it.

In Beatification. (a) The person beatified is not expressly declared to be a Saint or blessed, but it is only granted that this title may be given to him as in the words of Beatification : "*Facultatem facimus ut N.N. Beati nomine in posterum appelletur.*"* " We grant leave that N.N. may be called in future by the name *Blessed.*" (b) He is not to be called Saint, but Blessed. (c) He is not to be venerated by public honour, except within the limits of those places to which the concession has been made. (d) The sentence of Beatification is not final and definitive. We have to explain the difference between private and public worship (*cultus*) or honour, in connection with this subject.

Private worship is not offered in the name of the Church, and has not been appointed by the Church, but is that which may be offered by any private individual out of devotion, either in secret or in public.

Public worship is that which is offered in the name of the Church, and has been appointed by the Church as such, and this whether it be offered in a public place or in secret.

It is certain and of faith, or at least definible of faith,† that

---

* Litteræ Apostolicæ Pius. IX. quod juxta and ad excitandum. 1 Oct., 1852.
† Murray, de Eco. D. xvii. S. v.

the Church has the authority to canonize Saints.   That authority she has always exercised from the beginning.

Either she has that authority from God, and, as it is a spiritual authority, it could not be otherwise than from God, or it must be said that the Church has exercised from the beginning an usurped authority.   But this latter we cannot say; therefore the Church has this authority; therefore she has it by revelation, as that is the only way in which she could receive it from God; and therefore we may conclude that it is revealed that the Church has this authority from God.

6.   From this it follows that the Church is infallible in the Canonization of Saints.   This at least is the more common and more probable opinion of Theologians.   The Church in Canonization defines a person to be a Saint, and to be regarded as such by the whole Church, and in a matter of this kind her definition must be infallible.   That she declares those canonized to be Saints is evident from the Decrees and Rules of Canonization: as in the Decree of Canonization of 27 Saints by His Holiness Pius IX. on the Feast of Penticost, 8th June, 1862.   *Ad honorem Sanctae et Individuae Trinitatis, & exaltationem fidei Catholicae, & Christianae religionis augmentum, auctoritate D. N. Jesu Christi, Beatorum Apostolorum Petri et Pauli acnostra......Beatos Petrum Bapt. &c.,......Sanctos esse decermimus & defininimus ac sanctorum catalogo adscribimus; statuentes ab ecclesia universali illorum memoriam......quolibet anno......pia devotione recoli debere.*

"To the honour of the holy and undevided Trinity, for the exaltation of the Catholic faith, and the increase of the Christian religion, by the authority of Our Lord Jesus Christ, and of the Blessed apostles Peter and Paul, and Our authority, we declare and define the Blessed Peter Baptist......&c. to be Saints, and to be numbered in the catalogue of the Saints, determining at the same time their memory to be kept by the universal Church every year with pious devotion."

This was the practice of the Church in former times, as we may learn from the decree of Pius II. in the Canonization of St. Catherine of Sienna: "By the authority of Our Lord Jesus Christ, of His Blessed Apostles Peter and Paul, and Our authority, we declare Catherine of Sienna to have been received into the heavenly Jerusalem, and to have received the crown of eternal glory; and we decree and define that she be both privately and publicly venerated as a Saint."

The same truth may be proved from the Note of Sanctity in the Church.   The Church is holy, and were she to propose a wicked or ungodly person to be venerated and imitated as a Saint, the faithful would be deceived, and her sanctity would be impaired.

In concluding this subject it may be useful to explain the quality of certitude with which the proposition of the Church's infallibility in the Canonization of Saints is to be received.

Some, with Benedict XIV,* hold the proposition, which affirms the Church to be infallible in this to be of faith, but many others deny this, as the same author attests. We may therefore safely say—

(a) It seems that the proposition which affirms the infallibility of the Church in the Canonization of Saints is revealed, and therefore definable of faith, or one that may be defined.

(b) It appears certain that the proposition is not of divine Catholic faith, so that the opposite doctrine can be called heretical.† For although it is certainly of faith that the Church is infallible in the common doctrine of morals, it is not certain with the same certitude of faith that the Canonization of Saints pertains to the common doctrine of morals, nor do all agree that it does. There is no express definition of the Church as to its infallibility in this respect being the doctrine of divine faith, neither can it be gathered from the usual practice of the Church.

Hence we believe the infallibility of the Church in the Canonization of Saints, and those whom she has canonized to be Saints, not by divine faith, nor by purely human and fallible faith, but on ecclesiastical and infallible faith, founded on the assistance given by the Holy Ghost to the Church.

Any one who should deny a canonized Saint to be in heaven, would not thereby be actually a heretic, but he would be (a) temerarius, (b) scandalous, (c) impious, and suspected of heresy.

THE AUTHORITY OR POWER OF THE CHURCH IN RULING.

7. After explaining the Indefectibility of the Church as to her being and existence, and her Infallibility in teaching, it now remains that I explain what is meant by her power and authority in ruling.

The notion of ecclesiastical power. Power is the faculty of

---

* De Canoniz. 45. 14, &c.   † Benedict XIV., de Canoniz. N. 27.

doing something; it is either physical or moral, according as it is the principle of physical or moral action.

Moral power implies a right or authority to oblige other persons. Authority may be devided: — (a) By reason of its object into the power of commanding, and of binding or loosing. (b) By reason of the persons possessing it it may be either paternal, pastoral, or kingly. (c) By reason of Society it is either domestic, political or ecclesiastical. (d) By reason of its origin it is natural or positive, human or divine. All power is at least mediately from God, according to the words of St. Paul: *there is no power but from God;* and those of the Psalmist: *by me Kings rule.*

After this general reference to power and authority we have to ask what is meant by the power of the Church, and how manifold is it? The power of the Church means a moral faculty or authority divinely bestowed upon the Church, which gives her the right to command and to bind and loose all her children. It is three-fold: the power of teaching, of ministering, and of ruling; which three-fold power is generally signified by the *power of the keys, the keys of the Church.*

8. This three-fold power may again be divided into the power of *Order* and *Jurisdiction.* The *power of Order* is derived from a *Sacrament;* that of *Jurisdiction* from the *Mission* or being sent: the one affects the power given to a man; the other affects other persons who are given to him as subjects over whom he may exercise that power.

Mission is three-fold. (a) Of preaching the faith: *Go, teach all nations.* (b) Of dispensing mysteries and Sacraments: *Baptizing them......the ministers of Christ and the dispensers of His mysteries.* (c) Of providing for its own conservation and government: *teaching them all things that I have commanded you......and to the consummation of the world.*

9. Christ instituted in His Church a Hierarchy of Order, consisting of *Bishops, Priests* and *Ministers.* This is defined of faith by the Council of Trent.*

Hierarchy means a sacred power distinct in subordinate grades; one arranged under the other. It is either heavenly or *earthly.* With the heavenly hierarchy we have nothing to do in this place, but only with the terestial one. This means inequality of power and subordination, as it is established on earth between the pastors and ministers of the Church.

---

* Sess. xiii. Can. 6. 17., cap. 4.

The hierarchy of the Church is two-fold, one of *order*, the other of *jurisdiction*. The hierarchy of *order* is conferred by the Sacrament, and consists of the seven Sacramental Orders.

That of jurisdiction is made up of various grades of dignities and offices in the Church, which are, the Papacy, Cardinalate, Patriarchate, Primatial, Archiepiscopal Prelacy, and those inferior to Episcopacy. Of these some are established by divine right, and some are only ecclesiastical. Those that are of divine right in the hierarchy of *Orders* are Bishops, Priests and Ministers ; and in the hierarchy of *jurisdiction* : The Sovereign Pontificate or Apostolic Primacy, Episcopacy and Priesthood.

Of these the *Church teaching* is composed, and as they belong to the Constitution of the Church it will be necesrary to explain some of them more in detail, especially as regards the Pope, the Head of the Church.

CHAPTER II. (ARTICLE IX.)

THE ROMAN PONTIFF.

1. The signification of the word Pope.—2. Christ, the invisible Head of the Church, appointed a Vicar, or visible Head of the Church on earth.— 3. What is meant by the Primacy of honour and of jurisdiction.— 4. The Catholic doctrine regarding the Primacy of St. Peter and his successors. — 5. Scriptural proofs that Christ conferred the Primacy on St. Peter, (a) from St. John i. 42. (b) from St. Matt. xvi. — the text explained. (c) from St. John xxii. 22-6. St. Peter exercised this power, and it was acknowledged by the other Apostles. — 7. Dr. Lingard's Note on the subject.

1. By the word Pope is meant *Father*. The Bishop of Rome, the successor of St. Peter, is in fact the Common Father of all the faithful. Hence he is commonly called the Pope. He is also called the Sovereign Pontiff, or the Vicar of Christ on earth, and for this reason, in addressing him, we call him our Holy Father.

The Pope is elected by the College of Cardinals, as often as a vacancy occurs in the Holy See. These Cardinals are Bishops, Priests, or even Deacons, which former Popes chose as their Council. Their number is fixed at 70.

We have now to treat of the visible Head of the Church, and the importance and utility of this question is of the greatest magnitude, for as Cardinal Bellarmine says : " Our adversaries, that is heretics, whilst in almost all other dogmas they differ amongst themselves, all agree in opposing with all their strength the prerogatives of the Roman Pontiff. There were never any enemies of Christ and of the Church who did not at the same time wage war against the Chair of Peter."

2. That Jesus Christ in quality of *Our Lord* is the Head of the Church will not be disputed ; *for God appointed Him Head over all the Church.** But, since His ascent into heaven, He is invisible to us ; and the question is, whether He did not, before He left the earth, appoint a Vicar or deputy to be the visible Head in His place. From Sacred Scripture it is manifest that He did, and that St. Peter was the person on whom He conferred this high dignity. We have therefore to treat this subject in detail.

---

* Ephes. i. 22.

V

CHAPTER II.

SECTION 1. (ARTICLE IX.)

OF THE PRIMACY OF PETER.

8. By *primacy* is to be understood the pre-eminence of *honour* and *jurisdiction* over the whole Church.

By the *Primacy of honour* is signified a certain title to which is annexed certain honourable rights, such as taking the first place in assemblies.

The *Primacy of jurisdiction* is that which gives real power to a man to be exercised over others as over subjects, whom he rules by laws, and calls under His judgment, and obliges by penalties. It is of this primacy chiefly that there is question, when we speak of the primacy of Peter and of the Pope: for the primacy of honour is founded on the primacy of jurisdiction, and follows of necessity from it.

4. The Catholic doctrine of the Primacy of St. Peter and his successors in the Roman See is known to all from the manifest faith of the Church. It may be stated in the following proposition.

Christ instituted in His Church the primacy of Jurisdiction, which He conferred upon St. Peter, and He wished that it should last always in His Church. This is the doctrine of faith according to the Decree of the Council of Florence (*anno* 1438) for the union of the Greeks: "We define that the holy Apostolic See holds the primacy over the whole earth, and that the Roman Pontiff is the successor of Blessed Peter......and that to him, Blessed Peter, was delivered by our Lord Jesus Christ the fulness of power to feed, rule, and govern the universal Church."

It is evident from Sacred Scripture that the Church has one Supreme Head. She is compared in the Scripture to a Kingdom, an Army, and a Sheepfold. And these expressions indicate one King, one Shepherd, and one General: In the words of St. John, *one fold and one shepherd.*

By the divine ordinance or decree the supreme ruler of the Church should be one.

The Church is one in government; that is, all is subject to one supreme government. And either this supreme power resides in one ruler, or in many who form a combined government: but this latter cannot be; because from the beginning of the Church no such form of government existed. General Councils are not of this kind, for the form of government of any society should be permanent and continuous; but General Councils have been few, and celebrated after long intervals of time. Moreover, all or nearly all General Councils were held for the purpose of settling some particular controversy, and they did not so much rule the Church as form decrees of faith and morals by which she should be ruled.

Before giving the Scripture proofs of the proposition above stated, I have to note that all the arguments that go to prove the primacy of St. Peter, equally prove the primacy of the Sovereign Pontiff, inasmuch as the power conferred on St. Peter was transmitted to his successors.

5. That Christ conferred the primacy on St. Peter is proved (a) from St. John,* where it is mentioned that Christ changed Peter's name: *And he* (Andrew) *brought him to Jesus. And Jesus looking upon him said: Thou art Simon, the son of Jona; thou shalt be called Cephas, which is interpreted Peter.* Christ did not then assign the reason of this name: but on the authority of Cardinal Wiseman we know that it was a custom amongst the Jews, and especially the interpreters of the Law in the time of our Lord, and after that time, to change the name of some who amongst the disciples were more remarkable than, or excelled, others in merit or learning. But there is no need of recourse to the Jewish custom in this matter, as Christ Himself assigned the reason of this change of name, when He promised that He would build His Church on Peter. (b) This then is the second Scriptural proof taken from St. Matthew.† *Jesus came into the quarters of Cesarea Philippi, and He asked His disciples, saying, Whom do men say that the Son of man is? ......Simon Peter answered and said: Thou art Christ, the Son of the living God. And Jesus answering said to him: Blessed art thou, Simon Bar-Jona, because flesh and blood hath not revealed it to thee, but My Father who is in heaven. And I say to thee, that thou art Peter; and upon this rock I will build My Church, and the gates of hell shall not prevail against it.*

From these words we may form an argument thus: what Christ promised, He fulfilled; and He promised that He would build His Church on Peter, therefore He did so. Christ conferred

---

* St. John i. 42.   † St. Matt. xvi.

the primacy on St. Peter, and it is in this sense the foundation of
the Church is to be understood.   The texts clearly prove the promise of Christ, and yet the efforts of adversaries have been used
for the purpose of confusing and distorting the sense of our
Saviour's words, hence it is necessary to notice one or two of
their objections.

Against our application of this text and the word *Peter*—rock
(or *Petra* in Latin) the objections are—(*a*) according to some that
by the rock (or *petra*) Christ meant Himself; (*b*) others that He
meant the faith of Peter; and (*c*) some others say that by the
rock He meant the whole body of the faithful.

To these objections we answer :—

(*a*)   The rock or *Petra* in this place does not signify Christ
Himself, (1) because in the Syro-chaldaic language
there is no distinction of gender in the word, as there
is in Latin and Greek ; but both *Petrus* and *Petra* are
expressed by one and the same word, they have the
same sound and meaning, or object ; (2) because the
sentence or discourse of our Lord from beginning to
end was addressed to St. Peter, and Christ spoke to
Peter alone, face to face.

(*b*)   The word *Petra*, a rock, does not mean the faith of Peter
in the abstract.   That the text should bear this sense
it should be somewhere in it expressly stated, and in
nowhere, either in this text or any other, do we find
Petra or *rock* used for faith.

(*c*)   *Petra*, a rock, cannot be taken to mean the body of the
faithful, because the body of the faithful is the Church
itself; and the meaning of the text is not that the
Church would be build upon itself, which implies an
absurdity.   Neither is *Peter*, a *rock*, the body of the
Apostles, as some others have imagined, for neither by
usage or by any institution could this word be applied
to the body of the Apostles.   Moreover, in all this
discourse, no word of Christ is addressed to the
Apostles, but all is addressed to Peter, and to Peter
only.   Peter is therefore the rock ; and the Latin
Petrus is the same as *Petra*.   No one but Peter at the
time confessed the divinity of Christ.   No one but
Peter could be called Simon Bar-Jona ; and no one but
Peter was called Cephas.

We have now to proceed with the continuation of our Lord's
discourse to Peter, and obtain another argument from the figure

of the Keys. *And I will give to thee the keys of the Kingdom of heaven. And whatsoever thou shalt bind upon earth, it shall be bound also in heaven; and whatsoever thou shalt loose on earth, it shall be loosed also in heaven.** By the Kingdom of heaven is here meant the Church, of which He makes express mention in the preceding words. The possession, or giving up of the keys of any place, house, or city, &c., was, amongst the ancients, especially in the East, a symbol of possession, or the giving of power over such places: Scriptural usage is clear on this point, for the Sacred Scripture, wherever it uses the metaphor of the keys signifies real power and authority. Thus, in Isaias, when God wished to signify that He gave His authority to Eliacim in the hall of the King, He said: *And I will lay the key of the house of David upon his shoulder; and he shall open, and none shall shut; and he shall shut, and none shall open.*† And it is in the same sense our Saviour Himself uses it, when He says: *Woe to you lawyers, for you have taken away the key of knowledge*; that is, assumed to themselves the sole authority of interpreting the Sacred Scriptures. And in the Apocalypse, Christ, wishing to signify that He has the power of life and death, says that He has *the keys of death and hell.*

As the Scriptures, in these and in many other places, use the metaphor of the keys to signify power, it should in this place be taken in the same sense; to give the keys of the Kingdom of heaven therefore means the giving of supreme power to St. Peter, and constituting him the Vicar of Christ on earth.

The power of binding and loosing was afterwards conferred on the other Apostles, but here it is promised in a special and emphatic manner to St. Peter by himself, to show the supreme power that Christ would entrust to him: *whatsoever thou shalt bind on earth it shall be bound also in heaven, &c.*

(c) The third place of the New Testament from which we conclude the primacy of St. Peter is the Gospel of St. John,‡ where Christ, after His Resurrection, conferred on St. Peter the promised power. Three times He asked St. Peter in the presence of the other Apostles whether he loved Him more than they did; and to Peter's three-fold protestation of love He subjoined the three-fold command: *Feed My lambs, feed My sheep. When therefore they had dined, Jesus saith to Simon Peter: Simon, son of John, lovest thou Me more than these? He saith to Him: Yea, Lord, thou knowest that I love thee. He saith to him: Feed My lambs. He*

---

* St. Matt. xvi. 19.   † Isa. xxii. 22.   ‡ St. John xxi. 15 *et seq.*

saith to him again: Simon, son of John, lovest thou Me? He saith to Him: Yea, Lord, thou knowest that I love thee. He saith to him: Feed My lambs. He saith to him the third time: Simon, son of John, lovest thou Me ? Peter was grieved, because He had said to him the third time: Lovest thou Me? And he said to Him: Lord, thou knowest all things; thou knowest that I love Thee. He said to him: Feed My sheep.

From this whole text it follows: (a) That our Lord gave to St. Peter a special power and commission to feed not only His *lambs*, that is the faithful in general; but also His *sheep*, that is the Clergy and Bishops, etc.

(b) That to St. Peter was committed the universal Church, both the sheep and lambs of Christ, as embracing the whole fold by the Supreme Pastor, the pastor of pastors. Therefore we conclude from the promise of Christ, the metaphor of the keys, and the three-fold command to feed His lambs and His sheep, that our Lord conferred on St. Peter the Primacy over the universal Church on earth.

6. These arguments may be further confirmed by the fact that St. Peter exercised this power, and it was acknowledged by all the other Apostles. Peter, in the list of the Apostles, is always placed first by the Evangelists.* And St. Matthew says expressly: *the FIRST Simon who is called Peter.* Sometimes he alone is mentioned, the others being omitted. Thus in St. Mark's Gospel :† *And Simon and they that were with Him followed after Him.* And again :‡ *But go, tell His disciples and Peter that He goeth before you into Galilee.* In the Acts of the Apostles we find the same :‖ *But Peter and the Apostles, answering, said.* And in the first Chapter of the Acts we find St. Peter taking the lead : *In those days Peter, rising up in the midst of the brethren, said,* &c.

During the lifetime of Christ Peter speaks in the name of and for the other Apostles, as narrated in many places of the Gospel of St. Matthew (xv. 15., xvi. 16., xvii. 4, 23., xviii. 21., xix. 27.). Finally St. Peter presided at the first Council of Jerusalem, and when he spoke all the others remained silent. And St. Paul, who had received the Gospel by revelation, nevertheless tells us, that after three years he went to Jerusalem to see Peter, and that he tarried with him fifteen days.

7. I may here give, by way of summary of the foregoing proofs, Dr. Lingard's Note on this subject.

(a) "The name of this Apostle was originally Simon. The

---

* SS. Matt. x. 2; Mark. iii. 16; Luke vi. 14.   † St. Mark. i. 36.
‡ St. Mark. xvi. 7.   ‖ Acts v. 29.

moment he appeared before our Saviour, he received from Him a new name : — *Thou art Simon, the son of Jona ; thou shalt be called Cephas.* *

The true interpretation of Cephas is *rock*, though in the version of the English Church we read *stone*—probably to elude the argument drawn from this change of name. Now, why did our blessed Lord give to him, at first sight, before Simon had done or said anything to elicit it, this name of *rock*? The mystery was disclosed later, when, in consequence of Peter's confession, He said to him : *Thou art Cephas, and on this Cephas I will build My Church, and the gates of hell shall not prevail against it* ;† words in Hebrew equivalent to the following : *Thou art Rock, the Rock on which I will build My Church.*

(b) "He then proceeded thus : *I will give unto thee the keys of the Kingdom of heaven*, &c. The power of binding and loosing was afterwards conferred on the other Apostles, but not the keys, the badge of the chief office in the household. They were granted to Peter alone.

(c) "At the miraculous draught of fishes, figurative of the gathering of the nations into the Church, when Peter, with his partners James and John, *forsook all and followed* our Saviour, it was the bark of St. Peter into which Jesus entered in preference ; it was Peter whom He ordered to let down the net for a draught, and to Peter He said : *fear not ; henceforth thou shalt catch men* ;‡ that is, shalt be a fisher of men. From that period we find him always mentioned as the first, and the leader of the others ; to him is given the charge that he confirm his brethren ;§ and the office of feeding both the lambs and the sheep.‖ After the Ascension of our Lord we find him acting as the head of the whole body at the election of Matthias (Acts i.), in preaching the Gospel to the Jews (Acts ii. iii.), in rebuking Ananias and Saphira (Acts v.), in the calling of the Gentiles (Acts x.), and in the Council at Jerusalem (Acts xv.). All these passages and proceedings demonstrate in Peter a pre-eminence in rank and authority above the other Apostles.

---

* St. John i. 42.   † St. Matt. xvi. 18.   ‡ St. Luke v. 10.
§ Ibid. xxii. 32.   ‖ St. John xxi. 15. 16.

CHAPTER II.

SECTION 2. (ARTICLE IX.)

THE PRIMACY OF THE ROMAN PONTIFF.

1. The Office was not personal to Peter, but was to pass to his successors.—
2. Christ wished the primacy to continue in His Church.—3. The primacy conferred on St. Peter continues in the Roman Pontiff.—
4. The Roman Pontiff by divine right is the successor of St. Peter.—
5. An objection against the supremacy of the Roman Pontiff, and its answer.

1. DR. LINGARD, continuing his remarks on the Church and the primacy of St. Peter, says of the succession of that authority and supremacy:

"It may perhaps be supposed that the office might be personal to Peter, and therefore might not pass to his successors. But on what grounds does such a supposition rest? If Christ, when He established His Church, gave to it a visible Head, who could have authority to change that form of government afterwards? Whatever reason there might be why Peter should be invested with authority over *his* brethren, the other Apostles, the same will require that the successor of Peter should be invested with authority over *his* brethren, the successors of the Apostles. It is idle to require proof from Scripture on such matters, because the Scripture does not treat of them. We may glean from the inspired writers a few detached and imperfect notices of the form of Church government which was established in their time; but not one of them fully describes that form, nor alludes to the form that was to prevail in time to come. For such matters we must have recourse to tradition; and tradition bears ample testimony to the superior authority of the successor of St. Peter. For, says Irenaeus (*anno*167) 'It is necessary that all the Church, that is, the faithful wherever they are, should conform to (be in communion with) the Church of Rome on account of her Superior chiefdom.'" (Adv., Haer. 3.)

2. We may, however, state that Christ wished the *primacy* to continue in his Church.

No one denies that Christ wished his Church to remain always the same as He established it, but in its primary constitution, and by divine institution, the primacy was established in it; therefore it is always to remain in it, according to the will of Christ Himself.

Moreover, the end for which the primacy was instituted always remains; that end is the preservation of unity in faith and discipline; and that it is necessary to this end, that the primacy of authority and jurisdiction should exist in the Church, no one can reasonably deny. For, as we have already seen, there cannot be two Christian Churches; and those who cause a division in the one true Church, as to her faith and doctrine, can no longer belong to her. The Church is of necessity, and by divine institution, *one;* therefore she must always have a Primate or Chief Pastor; and as she is to last to the end of time, so the primacy must also last, and perpetually abide in her, as it belongs essentially to her nature and institution. This is evident from the words of Our Lord, addressed to St. Peter: *and the gates of hell shall not prevail against her;* and this, because she is built on the rock of Peter.

3. The primacy conferred on St. Peter continues in the Roman Pontiff. No other Bishop has ever claimed to be the successor of St. Peter, and no other has ever been acknowledged as such by the faithful, and by the Church. All the Roman Pontiffs, from St. Linus, the immediate successor of St. Peter, to the present Pontiff, Leo. XIII., have acted as the successors of St. Peter, have vindicated to themselves, and used that power and authority which belongs to the primacy. The Fathers of the Church, the Councils, and the whole Catholic world, recognised and recognise the Roman Pontiffs as the successors of St. Peter, and acknowledge now, as in the past, their primacy.

The same proposition may be proved from the fact of Peter's See at Rome, and his dying as Bishop of Rome, and the right of succession. That Pastor has the *primacy,* which was granted to Peter, who is the one and lawful successor of St. Peter. And as this is no other than the Roman Pontiff, he has the prerogatives of Peter and his primacy over the Church. According to the natural law of succession, where the predecessor dies, and there lays down his office, in that place we have to look for his successor. But Peter had his See at Rome; he did not transfer it elsewhere, and he died Bishop of Rome; and it was in Rome itself he gave up his life, and with it the primacy over the Church on earth; therefore, the Bishop of Rome only can be his successor. As to the coming of St. Peter to Rome, his living there, and his death in that city, it is useless to institute any discussion, as it becomes useless in the present day to doubt or discuss the question as to the fact of Alexander's dwelling in Greece, and Cyrus in Persia.

It would be useless to dwell on the arguments in proof of a fact which is not doubted by anyone of a sound and unprejudiced mind, for it may be said in all ecclesiastical history, there is no fact more known, none more certain or better attested, than this. But what we have chiefly to notice in regard to this question, is that St. Peter placed his See at Rome, and there remained Bishop until his death; and this is also attested by the testimony of all historians, and all ages.

4. There is a further question to be examined in connection with this matter, namely, whether the Roman Pontiff is not only the true and certain successor of St. Peter, but his successor by divine right (*jure divino*). This is a grave question, and we have four different opinions in regard to it; but two only of them are solid and tenable.

The first is that God left St. Peter free to choose his own See, and at the same time ordained that whatever See St. Peter should have at the time of his death, it should ever afterwards retain the primacy; in other words, the succession in the Episcopal See which St. Peter should make his own, should have connected with it, by divine right, the succession of his primacy.

The second opinion states that God not only ordained that some one particular See should be chosen, but revealed to Peter the See of Rome, and designed that it, in particular, should be the See of Peter and his successors. These two opinions are tenable, and in accordance with the decree of the Vatican Council (1870), in which we have the following definition: *Si quis ergo dixerit non esse ipsins Christi domini institutione, seu jure divino, ut Beatus Petrus in primatu super universam Ecclesiam habeat perpetuos successores ; aut Romanum Pontificem, non esse Beati Petri in eodem primatu successionem, anathema sit.*

"If anyone, therefore, say that it is not by virtue of Christ's institution and divine right that the Blessed Peter has perpetual successors in the primacy over the Universal Church; or that the Roman Pontiff is not the successor of Blessed Peter in the same primacy, let him be anathema."

The Councils of Nice, the first of Constantinople and of Ephesus, have the following statement: "St. Peter, the prince of the Apostles, and the head and foundation of the Church . . . . . up to this time, and in all future times, lives and exercises judgment by his successors."

It is, therefore, concluded from this doctrine, and according to the common teaching of Theologians, that the Primacy is inseparable from the See of Peter, and that Popes can indeed transfer their residence elsewhere, and leave Rome to dwell in other countries; but the See, or its title, cannot be transferred, and that, wherever the Pope is, he must always be the Bishop of Rome, otherwise he would not be St. Peter's successor.

5. The only objection to the supremacy of the Popes is that uttered by some Protestant writers, who say, that the supremacy of the Popes owes its origin to the astuteness, to the fraud, to the barbarity of the middle ages, and to the celebrity of the City of Rome.

To this sweeping and unfounded objection we answer : Astuteness and fraud cannot easily be reconciled with the sanctity and eminent virtue of a great number of the Popes, especially those of the first ages, all of whom suffered martyrdom for their faith. The Pontifical primacy does not date from the middle ages, but from St. Peter. In the middle ages they had as many able and learned men, and Theologians, and men of independent spirit, as in any other epoch of the world. In the middle ages, the Popes did not cease to defend the spiritual authority against the claims of the civil power. If the Papacy was founded in the middle ages, how does it subsist in modern times? This Papacy did not begin to flourish until the renown of Rome became obscure and the city was overrun by Barbarians, and until the seat of the Empire had been transferred to Constantinople.

Far, therefore, from being able to explain the Papacy by natural causes, and much less by political convenience and design, it is necessary to acknowledge the establishment and conservation of the Papacy as a supernatural and a divine fact. If it had been a human institution, the Papacy could not have lasted over eighteen centuries, in the midst of so many enemies who were determined on its ruin. Had she been a human institution alone, her action in this world could not have obtained for her the respect, the love, and obedience in every generation of millions of men, many of whom were the most illustrious for sanctity and learning that the world has ever seen.

She could not, without divine help and supernatural strength, have shown such invincible patience under persecutions ; such persevering courage in pursuing her work and its end, namely, the salvation of souls; and such indefatigable zeal in promoting the principles of true civilization. Without the intervention of

God, the Papacy would have followed the fate of all other institutions in the past; they have all disappeared or perished like the Patriarchate of Constantinople, which, sustained by the power of the Emperors of the East, had never more than the shadow of authority.

The Pope to-day, as in the first ages, is the Primate, and first of all. No other is known by all; no other is recognised by all; no other influences all; and has power to influence the whole body; because he is the head and foundation of Christianity.

I may, therefore, sum up the doctrine of the perpetuity of the primacy as continued in the Church. The primacy of jurisdiction, conferred on St. Peter, is to last to the end of time. For it was not given or instituted for him, but for the Church. The Church is a *kingdom*, it must, therefore, have a king; it is a *house*, it therefore must have a head or master; it is a *family*, and must have a father; it is a *sheepfold*, and must have a shepherd; a *ship*, and must have a pilot; it is a *body*, which must have a head; and a *building*, which must have a foundation.

CHAPTER II.

SECTION 3. (ARTICLE IX.)

THE INFALLIBILITY OF THE ROMAN PONTIFF.

1. The Infallibility of the Pope is the consequence of his Primacy.—2. The question as to whether the Roman Pontiff has *passive Infallibility*, that is whether his faith is infallible.—3. The Infallibility of the Pope in teaching and as defined by the Church.—4. When the Pope may be considered as speaking *ex cathedra.*—5. The Decree of the Council of the Vatican on the Papal Infallibility.—6. The Papal Infallibility proved from Scripture.—7. The Papal Infallibility proved from tradition.—8. No Pope has ever erred when speaking *ex cathedra.*—9. Facts quoted against the Papal Infallibility answered:—(a) the fall of Peter, (b) the fall of Liberius, (c) the case of Pope Honorius.

1. THE Infallibility of the Pope is a consequence of his primacy. The Church which will last on earth to the end of time ought to profess the true doctrine of Jesus Christ, and at the same time remain united to Peter and his successors as her centre, and obey them as her head and chief; in other words, she must recognise or acknowledge their supreme doctrinal and legislative authority. For, if Peter or his successor were to ordain that some doctrine be professed as the true doctrine of Jesus Christ, which would not be true, or be contrary to the true doctrine, it would follow that the Church would err in faith in obeying him; or otherwise she would be separated from her centre, and disobey her chief and supreme Pastor. But from the promises of Christ we know that the Church cannot err in faith, and from the institution of Christ the Church must remain united to the Papacy, and therefore it is necessary to conclude that the Pope is *infallible.*

Let us first understand what is meant by *infallibility* as belonging to the Pope. It is, as I have said above, the *gift of inerrancy*; and it is either *passive* or *active. Passive infallibility* belongs to the Church believing, or the whole body of the faithful. *Active infallibility* belongs to the Church teaching.

2. The Sovereign Pontiff may be considered as one of the faithful believing, or as a doctor, or teacher, of the Church. The question is not as to whether the Roman Pontiff is infallible as

one of the *faithful believing*; or in other words, we do not ask whether he has *passive infallibility* in himself. Doctors differ on this point. Some deny that the Pope could fall into *formal* heresy, and others affirm that he could. Bellarmine holds the opinion which denies this as probable, and Suarez thinks it the more probable.

This opinion receives strength and confirmation from the fact, that not one of the many Popes who have occupied the Chair of Peter has ever fallen into *formal* heresy; but whatever may be said as to *formal* heresy, it is certain, and not questioned or doubted by any one, that the Pope has not passive infallibility in the sense that he is preserved from all *material* dogmatic error, or from *material* heresy as a private man or a private doctor. As a private doctor he is not preserved from holding and teaching and propagating error, and much less as a private person is he preserved from holding error and being lead into it.

3. The question that we have to deal with now is the infallibility of the Sovereign Pontiff, that is *infallibility* as it is "a special providence and assistance of God, by which the Sovereign Pontiff in teaching or defining *ex cathedra* is preserved from all doctrinal error."

The Pontiff can teach (*a*) as a private doctor, as other men and Theologians, by writing and editing books, and even by writing doctrinal epistles; but it is certain that these writings have no pontifical authority, and are not to be looked upon as infallible documents. (*b*) He can teach as Pontiff, and he is considered to teach as such as often as he speaks *ex cathedra*, or by the authority of his primatial See. "He speaks as Pontiff," as Billuart says, "when, as supreme pastor and head of the Church, he proposes anything to the whole Church affecting faith and morals, obliging all the faithful, under pain or penalty of heresy, to believe it by divine faith." And this is what is to be understood by speaking or teaching *ex cathedra*: that is, from the plenitude of his power, because by the *Chair* is understood authority to teach and to command according to the meaning of the words of St. Matthew: *The scribes and pharisees sit upon the chair of Moses.**

4. That the Pope be considered as speaking *ex cathedra* other conditions are to be observed: (*a*) He must be free. (*b*) He usually gives the subject mature and due examination. (*c*) He calls into consultation his own Church of Rome, especially his Cardinals.

The reason of this diligence in examination and deliberation

---

* St. Matt. xxiii, 2.

is, that the help of the Holy Ghost in forming definitions, presupposes industry and careful attention on the part of the Church. That assistance is not given by way of inspiration; but rather by way of co-operation; therefore it supposes that the agent himself acts; that the Church, or the Pope, uses the ordinary and necessary means of ascertaining the truth. The assistance of the Holy Spirit is always present with the Church, or the Pope, to preserve them from error in their definitions; and if, therefore, in any particular case the necessary diligence in examination be omitted, the person defining would sin through his negligence, but he could not err in the definition. If therefore the Pope, or the Council, should have the intention of defining that which is false, then God in His wisdom would save His Church in some way according to His Providence, either by changing the mind of the person defining, or dissolving the Council, or taking the Pontiff out of this world. This last is not necessary, as God can easily change the mind and heart, and we need not have recourse to the supposition of either a sudden or a violent death.

All agree that the Church, or the Pope, cannot err in the definition itself, but they do not agree as to whether they will infallibly use the required diligence in the examination. Some, as Melchior Canus, contend that the Church, or Pope, can no more omit the due diligence, than err in the definition. Others contend that due diligence may be omitted by the Pontiff, and the omission on his part would be sinful, but the definition itself would always be free from error. Hence, all agree in these two things.

(a) Whether the antecedent examination infallibly takes place or not, the Church or Pontiff cannot err in the definition, and this is a *dogma of faith*.

(b) There is an obligation of using the previous diligent examination, and this is *certain*, and admitted by all. Take for example the case of the Apostles, and the first Council at Jerusalem; before the definition, not only were the Apostles assembled together in Council, but in that Council they held serious and careful deliberation as to the matters to be defined : *And the Apostles and ancients assembled to consider this matter, and when there had been much disputing, Peter, rising up, said.**

5. I here subjoin the Decree of the Vatican Council on the Infallibility of the Roman Pontiff. (1870.)

* Acts xv. 6, 7.

"Therefore we, adhering faithfully to the tradition received from the beginning of the Christian faith, to the glory of God, our Saviour, the exaltation of the Catholic religion and the salvation of Christian people, the Sacred Council approving, we teach and define that it is a divinely revealed dogma that the Roman Pontiff, when he speaks *ex cathedra*, that is, when performing the function of Pastor and teacher of all Christians, by virtue of his supreme and apostolic authority, he defines a doctrine of faith and morals to be held by the universal Church, has through that divine assistance promised to him in Blessed Peter, that infallibility with which our divine Redeemer wished His Church to be endowed, in defining a doctrine of faith and morals; and, therefore, that the definitions of the same Roman Pontiff of themselves, and not by the consent of the Church, are irreformable. If anyone should presume, which God avert, to contradict this, our definition, let him be anathema."

All that we have written, therefore, in explanation of the infallibility of the Church, and the object of this infallibility, equally applies to the Sovereign Pontiff and his infallibility, as according to the definition of the Vatican Council, he is endowed with the same infallibility, and to the same extent as the Church.

We can easily know when the Pope intends to define an Article of faith, and to oblige the faithful.

   (a) He intends to oblige the faithful when he affixes to a proposition a theological note of condemnation, especially if he condemns it as heretical.

   (b) When, by his Apostolic authority, he commands that this or that particular doctrine be held by all as of faith. How clear and unmistakable are the definitions, for example, of the Immaculate Conception of the Blessed Virgin, and of the Papal Infallibility itself. No one can mistake or fail to understand their meaning, and the mind of the Church in these, and in her other definitions, binding on the faithful.

6. Having given the definition of the Vatican Council on the Papal Infallibility, we may now proceed to give the proofs of Scripture on which this doctrine rests.

There are three principal Scriptural pronouncements by which the Papal Infallibility may be proved.

The first is from St. Luke :* *Simon, Simon, behold Satan hath*

---

* St. Luke xxii. 31,

desired to have you that he might sift you as wheat, but I have prayed for thee that thy faith fail not; and thou being once converted, confirm thy brethren.

The second is from St. Matthew:* *Thou art Peter, and upon this rock I will build my Church, and the gates of hell shall not prevail against it.* From these words it follows that if St. Peter should err, the Church resting upon his authority and assenting to it, would err also, which is repugnant to its gift of indefectibility.

The third is from St. John:† *Feed My lambs......feed My sheep*: from which it follows that if the Church could reform the decrees of the Sovereign Pontiff, it would not be the Pastor that would feed the sheep, but the sheep the Pastor. Therefore the decrees of the Sovereign Pontiff are irreformable, and therefore infallible, as Christ could not subject His Church to an irreformable decree that is not true.

Hence it follows (*a*) that St. Peter and His successors, by the concession of Christ, have the right and power to confirm the faithful, and to feed the lambs and the sheep. (*b*) That the judgment of the Sovereign Pontiff is supreme and final, from which there is no appeal. There are many other reasons given in refutation of Gallicanism, but the question of the Papal Infallibility is now defined and settled, and all are obliged not only to concede it, but to hold it.

7. The Infallibility of the Pope may also be proved from tradition.

The Fathers and Theologians understand and explain the testimonies above cited from Sacred Scripture, to refer to the Papal Infallibility. In this sense St. Agatho uses the words of St. Luke, in his Epistle to the Emperor Constantine Pogonatus, which was read and accepted by the Fathers of the Sixth Ecumenical Council, the third of Constantinople (A. D. 680—682).

Likewise St. Leo says : " In Peter, therefore, the fortitude of all is strenghtened, and the help of divine grace is so ordered that the firmness, which was given by Christ to St. Peter, through Peter was conferred upon the Apostles." Other Fathers have taught, as universally received, that this gift (of infallibility) belonged to the Roman Pontiffs, as it was necessary that all should be in conformity with the Chair of Peter, if they desired to remain faithful Christians.

Amongst many testimonies from the early Fathers it will

---

* St. Matt. xvi. 18.   † St. John xxi. 15.

W

suffice to refer to the following : "It is in the Roman Church that the faithful have always preserved the tradition that has come down from the Apostles. It is to this Church, because of its superior authority, that every other Church ought to be conformed." (St. Ireneus.)

"It is with the Chair of Peter that all should keep united." (St. Optatus.)

"Know that the Roman faith is inaccessible to heresy." (St. Jerome.)

"The causes relative to faith ought to be to that place where faith cannot fail. This is the prerogative of the Holy See." (St. Bernard.)

Moreover we see that in every age all discussions in matters of faith and morals were submitted to the judgment of the Pope, and his judgment was always regarded as irreformable.

The Roman Pontiffs themselves have very often declared that there can be no appeal from their sentence, and have often forbidden such appeals under penalty of excommunication.

The Councils have also borne testimony to the doctrinal infallibility of the visible head of the Church. The Fathers of the Fourth Council of Constantinople declared that, "in the Apostolic See the Catholic religion had been always preserved immaculate, and a holy doctrine always taught."

Those of the Second Council of Lyons declared that, "when questions arise concerning faith, these questions should be defined by the judgment of the Holy Roman Church." The Council of Florence, that "the Roman Pontiff is the Father and Teacher of all Christians." Those of the Council of Vienne, that "it belongs to the Apostolic See alone to pronounce on doubts in matters of faith."

We have the public facts of history in proof of this doctrine. (a) All heresiarchs and innovators have been condemned by the Holy See or Sovereign Pontiff. (b) All Ecumenical Councils have been approved by the Popes. (c) All the encyclicals, allocutions and epistles of the Roman Pontiffs are received as irreformable. (d) All Catholics have invariably submitted to the Popes' decrees and doctrinal decisions ; and the Gallican Church itself, up to the celebrated declaration of the year 1682, professed the same doctrine.

8. All this tradition may be confirmed by the fact that no Pope has ever erred when speaking *ex cathedra*. It is very useful and indispensable, from this question, to prove the truth of this assertion ; for if even one Pope ever defined *ex cathedra* a false

doctrine, all our arguments in favour of the Papal infallibility are of no avail. If, on the contrary, it can be shown, that out of the long role of Pontiffs not one of them erred when speaking *ex cathedra*, we have a very strong and convincing proof of the divine assistance of infallibility given to the Popes. For it would be almost impossible that men without a special divine assistance, which we call infallibility, should make declarations in all matters affecting religion without falling into any error; and this the Roman Pontiffs have done all along up to the present day, and that without heresy or error.

This argument is stated as certain, and it is the duty of our adversaries, who deny it, to tell us what Pope erred, and when did he err when teaching *ex cathedra*. To do this two things must be certain.

(a) That the error is certainly against faith, and that it does not admit any Catholic interpretation.

(b) That it is an error of a dogmatic definition, or of a definition of the Pope speaking *ex cathedra*. If either of these two be wanting, the case cannot affect the Infallibility which we attribute to the Roman Pontiff. All the facts which our adversaries can bring forward against us, are wanting in one or other of these conditions, and they do not, therefore, affect the question.

9. There are three principal facts quoted against the Papal Infallibility. (a) The fall of Peter. (b) The fall of Liberius. (c) The fall of Honorius.

(a) As regards the fall of Peter, there was clearly no definition of faith, since neither the Church itself was solemnly instituted, nor the primacy actually conferred upon St. Peter, but only the promise of that, on account of which he and his successors were gifted with infallibility. St. Peter, although he denied Christ in words, did not do so in his heart, according to the more common opinion of Commentators; and even if he did in his heart deny the faith, he was not yet, at that time, constituted the head of the Church, nor was he teaching the universal Church in any sense.

(b) As to the fall of Liberius, there is no difficulty. He was not making any definition of faith, but he subscribed a *formula*, which contained a Catholic sense, but had also an heretical sense, and in itself was erroneous. Besides, it has been asserted by many critics, that the fall of Liberius is entirely ficticious, or, at least, so doubtful that no certain argument can be concluded from it against the personal character of that Pope. Dr. Döllinger, in his Ecclesiastical History, speaking of Liberius, says : " It is said that in 357 the above Pope renounced all communion with St. Athanasius, associated himself with the Arians, and subscribed one, probably the first, of the three *formulas* that had been compiled at Sirmium. This formula was so drawn up that, in the true signification of the words, it was not heretical, but was of such a nature that orthodox Catholics might, without diffi- culty, subscribe to it."

(c)   Honorius did not define a dogma on the occasion of the fall attributed to him. On the contrary, he openly and expressly asserted the two-fold operation and will in Christ by reason of His two-fold nature, and he uses a form of Catholic doctrine, which was accepted by an Ecumenical Council. Besides, he himself declared openly that he did not wish to give a dogmatic definition at the time, as is clear from the very letters on account of which he is accused.[1]

---

* See Perrone, *de Locis Theologicis*, p. 1., s. 11. Billuart *de locis.*

CHAPTER II.
SECTION 4. (ARTICLE IX).
THE PAPAL INFALLIBILITY. (CONTINUED).

1. The conditions required that a Papal definition be infallible.—2. The *assistance* of the Holy Ghost, as distinguished from Inspiration or Revelation.—3. The distinction between faith purely *divine*, and divine-Catholic faith.—4. The *Magisterium* of the Church—*special* and *ordinary*.—5. The objections of the heresiarch Döllinger against the Papal Infallibility answered.—6. The four propositions of the Gallican convention held in 1682,—7. Arguments from reason in favour of the Papal Infallibility.

1. THAT a definition of the Pope be considered infallible, according to the Decree of the Vatican Council, the following conditions are required : (*a*) That the Pope speaks as a public doctor or teacher, and not as a private person or particular doctor in a theological work. (*b*) That he acts out of the plenitude of his power and authority, and imposes an absolute and irrevocable obligation. (*c*) That he defines a doctrine as divinely revealed. (*d*) That he defines it as a doctrine to be held by the universal Church. If one or other of these conditions be wanting, the sentence need not be regarded as infallible.

2. According to the same Decree, the efficient cause of the infallibility of the Pope speaking *ex cathedra* is the divine *assistance*, which preserves him from error in the exposition of truths contained in the deposit of faith. It is not *inspiration* nor the *revelation* of truths before unknown. The Pope is the interpreter of truths already inspired or revealed. He only interprets them and pronounces their revelation or inspiration. He does not invent them or claim inspiration, but only the divine assistance when teaching, as the Pastor of the Universal Church, by which he is saved and preserved from error.

In order to answer the objections of modern innovators, who attack the dogma of the Papal Infallibility, it is necessary to refer to some things which I have already explained, when treating on the infused virtue of faith.

3. Faith, as a habit, can be defined : "A theological virtue by which a man, on the authority of God, firmly assents to all the truths certainly revealed by Him."

This faith may be *purely divine*, or divine-Catholic faith. The first is that which we have defined; the other requires the addition, *and proposed by the Church to all to be believed*.

An act of faith is " the actual firm assent of the mind given to any or every truth revealed by God, on account of His authority." Thus he believes by divine faith, who, through grace and the virtue of faith, assents to a truth, because God has inspired or revealed it.

Moreover, every truth revealed or inspired by God, and proposed by the Church as the revealed or inspired word of God, belongs to and is the object of divine-Catholic faith, because no one can be in the Church who does not believe a truth of this kind; but not all revealed truths are defined by an express definition of the Church. There are many such truths revealed by God, on which the Church has not yet pronounced any definitive judgment.

A Catholic, therefore, who, by the study of Scripture or tradition, would come to the certain knowledge of these truths and their inspiration would be bound to believe them. The faith by which such truths are believed is not human, because they are not found in the words of men, but in the pure word of God; and, therefore, they are believed on the authority of God through grace and the divine virtue of faith. Nevertheless, a man denying one of these truths would not thereby be a heretic, because they are not yet proposed by the Church as revealed and to be believed by all.

From the state of divine faith, to the state of divine-Catholic faith, the truths to be believed pass by the virtue of the living *Magisterium* of the Church.

4. The *Magisterium* of the Church is nothing else that her doctrinal authority. And this is two-fold. *Special* and *ordinary*.

Her special *Magisterium* is exercised when the Church, in reference to any dogma, solemnly pronounces a sentence, either of condemnation or of definition.

The ordinary *Magisterium* is that authority which is daily used by her pastors and doctors. By virtue of this second *Magisterium*, a truth can be proposed as Catholic, or such a truth remaining in a state of truths of faith purely divine, may so far progress as to attain almost to the state of defined truths, and then it may be said to be a truth proximate to divine-Catholic faith. A person denying such a truth would not thereby be a heretic, but he would be proximate to heresy; thus, for example, the dogma of the Immaculate Conception, before its definition in 1854, and the dogma of Papal Infallibility, before the definition of the Vatican Council (1870), were truths to be believed by divine faith; but by the special *Magisterium* of the Church, they are now defined and to be believed by all, so that he would be a heretic who should deny either of them.

5. By these remarks we have the key to the solution of the objections of the Heresiarch Döllinger, against the definition of the dogma of Papal Infallibility.

The objection of the Heresiarch, which was so sharply and maliciously published a little before the time of the assembly of the Bishops at the Vatican Council, may be briefly stated. " By such a definition," he said, " the Church will place Catholics under an obligation of believing a truth which before they did not believe, and which the Church never believed, nor ever taught."

The Church, he says, did not believe in it, because those who held it, could not be said to believe it, taking the word belief in its Christian sense. There is a great difference between those things which are to be believed by divine faith, and those that are only perceived as probable by the human intellect. A Catholic can and is bound to believe only those truths which, as revealed, belong to the doctrine of salvation, and in reality are, without doubt, proposed by the Church, or the opposite of those which have been condemned as heretical by the same authority. "But," he continues, " no one from the beginning of the Church to our day believed in the dogma of the Infallibility of the Sovereign Pontiff, that is, by the same faith by which we believe in God, in the Trinity and the Incarnation, but there were many who thought it probable, or at most believed on human faith, that this prerogative belongs to the Pope."

In answer to this objection, we may refer to the above remarks, and the distinction between faith purely divine, and divine-Catholic faith. We deny that, before the definition, no one believed in this dogma by *divine faith*; but we concede that it was not the object of divine-Catholic faith until it was defined by the Church. The distinction has been already explained. Besides, this objection would prove too much, because it would follow from it that the Church herself is not infallible, and that the *Magisterium* of infallibility does not belong to her, and she could not therefore ever declare either in her Councils or out of them what are, and what are not, the dogmas of faith, which no Catholic ever asserted, or could assert, without falling into heresy.

Besides, the Church has always acted on the belief in this truth, even before it was defined, and the contest with the Gallicans was, according to Cardinal Deschamps, carried on in good faith by the greater number of them; for the French School, although in recent times it contradicted this truth in theory, always confessed it in practice with a fidelity truly worthy of the French Clergy.

A second objection is proposed against the definition, to wit; in the definition of Papal Infallibility, the Pope bears witness of himself, because the Bishops, even in Council assembled, are fallible without the Pope; the Pope alone is infallible, therefore, in defining his infallibility, he gives testimony of himself.

To this we may answer: first, that every supreme power has the right and faculty of bearing testimony to or of itself, and of vindicating itself. God vindicates Himself. *I am who am;* and Christ says of Himself: *I am the Alpha and Omega, the beginning and the end. No one cometh to the Father except through me.* A king vindicates himself, and justly judges and punishes those who offend against him. The same applies to the Pope, who is the supreme King, the Vicar of Christ. He can give testimony of himself, and declare the prerogatives conferred upon Him: He is the supreme head of the Church, and he holds the *primacy* over her.

Secondly, we can reply that the authority and infallibility of a Council is not only Papal, but also Conciliary (*conciliaria*), by virtue of that universal authority which Jesus Christ conferred on St. Peter, and the College of the Apostles. And, although this gift belongs to the Church teaching, by reason of the unity whose centre and fountain is the Sovereign Pontiff, and the infallibility proceeds from him as from the head; although objectively considered the infallibility of the Pope is prior to the infallibility of the Church, subjectively, however, and as to us (*quoad nos*), the infallibility of the Church teaching with the Pope, is prior to the infallibility of the Pope alone. The former was always held as a truth of divine-Catholic faith, but not the latter. An argument may, therefore, lawfully proceed from a truth known by divine-Catholic faith to that which is known only by purely divine faith. Properly speaking, it is not, therefore, the Pope that bears testimony of himself in the Vatican Council, but it is the whole teaching Church in conjunction with the Pope; it is an Ecumenical Council, which was always acknowledged as infallible, that declares the subject of infallibility to be the Pope with the Episcopate, and the Pope alone when he speaks *ex cathedra.*

6. I may mention in connection with this question the four propositions of the Gallican Convention held in the year 1682; their sense may be briefly stated in the following terms:—

(a)   That to the Roman Pontiff belongs no power, not even indirect, over Kings or in civil affairs.

(b)   That the authority of a general Council is superior to the authority of the Roman Pontiff.

(c)   That the power of the Apostolic See may be restricted (1) by canons already formed and consecrated by the reverence of the whole world, (2) by the Constitutions and institutions received by the Kingdom of France, and the Gallican Church.

(d)   That the judgment of the Roman Pontiff is not infallible, unless the consent of the Church be given to it. This last proposition is now heretical after the Decree of the Vatican Council. It is therefore no longer asserted by any Catholic, and with it Gallicanism died. There is no such school or system now recognized in Catholic Theology.

7. In concluding this subject I may sum up a few of the arguments from reason, in favour of the Papal Infallibility.

That judgment in matters of faith is irreformable which is supreme and final; above which there is no other to which we can appeal, and such is the judgment of the Roman Pontiff.

In judicial tribunals and cases, sometimes there is an appeal allowed to a higher tribunal. Thus, for example, it is lawful to appeal from the judgment of a Parish Priest to that of the Bishop, and from the judgment of a Bishop to the Pope; or to one of the tribunals appointed and sanctioned by the Pope for the hearing of Papal cases. Now the necessary condition of our appeal is, that the person who appeals withdraw himself from obedience, and the jurisdiction of the tribunal from which he appeals; but no Catholic can withdraw himself from the jurisdiction of the Pope and from obedience to him in matters of faith. If such an appeal were ever lawful it would be an appeal to a General Council; but such an appeal is not, strictly speaking, an appeal from the judgment of the Pope; because it belongs to the Pope to convoke a General Council, to preside over it, and to confirm its decrees, and these are not irreformable unless they are confirmed by Pontifical and Apostolical authority. Besides, we must bear in mind, that the Church is a perfect society, and well ordered; therefore it must have a permanent and living supreme judge. Christ made sufficient provision for His Church; and since errors, and errors

in faith, rise up every day, it is necessary that there be a permanent and living judge to correct such errors, and to preserve
inviolate and pure the faith of the Church, and this judge is no
other than the Roman Pontiff; only at rare intervals, and with
great difficulty, are General Councils assembled.

It is absurd to suppose that the judgment of the Roman Pontiff is not infallible without the consent of the Church, because
from this it would follow (*a*) that the Pope would receive his infallibility from the Church, and this cannot be said or held,
because the Church is founded on Peter, and it is Peter who is appointed to feed and to confirm his brethren. It is for this reason that
Pius VI., in the Bull *auctorem fidei*, condemned the proposition
which asserted that power was given by God to His Church that
she might communicate it to her Pastors, who are her ministers
for the salvation of souls, which proposition, understood in the
sense that the Pastors of the Church derived the power of their
ecclesiastical ministry and government from the communion of
the faithful, is heretical. It would follow (*b*) that the Sovereign
Pontiff would have no more the gift of Infallibility than the Bishop
of any, even the least and most insignificant, diocese. For any
Bishop who enunciates a dogma of faith, if to his judgment the
consent of all the other Bishops be added, would be infallible.

In regard to the consent of the Church, it may be further
asked what kind of consent must be obtained? whether the consent of the whole Church, or of the lesser part, or the greater
part of the Church.

The consent of the whole Church is certainly not required,
or attainable before a definition; as in this case the dissentient
voice of even one, and that might be a Bishop deficient in intelligence or learning, would be sufficient to cause the declaration to
be wanting in Infallibility; and how could the consent of every
single one of the Bishops be obtained before any one point of
heretical, or depraved doctrine, could be condemned by infallible
authority?

The consent of the lesser part of the Church could not make
the judgment of the Pope infallible; for by what right can this
or that part, say one or more dioceses, or provinces, give to the
Pope that Infallibility which they have not got themselves. As
to the greater part of the Church the same question may be asked,
by what right can it give infallibility? Besides, who could count,
or enumerate, the consenting parties throughout the world? and
in such a case how could the faithful be ever sure of their faith.
And if the consent of the greater part is sufficient, then we have

that consent freely given against all the Gallican propositions, and in favour of the Papal Infallibility in the Vatican Council.

I have only to add a word of explanation as to the expression— the *personal infallibility* of the Pope. This expression is equivocal. As applied to the Roman Pontiff, considered as a private person, it is not correct, because to him, in this capacity, infallibility is not promised ; but applied to the Sovereign Pontiff as a public person, and to the authority with which he is invested, it may be correctly used and received in the true sense of the Papal Infallibility.

CHAPTER III. (ARTICLE IX.)

BISHOPS AND GENERAL COUNCILS.

1. The divine institution of Bishops.—2. The meaning of a Council and the various kinds of Councils.—3. The distinction between a *General* and an *Ecumenical* Council.—4. The necessity and utility of Councils. —4. Conditions required that a Council be Ecumenical (a) in its convocation. (b) In its celebration. (c) In its conclusion.—5. The definitions of an Ecumenical Council are Infallible.—6. The confirmation of decrees of an Ecumenical Council.—7. The names and dates of the General and Ecumenical Councils of the Church.—8. The authority of Councils.

THE DIVINE INSTITUTION OF BISHOPS.

1. BESIDES the Sovereign Pontiff there exists in the Church, and by divine right, pastors, who, with him and under him, teach and govern the faithful. These pastors are the Bishops, the successors of the Apostles.

In effect it was said to them in the persons of the Apostles : *Whatsoever you shall loose upon earth, shall be loosened also in heaven.*[*] *I will ask the Father and He will send you another Paraclete.*[†] *As the Father hath sent me so I also send you*[‡] *Receive ye the Holy Ghost: whose sins you shall forgive, they are forgiven ; and whose sins you shall retain, they are retained.*[§] *Going therefore teach ye all nations . . . . . teaching them to observe all things whatsoever I have commanded you : and behold, I am with you all days, even to the consummation of the world.*[||]

Catholic tradition, by the organs of the Fathers and the Councils, has always interpreted these texts in the sense that the episcopal body, united with the Sovereign Pontiff, possesses doctrinal and legislative authority that is required to teach and to govern the Church ; what the Pope possesses primarily and absolutely, Bishops possess secondarily, and with dependence on the Pope : and thus the Pope and Bishops constitute the Church teaching, which the Church hearing or learning (*discens aut*

---

[*] St. Matt. xviii. 18.   [†] St. John xiv. 16.   [‡] St. John xx. 21.
[§] St. John xx. 22, 23.   [||] St. Matt. xxviii. 20.

credens), comprising simple priests and the faithful laity, should obey. The result of the teaching, and the constant practice of the Church is, that simple priests, even though charged as Curès, or Parish Priests, with the care of souls, and who are called pastors of the second order, do not fully participate in the doctrinal and legislative authority of the Church. They teach and rule, under the orders of the bishops, the faithful committed to their charge, but they are not judges of the faith, nor necessary councillors or accessories to the Bishop in the administration of the diocese. And as to lay persons, who by reason of their talents may be called to defend the Church against the attacks of the impious, they should always act with reserve and prudence, they should ask the advice of the Bishops, and never outstep the rules which may be given for their guidance.*

COUNCILS.

2. By natural and divine right, the pastors of the Church teaching have the power of assembling, for the purpose of deliberating and judging of matters of doctrine, and of Christian discipline. An assembly of this kind is called a Council; and this leads me to speak of the nature and authority of an Ecumenical Council, in connection with the constitution and authority of the Church.

A Council in general means an assembly of chosen men in one place, for the purpose of deliberating on certain things. A Council of the Church is an assembly of the Prelates of the Church for the purpose of ordering, or regulating, the public affairs of the Church.

Councils are various, and may be divided into General, or Ecumenical, National, Provincial, and Diocesan.

(a) A *General* or *Ecumenical Council* is that to which all the Bishops of the world are convoked, and over which the Roman Pontiff presides, either by himself or by his Legates.

(b) A National Council, or Synod, is that in which the Archbishops and Bishops of a whole Kingdom, or Nation, assemble, and over which the Patriarch, or Primate, presides.

(c) A Provincial Council, or Synod, is the assembly of the

---

* Concerning the Sacerdotal character, and the Sacrament of Order, and the divine grace conferred by it, enabling Priests to offer Mass and administer Sacraments, we shall speak when treating of Holy Order.

Bishops of one province, under the presidency of the
Archbishop or Metropolitan.

(d)   A Diocesan Council, or Synod, is that which a Bishop
convokes, of the Parish Priests, and the other Priests
and clergy of his diocese, over which assembly he himself presides.

I must in this instruction confine myself to the General or
Ecumenical Council.

3.   Some Theologians make a distinction between a General
and an Ecumenical Council.   An Ecumenical Council has the
authority and approval of the Pope, and a General Council has
not.   There are four General Councils that are not numbered
with the Ecumenical Councils. 1, Sardis (347) ; 2, Pisa (1,409) ;
3, Constance (1,414) ; 4, Basle (1,431-43).   Councils are called
General (a) because all the Bishops are convoked or called to
them ; even though all may not attend.   (b) On account of the
universal kind of causes which are treated of, or can come under
discussion, on faith, morals, and discipline.   (c) Because of the
universal decrees which bind all.

THE NECESSITY AND UTILITY OF COUNCILS.

4.   The Jansenists affirm that it is absolutely necessary
sometimes to hold Councils, but all Catholics deny this.   It is
not absolutely necessary ever to hold a Council, because : (1)
There is always the Pope in the Church, who is the supreme
judge and infallible teacher.   (2) The Bishops are always ready,
even though dispersed throughout the world, to act with the
Sovereign Pontiff.

Although not absolutely necessary, it may be said to be
sometimes morally necessary, i.e., very useful.   (1) Because by
them, heretics are more efficaciously condemned and silenced.
(2) In making laws that are binding everywhere, Bishops who
come from various places and countries, can better testify to the
wants of these countries, and judge of those things that are most
suitable for the welfare of the Church and the people.

The end for which Councils are held is that the unity of
government of the Church may be preserved and strengthened.
This unity would be endangered.   (1) In the case of an heretical
Pope ; (2) in the case of a Pope suspected of heresy.   (3) In
case of a doubtful Pope.   (4) In a case when the Cardinals
would persistently refuse to elect a Pope, or delay too long
before doing so.   The first and second cases have never happened

in the history of the Church. The fourth case also has never happened, and the third case only once.

4. That a Council be in every respect General and Ecumenical, certain conditions are required.

(1) It must be General in its convocation. That is, it must be convoked by the Sovereign Pontiff. He alone has universal jurisdiction. The Bishops, without the Pope, have not perfect jurisdiction. If the convocation cannot be made by the Pope, then the congregation of the Bishops will be either necessary or not; if not necessary, then we need not discuss the matter, as they need not assemble; if necessary, then the congregation, God providing, can be lawfully and validly convoked by the Cardinals; or, the Bishops themselves, moved by the Holy Spirit, may assemble together. But this convocation would not be a Council, except to the extent of electing a Pope or causing a Pope to be elected. And apart from the election of a Pope, it has no right of decreeing or defining other things in regard to faith or discipline; and if it should make any definitions of the kind, they would have no force unless afterwards approved and confirmed by the elected Pope, and only to the extent of his confirmation. The Roman Pontiff is superior to the Bishops, even when assembled in Council. He holds the primacy. He is infallible and the Chief Pastor. All the Fathers in this sense affirm the supreme jurisdiction of the Pope. The Bishops, without the Pope, do not represent the entire Church. By the whole Church is signified the Church as it in reality exists, one and entire body under one head. And hence the Roman Pontiff can dispense from the laws of a General Council, or abrogate them altogether.

All Theologians agree that (1) in the supposition of a Pope becoming openly a heretic, he would be subjected to a General Council. It is the most common opinion that by formal and public heresy, either by the very fact itself, or at least after the declaration of his error, he would cease to be Pope. He would cease to be a member of the Church, and *a fortiori*, he would cease to be her head. (2) Should the Pope become a scandalous sinner and contumacious, he could be admonished by a General Council, but this admonition is not coercive. The Council cannot oblige him to resign, or in any sense to obey it, more than by advice and counsel. (3) In the case of a doubtful Pope, on account of a probably invalid election; if there be many doubtful Popes, they are all bound to submit themselves to the Council, for this the good of the universal Church demands. In such a case there is no true Pope in the sight of the Church, and, therefore, no one is bound to obey any one of them; and, therefore, the right of electing a true Pope abides in the Church. (4) If the Pope should fall into a state of permanent insanity, then by divine law he would be deprived of the Pontificate.

The Members of a General Council. For various reasons, and under various titles, different persons are called to Councils.

(a) Secular Princes, or their Legates, may be called in order to protect the Fathers of the Council, and to prevent sedition; thus, in the earlier ages of the Church, we hear of the convocation of secular princes or rulers to General Councils.

(b) Heretics and Schismatics of every condition, in order to treat of matters affecting them, or to give an account of themselves before the Council, or to be reconciled to the Church.

(c) The learned, Theologians and Canonists, that they may discuss the questions to be treated of or dealt with in the Council. The Bishops of the Council usually have two Theologians, or at least one each with them at the Council.

(d) The Bishops, who are the proper members of the Council. These alone, by the ordinary law, have the right of suffrage in the definitions and decrees of the Council. That Bishops alone are the members of the Council by ordinary right, we gather from the Acts of the Apostles,* where it is said: *Take heed to yourselves, and to the whole flock, wherein the Holy Ghost hath placed you bishops to rule the Church of God, which He hath purchased with His own blood.* This is also shown from the practice of the Church, which proves the Bishops alone acted as the ordinary judges in all the General Councils of the Church. They only are the ordinary judges in the external tribunal (externo foro) of the Church; and in General Councils, not only do they treat of cases of conscience and of matters regarding faith and morals, but they also make laws, and appoint or determine penalties such as ecclesiastical censures.

I have said by ordinary law, because the Pope, if he thinks it expedient, may communicate to other ecclesiastics the privilege

---

* Acts xx. 28.

of voting and taking part in a General Council. Other Ecclesiastics, besides the Bishops, are capable of exercising the rights and privileges required in a Council, because the acts that are effected in a Council do not proceed from or require episcopal consecration. The following persons usually enjoy this privilege:—(1) Cardinals, who are not Bishops. (2) Abbots and Generals of Religious Orders.

The Bishops in the Councils are not merely counsellors of the Pope, but they are really judges and legislators. Counsellors are those who investigate matters after the manner of the Doctors of the Church and Theologians, and make their comment-aries on points of doctrine. The Judges are they who decree and give sentence. Thus the Bishops, in signing the decrees of Councils, use the *formula* in subscribing—*I., N., defining, have subscribed*: (*Ego N. definiens subscripsi*).

That a Council be General, it is required that all Catholic Bishops, except any excommunicated, be called. It is required that as far as possible all be called to the Council, who have the right of suffrage, and that none be excluded. It is a probable opinion that Bishops, *in partibus infidelium*, as it is expressed, that is Bishops who have actually no Sees and no Jurisdiction, have no right to sit in a General Council; and that if they are called to the Council, it is by custom and privilege, in the same sense that Cardinals, who are not Bishops, Generals of Orders, and Abbots, are called to General Councils.

(2) The second condition required in order that a Council be General or Ecumenical is, that it be General in its cele-bration. For this purpose it is required:—(a) That there be as many Bishops present, and from as many places, as to represent the entire Church. The general rule laid down on this point is that some come from the greater part of the Provinces of Christ-endom. (b) That the Council be presided over by the Sovereign Pontiff, or his Legates. Because a Council is a well-ordered meeting, and such a meeting should have a head or president, and this can be no other than he who, by divine right, is the Chief Pastor of all the Bishops. (c) The members must act as councillors, that is, use diligence in examining causes and questions before forming decrees. (d) The Council must enjoy full liberty.

(3) Finally the Council should be General in its conclusion; that is, that it be confirmed by the Sovereign Pontiff. This confirmation of the Pope is required, because the decrees and laws of a General Council are made for the whole Church, and

X

oblige all, therefore they need to be confirmed by the universal Pastor. It suffices for this confirmation, if the Pope send his Legales with definite instructions, and if these instructions be exactly observed. Although the Pope can communicate his jurisdiction to his Legates, he cannot communicate to them his prerogative of *Infallibility*. If, therefore, the decrees of a General Council are approved by the Legates, without any definite instructions from the Pope on the matters defined, they would need the further confirmation of the Pope to make them irreformable, and binding on all. A Council is not infallible in its decrees, unless these are confirmed by the Pope.

5. It is the received and constant faith of the Church, that a Council which is General or Ecumenical in its convocation, in its celebration, and in its (exitu) conclusion, is infallible in its definitions of faith and morals, and becomes immediately the rule of faith without any further reception or approval of its decrees on the part of the Church dispersed.

It is a doctrine of Catholic faith that a National Council is not of itself infallible. The proposition stating this was condemned by the Constitution *auctorem fidei* as heretical; understood in the sense, that controversies regarding faith and morals, whenever they should arise in the Church, might be decided by a National Council, by an irrefragable judgment, as if inerrancy in questions of faith and morals should belong to a National Synod. Such a proposition is condemned as Schismatical and heretical.

THE CONFIRMATION OF COUNCILS.

6. Under this head we may consider three things. (a) The necessity of Papal confirmation of Councils, and the manner in which that may be given. (b) The number and names of the General and Ecumenical Councils. (c) The authority of these Councils.

(a) I have already referred to the necessity of the Papal confirmation for the decrees of Councils. That such a conformation is sufficient to give them force and authority cannot now be doubted, as the infallibility of the Pope is a dogma of faith.

As to the necessity of such a confirmation, objections are sometimes raised to the effect (a) that a General Council, over which the Papal Legates preside, represents the whole Church; and as the whole Church teaching is infallible, the confirmation of the Pope in such a case is not necessary. To this we answer, that the General Council, with the Papal Legates presiding, represents the whole Church incompletely and imperfectly only. They are Legates, and not the head of the Church, and the prerogative of infallibility, which belongs to the Pope, cannot be claimed by the Legates.

The judgment of a General Council lawfully convoked, and presided over by the Papal Legates, is irreformable, if it defines any decree according to the previous instruction of the Pope. Thus the Legates may be sent with instructions to this effect ; if the Council agrees to the instruction, then let the decree be made and formulated ; if the Council does not agree, then let the decree be suspended until the Pope be again consulted. Nevertheless, even in this case, according to safe Theologians, the confirmation of the Pope is necessary, not that the decrees of the Council should obtain force and authority which they have already received, but that the Church may know that all has been properly done in Council, and in accordance with the mind of the Pontiff, and that the decrees have been formed according to his directions.

7. (b) In the history of the Church we find that nineteen General or Ecumenical Councils have been held, to which we now add the Vatican Council. They may be known with their dates, in the following abbreviated form :

Ni. (325) ; Co. (381) ; E. (431) ; Ca. (451) ; Co. (553) ; Co. (680-81) ; Ni. (787) ; Co. (869-70) ; La. (1123) ; La. (1139) ; La. (1179) ; La. (1215) ; Lu. (1245) ; Lu. (1274) ; Vi. (1311-12) ; Con. (doubtful 1414-18) ; Flo. (1438-9) ; La. (1512-17) ; Tri. (1545-63) ; and Va. (1870).

8. (c) The authority of Councils. The definitions of an Ecumenical Council in matters of faith and morals approved and confirmed by the Pope are infallible. But the question is, how are we to know in these decrees those things which the Church wished to define, and that are to be believed from those things that are not defined? And how are those things which are *of faith* to be discerned from those things that are not defined *of faith ?*

As to the first question. In General Councils, those things only are proposed to be believed which are contained in the Canons and decrees. The reason is, because in this only the Bishops intend to teach definitively ; and although they teach in some way

in the chapters and explanations, they do not teach by defining.
As to the second question. A definition is of faith, no matter
what form of words may be used, if it plainly signify that the
doctrine is revealed, or that the opposite is heretical. One way of
knowing this is by the form used in the canons and decrees. *Si
quis hoc vel illud senserit aut dixerit anathema sit.* "If any one
say or think such or such a thing, let him be anathema."

All are bound by any definition of the Church in matters of
doctrine, and it would be a grievous sin to oppose the judgment
of the Church, and maintain a proposition which she may have
condemned as heretical, or which she has stamped as forbidden
by any theological censure. Moreover, the assent which is given
to the definitions of the Church, either in matters of faith or other
points of doctrine, proceeds from the virtue of faith; and when
we do not know whether a doctrine is expressly defined by the
Church as of Catholic faith, or only certain in some other way, it
suffices to submit to it, and to receive it in general as Catholic
doctrine. Particular Councils have only the same authority as
the Churches they represent. They may have great authority,
but never infallibility, unless solemnly confirmed, and in a special
manner, by the supreme authority of the Roman Pontiff. Acts of
Provincial and National Councils are to be sent to Rome by order
of Pius V., that they may be examined by the Sacred Congregation of the Council; not that they may receive any positive confirmation; but they may be corrected in case they should
contain anything at variance with sound doctrine, or the principles
of ecclesiastical law. Sometimes, at the request of the Bishop, the
Pope confirms the Acts for that Province, or that Church, but not
for the universal Church.

CHAPTER IV. (ARTICLE IX.)

THE EXERCISE OF THE LEGISLATIVE AUTHORITY OF THE CHURCH, AND HER RELATIONS TO CIVIL SOCIETY.

1. In what consists the authority of the Church ?—2. The object of this authority.—3. The conditions required for its exercise.—4. The independence of the Church.—5. The rights of the Church: (a) To propagate her teaching. (b) To establish a hierarchy. (c) Free communication with the Sovereign Pontiff. (d) To train and educate her clergy. (e) To teach not only Theology but all the other Sciences. (f) To determine the conditions of marriage. (g) To possess both moveable and immoveable goods.—6. The obligation of Society to be Christian.—7. The duties of the State towards religion.—8. The teaching of the indifference of the Civil power towards religion, or the separation of Church and State not to be admitted.—9. Tolerance, as regards religion, properly understood.—10. The most strenuous opponents of a Christian State are they to whom the alliance of the Civil power with the Church is intolerable.—11. The Temporal power of the Pope. (a) Its origin. (b) Its lawfulness. (c) Its necessity.—12. Summary of conclusions drawn from the teaching of the Church in regard to the temporal dominion and the temporal power of the Pope.

THERE are many questions concerning the Church that are of interest to Catholics, on which it is necessary to have clear definite knowledge in our day. These regard the exercise of her authority; her independence; her principal rights; the duties of the Civil rulers towards her; her relations to the Civil power; and the temporal power of the Pope. I may briefly explain her position and her tenets in regard to these points, as far as they affect the constitution of the Church. And for the sake of order and clearness, I shall follow the plan, and also the mode of treatment of the Abbé Moulin.*

IN WHAT CONSISTS THE AUTHORITY OF THE CHURCH.

1. The Church being a true and perfect society, the authority which she possesses must not only be a legislative power, but also an executive and administrative power, and a

---

* Demonstration de la divinité du Catholicisme. Ch. v., Art. 11, pp. 308 et seq.

judicial and coercive power. Ecclesiastical authority would not be effective unless it could enforce the laws which it makes; and exercise judgment, and inflict penalties, on those who violate them. Like her doctrinal authority, her government authority is whole and entire in the hands of the Sovereign Pontiff, and subordinate to his authority and directions is the authority of the Bishops, each within the limits of his diocese.

THE OBJECT OF THIS AUTHORITY.

2. As the proper and direct end of the Church is the spiritual good and welfare of the faithful, it follows that her legislative authority has, for its direct and proper object, the actions of the faithful, as they are ordained towards that end. As a consequence, it belongs to her to regulate all that appertains to exterior religious discipline; such as the preaching of the Gospel, the divine worship, festivals, sacred rites, the administration and reception of the Sacraments, the appointing of the ministers of the Church, vows and religious orders, fasts and abstinence, canonical penalties, censures and irregularities.

THE CONDITIONS REQUIRED FOR THE EXERCISE OF THIS AUTHORITY.

3. That the Church may fully and efficaciously fulfil her mission, it is necessary (a) that she have entire independence in exercising the rights which she has received from Jesus Christ. (b) That she be aided and protected in her work by the civil power. (c) That the Pope possess temporal sovereignty. These three principles, which have been specially attacked in our day, should be brought to light and fully maintained.

THE INDEPENDENCE OF THE CHURCH.

4. The Church is distinct from, and independent of, the State. The Church is composed of men, as civil society is, nevertheless, she is distinct, and differs from it: in her *origin*, for she exists by an institution directly from God; in her *end*, which is to conduct men to eternal happiness; in her *means* to attain that end. She is also a supernatural and spiritual society; and as a consequence, she is a perfect society in that sphere, possessing in itself, and by itself, all the resources that are necessary for its existence, and for its action. And as the end towards which the Church aims is the highest and most excellent

of all, her power must be above all other power, and in no one point can she be subordinate or subject to the civil power. This doctrine is founded on the Gospel, on tradition, and on the practice of the Church.

When Jesus Christ said: *Render to Cæsar the things that are Cæsar's, and to God the things that are God's,* He established an essential distinction between the spiritual and the temporal power, which the pagan world had confounded. Thus St. Peter and the other Apostles, before the Council of the Jews, proclaimed this principle courageously when they said: *We must obey God rather than men.* They and their successors received the Commission: *Go and teach all nations; to baptize them; to teach them to observe all that Jesus Christ had commanded.* In giving them their mission, Jesus Christ said to them: *All power is given to me in heaven and on earth; go ye, therefore, and teach,* etc. Now Jesus Christ is independent of all earthly power; and He has communicated this independence to the Church. This independence is necessary in order to preserve the unity of faith; and this the Church has always, and in every place, proclaimed and vindicated with invincible constancy against all tyrannies.

The following objections are proposed against this doctrine:

(a) It is said that the Church is in the State, and not the State in the Church; and the Church is, therefore, dependent on the State. To this we answer: It is true that the faithful who compose the Church are members of some State, to which they owe allegiance and obedience in civil and political things; but it does not follow from this that the Church is in the State as a part in the whole. The Church being a universal society, it would be more true to say that the State is in the Church, or, better still, to say with St. Thomas, that the Church is in the State in the same way as the soul is in the body, inasmuch as it gives the State moral life.

(b) It is said that we cannot deny that the State has the right to procure social well-being. But religion is the chief means of obtaining this, and that, therefore, the State can lawfully regulate religious affairs. To this we reply, that the end of the State being natural, the civil power has the right to employ all natural means to obtain its end, but in no sense has it a right over Christian Society, which, although visible, is nevertheless essentially a spiritual and supernatural society. To make religion the instrument of the Civil power, a means only of governing a State, is to degrade it, and to paralyse its action. It is in this respect, namely, in the supreme independence of the Church, that the State obtains inappreciable advantages for civil society.

(o) They say, the Church being an establishment independent of the State, there will result a source of conflicts and of quarrels between the two powers. The only means to prevent this is to acknowledge, both in theory and in practice the supremacy of the State. To this we answer: If the civil power confines itself within its own sphere and limits, no conflict will take place. It has for its principal and proximate, or immediate end, to promote and protect temporal interests; the Church to procure the spiritual and eternal interests of men. And as a matter of fact, whenever public order has been disturbed by quarrels between the two powers, the fault has always been on the side of the Civil power, which, obeying the dishonest inspirations of ambition and pride, has outstepped its limits in order to govern with tyranny.

There are matters which appertain both to the temporal and spiritual power at the same time, such as burials, the goods used for the support of religious institutions, property, &c., and which may be called *mixed*, partly temporal and partly spiritual. It is easy to regulate such matters by concordats. The Church in such questions is ever ready, as far as possible, to make concessions, and to facilitate arrangements with the State.

The Rights of the Church.

5. As a consequence of her independence the Church has certain rights, the exercise of which is necessary for the attainment of her end, and whose violation by the State is an impiety, an injustice, and, at the same time, a source of evil to society. These rights may be enumerated as follows:—

(a) The Church has a right to propagate throughout the world the Gospel, by preaching the faith according to the command which she received from Christ.

(b) She has a right to establish, wherever the faithful exist, a hierarchy necessary for their care and direction.

(c) She has a right to claim for her Bishops, and for all the faithful, free communication with the Sovereign Pontiff; the execution of her spiritual laws; the free preaching of the Gospel; the censuring of errors, and the convocation of Councils and other assemblies.

As a consequence the right, called in French *Appel comme d'abus*, that is, the right to judge episcopal actions; and the *Placet* or *Exequatur*, that is, the pretension of temporal rulers that the promulgation and execution of ecclesiastical acts should be submitted to their will and pleasure, are usurped rights. " We condemn and reprobate," say the Fathers of the Vatican Council, "the maxims of those who say that the communication of the chief Head with the pastors and the flock may be lawfully impeded, or that it ought to depend on the secular power, pretending that the things established by the Apostolic See, or by virtue of her authority, have no force or authority unless confirmed by the sanction of the secular power."*

(d) The Church has the right to train and educate her Clergy with absolute independence. To take from her the education of the Clerics, who later on are to exercise ecclesiastical functions, is to design her ruin. The same may be said of measures enacted to impede their vocation, and their training.

(e) Being essentially a spiritual and doctrinal society, the Church has the right to teach, not only revealed Theology, but all sciences, for there is no science but has some connection and relation to Theology. Besides, as she is a perfect society, and independent of the State, she has a greater right even than the State to open Schools, to choose teachers, to prescribe programmes and methods of education, and to confer degrees.

We ought to recognize it as the right and duty of the State to promote intellectual and moral education, so that fathers of families may be provided with the means of bringing up well their children; and also the right and duty of the State to watch over the systems of instruction, to prevent or eliminate from them anything opposed to honesty and justice; but the State has not the right to enforce on fathers of families, its masters or teachers, its schools, its programmes and its methods. The education of children belongs by natural right to the parents. The State

*4 Sess. Chap. iii.

cannot interfere with this right without incurring the guilt and blame of odious tyranny. And as parents are obliged to bring up their children in a Christian manner, it belongs to the Church to see to the fulfilment of this obligation on the part of the faithful.

(f) It is the right of the Church to determine the conditions to be observed for the validity of the marriage contract. It is a dogma of faith that Christ raised the contract of marriage to the dignity of a Sacrament, in such a way that amongst Christians the contract of marriage is inseparable from the Sacrament. And as the Sacraments belong to the Church, and not to the State, it follows that the conditions of Christian marriage depend, not on the civil power, but on the ecclesiastical authority. The State has only the right to regulate the civil effects of marriage.

(g) The Church has the right to possess goods moveable and immoveable : and as a consequence, to acquire them, and administer her temporal affairs. The right of proprietorship is a natural right in every individual, and much more does it belong to a Society which is nothing else than a collection of individuals. Now the Church is an independent Society, she has therefore as much as the State itself the right to possess goods and property. In order to build Churches, to sustain her ministers and her worship, to propagate the faith, and to succour the needy and the poor, it is necessary that she should have fixed and determined means, the possession and administration of which are inviolate rights, and in no way belong to the civil power. Experience also shows that the confiscation of the goods and property of the Church has been the great cause of pauperism in modern nations, and that it opens a road to Socialism.

(h) The Church has the right to establish within her own communion other societies, subordinate to her, and subject to her direction, in order to aid more easily and more efficaciously in obtaining her end ; such, for example, are Religious Orders. It is the natural right of individuals to form amongst themselves an entire society, as long as it does not interfere with public order. In the State there are innumerable particular societies formed, that have for their object—sciences, letters, arts, industry, commerce.

Why, therefore, may not the faithful be free to associate in a like manner for the service of God, under the approbation of the Church ? Religious Orders are most useful for promoting the divine worship and the salvation of souls ; they are in the Church a part of her sacred army, and the service which they render the world in all things is immense and invaluable. When the State suppresses them, or prevents their establishment or development, it commits an act of injustice and of tyranny, and causes great harm to itself.

Having enumerated some of the principle rights of the Church, we have now to consider the chief obligations of the State towards religion.

THE OBLIGATION OF SOCIETY TO BE CHRISTIAN.

6. If each man in particular is bound to render due worship to God, because he came from Him, and should return to Him, the Civil Society is bound by the same law. In effect, men who are united by social ties and in social life, are no less dependent on the divine power than men taken separately and alone. Therefore, both the individual and society are bound to give thanks to God, from whom they proceed, who preserves them by His providence, and bestows so many favours upon them. It is for this reason that it is a crime in political societies, as it is in individuals, to conduct themselves as if there were no God, or to treat religion with disrespect, as if it were a thing dangerous to the public good, and of no utility to it whatever. As to the religion which Society is bound to profess, it is not a religion of any kind, but that religion which God Himself has imposed, and of which the most manifest proofs show to be the true religion amongst all others. That is the religion of which Jesus Christ is the author, and which He has confided to his Church to guard and to diffuse. Society ought then to be Christian, and recognise as its King, Jesus Christ, to whom God the Father has given all Kingdoms and all Nations.

THE DUTIES OF THE STATE TOWARDS RELIGION.

7. The obligation by which the Social body is bound to practice the Christian religion in its true form, which is Catholicism, evidently imposes on the Rulers of the State the duty of favouring that religion, to protect it by their goodwill, to guard it by the authority of the law; and to establish or

order nothing injurious to it, or contrary to its action. They are responsible for all this to the citizens over whom they preside. In causing the true religion to be respected, they promote and ensure the public prosperity, of which religion is the fundamental condition. In this way they discharge their principal obligation. A well-regulated society is impossible without religion, as Leo. XIII. says. And Pope St. Gregory, as Bossuet tells us, writing to the pious Emperor Maurice, represents to him in the following words the duties of a Christian King: "Know, O great Emperor, that the Sovereign power has been accorded to you from on high, to the end that virtue may be aided; that the roads to heaven may be enlarged; and that the Empire of earth may serve the Empire of heaven." It is truth itself that dictated these beautiful words: for what can be more becoming than that power should be used to succour virtue? That strength should be used to defend right? And for what purpose do men command and rule, unless it be to effect obedience to God and His law?

8. We cannot, therefore, admit the doctrine of the indifference of the civil power in regard to religion, or the separation of Church and State. The separation would mean inevitable war for the State, which police or soldiers could not control without religion; it would also be to the great detriment of religion, and to the civil society itself.

The normal situation, according to the design of God, is that Church and State be united as soul and body; that the power of Christian wisdom and of divine virtue should penetrate the laws, the institutions, and the manners of the people, and pervade all the ranks and relations of civil society. Where religion, occupying that degree of dignity which is its right, is flourishing, society is also well organised, and gives results far superior to those which are usually expected from it. "If," says Leo. XIII., "Christian Europe has subjected barbarous nations, and caused them to pass from ferocity to meekness, from superstition to truth, if it has repelled victoriously the invasions of the Mussulman; if civilization has taken the advantage in preparing the way for the rest of the world, and in teaching it all that it can know to its honour and advantage; if it has satisfied the people with true liberty in all its forms; if it has wisely founded numbers of institutions for the comfort and solace of men in their miseries and sufferings; it must be confessed that all this is greatly owing to religion, which it has as its inspirer and its helper in attaining this desirable end. The world would enjoy now all these advantages had the two powers been preserved in accordance with one another; and there would be hope of greater things if the world would submit with more faith, and in a more durable manner, to the counsels of the Church."

It is said against this doctrine, that the theory of a Christian State is a theory of absolutism, which is directly opposed to the modern world.

If by absolutism is meant a system of government which accepts as law the will and pleasure of the ruler, there is nothing similar to it in the Christian State, whose fundamental principle is submission to the divine law as taught and interpreted by the Church. The essential principle of the Roman claim was: *Quod principi placuit legis habet vigorem. If the King wills it, the law wills it.* Modern Cæsarism, the King or the sovereign people, cannot put this principle in force unless it separate the State from the Church. So that wherever the divine law is respected, there, no matter under what form of government, authority is strong, and true liberty is found.

It may be said that this is an intolerant doctrine, for it gives the right, and imposes the duty, on the civil power, not to tolerate the enemies of the Catholic religion.

9. There are two sorts of tolerance—dogmatic tolerance and civil tolerance. The first regards with indifference all religions; it places all on an equal footing, as if they were all equally good or equally bad. Such a tolerance is impious, injurious to God, who has revealed the Christian religion, and obliges all men under penalty of eternal damnation to submit to it.

The Church cannot admit this tolerance, for it is equivalent to Atheism. But if the Church is intolerant in respect to error, she is full of meekness and charity towards those who are in error. She uses the greatest vigilance that no one be forced against his will to embrace the Catholic faith (no priest would receive into the Church an unwilling subject), and she has not forgotten the wise saying of St. Augustine: "Constraint can obtain everything of man, everything save the faith." This it can neither give nor take away.

But it is one thing to use force to oblige men to believe and to sanctify themselves; another thing to repress exterior and public impiety, which threatens the faith of the weak, and carries trouble and disorder into the midst of civil and religious society. We punish the attacks made on political sovereignty, the violation of the laws on which the peace and security of citizens depend. Why should it be forbidden to punish those who attack God, religion, morality, and fundamental truths, without which society could not exist?

It follows, therefore, that the civil power has the right and duty, as far as it is possible, to make people respect the divine law. In a society composed entirely of Catholics, it should be used against turbulent spirits who attempt to introduce schism and heresy; for it should prevent the rupture of religious unity, which is the principal foundation of social unity.

If heresy has divided nations, and obtained a sort of legal existence strengthened by time, granted or accorded to them by treaties or agreements, the Sovereign, whilst condemning in his conscience all that is false and erroneous, may accept the situation brought about by circumstances, and tolerate different forms of religion in the state, in the hope that he may yet bring about or promote Catholic unity or unity with Catholicism. To avoid a greater evil he would be sometimes obliged to tolerate the practice of different forms of religious worship.

10. We may observe that the most strenuous opponents of a Christian State are they to whom the alliance of the state or civil power with religion is intolerable. They labour with all their strength to create an anti-Christian state, a state of Freethinkers, where the government will take in hand the cause of incredulity in order to establish and to spread Atheism. We have seen in 1798, and we see in our own day in France since 1879, the anti-religious homogeneousness, which is the end and object of the French Freemasonry. It is by the enforcing of true religious unity that nations are rendered great and prosperous, and that men are led to respect the truth of this teaching.

But it may be further stated that modern society rests on liberty of conscience and of worship, liberty of speech and of the press, which liberties are irreconciliable with the principles of a Christian state.

To call the above-named rights *liberties* is nothing less than to take evil for good; it is an odious abuse of language, the reverse of all morality. Liberty, as Montesquieu says, consists in this, that one should have the power of doing what he ought to do, and of not being forced to do that which he ought not to do. Now if there is anything which a man, or a Society, ought to wish to do, it is that which is good, namely the fulfilling of the law of God.

When liberty outsteps the limits prescribed by truth and justice, it does not merit that name, it becomes licence, that is the liberty of perdition, as St. Augustine says : and in that case it becomes injurious to the moral and religious interests of the people, and the civil power should restrict its manifestations. But it may be asked, would it not be preferable, before the law, to give equal liberty to truth and error? Truth will always prevail, and tolerance will gain to the Church rebellious spirits. As error is of itself bad, it is unlawful to recognise any right for it or its existence. All that is permitted in regard to it, is to tolerate it under certain grave and necessary circumstances. To suppose that truth, without support or protection, will triumph over error, is to be under a strange delusion. Men are naturally prone to evil, and for the most part, incapable of solving the captious sophisms in which error is usually enveloped. That which flatters men's passions is regarded with favour : truth is misrepresented, virtue is ridiculed, and a frightful moral and intellectual perver sion is produced in the masses.

This *tolerance*, they say, will gain to the Church rebellious spirits, instead of the estrangement caused by severity. To this experience gives the reply. When religious truth is not protected, its enemies increase every day, faith becomes weakened, and with faith the good and well-being of the people fails. In society good is not practised, except under the condition that the teaching of the truth be sustained by salutary fear. The citizens, on their part, have a right to exact from the State that they be preserved from error, and that the poisoners of the public spirit be treated as pestiferous criminals.

It is also represented that the system of liberty of worship, if universally recognised, will authorise the introduction of the true religion into all lands, whilst the system of protection would only shut it out, or expose it to persecution.

Revealed truth alone has the right to reign in this world ; it has every right of liberty. It alone presents itself with motives of credibility of such a kind that every government can recognise its divine origin. In consequence, a government that makes itself the defender of a false religion to the exclusion of the true worship, is not within its right ; it abuses shamefully the one true and salutary principle. But the abuse of a thing ought not to stop its usage ; because the bad persecute the good, that is no reason why they should have licence to do so when they can be prevented. We must therefore acknowledge that the protection of the Church by the State is the only principle admissable, and that it ought to be put in practice whenever circumstances permit.

THE TEMPORAL POWER OF THE POPE.

11. (a) The origin of the Temporal power. Even in the days
of persecution, before Constantine, the Papacy received from the liberality of the faithful consider-
able means to be employed for the maintenance of
the Christian religion, and the relief of the poor.
This patrimony increased so much under Constantine and his successors, that it served as a means to
propagate the faith, to build Basilicas, and to succour the needy of every description.

About the middle of the eighth century, the Roman Empire
perished, and Europe became covered with a host of new nations,
often opposed to each other, and divided in their interests ; these
circumstances brought about the foundation of the temporal
power, which was destined in the designs of Providence to preserve and ensure the independence of the supreme Head of the
Church.

Rome at this epoch saw itself abandoned and illtreated by the
Emperors of the East, its masters.   During the invasions, continued without ceasing, of the Huns, the Vandals, the Ostrogoths,
and Lombards, Rome was thrown into the arms of the Papacy.
The Papacy, which had exercised since Constantine a great influence on public affairs, took on itself the guardianship of forlorn
Italy, saved Rome from the terrors of Attila and Genseric, and
raised it up from ruin nine times.   Not being able in the end to
defend it against the attacks of the Lombards, she appealed successively to Pepin and Charlemagne, who lent her their victorious
arms, made the King of the Lombards restore all the towns and
principalities which he had taken, and extended generously the
dominion of the Pope by ceding to him the provinces which they
came to conquer.

As a fact, the temporal sovereignty of the Holy See in the
duchy of Rome and the exarchate of Ravenna, commenced under
the pontificate of Gregory II. (715-731.) After the grant of
Pepin, the Popes acted as the Sovereigns of Rome, and considered themselves definitely enfranchised from all dependence
on the Emperors of Constantinople.   They have been ever
faithful, although the evils with which they have had to contend,
as well as the impotence of these Emperors in Italy, have never
been clearly manifested or known.

(b) *The Lawfulness of the Temporal Power.* If there is a
temporal power lawful and legitimate in this world,

assuredly it is the temporal power of the Popes. There is nothing more sacred or more incontestible than that it rests upon the strongest titles that can be assigned for temporal rights. (1) On the election and the voice or wish of the people who, forsaking their ancient masters, took refuge under the guardianship of the Sovereign Pontiffs. (2.) On the rightful conquests of Pepin and Charlemagne, and the free concession of the Princess Matilda, who willed at her death her patrimony to the Holy Sec. (3) On the prescription of more than ten centuries. (4) On public European right, which in all its congresses and treaties has recognised the Pontifical States. (5) On the invaluable services rendered by the Popes to Italy, of which they have been so often the saviours and the peacemakers; and the salutary influence which their temporal independence enabled them to exercise over the whole world.

(c) *The Necessity of the Temporal Power.* If this power be not of divine institution, it is at least apparent that in the actual condition of the political world, it is a providential means of protecting the spiritual power, and of efficiently securing its honour and its liberty.

Under a strange or alien Sovereign, the Chief Pastor of the Church would not enjoy that full independence which is necessary for the exercise of his doctrinal and legislative authority. History furnishes us with the proof. Before Constantine, thirty Popes suffered martyrdom; all more or less had to keep secret their sovereign dignity. Later on they have been imprisoned, banished from Rome, and condemned to die in exilo. We have always seen a troubled world when their temporal sovereignty has ceased for a time. In our day, since tho Piedmontese army invaded Rome (20th Sept., 1870), Popes Pius IX. and Leo XIII. have on many occasions complained of the intolerable situation in which they have been placed.

Heretics and impious men of every age understood full well the importance of the temporal power; and so Frederick of Prussia wrote to Voltaire, "There is nothing to be done but to bring about the downfall of the temporal power; the temporal power once destroyed, the spiritual will become that which it ought to be, and we shall come to have national Churches as we have national languages."

From this we can understand the reason why the Catholic

x

Church vindicates so strenuously the rights of the Holy See to its temporal dominions and princedom. The Council of Trent declares that the temporal States of the Church are sacred property, and to protect them against usurpation, it pronounces excommunication against any who should dare to attack them either directly or indirectly.*

Having given the Catholic views as stated by the Abbé Moulin, I wish to add briefly some remarks on the temporal power of the Church as they have shaped themselves in my mind.

12. The first question to be asked is: Whether the Church or the Pope should have any temporal power? In answer to this question, I assert: (a) It is certain that the Pope has not dominion over the whole world. The Lord committed only His sheep to Peter. Infidels, or not baptized people, are not the sheep of Christ's flock, and therefore the Pope has no power over them, or to judge them according to the words of St. Paul: *For what have I to do to judge them that are without?‡*

Infidel and Pagan rulers are therefore true and supreme princes and rulers of their territories, as dominion is not founded on grace or on faith, but on reason and free will. It does not descend by divine right, but by the laws of nations according to which our Saviour said: *Render therefore to Cæsar the things that are Cæsar's, and to God the things that are God's.*

It is certain, in the second place, that the Pope has not the dominion of the whole Christian world. From the Scriptures we do not learn that more was bestowed on the Pontiff than the Keys of the Kingdom of Heaven; there is no mention of the keys of earthly kingdoms.

It is certain in the third place that the Pope has no temporal jurisdiction directly *jure divino*, by *divine right*. That is, the Pope is not, by divine right, the King or Supreme temporal Sovereign of any place. Christ as man, whilst on earth, received no temporal dominion, therefore, the Sovereign Pontiff has not, by divine right, the temporal dominion or direct temporal power over any country or province.

The next question is: Whether the Pope has the Supreme temporal power indirectly? Here we must distinguish temporal power from temporal dominions or possessions, under the title of King or Sovereign. His temporal possessions and dominions are

---

* Thus far in this instruction I have quoted the Abbé Moulin.
‡1 Cor. v. 12.

entirely human, and of human origin, and of human duration; in the sense that they may pass away in time; but as to indirect temporal power, as connected with the spiritual power, and as necessary for its exercise, we must say that, although the Pope, as Pope, has not any direct temporal power, he has the power for the spiritual good of the faithful, of disposing of the temporalities of Christians, whenever this may be necessary. And he has *jure divino*, by *divine right*, temporal power indirectly, that is in so far as this is necessary for the exercise of the spiritual power bestowed upon him by Christ. In the Civil State there are rulers, laws, and judgments; in like manner in the Church there are Bishops, Canons, and judgments. The former have for their direct object and end the temporal peace and welfare of the State; the latter, the salvation of souls. Nevertheless, for this object we know that temporal power is sometimes most useful and necessary, and, therefore, when necessary for the end of the Church, we must suppose that it was granted to her in connection with the spiritual authority.

It is further asked whether the Pope has any authority over the temporal affairs of Kings? Here we must remember that the temporal end is subordinate to the spiritual, and if in temporal administration spiritual good should be impeded, in the judgment of all, the temporal prince would be bound to alter the mode of administration. Therefore, the spiritual ruler can command temporal sovereigns, that they may regulate their temporal affairs, in order to the spiritual good of the faithful, as every superior can command his subjects.

Although the Pope, as such, cannot command or ordinarily depose secular princes or sovereigns, even for a just cause, in the same way as he can remove a Bishop from his See, that is as ordinary Judge, he might, however, change Kingdoms, and take them away from one and give them to another, as the Supreme Spiritual Pontiff, if that were necessary for the salvation of souls. Otherwise, bad kings and rulers could favour heretics with impunity, and overturn religion in their states.

We may add that if the Sovereign Pontiffs be selected as the arbitrators of quarrels between princes and people, and between kings themselves, then by human right they would obtain a certain power and authority over the temporal affairs of kings. And according to this right many historical facts can be properly explained and understood, such as that of Alexander VI., dividing the New World between the Kingdoms of Spain and Portugal.

Then it is well known that for many ages there were Superior rulers and inferior ones. The inferior rulers, although they governed their Kingdoms by their own authority, were, neverthe-less, subject in many things to the greater or superior Sovereigns; and the Pope was recognised as the arbitrator between them and their people in all matters of dispute and of government; and especially in whatever affected the Church or religion, his authority was acknowledged as supreme and unquestioned.

Bearing this distinction in mind between the direct and the indirect temporal power, we have to refer again to his temporal possession and dominion, because, although in this we need not claim any divine right, we assert, however, that the Sovereign Pontiff is capable of temporal sovereignty, and the same man may be at the same time a political king and an ecclesiastical Pontiff. This statement is against Calvin and Brentius and others, who consider the two powers incompatible.

The union of this two-fold power in one man is in no sense repugnant either to the *natural,* the *divine,* or *human* law. Not to the natural law, because, as far as the nature of things goes, there is no opposition between the two powers.

Not to the divine law, which in no place is adverse to this doctrine or arrangement. On the contrary, we see the two often united in Scriptural history, as in the case of Melchisedeck, who was at the same time King and Pontiff. Also Moses was at the same time the greatest prince and the chief priest, or Pontiff, of the Jews. Both powers are good, both are from God, both are praiseworthy, one helps the other; there is, therefore, no opposi-tion between them, and both may be possessed by the same person.

As to the lawfulness of the temporal sovereignty of the Pope, that which he claims, and of which he was robbed, there can be no doubt. It originated in the most lawful manner, as is certain from history. Many temporal dominions were bestowed on the Holy See by Christian Kings in the very first ages, which Con-stantine the Great afterwards augmented (in 330). Pepin (752) gave to the Popes dominion over the exarchate of Revenna; which Charlemagne afterwards (772) confirmed. To these were added the territory of the Countess Methilda, which by a solemn act she made over to the Holy See.

The Popes had and retained these by the best title of pre-scription, or peaceful and indisputed possession, for many cen-turies. From the time of Pepin and Charlemagne, even to our own day, the Holy See retained dominion over the States of the Church, and her right in this respect was recognised by the public law of nations.

Hence Pius IX. in the Syllabus condemned the following propositions:

"The Church has no temporal power, either direct or indirect."

"The Church has not a natural or lawful right to acquire or possess."

"The Sacred ministers of the Church, and the Roman Pontiff ought to be excluded entirely from all dominion over, and care of, temporal things and possessions."

The civil power of the Holy See ought to be liberated and preserved, because of the many advantages which it brings with it, not only to the Church, but to the whole Christian world. The supreme Pontiff ought not to be the subject of any king, and he should be fully independent of every temporal prince and ruler, that he may be able, fully and freely, to discharge his sacred authority over the faithful.

In these few remarks I have endeavoured to show (a) that the Church, or the Pope, has supreme temporal power only indirectly, inasmuch as it is necessary for the salvation of souls. (b) That the Church, or the Pope, has indirectly some authority over the temporal affairs of kings, and (c) that the Pope is capable of temporal authority and dominion: that the temporal and civil princedom, or sovereignty of the Pope, is perfectly lawful, and to be preserved and defended

CHAPTER V. (ARTICLE IX.)

THE COMMUNION OF SAINTS.

1. What is meant by the Communion of Saints.—2. The states of the Church *militant, suffering, and triumphant.*—3. Who are they that are included in the Communion of Saints ?—4. Are sinners included in this Communion ?—5. Are those outside the Church to be included? —6. The Communion of Saints extends to the souls in Purgatory, and to the Blessed in heaven.—7. That in which this Communion consists—(*a*) Communion of the Saints with God and with the three Persons of the Blessed Trinity. (*b*) Communion between the Saints and Angels. (*c*) Communion with each other. (*d*) Communion of the Saints in heaven with the souls in Purgatory, and the faithful on earth. (*e*) Communion of the faithful on earth with the souls in Purgatory. (*f*) The Communion of the faithful on earth with each other.—8. The external manifestations of spirits in this world.—9. These spirits that can and do appear.—10. Rules by which true and good visions may be distinguished from those that are false or diabolical.—11. Difference between the teaching of Ascetical Theology and Modern Spiritualism, in regard to communication with spirits and departed souls.—12. Spiritualism a dangerous and unlawful practice.—13. Exhortation of Bishop Milner on the subject of the invocation of Saints.

1. ACCORDING to our Catechism, by the communion of Saints, we mean that all the members of the Church, in heaven, on earth, and in purgatory, are in communion with each other, as being one body in Jesus Christ.

The faithful on earth are in communion with each other by professing the same faith, obeying the same authority, and assisting each other with their prayers and good works.

We are in communion with the Saints in heaven by honouring them as the glorified members of the Church ; and also by our praying to them, and by their praying for us.

We are in communion with the souls in Purgatory by helping them with our prayers and good works. *It is a holy and a wholesome thought to pray for the dead, that they may be loosed from their sins.**

The word Communion is taken here for fellowship or intercourse.

---

* Mac. xii. 46.

2. The members of the Church of Christ may find themselves in one or other of three different states. Either they are engaged on the battle-field, sustaining the combat against the enemies of their salvation; or they have gained the victory in this world, but gone out of it wounded, and are in a place where all their wounds are being healed; or they are already in a place where they enjoy the glory of their triumph.

In the first state they form part of the Church *militant, i.e.,* fighting, because its duty is to be always in arms against sin and wickedness. In the second they form part of the Church *suffering* in Purgatory; and in the third of the Church *triumphant*; namely, that part of which the Apostle speaks in his Epistle, and calls *a glorious Church, not having spot or wrinkle or any such thing.**

This three-fold Church is only one, because it has only one Head, who is Jesus Christ. All its members are united under that one head, and in the sense of this Article of the Creed, have communion with each other.

The dogma of the Communion of Saints means the fraternal union of all the members of the Church, and their participation in the same spiritual benefits.

The instruction on this dogma may be divided into two parts. (a) Who and what kind of persons are called Saints. (b) In what the nature of their communion consists.

WHO AND WHAT KIND OF PERSONS ARE CALLED SAINTS.

3. By sanctity we mean holiness, and holiness in its literal * sense signifies separation, both (a) in regard to that from which the separation is made, and (b) that to which what is separated is applied. The holy things under the law were separated from common use, and applied to the service of God. Thus, all persons called or separated from the common condition of the world, to any peculiar service or relation to God, are thereby denominated holy, and in some sense receive the name of Saints.

The separation from the world, and appropriation to God, is under the New Law, effected by the Sacrament of Baptism, inasmuch as this Sacrament is a washing away of sin; it is a sanctification and purification, and it also enriches the soul

----

* Ephes. v. 27.

with the theological gifts of faith, hope, and charity, in which true sanctity consists.

Those, therefore, may be called holy, or saints here on earth, who have been baptized; and who are sanctified in Christ Jesus by the virtues of faith, hope, and charity, and who, as a consequence, are holy in respect of their conversation, that is their behaviour and their manner of life, according to the words of St. Peter: *But according to Him that hath called you, who is Holy, be you also in all manner of conversation holy; because it is written "you shall be holy for I am holy."**

From this it follows that in the Communion of Saints are included:

(a) Souls that lead lives of perfection, and practice virtue in an heroic degree.

(b) Those who only enjoy the first degree of holiness, namely, freedom from mortal sin, or from formal disobedience in matters of moment to one or more commands of God or His Church, although they may have slight faults, for the Scripture tells us that the just man himself *falls seven times.*

4. It may naturally be asked whether sinners are excluded from this Communion of Saints? Sin places a soul in a state of revolt against God, consequently in a state of spiritual death. Yet even the sinner who has not been cut off from the body of the Church by excommunication, remains attached to it as a withered member, and many graces continue to flow upon Him through various channels. "The instructions he hears, the good examples he sees, the prayers offered for his conversion, and that secret influence which a living body always possesses over even its withered members, all serve as so many stimulants to urge him to arise from his fallen state. He has lost Charity which can never co-exist with mortal sin; but so long as he does not complete his separation by abandoning faith and hope, he still possesses within him a germ of life, which at any moment, if he so wills, may spring up to transform him once more into a Saint."

5. It may further be asked whether, to belong to the Communion of Saints, it is indispensable that one should belong to the Catholic Church? Yes, he must belong to the Church in one of these two ways, either he must be actually aggregated to the body and soul of the Church, or he must be fully disposed and

---

* 1 St. Peter i. 15, 16.

entirely resolved to enter into her communion the very instant he is satisfied that she is the true Church.

To understand this I must refer you to the fact that we must recognize in the Church, or mystical body of Christ, a soul as well as a body, and hence the distinction between the soul and body of the Church.

The soul of the Church is the union, in different degrees, of all who live in the spirit of Jesus Christ, which is a spirit of faith, hope and charity. The body of the Church is the assembly of all who exteriorly profess the same faith, participate in the same Sacraments, and are governed by the same pastors. Hence we may conclude that a person may belong to the soul of the Church without being actually a member of her body, in the same manner as many belong to the body without belonging to her soul. Some who do not care to retain anything of communion with us may call this a tardy distinction, but it is a distinction used by the ancient doctors of the Church, founded on Catholic tradition, and on the general principles of Christianity, according to these words of our Saviour : *And other sheep I have that are not of this fold ; them also I must bring, and they shall hear My voice, and there shall be one fold and one Shepherd.**

We may, therefore, include in this communion (*a*) all children who have been validly baptized (even by a pagan), and who die either before they come to the use of reason or before they commit an actual mortal sin. (*b*) All adults, even if externally in communion with some heretical or schismatical sect, who on account of their entire sincerity, and the good use they make of the truths which they conscientiously believe, preserve their baptismal innocence, or recover grace after it has been lost, by works of penance and charity. (*c*) All those men of good will who, purified from the stain of original sin, and from the defilements of actual sin have been reconciled to God by an act of perfect charity, which always includes an implied desire of baptism, and of all the regular means of sanctification.

The *Communion of Saints*, therefore, in the sense in which we understand it, is truly *Catholic*, for it includes all the servants of the true God, whatever the circumstances of time or place, or whatever may be the moral, or social condition in which they have lived, or still are living.

6. The Communion of Saints extends further. " It follows its members wherever they go (as long as they do not die in a

---

* St. John x. 16.

state of mortal sin and final impenitence). It is in fact the everlasting society of the friends of God, a society beginning here
below, on the field of battle and trial, continued in that place of
temporal punishment called purgatory (the temporary abode of
souls that depart indebted to Divine justice, which they must
satisfy before they can enter into the possession of the Kingdom
of perfect purity); and finally consummated in the everlasting
city of heaven."

These three divisions of the mystical body of Christ are, as I
have already said, known under the titles of the Church *triumphant*, the Church *suffering*, and the Church *militant*.   But in
reality these three Churches are one.   They are but one, because
the saints in glory, the saints in purgatory, and the saints on
earth, are closely united to each other under their one Head,
Jesus Christ, and live one common life, derived from its Head,
and from the sanctifying Spirit, which life is charity itself, perfect
in the Saints in heaven, imperfect as yet in the souls in purgatory,
and far more imperfect in the saints on earth ; but still in each
the same Divine Charity, which Jesus Christ came to enkindle on
earth, and which is infused into our hearts by the Holy Ghost."*

7.   Having explained what kind of persons are called saints,
we may now proceed to examine the second question, namely, *in
what does their Communion consist ?*

In this communion we have to consider (*a*) those who differ
from the Saints in nature, as the angels, (*b*) those saints who
differ in person only from each other, (*e*) those whose condition
is different.

(*a*)   We may notice by itself that the saints living in the
        Church have communion with God, that is with the
        three Persons of the most Holy Trinity :
                  WITH THE FATHER—
        And truly our fellowship may be with the Father.
                  WITH THE SON—
        And with His Son, Jesus Christ.   (1 St. John iii.)
                  WITH THE HOLY GHOST—
        *The grace of our Lord Jesus Christ, and the charity of
        God, and the communication of the Holy Ghost be
        with you.*   (2. Cor. xiii. 13.)

(*b*)   Communion between the Saints and the Angels.

It was an angel foretold the birth of John the Baptist, that
announced the conception of Christ, and sang a hymn at His

---

* The Philosophy of the Cath. Catch. by the Abbé Martinet.

Nativity, that carried Lazarus into Abraham's bosom, that appeared from heaven to strengthen our Saviour in His agony, that brought the Apostles out of prison. Angels will come at the end of the world to separate the just from the wicked. From these evidences it is certain that the Angels have a perpetual relation and intercourse with the children of men. *Are they not all ministering spirits, sent to minister for them who shall receive the inheritance of salvation.** *And thus there is joy before the Angels of God upon one sinner doing penance.†*

Then we have the Catholic doctrine of Guardian Angels, which teaches that every human being has an Angel appointed by God to watch over him in this life. Hence our Saviour, speaking of children, said : *See that you despise not one of these little ones ; for I say to you that their Angels in Heaven always see the face of my Father who is in heaven.‡*

(c) There is communion with one another   Here on earth the saints have some communion with men not saints. We have the same Baptism, the same Creed, the same means of grace, &c. And the living saints in the same Church of Christ have still closer communion with each other in grace, in charity, having the unity of the spirit in the bond of peace, according to the words of St. Paul : *One body and one spirit, as you are called in one hope of your calling. One Lord, one faith, one baptism. One God and Father of all, who is above all, and through all and in us all.§*

I shall now give the manner in which the members of the Church help each other according to their various conditions, whether as belonging to the Church *militant, suffering,* or *triumphant.*

(d) The Saints in heaven intercede for the souls in Purgatory, and for the faithful on earth. They see in God, as in a mirror, all that concerns creatures, especially those related to them by the ties of family and of friendship. They do not now require the corporal senses—ears to hear, or eyes to see ; and distance and time cannot intercept their knowledge.

Their charity makes them take a great interest in the sorrows of the Church *suffering,* and in the combats of the Church *militant.* They are aware of all the appeals that are made to their intercession and mediation, and they supplicate

---

* Heb. i. 14.   † St. Luke xv.10.
‡ St. Matt. xviii. 10.   § Ephes. iv. 45.

the bounty and goodness of God to grant the prayers of those who invoke their aid. Hence the doctrine of the invocation of Saints. The mystical union between Christ and His Church, and between all its members, is not dissolved by death; but true holiness is improved by death, and consequently the prayers of the Saints are more efficacious now than they were during life.

In exchange for their good offices towards men, the honour and respect and devotion of the faithful here, and of the souls in purgatory, are a cause of joy to the Saints in heaven, and add to their accidental glory.

(e)   The faithful on earth intercede for the souls in Purgatory by praying for their deliverence and for the alleviation of their sufferings. (This matter I shall explain more fully in the instruction on Purgatory). The souls in Purgatory, on their part, pray for the faithful on earth, especially for those to whom they were united here below, and for those who, moved by pity and compassion, succour them by their prayers and good works.

(f)   Finally, the faithful here on earth intercede and pray for one another. Fervent prayers are incessantly going up before the throne of God for the conversion of sinners, for the perseverance of the just, for the exaltation of the Church of which we are members, and for the cessation of the scourges that afflict human society.

8.   Having explained the nature of this spiritual union that exists between the members of the Church, it may interest us to know something of the external acts and operations and appearances which are sometimes manifested to men here by the spirits of another world.

That there can be some such communication is undeniable; but as to how it is brought about is not so certain.

It is clear that the spirits of the other world are either Angels, devils, or departed souls; and these are either in heaven, in purgatory, or in hell. And, therefore, visions and apparitions may be either of good or bad spirits, that is, they may be either divine or diabolical, either from God or from the devil.

This leads me into a portion of mystical Theology that requires a long and detailed treatment. Here I refer only to certain propositions that are admitted by all who treat on this subject.

9. (a) The good Angels can assume bodily forms, and appear manifest to our senses.

(b) The devils can and have also appeared to men.

(c) The souls of the blessed can also appear in visible form, as Moses and Elias appeared at the Transfiguration.

(d) The souls in Purgatory, God permitting them, can also appear to men for our instruction, and for the purpose of obtaining the aid of our prayers. The apparition of these souls is commonly made by the agency of Angels in assumed bodies, especially the guardian Angels of these souls.

(e) Even lost souls, as warnings of the divine justice, have been allowed to appear visibly to men, to teach us so to order our lives as not to incur like penalties.

(f) There is no record of an apparition of any infant, who died without Baptism ; for these cannot be helped by our suffrages, and no utility or example of virtue could be drawn from their apparitions.

10. I shall now give some rules by which true visions can be distinguished from false ones. These rules may refer either (a) to what is seen, or the apparition itself. (b) The person seeing the vision. (c) The effects of such manifestations.

(a) As regards the vision itself. (1) It is not from God if it announces anything contrary to faith or morals. (2) If the form in which the spirit appears is deformed : demons do not appear in perfect human form as a rule, and Angels do not take the form of beasts or irrational creatures.

(b) As regards the persons receiving the supernatural manifestations. Although Pharaoh and some other men, who were not very holy, received manifestations of this kind ; although in themselves these supernatural manifestations do not constitute an absolute proof of sanctity, yet as a rule Angels do not appear to non-Catholics or to sinners ; but it may happen sometimes that a departed soul may give warning to such as are still in the flesh, and not leading a very good life.

(c) As regards the saints who received these visions, they were humble and diffident ; they did not seek them, they did not of their own accord publish them to the world ; and they were guided in regard to them by the directions and advice of prudent and experienced priests.

11. All this is very different from modern Spiritualism, which is only another name for vain observance and superstition. Spiritualism, or Spiritism, is to seek to communicate with the spirits of the departed by observances such as the following: *Seances:* a number of people sitting in a dark room; with hands joined with an entranced medium in a cabinet; they hear the rapping and tapping of spirits; the writings are given on slates; messages from the other world are given, and they see their dead friends and relations, and hold communion with them. In all this I do not deny the fact when attested by trustworthy witnesses, because, in the matter even of divine visions, we have only the word or testimony of the saint who receives them for their truth; but I do question the origin of these apparitions. Apart from all the allowances that must be made for the imagination and derangement of the minds of some people on certain matters, these things do not stand any of the tests by which we can show that they are from God or from good spirits.

12. The practice of Spiritualism is a means of seeking to know hidden things by means not ordained by nature or by God for that purpose, and hence it is a dangerous practise when it imples a direct or indirect intercourse with evil spirits. Whilst avioiding all these dangerous practices, I would exhort to that practice which is safe, good, and profitable, namely, the invocation of the saints who are reigning with God in heaven.

13. I think I may appropriately conclude this instruction with the words of Bishop Milner on this subject.

" You will observe that the Council of Trent barely teaches that it is *good* and *profitable* to invoke the saints; hence our divines infer that there is no positive law of the Church incumbent on all her children to pray to the saints. Nevertheless, what member of the Catholic Church militant will fail to communicate with his brethren of the Church triumphant? What Catholic, believing in the *Communion of Saints*, and that the Saints reigning with Christ pray for us, and that it is *good and profitable for us to invoke their prayers*, will forego this advantage? How sublime and consoling! how animated is the doctrine and practice of true Catholics compared with the opinions of Protestants! We hold daily and hourly converse, to our unspeakable comfort and advantage, with the angelic choirs, with the venerable patriarchs and prophets of ancient times, with the heroes of Christianity, the blessed Apostles and martyrs, and with the bright ornaments of it in later ages, the Bernards, the Xaviers, the Teresas, and the Sales. They are all members of the Catholic Church. Why should not you (to a Protestant) partake of this advantage? Your soul, you complain, dear sir, is in trouble; you lament that your prayers to God are not heard; continue to pray to Him with all the fervour of your soul; but why not engage His friends and courtiers to add the weight of their prayers to your own? Perhaps His divine Majesty may hear the prayers of the Jobs, when He will not listen to those of Eliphaz, or Baldad, or a Zophar.* You believe, no doubt, that you have a guardian angel appointed by God to protect you conformably to what Christ said of the children presented to Him: *Their angels do always behold the face of my Father who is in heaven†* Address yourself to this blessed spirit with gratitude, veneration and confidence.

You believe also that among the saints of God there is one of supereminent purity and sanctity, pronounced by an Archangel to be not only gracious, but *full of grace*, the chosen instrument of God in the Incarnation of His Son, and the Intercessor with this her Son in obtaining His first miracle, that of turning water into wine, at a period when His time for appearing to the world by *miracles was not yet come.‡ It is impossible*, as one of the Fathers says, *to love the Son without loving the Mother;* beg then of her with affection and confidence to intercede with Jesus, as the poor Canaanites did; to change the tears of your distress into the wine of gladness, by affording you the light and grace which you so much want. You cannot refuse to join with me in the angelic salutation: *Hail full of grace, the Lord is with me:* nor in the subsequent address of the inspired Elizabeth: *Blessed art thou among women, and blessed is the fruit of thy womb.* Cast aside, then, I beseech you, dear sir, prejudices, which are not only groundless, but also hurtful, and devoutly conclude with me in the words of the whole Catholic Church on earth: *Holy Mary, Mother of God, pray for us sinners, now and at the hour of our death. Amen."||*

---

* Job xlii. † St. Matt. xviii. 10. ‡ St. John iii. 4. || Letter xxxvi.

CHAPTER VI.   (ARTICLE IX).

PURGATORY.

1. What is Purgatory?—2. The doctrine of Purgatory as defined by the Council of Trent, and the proofs of the doctrine from Sacred Scripture. —3. The doctrine of Purgatory proved from tradition, and the reasons for this doctrine.—4. The Place of Purgatory.—5. The pains of Purgatory.—6. The duration of the sufferings of the souls in Purgatory.—7. The state of the suffering souls.—8. Prayers for the Dead.—9. The tradition of the Church in regard to prayers for the Dead.—10. Suffrages to be offered for the souls in Purgatory. —11. The suffrages of the living can benefit the dead.—12. The manner in which the souls in purgatory can help themselves and others by prayer.—13. Motives for devotion to the souls in Purgatory.

UNDER this Article of the Creed, Purgatory is explained in our ordinary Catechism, as it is so closely connected with the Communion of Saints, and the following five questions with their answers are given.

What is Purgatory?

1. Purgatory is a place where souls suffer for a time after death, on account of their sins.

What souls go to Purgatory?

Those souls go to Purgatory that depart this life in *venial* sin, or that have not fully paid the debt of *temporal* punishment due to those sins of which the guilt has been forgiven.

What is temporal punishment?

Temporal punishment is that punishment which will have an end either in this world or in the world to come.

How do you prove that there is a Purgatory?

I prove that there is a Purgatory from the constant teaching of the Church, and from the doctrine of the Holy Scripture, which declares that God will render to every man according to his works; and that some will be saved, *yet so as by fire.**

How are we in communion with the souls in Purgatory?

We are in communion with the souls in Purgatory by helping them with our prayers and good works : *It is a holy and a whole-some thought to pray for the dead, that they may be loosed from their sins.*†

---

* St. Matt. xvi. 27; Apoc. xxi. 27; 1 Cor. iii. 15.   † Mach. xii. 46.

" Purgatory is a word that has been formed from a Latin root, which signifies to cleanse or purify, and was gradually introduced and adopted to express more conveniently, by one word, what was previously expressed by metaphors and circumlocution. In this manner many new terms have been admitted into Christian Theology. Men believed in the three Divine Persons long before they adopted the word *Trinity.*"*

Purgatory is therefore a place in which the souls of the just departed suffer punishment for a time. Souls after leaving this world can no longer merit, nor, properly speaking, satisfy for the penalty due ; but they are said to pay the debt of punishment by suffering (satispatiendo), in such a way that they cannot help themselves, or liberate themselves from the penalties in any other way than by bearing them and suffering.

2. The Council of Trent,† in the beginning of its decrees on Purgatory, defines two things of faith regarding it. (*a*) That there is a Purgatory. (*b*) That the souls therein detained are helped by the suffrages of the faithful, and especially by the holy Sacrifice of the Mass. This same faith was professed by the Greeks as well as the Latins, in the Council of Florence.

The proofs of the existence of Purgatory may be found in the Old and New Testament. From the Old Testament, the first proof usually quoted is that from the 2 Machabees,‡ where the valiant soldier and Priest Judas collects and sends to Jerusalem twelve thousand drachmas of silver, for sacrifice to be offered for the sins, or rather for the remission of the punishment of the sins of the dead. *It is therefore,* says this passage, *a holy and a wholesome thought to pray for the dead, that they may be loosed from their sins*. We conclude from this passage that, besides heaven and hell, there is a middle state ; because as the souls in heaven require not the aid of prayers, so the souls in hell can receive no benefit from them ; hence there must be some third state of souls in which prayer is beneficial to them.

The book of the Machabees has been recognised as a canonical book containing God's word from the earliest ages, and has been received as such by the Councils of Florence and Trent. St. Augustine (Civit. Dei. 36) says : " The Church of God has always acknowledged the Machabees as a canonical book." This book, like some other books and portions of Sacred Scripture, has been rejected by Protestants, because it contains doctrine contrary to

---

* Dr. Lingard's Catechism. Arch. xi. † Sess. 25. ‡ xii.

Z

their errors. They only know the Scriptures which they admit to be God's word on the authority of the Catholic Church, and that authority declares the book of Machabees to be inspired and a canonical book as well as the rest. Even admitting that it were not canonical, it would, at all events, be worthy of historical faith, the same as is given to profane and heathen authors; and on this account the narrative testifies to the practice amongst the Jews, several years before Christ, not only to pray for the dead, but also to offer up public Sacrifices for them. That practice, and the traditions of praying for the dead, continued from that time up to the present, are proofs of the existence of Purgatory.

There are also other places in the Old Testament where Purgatory is referred to; as for example: *A gift hath grace in the sight of all the living, and restrain not grace from the dead.** And again: *Lay out thy bread and thy wine, upon the burial of a just man, and do not eat and drink thereof with the wicked.*†

The doctrine of Purgatory may be proved from many places of the New Testament. (a) From St. Matt.‡ *Whosoever speaketh a word against the Son of man it shall be forgiven him; but whosoever speaketh a word against the Holy Ghost, it shall not be forgiven him either in this world nor in the world to come.* St. Augustine, with all other commentators, draws from the passage that some sins are forgiven in the next world. Now sins are not remitted in heaven, for no sin can enter there; nor in hell, for out of hell there is no redemption; therefore there must be some third place where some sins, or their penalties, are forgiven.

Secondly, St. Paul, writing to the Corinthians, says: *Now if any man build upon this foundation, gold, silver, precious stones, wood, hay, stubble. Every man's work shall be manifest, for the day of the Lord shall declare it, because it shall be revealed in fire; and the fire shall try every man's work, of what sort it is. If any man's work abide which he hath built thereupon, he shall receive reward; if any man's work burn he shall suffer loss; but he himself shall be saved, yet so as by fire* §

On this last we may remark that by the *wood, hay*, and *stubble*, are meant the venial sins and imperfections that are mixed up with our good works. The remainder of the passage must be interpreted of Purgatory: for there can be no pain, or suffering, or fire, in heaven; nor is the fire of hell for salvation, but damnation; therefore the fire which worketh unto salvation must be in Purgatory.

---

* Eccles vii. 27. † Tobias ix. 18.
‡ St. Matt. xii. 82. § 1 Cor. iii. 12, *et seq.*

3. The teaching of the Holy Fathers on this point is exemplified in the whole book written by St. Augustine, *de cura pro mortuis*, "on the care of the dead," in which he teaches the doctrine of Purgatory, and that the souls therein detained are helped by the prayers of the faithful. Not only does he teach this doctrine in his writings, but he practised it in his daily prayers for the repose of the soul of his Mother, St. Monica, as he himself tells us in his Confessions.†

The following reasons are assigned for this dogma : (*a*) When the guilt of sin is pardoned, often the temporal punishment remains, and must be undergone either in this world, or in the next; ex. gr. *David.* It may happen that persons die before having paid this temporal punishment, or debt, in this life, and therefore they must do it in another life. Justice requires this, that those who die with little or no debt of sin, and those who die with a great debt of sin, may not be equal until the latter be purified and perfected. Again, it may happen that some die in venial sin. In such a case, according to the teaching of St. Thomas, the guilt of the sins is remitted by the perfect act of charity which the just soul makes in the instant of its release from the body. By this act, however, the liability to punishment is not taken away or diminished ; and therefore, the punishment of these sins must be endured in Purgatory. The reason assigned by St. Thomas for this explanation is, that after this life the soul can neither merit nor satisfy, and that the act of charity made by the soul the instant after its separation from the body is not meritorious and satisfactory, and although it removes the impediment of venial guilt it cannot merit the absolution or diminution of the penalty of the same as it could in this life.

That there must be some place for the punishment of souls after death is clear from the text of the Apocalypse,* where it is so distinctly declared that nothing evil shall enter heaven. We are told that even the just man falls seven times, and we must admit that many will die without expiating altogether their small faults. With these they cannot enter heaven, which receiveth nothing defiled ; they cannot be sent to hell, for they are, according to the Scripture, *just.* Therefore there must be a third place where these failings, of even the just man, will be expiated. It is true that the Scripture says : *Blessed are the dead who die in the Lord, for they shall rest from their labours.* Yes, thrice blessed we say. But this text only alludes to martyrs, and such as die free from all sin and debt of temporal punishment; and such, of course, require no purification. They really die in the Lord. Then again, the Scripture says: *As the tree falls, there it shall lie*; but this simply means that every man who dies is either saved or lost: it may also refer to the state of the soul after the last judgment. The moment man dies, his ultimate fate is decided either for heaven or hell.

In regard to this place, after explaining the dogma and proving that there is a middle state, or Purgatory, the following questions naturally present themselves to the mind. (a) Where is this place? (b) What are the pains of Purgatory? (c) How long will they last? (d) What is the state of the souls there? And as the Church has not defined any doctrine of faith on these questions, I shall give the more commonly received teaching in my answers to them.

4. (a) As to the place of Purgatory. It is somewhere under the earth and near hell. St. Thomas thinks that some souls, by an extraordinary arrangement of Providence, are purified out of that place, and undergo their purgatory in various places of this world, either for the instruction of the living, or as a means of help to the dead, that sometimes they may appear and make their wants known to the living. Thus St. Gregory in his dialogues* refers to the example of a certain Pascharius, who endured his purgatory in the locality, or neighbourhood, of the public baths.

5. (b) The pains of Purgatory are two-fold; namely, the *pain of loss*, and the *pain of sense*, both temporal or temporary.

The pain of loss is the delay of the beatific vision, in punishment of sins. This pain is the most vivid and most severe for poor souls. The knowledge which they have of God is most perfect, and their love for Him most intense, which causes them the most inexpressible sufferings.

The pain of sense is a physical suffering produced by fire of some kind which, by a mysterious power, acts on the soul, the same as if it were a body. It is commonly received that this is real material fire, and hence the Church, in praying for the faithful departed, asks for them a place, not only of light or peace, but also of *refrigerii*, that is, of coolness from the heat of the fire, which torments them. This opinion as to the fire being material,

---

* lib. 4., chap. 40.

is not of faith; for the Greeks in the Council of Florence would not admit this, but only that purgatory was a place full of labour and sorrows which caused the pain of sense; and that opinion is not condemned either by the Council of Florence or the Council of Trent.

In respect to the intensity of these sufferings and their duration, nothing is defined by the Church. St. Bonaventure and Bellarmine teach that the greatest pain in Purgatory is greater than the greatest pain of this life, but that the least pain in purgatory is not greater than the greatest pain in this life. I do not know how far the comparison applies. When we speak of Purgatory we are speaking of another order of things than is found here below. It is another state, and in another sphere altogether, and we do not know how far the comparison can be made, as things that are thus in different orders and states cannot be compared. Although this matter is uncertain as far as the comparison goes; it is nevertheless certain that the sufferings in Purgatory are very severe and bitter, as appears from the solicitude of the Church in exhorting us to prayers and good works, and to apply Indulgences for the souls of the faithful departed; also because that future state is one of retribution and of punishment, and the teaching of the Fathers is very distinct as to the severity and intensity of the pains of Purgatory.

It is certain that they are less severe than the pains of hell. They are necessarily alleviated by the friendship of God, the security as to the possession of future glory; and by the resignation of the sufferers to the most just will of God.

St. Thomas teaches that the souls in Purgatory are not tormented by demons, as they have triumphed over these; neither do the good Angels inflict the punishments, because these are not likely to afflict their companions and friends.

The pains and sufferings of all are not equal in Purgatory; but they are greater or less according to the debt of punishment due, and this applies to both the *pain of loss* and *the pain of sense*. Although the pain of loss may be said to be equal, inasmuch as all are deprived of the Vision of God, it may be felt unequally.

6. (c) We do not know anything certain about the duration of the punishment, or how long the souls are detained in Purgatory. It would appear from the practice of the faithful in the pious foundations left for Masses for the souls in Purgatory, that some souls are detained in Purgatory for many years; and Alexande VII. condemned a proposition which said that nor

legacy left for a soul should last more than ten years.

St. Augustine prayed for the soul of his mother for more than thirty years after her death, and asked all who might read his Confession to remember her at the altar.

There is no reason for saying that the souls in Purgatory are kept there until their heirs make restitution, or carry out their legacies or "wills," because the duration of the pains is determined at the moment of the particular judgment according to the measure of the debt due, and is not left to the determination of any one in this world. Restitution may benefit the souls departed inasmuch as it is a good work, and may move the creditors to prayers for their departed friends.

Souls are not all kept in purgatory an equal length of time, for, as St. Thomas says, the greater the venial sin the longer will it take to cleanse the soul of the debt corresponding to it. Again, we can suppose that the penalty is longer or shorter, according to the manner in which the habit of the sin is rooted in the soul, by the greater or less attachment; so that, according to the same holy doctor it might happen that a soul might be kept longer in Purgatory, and be less afflicted than another who would have more intense suffering but of shorter duration. The acerbity of the pains corresponds to the quantity of the fault, and their duration to the greater adherence which the sin had in the soul in this life. And it might happen that one might be more helped by the suffrages of the living than another, and obtain its liberation quicker and sooner. And we do know, on the authority of Scripture, that the souls, whether the time be long or short, will not come out of the place of suffering until they pay the last farthing of the debt, according to the determination of Divine justice :* *Be at agreement with thy brother betimes, whilst thou art in the way with him; lest perhaps the adversary deliver thee to the judge, and the judge deliver thee to the officer, and thou be cast into prison. Amen I say to thee, thou shalt not go out from thence till thou repay the last farthing.*

7. (d) In regard to the state of the souls whilst in Purgatory we know the following few things : (1.) They are certain of their salvation and entirely secure, because of the revelation made to them at the particular judgment; and also because they know that they have persevered in grace to the end of their lives, and

---

* St. Matthew v. 25, 26.

Christ has said : *He who shall persevere to the end shall be saved.* (2.) The souls in Purgatory are confirmed in grace, so that they can never lose it, or ever again sin, through the special protection of God. (3.) They bear their sufferings with the greatest patience ; and St. Thomas, on this account, says that they are not sufferings absolutely and strictly speaking, because voluntary, inasmuch as they know that they are required by the justice of God, and that they cannot otherwise attain their beatitude. (4.) These souls continually exercise acts of virtue, especially of *charity* ; and also of *faith,* because they do not yet see God clearly ; and of *hope,* because, although they are certain of the possession of God, they do not yet actually possess Him in Heaven. These acts are not meritorious because these souls have reached their term, and can no longer merit or demerit.

In the prayers of the Church which are offered for the dead we have expressions such as the following : That they may be liberated from the pains of hell ; that darkness may not envelope them ; that they may not fall into the obscure place, &c. *Ut liberentur de poenis inferni, ne abserbeat eas tartarus, ne cadant in obscurum,* &c. When these and such like expressions are used, souls are considered and represented as in the act of going out of the body. Such representations are usual in the Church's prayers ; thus in Advent we pray : *Rorate Coeli desuper et nubes pluant justum,* representing a mystery that has taken place long ago, but asking that its fruits may be now applied to us. Also we have to notice that the Church in the Office of the Dead (and the same may be said of the Office of any Feast or Saint) may use some Psalm, or other form of prayer, on account of one or more suitable verses ; and from this it does not follow that all the verses of the Psalm, or expressions in the Office should be understood as applying to the dead. The whole Psalm is recited as a manner of prayer or praise to God, by which the souls departed may be helped.

PRAYERS FOR THE DEAD.

8. It is of faith, defined in the Councils of Florence and Trent,* that the souls in Purgatory can be helped by the suffrages of the faithful on earth. This may be proved from the doctrine

---

* Sess xxii, Cap. 2, Can. 3, item initio Secreti de Purgatoria.

of the Communion of Saints which exists between the Church *militant* and the Church *suffering*, for, according to the teaching of St. Paul,* members of the same body are solicitous for each other, and mutually sympathise and assist each other.

The same doctrine is clear to us from the constant, perpetual and universal practice of the Church. This doctrine follows from the doctrine of venial sin, and the existence of Purgatory.

"As a Christian may die guilty of only venial sin, and as nothing defiled can enter heaven, by praying for such a Christian we appease God's anger against him, and shorten the duration of his sufferings in a middle state, in the same manner as we benefit the living by praying for them. Purgatory exists as we have already proved ; if so, then we, by praying for the dead, shorten the period of their sufferings in a middle state ; we make for them by prayers and oblations a satisfaction which they themselves cannot make, as they are not now in a state of merit."

9.　The tradition of the Church in regard to prayers for the dead is handed down from the earliest ages of Christianity. The third Council of Carthage (*anno* 253) decreed prayers for the dead. The Council of Chalons (in 579), the Council of Worms (in 829), came to the same decision as the Councils of Florence and Trent. The Emperor Constantine wished to be buried in a Church, that the faithful might remember him in their prayers to God. St. John Chrysostom (Hom. 1, Ep. ad. Cor.), says, " The tears of the living are not useless to the dead ; prayers and alms relieve them." St. Jerome, in his Epistle to Pammachius, remarks : " It is customary to strew the graves of the female dead with flowers, but you have followed a better usage in strewing the grave of your wife with alms for the solace of her soul." I have already referred to the testimony of St. Augustine, and I may now conclude that if the Church always prayed for the dead, she believed the dead were in a place where prayer could be beneficial to them ; this place was not heaven, nor could it be hell, therefore it was Purgatory.†

10.　The suffrages to be offered for the souls in Purgatory are :—

(a)　That specially mentioned by the Council of Trent, the Holy Sacrifice of the Mass.

(b)　The indulgences that are applied to the souls in Purgatory.

---

* 1 Cor. xii. 12 *et seq.*
† See Rev. S. Keenan's Controversial Catechism in loco.

(c) Prayers, such as, the *Way of the Cross*, the *Rosary,
Communion*, &c.

(d) Alms, and other good works, *performed through charity.*

In saying that the prayers, alms and good works, *performed
through charity*, benefit the dead, I mean that they ought to be performed by a person in a state of grace, that they may benefit the
Holy Souls; because the works of a sinner are not, properly
speaking, either meritorious or satisfactory. The Holy Sacrifice
of the Mass has its own intrinsic value independently of the disposition of the priest, and it will always benefit the dead. The
same may be said of the prayers that are offered in the name of
the Church. They always avail by way of impetration, as when
the Office of the Dead, and the *exequies*, are offered according to
the rites and ceremonies of the Church.

11. The *suffrages* of the living can benefit the dead by way
of *impetration, of satisfaction,* and of *congruous merit.* That is,
we can obtain by prayers favours for them; we can offer the
satisfactory part of our works for them; and, as the friends of God,
it is reasonable to suppose that through His love and goodness
towards devout souls, He will regard their prayers and good works
in such a way that He will grant His relief to the souls in purgatory, which may be said to be a reward merited, not strictly, but
by congruity.

Good works offered for the dead are at the same time beneficial to the person who performs them. They merit an increase
of grace inasmuch as they proceed from grace, and the merit of
having done a good work, and the reward in store for it, are inseparable from the person who does it. The merits are personal
and cannot be given away; but the satisfactory portion of our
works may be given away to others to pay the debt of their sins.
The suffrages therefore, inasmuch as they are satisfactory, do not
directly benefit the person who offers them for the souls in Purgatory, because he gives them away to the departed souls; and the
same satisfaction cannot pay a two-fold debt; if however the person for whom the suffrages are offered does not need them, then
they may profit by way of satisfaction the person himself who
offers them.

It is sometimes asked whether the suffrages infallibly benefit
the souls for whom they are applied? It is most probable that
they do. There is no impediment in the way as far as the faithful departed are concerned, and it would appear that God wills to
apply them for the relief of those for whom they are offered. And
this is also the mind and belief of the faithful.

But it is not certain that they benefit the particular souls to the full extent. Some say, Yes; and some say that they always lessen their sufferings; but they do not always absolve from the full penalty, even though the suffrages be condign and redundant. All this entirely depends on their application according to the Will of God; and we are not to cease offering our suffrages for the departed, until we are sure that they are in heaven.

Suffrages cannot benefit the lost souls; neither can they benefit the blessed in heaven; and therefore, when we know for certain that they are saints, we should not, and cannot, offer suffrages for them. Neither are suffrages offered for children who die without Baptism.

We can, however, invoke the aid of the Saints, and beg them to intercede with God for the souls in Purgatory.

There is one other question that remains to be answered as regards the souls in Purgatory, that is, as to their praying for themselves and others.

12. Although these souls are beyond the state of *meriting* and *satisfying*, they may nevertheless, by praying to God, obtain some favours from Him, such as the remission of their punishment, or that the living may apply suffrages and indulgences for them. There is no reason whatever to doubt that they can pray for themselves.

As to whether they also pray for us is not so certain. According to the more probable opinion they do pray for us, and especially for those souls who pray for them. There does not appear to be any reason against this, as the souls in Purgatory are with us in the Communion of Saints, and they know that we need the suffrages of others. It is not necessary that they should know those who pray for them, and yet they may know; for Angels may let them know, or God Himself in some special way. And although they do not know in particular what goes on here on earth, they know in general many of our necessities; and these they can know from the knowledge which they had in their life, concerning the necessities of their families and friends, and of the Church. Thus we read of Moses and Jeremias, that they prayed for the people out of the knowledge which they had of them here on earth. We may, with greater certainty, suppose that as soon as these souls go to heaven, they will know at once their friends on earth, and especially those who helped them by prayers and good works when they were in Purgatory; and then these Holy Souls will be certainly able to intercede for their charitable friends before the throne of God.

We may invoke the aid and prayers of the souls in Purgatory, as we invoke the prayers of devout people; although the Church does not in her public prayers ask their suffrages, or invoke them, because they do not know the prayers directed to them, and it is not certain that they can help us.

13. There are many motives that should influence us in our devotions and prayers for the souls in Purgatory.

(a) It is a duty of *religion*, because it is most pleasing to God that we promote His glory in satisfying His justice for those souls who are infinitely dear to Him.

(b) It is a duty of *justice* towards those souls who are now suffering for the evil which we have done them in life by our example or influence.

(c) It is a duty of *gratitude* towards those souls who have loved us and benefited us in many ways.

(d) It is a duty of *charity towards our neighbour*; for those souls have no less a claim to our charity in their present misfortune, than if they were enduring the trials of this life. Their claim is stronger now, as they cannot help themselves.

(e) It is a duty of *charity towards ourselves*. God will bless and favour those who help the souls in Purgatory, and they themselves in their gratitude will pray to God for us.

"It is a great charity to pray for the souls in Purgatory, whether we consider who they are, what they suffer, or how easily they can be relieved by us, though they can do nothing for themselves: *for the night has come upon them, when no man can work.*"*

The souls in Purgatory are the beloved Spouses of Jesus Christ, united to Him by grace, and secure of their eternal salvation. Now if Christ assures us that a cup of cold water, given for His sake in this life, shall not lose its reward, what reward will He not give to those who, for His sake, confer such a benefit on the souls in Purgatory, as to relieve their sufferings, and procure for them a more speedy admission into His Divine Presence?

If we could get a look into Purgatory, perhaps we should see a parent, brother, or sister, or some dead friend, crying out to us in the words of holy Job: *Have pity on me, have pity on me, at least you my friends, because the hand of the Lord hath touched me.*†

---

* St. John ix. 4. † Job xix. 21.

ARTICLE X.

APOSTLES' CREED.
The forgiveness of sins.

NICENE CREED.
I confess one Baptism for the remission of sins.

SECTION 1.

THE FORGIVENESS OF SINS.

1. The forgiveness of sins—its meaning.—2, Christ gave the power of forgiving sins to the Apostles and their successors : *whose sins you shall forgive they are forgiven them, and whose sins you shall retain they are retained.*—8. The means of forgiveness, the Sacraments of Baptism and Penance.—4. Sin—its definition and meaning.—5. The guilt and stain of sin.—6. The distinction of sins as to their species or kind, and as to their number.—7. The division of sins according to their specific and numeric distinction.—8. Sins are not all connected together, and they are not all equal.—9. The causes of sin—*internal* and *external.*

FAITH, in the remission of sins, means to believe that Jesus Christ has given to His Church the power of forgiving sins.

1. To remit sins means to pardon them, to efface them, to annihilate them, as if they had never been. It means the absolution from the guilt of sin, and the restoration of the soul to the favour of God, as in the parable of the Prodigal Son.*

The power of forgiving sins belongs to God alone ; because it belongs to the offended person to pardon the offence, as it belongs to the creditor to remit a debt owing to him.

Jesus Christ, inasmuch as He is God, has, the same as the Father, the power to forgive sins ; and, as Man, He received this power from His Father. By His death on the Cross He satisfied entirely the Divine Justice, and merited grace and pardon for all sinners. Thus, in His life-time, our Divine Lord, in absolving the man sick of the palsy, expressly mentions that they might *know that the Son of man hath power on earth to forgive sins.*

The grace of the remission of sins has to be applied to each one individually and personally ; as it is not a grace accorded to all in general, even to those who neither wish for or desire it, as

---

* St. Luke xv. 11-82.

God will not forgive the sins of the impenitent. The sinner, in order to be pardoned, must freely participate in the sacrifice of redemption; that is, the merits of Jesus Christ must be applied to his soul. And as Christ has established His Church to continue His mission, it is from the ministers of the Church, as representing Jesus Christ, that sinners must obtain the pardon of their sins. As God is the Sovereign Lord, He can give the power of remitting sins to others, and grant remission to the sinner in any way He chooses.

2. In effect, on the day on which He left the tomb, He gave to His Apostles, and to their successors, the power of forgiving sins by the words: *Receive ye the Holy Ghost: whose sins you shall forgive they are forgiven them; and whose sins you shall retain they are retained.*[*]

Receive ye the Holy Ghost. The Apostles therefore received the Holy Ghost Whom Christ gave, and at the same time they received the power of forgiving the sins of those who should demand pardon of their sins from them. It is by the grace of the Holy Ghost that the sinner is justified. By virtue of this grace, sins not only cease to be imputed, but they are taken away from the soul which is purified from them, becoming thereby the friend of God and the temple of the Holy Ghost. The Apostles, as regards this power, are the representatives of the future bishops and priests of the Church.

Whose sins you shall forgive they are forgiven. All sins without reserve, no matter how numerous or how grievous they may be. So that the power of forgiving sins was conferred by Christ on His ministers to the fullest possible extent; they have power to forgive all sins that can be repented of.

Whose sins you shall retain they are retained. The remission of sins is subject to certain conditions. The minister of Christ, who has delegated authority from Him, has to judge whether these conditions are present or not; and if the sinner does not observe them, his sins are to be retained; as the priest cannot absolve a person who is indisposed, or does not comply with what is required for the worthy reception of the Sacrament of Penance.

3. It is principally by the Sacraments of Baptism and Penance that the Church remits sins. The first blots out original sin in the case of infants, and all sins in the case of adults. The second forgives the sins committed after Baptism. The nature

---

[*] St, John xx. 22, 23,

and conditions of these two Sacraments are treated of in the explanations of these Sacraments, which do not belong to this portion of the Christian doctrine.

Besides the power of forgiving sins, the Church has also the power to remit either entirely or in part the temporal punishment due to sin, under certain conditions which She imposes on the faithful. This power, known by Catholics as the power of granting Indulgences, is founded on the words of Christ : *whatsoever you shall loose upon earth, shall be loosened also in heaven.*

As the Catholic Church is alone the true Church of Christ, She alone has received from God the power of forgiving sins, and remitting the temporal punishment due to sin. Any sect separated from her has no right to claim for itself this divine power. It is, therefore, in the Catholic Church alone, that sinners can hear the voice which declares on the part of God that their sins are forgiven.

In connection with this Article of the Creed, I find in nearly all Catechisms sin itself treated of and explained as to its nature, its different kinds, its causes and effects, as well as its remission ; and it may be well in this matter to follow the usual plan, in order that this Article of the Creed may be fully explained and understood.

SIN.—ITS DEFINITION AND DIVISION.

4. The Greek word signifying sin is ἁμαρτια—missing a mark. Sin is defined by St. John as the *transgression of the law* ; and by St. Augustine as "any word, deed, or desire against the eternal law." It is, therefore, any thought, word, deed, or omission against the law of God. *Whosoever committeth sin, committeth a transgression of the law ; for sin is transgression of the law.*[*] By the law of God is here understood, not only the natural law and the divine law, but also ecclesiastical laws, and the laws and commands of those who have legitimate authority over us ; as far as all these are subordinate to or in conformity with the law of God. Also whatever is opposed to right reason is opposed to the eternal law, and hence there is no such thing as a *philosophical* sin that is not at the same time a *theological* sin, although it may be considered in different ways by the philosopher and the theologian. God, the Author of our being, in creating men and angels, gave them wills wholly free, and He set before them His law as the way of happiness. His

---

* 1 St. John iii. 4.

Will is the absolute law of all created things. Both Angels and men abused the freedom of their wills, and revolted against God. Satan and the bad Angels set their wills in opposition to the Will of God. Adam and Eve turned away from God's Will, and transgressed His commandment in one particular. Sin may, therefore, be either a direct revolt against God and His Will, or an indirect revolt by the transgression of His commandments, or a turning to the creature in things unlawful. It is not often that we have open and directly rebellious sins, yet they are to be found in those who (a) profess Atheism, (b) who actually think of God, and directly wish, to offend Him ; (c) who resist the known truth, (d) who resist God's Church.

5.   Two things may be considered as belonging to the nature of sin, besides the actual revolt against the law of God. They are called the effects of sin; but as they are its necessary results, we must consider them with the nature of sin itself. These are the *stain* and the *gilt*. The *stain* of mortal sin is the privation of the supernatural lustre or brightness of the soul ; that is, the privation of grace or charity ;   the stain of venial sin is the lessening of that brightness, or the privation of the fervour of charity ; and the stain of both mortal and venial sin is the privation or diminution of the supernatural cleanness or brightness of the soul.

The *stain* contracted by sin, and remaining after the act of sin in the soul until the sin is remitted, may be considered the same as habitual sin, or the state of sin.

The *guilt* of sin is two-fold.   (1) That of the *fault*, which is the debt or obligation of repairing the injury or the offence offered to God by sin.   (2) The *punishment* or penalty, which is *eternal* for mortal sin ; *temporal*, for venial sin, or for mortal sin which has been pardoned as to the fault.

Penalty, properly speaking, is inflicted only for one's own sins, in punishment of one's sins, and it is in this light called *vindictive* or *avenging* ; SATISFACTORY punishment may be endured and offered for the sins of others as well as for our own.   The punishment is called medicinal when it is intended to preserve the soul against future sin, or to heal the wounds and remnants of past transgressions.

THE DISTINCTION OR DIVISION OF SINS.

6.   Sins may be distinguished in *species* or kind, and in *number*. They are specifically distinct when they have a special and dis-

tinct repugnance or opposition to the law of God, and to right
reason. *v.g.* (*a*) When they are opposed to different virtues,
such as theft and fornication. (*b*) When they are opposed to
the same virtue, but in contrary ways, such as presumption
and despair. (*c*) When opposed to the same virtue and in the
same way, but under a different reason, such as theft and
rapine.

This three-fold rule will suffice for our present purpose.

THE NUMERICAL DISTINCTION OF SINS.

Sins are numerically distinct in the same species if committed
(*a*) by many acts of the will. (*b*) If the same act has many
objects which do not coalesce in one. Acts are considered
different when they are disconnected, such as two distinct acts of
theft, or when they are morally interrupted; that is, when re-
tracted by the will and then renewed. As to whether an involun-
tary cessation from an act caused by sleep or inadvertence is to
be considered a moral interruption, so that the act renewed
afterwards becomes numerically a distinct sin, is not quite
certain. All depends on the nature of the act, whether it is
internal or *external*, and on the interval of time between the
renewal of the act.

The same acts may have many objects, when one object is
distinct from another and forms no part of it, and has distinct
rights, as for example: different persons (*a*) in their corporal
life; (*b*) in their spiritual life; (*c*) in their character and repu-
tation. Even temporal things of fortune and the like may
coalesce into one property, and then we must see how many have
dominion or distinct rights over it in order to judge of the number
of sins.

7. After stating in general how we may judge of the specific
and numeric distinction of sins, we may give in particular the
divisions of sins according to their specific and numerical
distinction.

(*a*)   Sins are said to be *carnal* or *spiritual*, as they are
determined by the carnal pleasure of the senses, as
in luxury and gluttony; or independently of any such
carnal pleasure, as pride. These are certainly specifically different.

(*b*)   Sins may be in *thought, word, and deed.* (*Cordis, oris et
operis.*) Sin is committed in *thought* when one takes
wilful pleasure in considering those things which he

knows to be forbidden by the law of God. The thought of evil is not necessarily sinful, for we cannot avoid the knowledge of evil; but when the will consents to a thought of evil, and gives it a place in the heart, then it becomes sin, and especially if it be accompanied by evil wishes, and desires to do that which is sinful. We sin by *speech* when, knowingly, words are uttered either (1) contrary to truth; (2) contrary to charity; (3) contrary to religion. Sins of *thought*, *word*, and *deed*, may be only three grades of one and the same sinful act. And some sins are begun in the heart and consummated in word and deed.

(c) Sins may be either against *God, our neighbour*, or *oneself*; that is, directly and specially against God, as *blasphemy*; against our neighbour, as *injustice*; or against oneself, as *drunkenness*. These are evidently specifically distinct.

(d) Sins are either of *commission* or of *omission*, as they are opposed either to a negative, or an affirmative precept. *Negative*, that which prohibits, v.g., *Thou shalt not steal*; *affirmative*, that which commands, v.g., *Remember that thou keep holy the Sabbath Day*. Sins of commission are obvious, and we become guilty of them when we transgress any of the commandments of God in the spirit as well as in the letter. We sin by omission when we omit to do those things (1) which are commanded by the law of God, (2) which our conscience tells us are obligatory, (3) which are commanded by lawful authority.

These may be of the same or a different species.

The *internal* sin of omission is committed when there is the will, either direct or indirect, of omitting that which is commanded. The *external* sin, when the time for fulfilling the precept elapses. That which we do during the time of omitting an obligation is not thereby sinful unless it be the cause of the omission.

The nature and species of a sin of omission must be judged from the virtue by which we are obliged to do that which has been omitted; and the gravity of the sin must be judged in like manner, and also according to the graver or lesser motive or reason, on account of which the precept was given.

8. There are one or two other things to be remembered as regards the nature of sins. (a) They are not all connected with each other. (b) They are not all equal. They are not all

AA

necessarily connected, because a person can commit *one sin* without being guilty of the others. By theft, a man is not guilty of murder ; but, inasmuch as mortal sins are all an aversion from God, and banish His grace from the soul, and one cannot be forgiven without the rest, they may be said to be connected as to the aversion : and it is in this sense we must understand the words that a person sinning against one commandment becomes guilty of all. By one mortal sin a man loses the grace of God, and as long as he remains in that state, the keeping of the other commandments cannot avail him to eternal life.

THE INEQUALITY OF SINS.

It is of faith that all sins are not equal. And it is evident that one sin may be a greater privation of rectitude than another, such as one disease may be worse than another.

All mortal sins contain an infinite malice, not absolutely, but in the sense that they contain, at least tacitly, a contempt of an Infinite Being—namely God. He who sins mortally is thought to place God beneath the creature, and turns to the creature as to his last end, in which is involved contempt of the divine majesty.

In general those sins are considered more grievous than others that are principally and directly opposed to the more noble or worthy virtues. The virtues are placed in the following order of dignity: (*a*) Charity. (*b*) Faith. (*c*) Hope. (*d*) Religion. (*e*) Penance. (*f*) Prudence. (*g*) Justice. (*h*) Fortitude. (*i*) Temperance.

In particular, as to sins against our neighbour, those sins are the more grievous which do him the greatest injury. Carnal sins are less than spiritual ones, but they have deeper root in the heart, and are accompanied by greater disgrace and dishonour.

The will is the cause of all sins, and those motions or temptations that precede the determination of the will, or that do not depend upon the will, are not formal sins. There are, however, many causes that influence the will towards evil, and these may be said to be the causes of sin.

9. We may here ask, What are the causes of sin?

Besides some sins themselves (as in the case of the Seven Capital Vices) there are other causes, both *internal* and *external,* that lead the soul into sin.

The internal causes are four, according to the four powers of the soul. These are : (*a*) Culpable ignorance in the intellect. (*b*) Malice in the will. (*c*) Frailty in the sensitive appetite. (*d*) The imagination.

·Human frailty, that is, the weakness of our moral nature, is prone to evil, and easily lead into evil through (*a*) the violence of temptation, (*b*) the weakness of our resolution, (*c*) the force of habit, or the warmth and concupiscence of the imagination.

The sins of malice are exemplified in the six sins against the Holy Ghost, and the four that cry to heaven for vengeance.

THE EXTERNAL CAUSES OF SIN.

It is of faith, against the Calvinists, that God cannot be said in any sense to be the author of sin, or of the deordination of any act that can be called a formal sin.

The various objections brought forward to prove that God is said to be the cause of sin may be answered by showing that those texts of Scripture are to be understood in the sense—(*a*) That God permits sin. (*b*) That He sometimes withdraws His grace from sinners through their own fault. (*c*) That He governs and exercises dominion over the wills, even the evil wills, of men ; but He does not take away their freedom.

The external causes of sin are these :

(*a*) External objects. (*b*) The devil, either through jealousy of men or hatred of God, goeth about like a roaring lion seeking whom he may devour. The devil is the cause of sin indirectly only either by interior suggestion through the phantasy or the sensitive appetite, or exterior trials ; he has no direct power over our free wills, and he cannot be said to be the cause of all sins. (*c*) Men, or our fellow creatures, who endeavour to draw away our affections from God, and to fix them on themselves. Those who lead· others to sin, or co-operate with sinners, by counsel, command, consent, &c. (*d*) The world which has formed its own moral code. It is an easy and indulgent one, it glosses over faults and permits laxity. It does not enforce self-denial, but, on the other hand, encourages indulgence and extravagance ; a very great number of people take public opinion as their rule of life, and so long as they conform their lives to what society expects and demands, regard themselves as in the way of salvation. Now the social code is well enough as far as it goes, but it is not

intended to be the supreme code. The law of God is that which
we must obey first, and that always points out to us a higher
life, a purer life, and an unselfish one, whereas the world insists
on a life which is selfish and without any noble aims.*

* "Conscience and Sin." (Baring Gould.)

SECTION 2. (ARTICLE X.)

ORIGINAL SIN.

1. Original Sin—its meaning.—2. The existence of original sin as defined by the Church.—3. The manner in which original sin is transmitted. —4. Those who contract original sin. The Blessed Virgin exempt from it.—5. In what consists the essence of original sin.—6. The effects of original sin in this life.—7. The effects of original sin in the next life.

THERE are two kinds of sin. *Original sin* and *actual sin.*

1. Original sin is that guilt and stain of sin which we inherit from Adam, who was the origin and head of all mankind. It is the sin which we inherit from our first parents, and in which we were conceived, and born *children of wrath.**

THE EXISTENCE OF ORIGINAL SIN.

2. Against the Pelagians, and modern rationalists, it is a dogma of faith that there is such a thing as original sin, that is, that there exists a sin truly and properly so-called, a sin proper to each one, which is transmitted by our first parents to their posterity by origin or generation.

This dogma was defined in the Council of Trent,† and may be proved from the Scriptures, both from the Old and from the New Testament. It has also been handed down to us by the constant tradition of the Church, as is evident from the continued custom of baptizing infants for the remission of their sins: it is confirmed by the miseries of this life, both of body and soul.

Many think that even without revelation, we could come to the knowledge of original sin (or at least conjecture it, if we could not prove it for certain), from the miseries of men in this life. Their reason is that these miseries are not necessarily penal, but they could be natural if God had created man in a state of pure nature, as was possible. But in such a case, they say that the miseries of life would have been much less in that

---

* Eph. ii. 3. † Sess. v.

state than they are in our state of fallen nature. There would be less concupiscence and less inclination to evil. But, once having the revelation of God concerning original sin, the doctrine may be confirmed and illustrated from our present miseries, and from the ruins and vestiges of his primitive nobility which man can study in himself.

Original sin transmitted to us, is the sin of the disobedience of Adam in the eating of the forbidden fruit; containing at least, as far as Adam was concerned, the deformities of pride, gluttony, &c. Besides this sin, it is not certain that Adam's other sins did any injury to his posterity, although it is certain that they injured himself.

Original sin is a mortal sin, as the Council of Trent declares,* when it calls it the death of the soul; it is, however, less than a mortal personal or actual sin, because it is not in us voluntary, in the same way as our personal sins. It is, indeed, voluntary, but not by the personal will which is required for our own personal sins and defects in our works, but by the will of another, namely, by the will of Adam, which was sufficient for the sin of nature, or the sin of our whole race. And as Adam was the father and representative of the human race, we all sinned in him.

Original sin in us is not an actual sin, or any sinful act; but an habitual sin or a sinful state, which is, properly speaking, the sin, that is, the stain consequent on Adam's actual sin which is the privation of holiness and original justice. This, by the decree of God, was destined for all men until Adam lost it to himself and to his posterity.

Original sin cannot be said to be the actual transgression of Adam, morally persevering in us, and imputed to us; for that transgression has passed away, and our original sin is a sin proper to each one. The opinion that our will was contained in Adam's will, is not teneable, and involves an absurdity; and the agreement between God and Adam, that, on his fidelity the future of the human race would depend, is not to be held otherwise than as a pure supposition and a groundless one.

We may, therefore, conclude that original sin is a true and real sin, that is, the habitual sin of Adam transfused by propagation, inasmuch as it deprives us of that which was due to us by the Divine decree: It is a sin of its own kind (not the object

---

* l. c., can. 2.

of repentence), because it is not committed by our will, but by the will of another; hence it has effects proper to itself, especially in the next life.

THE MANNER IN WHICH ORIGINAL SIN IS TRANSMITTED.

3. It is of faith that original sin is transmitted (not by imitation) but by propagation, that is natural generation. As to the manner how this is done, we have no definition of the Church, and we have to say that the communication of original sin is a mystery. It cannot be fully explained, but we can show that it is not against any rational principle. Two things have to be considered in connection with original sin. (a) The soul is created by God, devoid of original justice and of sanctifying grace; this was a gift not due to our nature. According to Catholic doctrine, as to the origin of the soul, we teach that all souls are immediately created by God, and infused into the body at the same time that they are created. (b) This absence of original justice has some relation to the sin of Adam, inasmuch as the soul, although created immediately by God, when infused into the body, which is by propagation descended from Adam, becomes part of man, to whom original justice would have been given were it not for Adam's sin. Therefore, the soul created pure by God, when at the same moment as its creation it is infused into the body which descends from Adam, on account of the sin of Adam, suffers a privation of that gift which, by the former decree of God, it should have had.

Parents, although just, do not communicate sanctifying grace to their children, because this grace is a supernatural gift which cannot be propagated by generation, the same as original justice, which was not to descend by nature, but by the positive will of God to the posterity of Adam. But parents do communicate human nature to their children, and nature as descending from Adam, that is deprived of original justice, in the manner just mentioned, that is, nature stained by original sin.

THOSE WHO CONTRACT ORIGINAL SIN.

4. It is of faith that all men who descend from Adam, in the natural way of generation, contract original sin, unless some-one, by a special privilege, be exempted from the common law.

Christ our Lord is excepted, because He does not proceed in the natural way of generation, having had no man for a father, and because of the hypostatic union He could not be subject to sin.

The Blessed Virgin was exempted from original sin by a special privilege, as it is now defined of faith by the Bull *ineffabilis* of Pius IX. of the 8th Dec., 1854. "The Blessed Virgin, in the first instant of her conception by the singular favour and privilege of the omnipotent God, through the merits of Jesus Christ, the Saviour of the human race, was exempt from all stain of original sin." And the Council of Trent, in its fifth Session declares, that it is not its intention to comprehend in its decree concerning original sin the Immaculate Virgin Mary, Mother of God.

All the other members of the human race are subject to this sin. It is our state and condition, as represented by St. Paul, when speaking of himself: *When we were in the flesh, the passions of sin which were by the law did work in our members to bring forth fruit unto death. . . . . For we know that the law is spiritual, but I am carnal, sold under sin. For that which I work I understand not. For I do not that good which I will: but the evil which I hate that I do. . . . . For the good which I will I do not, but the evil which I will not that I do.*[*] It is of this original sin holy Job speaks in the words—*Man born of a woman, living for a short time, is filled with many miseries. Who cometh forth like a flower, and is destroyed, and fleeth as a shadow, and never continueth in the same state. . . . . Who can make him clean that is conceived of unclean seed ? Is it not Thou who only art ?*[†] And holy David exclaims : *Behold I was conceived in wickedness, and in sin did my mother conceive me.*[‡] And St. Paul, writing to the Romans, says : *Wherefore as by one man sin entered into the world, and by sin death; and so death passeth upon all men in whom all have sinned.*[§]

The Sacrament of Baptism was instituted principally as a remedy for original sin. Our nature is a fallen nature, degraded through the fall of our first parents ; by Baptism we are restored to a state of grace and friendship with God.

5. Having explained the doctrine of original sin, we may now conclude that the essence of this sin consists in the privation of original justice, or sanctifying grace, inasmuch as we inherit that privation through the sin of Adam. It is clear from the Council of Trent that it is the death of the soul. The life of the soul is its union with God by grace, or *sanctifying grace itself*. Death is the privation of life, therefore the death of the soul is the privation of sanctifying grace. This is the same as aversion from God, not a positive aversion, but a defect of conversion

---

[*] Rom. vii. 5, 14, et. seq.   [†] Job xiv. 1, et seq.
[‡] Ps. l. 7,   [§] Rom. v. 12,

towards God or union with Him. This privation of sanctifying grace must be considered in relation to its cause, namely, the sin of Adam ; otherwise it would be in us only as a mere want or absence of grace, as would be the case in a state of pure nature ; and it would not constitute us sinners ; wherefore not every privation of sanctifying grace constitutes the essence of original sin, but only that privation which arises from the sin of Adam.

Original justice, of which we are deprived by sin, as to its principle part, was constituted by sanctifying grace, by which the reason and will were subject to God ; from this, however, as from a cause, two other gifts followed, namely, the subjection of the inferior part of the soul to the superior, and of the body to the soul. Hence, when the cause was removed by the rebellion of man against God, the result was a rebellion in man himself, namely, that of the inferior against the superior part of his nature, and of his body against his soul.

The privation of sanctifying grace is called the *form* of original sin ; and the two-fold rebellion consequent on it is called the *material* of original sin, or concupiscence taken generally, which is the penalty or the effect of original sin.

Protestants commonly place the essence of original sin in concupiscence taken generally, that is in the deordination of all the powers of the soul ; and they extend it to the taking away of many natural powers, and even to a positive evil quality born with man. This notion of original sin is refuted by the fact that concupiscence remains after Baptism, and according to the teaching of the Church, expressly declared by the Council of Trent*— all that has the reason or nature of sin, properly so called, is taken away by Baptism. The Council further adds that even in the baptised the inclinations (*fomes*) to sin, and the concupiscence, remain ; and this concupiscence is sometimes called sin by the Apostle, not that it is sin in those regenerated, but because it proceeds from sin, and induces to sin.

THE EFFECTS OF ORIGINAL SIN.

6. The effects of original sin in this life are first as to the soul. (*a*) The enmity of God, that is the loss of the friendship of God. (*b*) Concupiscence taken in its general sense, that is the deordination of the powers of the soul.

As to whether that concupiscence, or the deordination of the powers of the soul (*vulnera animæ*), causes a real and true hurt or

---

* Sess. 5, can. 5.

wound to our nature is controverted. Some hold that man, by original sin, is not injured in his natural powers, but that his nature is despoiled of its supernatural and gratuitous gifts, and left to its own natural inclinations, as it would be in a state of pure nature ; only, that then it would belong to nature and be the result of nature, now it is a *penalty*, that which suffices, and gives us reason to call those natural infirmities *wounds*. On the other hand, many hold that by original sin, not only the gratuitous gifts of God are taken away, but that our natural gifts were greatly impaired by four wounds. (*a*) Ignorance obscured the brightness of man's intelligence. (*b*) Malice corrupted the integrity of his will. (*c*) Desire tyrannised over his concupiscible appetite, and (*d*) weakness paralysed his irascible appetite. This is illustrated by the parable of the Good Samaritan, in the example of the man going from Jerusalem to Jericho, who fell among thieves ; they not only stripped him, but also wounded him, and left him half dead.*

It is true, the Council of Trent declares that the whole man, as to body and soul, is placed in a worse state by original sin, and that man's will is weakened, but it does not decide whether this comes from his nature being impaired, or is the result of the taking away of the supernatural gifts ; and in contrast with a state of innocence man must now, no matter how it happens, be regarded as weakened and impaired in his natural powers.

Secondly, the effects of original sin as to the body are death, diseases, sufferings, pains, and all other bodily defects.

7. The effects of original sin in the next life are :—

(*a*) Certainly the pain of loss, that is, the privation of the beatific vision.

(*b*) It is doubtful whether also the pain of sense belongs to it. It is the more common and probable opinion that it does not, and St. Thomas teaches that those who die with only original sin will be able to enjoy God by natural knowledge and love.

In conclusion, let us not fail to remember what St. Paul proves in the fifth Chapter of the Epistle to the Romans, that Christ has benefited us more than Adam injured us, and hence, in the words of St. Augustine, the Church sings : *O felix culpa quae talem ac tantum meruit habere Redemptorem.* Now, again, supernatural grace is given, which strengthens and perfects nature, and which renders us holy, and capable of eternal life.†

---

*St. Luke x.   † See the Tractatus de Peccatis. Auctore, A. B. Van der Maeren.

SECTION 3. (ARTICLE X.)

ACTUAL SINS AND THE DEADLY VICES, &c.

1. Actual sin—its definition and the conditions required for it.—2. The division of sin into *mortal* and *venial*, and how they may be distinguished.—3. The various ways in which sins may be regarded as *mortal* and as *venial.*—4. What is meant by light and grave matter in regard to sin.—5. Conditions that diminish the guilt of sin, and that aggravate its guilt.—6. Seven circumstances that may cause a venial sin to be grievous.—7. The Capital Sins or Deadly Vices : (*a*) *Pride,* (*b*) *Avarice,* (*c*) *Luxury,* (*d*) *Envy,* (*e*) *Gluttony,* (*f*) *Anger,* (*g*) *Sloth.*—8. The six sins against the Holy Ghost.—9. The four sins that cry to heaven for vengeance.—10. The different ways in which one may be answerable for the sins of another.

1. ACTUAL sin is the sin which we ourselves commit. It is personal to each one, and has for its principle the abuse of our free will. It is that which we have already defined when speaking of the nature of sin : any thought, word, deed, or omission against the law of God.

Certain conditions are required that a man may be guilty of actual sin. These are : (*a*) Knowledge of what is proposed to do. (*b*) Liberty to do it or to forbear. (*c*) Will which determines the sinful act. When any of these conditions are wanting, there can be no actual sin.

2. Actual sin is of various degrees of guilt, and on this account it is usually divided into *mortal sin* and *venial sin.*

A sin is called *mortal* or *venial* as it is grievously or only lightly opposed to the eternal law ; or in defining them by their effects, it may be said that *mortal* sin causes the spiritual death of the soul by depriving it of sanctifying grace. *Venial* sin does not deprive the soul of grace, but it weakens it and disposes it to mortal sin.

It is certain that some sins are only venial, and this not only by reason of the condition of those sinning, or out of the divine mercy, but from the very nature of things, just as in every society there are slight offences that do not dissolve friendship.

Mortal sins may be distinguished from venial sins in a general way by certain rules that are laid down. (*a*) Those are mortal which the Scriptures designate as grievous, or condemn solemnly by the *Wo !* or some such expression ; or to which it attaches grave or everlasting punishment. (*b*) *Tradition* which tells us those sins that have always been regarded as mortal. (*c*) The common opinion of doctors and theologians. (*d*) Natural reason.

Outside these general rules it is difficult to decide in particular what sin is mortal and what is venial; and it is necessary for instructors to be careful in this matter lest they should convert theological opinions into Articles of faith, counsels into precepts, and light obligations into grave.

We must remember that for mortal sin two things are required, namely, (*a*) The full and perfect consent of the will. (*b*) Grave matter.*

MORTAL SINS.

Some sins are mortal of their own entire nature, such as blasphemy ; and some may be mortal in their own kind and species, as theft in a notable quantity ; and some may be mortal not in themselves, but by reason of some mortal circumstance in connection with them, such as a jocose lie, in order to do a serious injury to another.

Sin may be venial, (*a*) because of the imperfect assent of the will; and this applies in all cases ; (*b*) because of light matter. When it is venial, so that of its own kind it can never amount to grave sin, it is called venial (*ex genere suo*) of itself, as a simple lie. An example of a sin venial, by reason of levity of matter, would be small thefts.

4. It may be asked, what is meant by light and grave matter in regard to sin.

That matter is called light which only slightly affects the love of God, or our neighbour ; or the end of the law or precept. Many small things may coalesce, and become grave matter when they fall under the same precept, and belong, morally speaking, to one continued transgression of the precept ; such as a small theft, proceeding from the same uninterrupted will of stealing, may accumulate into a grave injustice.   There are some things in

---

* " So that those evil thoughts which pass through the mind to which we give no consent, direct or indirect, are not sinful to us, and entail on us no guilt.   Living in this evil world, in the midst of sin, we cannot avoid the knowledge of it ; that knowledge may, however, pass over the minds, darkening momentarily, but not staining like a shadow of a cloud on a hill-side."   Baring Gould.

which moralists do not admit levity of matter, as for example :
(a) In sins directly against God or His attributes, such as blasphemy. (b) In sins whose matter, unless gravely prohibited in all cases, would lead men into the greatest sins, to their utter ruin ; such as sins against purity outside married life. (c) In sins whose malice in any matter, great or small, would violate the end of the law, or gravely injure it, such as the breaking of the seal of confession, the violation of the natural fast.

5. There are conditions that diminish the guilt of sin so that a mortal sin may become venial ; and conditions that aggravate guilt so that a venial sin may become mortal. A mortal sin may become venial by reason of the imperfect consent of the will, or through levity of matter. The extenuating causes or circumstances on the part of the will may be : (a) excusable ignorance ; (b) grave fear ; (c) compulsion ; (d) inadvertence, or excusable want of attention. These are not given for the purpose of making excuses for sins, but for the comfort and peace of such souls that fear to fall into sins which they in their hearts hate. A venial sin may become mortal when the consent of the will, from being imperfect becomes full and perfect, and when light matter becomes grave.

6. There are circumstances grievously sinful that may accompany some sins that are only venial of themselves. These may be enumerated seven.

(a) *Grave scandal*, that is when a sin, venial in itself, becomes the occasion of grave sin to another.

(b) *Contempt*, which means formally to despise the law or the legislator as such, which is a grave sin against religion or piety.

(c) *The end proposed*, that is when one sets his heart on some venial sin as his last end.

(d) *The intention*, when one commits a venial sin in order to attain an end, grievously evil.

(e) When the venial sin leads one into the proximate danger of mortal sin.

(f) An error of conscience, which leads a person committing a venial sin to believe at the time it is mortal.

(g) Grave injury, which the person foresees will follow from his act.

Among these various ways in which a venial sin may become mortal, we do not include the multiplying of venial sins, for no number of venial sins could make up one mortal sin, as no number of finite things can amount to an infinite thing. But venial sins dispose one to mortal sin, and this they do (a) *directly* in the case where sins in themselves mortal are venial, only on account of the imperfect consent of the will, or the levity of the matter; (b) *indirectly*, inasmuch as all venial sins diminish the fervour of charity, and impede actual graces.

THE CAPITAL SINS, OR THE DEADLY VICES.

7. Certain sins or vices are called Capital or Deadly, because they lie at the head or source of all sin, and because they mortally affect the soul. They are not called Capital as if they were the greatest of all sins, or the worst, but because they are the principles, or springs, out of which so many other sins issue.

They are seven in number, and are as seven mothers which, when taken into the heart, settle there, and produce large families of sins, which are enumerated and explained by St. Thomas in various places.

The Seven Capital vices, or sins, are :—(a) Pride, (b) Avarice, (c) Luxury, (d) Envy, (e) Gluttony, (f) Anger, (g) Sloth.

Of these, Pride, Avarice, and Envy are vices of the soul ; Luxury, Gluttony, Anger, are vices of the body. Sloth is a vice of the soul and of the body.

(a) *Pride* is an excessive love of oneself, and an inordinate desire of being above others. There is no sin more ancient, more grievous, or more dangerous, for it is the sin of the fallen angels, and of the first man ; it is the sin which we have the greatest difficulty to preserve ourselves from, the last we overcome.

It may of its own nature be a grievous sin, and it is mortal when a man loves his own self so much as to refuse to be subject to God or to lawful superiors ; or, so as to contemn and oppress his neighbour seriously. It may be only a venial sin if the matter is light. Pride is opposed to humility.

(b) *Avarice* is an inordinate love and desire of riches, or the things of this life. It may be a mortal sin of its own nature when it violates justice, charity, or any other virtue, when these bind under grave sin. It is only a venial sin in itself when it is opposed only to liberality. It is opposed by defect to liberality, to which prodigality, in itself a venial sin, is opposed by excess.

(c) *Luxury*, which is the desire of the sin of the flesh, that sin which, in the words of St. Paul, ought not to be so much as named among Christians.* This is of its own entire nature a mortal sin, and does not admit levity of matter whenever there is the full consent of the will to a sin of this kind. Luxury is opposed to chastity.

(d) *Envy* is an inordinate sadness or repining at the worldly and spiritual good of our neighbour, or rejoicing at his injury or distress. Of its own nature it may be mortal, and is mortal when one yields intensely to this vice. It makes man resemble the evil spirits who go about continually to hurt us. Envy is opposed to benignity.

(e) *Gluttony* is an inordinate desire either of food or drink. Gluttony in eating and drinking, when it does not inebriate, is only a venial sin in itself ; but drunkenness or inebriety is a mortal sin of its own nature. Gluttony is opposed to temperance.

(f) *Anger* is a violent and inordinate motion of the heart against such persons or things as displease us. It leads to an inordinate desire of revenge. Of its own nature it may be mortal, when it leads to a grave violation of justice or charity. It is only venial when considered as to the manner in which one is angry. Anger is opposed to patience and meekness.

(g) *Sloth* is a laziness or weariness, that makes us omit the service of God, or perform it with neglect or indolence. It may be mortal of its own nature, and is mortal when it affects those things that are necessary for salvation, or that are of grave obligation, so as to prevent their fulfilment or observance. It is, however, often only a venial sin. Sloth is a vice opposed to devotion and piety.

Besides the Capital sins or vices, two other classes of sins in particular are mentioned in our Catholic Catechisms.

8. (a) *Sins against the Holy Ghost.* (b) *Sins that cry to heaven for vengeance.*

The sins against the Holy Ghost are chiefly six. (a) Despair

---

* Ephes. v. 3.

of salvation. (*b*) Presumption of God's mercy. (*c*) To resist the known truth. (*d*) Envy at another's spiritual good. (*e*) Obstinacy in sin. (*f*) Final impenitence. These are especially sins of malice, which involve an obstinate resistance to the inspirations of the Holy Ghost, and formal contempt of His gifts. It is said that sins against the Holy Ghost, such as the above, shall not be forgiven in this world or in the world to come, in the sense that it is very difficult to obtain the forgiveness of them; for men seldom truly repent of them. God and the Church, or its priests, can forgive them however, like all other sins, if we truly repent. All can be forgiven except final impenitence.

If we confess our sins, He is faithful and just to forgive us our sins, and to cleanse us from all iniquity.

10. There are *four sins that cry to heaven for vengeance*; that is, sins of so great an enormity that they are often punished by God even in this life. They are (*a*) wilful murder; (*b*) Sodomy; (*c*) oppression of the poor; (*d*) to defraud workmen of their wages.

10. Besides our own personal sins, we have to remember that one may make himself partaker in, and guilty of, the sins of another. This is the case for every one who counsels, commands, consents to, or commends, the commission of sins; he also sins who provokes another to do evil by assisting him to do it, by defending him in his wickedness, and who does not prevent him when he can, or when it is his duty to do so. Hence, St. Paul tells us: *Who having known the justice of God, did not understand that they who do such things are worthy of death; and not only they that do them, but they also that consent to them that do them.**

At the end of this Article on Sin, I may give two special catechetical questions and answers.

(*a*) When are we answerable for the sins of others?

We are answerable for the sins of others, whenever we either cause them, or share in them through our own fault.

(*b*) In how many ways may we either cause or share the guilt of another's sin?

We may either cause or share the guilt of another's sin in nine ways. (1) By counsel. (2) By command. (3) By consent. (4) By provocation. (5) By praise or flattery. (6) By concealment. (7) By being a partner in sin. (8) By silence. (9) By defending the ill done.

---

* Rom. i. 32.

ARTICLE XI.

APOSTLES' CREED.	NICENE CREED.
The Resurrection of the Body.	And I expect the Resurrection of the Dead.

1. What is meant by the Resurrection of the Body?—2. The Resurrection of the Body proved from Scripture—(a) from the Old, (b) from the New, Testament.—3. Pledges of the future Resurrection.—4. The dogma of the Resurrection of the flesh demonstrated by reason.—5. Objections of rationalists to the dogma, and their refutation.—6. All men shall rise again.—7. The Time of the Resurrection.—8. The state or condition of men in the Resurrection.—9. The age, size, and sex of resuscitated bodies.—10. The four qualities or gifts of a glorified body; and the corresponding defects or penalties inflicted on the damned.

1. In the Greek and Latin forms we have " the resurrection of the flesh," so that all ambiguity is avoided in relation to *celestial* and *spiritual* bodies, and our earthly bodies. As by flesh is understood the body of man, and no other flesh, so in translating it body, we understand no other body than that of man, the same body of flesh, of the same frail nature as man had, before it was by death separated from his soul.

To believe in the resurrection of the body, means to believe that at the end of the world, before the last judgment, all shall rise with the same bodies that they had in this life.

The resurrection is the restoration to life of our bodies. Although I have already explained the nature of a resurrection in treating of the fifth Article of the Creed, I think it well to refer again to the essential characters of a true resurrection. A resurrection means a substantial *change* by which what was before and was corrupted, is reproduced in the same thing again. (a) A change, not a second or new creation, as if a man or angel were annihilated and made again out of nothing. (b) A substantial change; not an accidental alteration as from sickness to health. (c) A change of what was before, and was corrupted; (1) things incorruptible cannot be reproduced; (2) and of things corruptible, some, the forms of inanimated bodies and all irra-

BB

tional souls when corrupted cease to be, consequently, even if such were reproduced out of the same matter, there would not be the restitution of the same individual, only of the same species by another individual. But when a rational soul is separated from its body, which is the corruption of a man, the soul still exists, and is capable of reunion with the body ; and if these two be again united by an essential and vital union, from which life necessarily flows, then the same man lives who lived before, and, consequently, the reunion is a perfect and proper resurrection from death to life.*

2. There shall be a resurrection of the body.

This is proved not only from this Article of the Creed, but from many passages of holy Scripture.

(a) From the Old Testament. The heathen did not believe in the Resurrection of the body, although many of them believed in the immortality of the soul. The Jews believed in the Resurrection of the body, and in Christ's time all, except the Sadducees, believed in it. Martha, we read, said to our Lord: *I know that he* (Lazarus) *shall rise again in the resurrection at the last day*, thus giving expression to the common belief of the Jews in her day. The resurrection is made known in the following revelation of the Old Testament. Job says: *For I know that my Redeemer liveth, and in the last day I shall rise out of the earth. And I shall be clothed again with my skin, and in my flesh I shall see God.*†

Daniel says yet more plainly : *And many of those that sleep in the dust of the earth, shall awake; some unto life everlasting, and others unto reproach, to see it always.*‡

Also in the vision of the dry bones of Ezechiel, the bones are clothed again with flesh.§

(b) In the New Testament, Our Lord stated to the Jews : That *the hour cometh, wherein all that are in the graves shall hear the voice of the Son of Man. And they that have done good things shall come forth unto the resurrection of life, and they that have done evil unto the resurrection of judgment.*||

Christ refers to this doctrine of the resurrection in St. Matthew's Gospel,** and in many other places : *And concerning the resurrection of the dead, have you not read that which was spoken to you by God, saying to you : I am the God of Abraham,*

---

* Pearson. Analysis, Article V.   † Job xix. 25, 26.   ‡ Dan. xii. 2.
§ Ez. xxxvii. 8, 16—20. || St. John v. 28, 29.   ** St. Matt. xxii. 31, *et seq.*

and the God of Isaac, and the God of Jacob? He is not the God of the dead, but of the living.

According to St. Paul, in the whole of the fifteenth Chapter of his first Epistle to the Corinthians, the resurrection is so certain, that to deny it is the same as to deny the resurrection of Jesus Christ Himself. But as Christ is certainly risen from the dead, so is our resurrection certain. Death came by the first Adam; Christ, the new Adam, came to destroy death.

PLEDGES OF THE RESURRECTION.

8. We have not only scriptural texts in proof of the resurrection, but pledges of our future restoration to life.

The Old Testament records three instances of restoration to life.

(1.) The dead son of the widow of Zarephath raised by Elias. (3 Kings xvii. 22.)

(2.) The child of the Sunamite woman raised by Eliseus. (4 Kings iv. 32.)

(3.) The dead man who was cast into the grave of Eliseus. (4 Kings xiii. 21.)

The New Testament records three miracles of raising from the dead by our Lord.

(1.) The daughter of Jairus, just dead, lying in the death chamber. (St. Matthew ix. 25.)

(2.) The son of the widow of Naim on the way to the tomb. (St. Luke vii. 11—15.)

(3.) Lazarus, who had been in the tomb, and had been dead four days. (St. John xii. 43.)

Two miracles of this kind are recorded of the Apostles.

(1.) The raising of Tabitha, or Dorcas, by St. Peter. (Acts ix. 36—41.)

(2.) The raising of the youth Eutychus by St. Paul. (Acts xx. 9, 10.)

It is also recorded by St. Matthew that, after the resurrection of Christ, many bodies of the saints arose, and going out of the tombs, came into the holy city, and appeared to many.

But the most signal instance of all is our Lord's own glorious resurrection, when He rose triumphant from the grave, and showed Himself alive, after His passion, by many infallible proofs.

4. Human reason suggests two principal proofs of the dogma of the resurrection.

(a)   The soul of man is not, as an Angel, a pure spirit; it is
      naturally destined to be united to a body. The body
      is its essential complement. Hence it seeks to remain
      united to it, and does not wish to be separated from
      it. After death it will always retain the desire of
      being united to the body, that it may not always
      remain an incomplete being. This desire comes from
      God, the Author of nature, and it is not a deception,
      and hence the soul will again vivify the body.

(b   The body is here below the natural instrument of the
      soul, either for good or evil; it is, therefore, just that
      it should have its share of rewards or punishments
      in the life to come.

The doctrine of the resurrection of the body has many
illustrations in nature. "(1) In every twenty-four hours the day
dies into night, next morning it revives, opening the grave of
darkness; this is a diurnal resurrection. (2) Summer dies into
Winter; the sap is said to descend into the root, and there it
lies buried in the ground, which is crusted with frost. When
Spring appears all begins to rise; the plants, &c., revive and
grow; this is the annual resurrection. (3) The corn, by which
we live . . . . . is buried in the ground that it may corrupt, and
being corrupted may revive and multiply; our bodies are fed
with this constant experiment, and we continue the present life
by a succession of resurrections. Can we think that man, the
lord of all these things which thus die and revive for him, should
be detained in death for ever—that God should thus restore all
things to man, and not man to himself?"*

5. Freethinkers say that the resurrection of the dead is
impossible. Myriads of dead bodies have disappeared for so
many ages without any trace of them to be found. Their dust
has gone into the composition of other bodies, and has served to
form plants and animals, which in their turn have undergone
innumerable transformations. By nutrition, it happens that some
human bodies are organized by the atoms of other human bodies,
as in the case of cannibals. How, it is asked, can living men
be again reconstituted out of such scattered dust? How, in
the midst of so much confusion, will it be possible to restore to
each one what originally belonged to him?

To all this we may answer, that He who made all things
out of nothing, can easily remake anything which He has already

---

* Pearson. Analysis, Art. xi.

made. He is infinite in His knowledge. He knows all men who ever lived, or shall live; He knows whereof all things were made; from what dust we came, to what dust we shall return. He also sees and knows all ways and means by which these scattered parts should be re-united. He knows how every bone should be brought to its old neighbour-bone, how every sinew may be embroidered on it; what are the proper parts, and by what *gluten* to be joined. The resurrection, therefore, cannot be impossible in relation to the Agent, through any deficiency of knowledge. Then His power is unlimited. There can be no opposition against Him, because all power is His. All creatures must do, as well as suffer, what He will have them. There is no atom of dust or ashes, but must be where it pleases God, and be applied to, and make up what, and how, it seems good to Him. The resurrection, therefore, cannot be impossible in regard to any deficiency of power on the part of the Agent.

On the part of the creature there is no impossibility in the resurrection, as there is no contradiction in this, that he who was and now is not, should hereafter be what before he was. "As no creature could be made out of nothing but by Him, so can it not be reduced to nothing but by the same; though therefore the parts of the body of man be dissolved, yet they perish not . . . . . it is no more a contradiction that they should become parts of the same body of man to which they did belong, than that after his death they should become the parts of any other body, as we see they do. Howsoever scattered, wheresoever lodged, they are within the power and knowledge of God, and can have no repugnancy by their separation to be re-united when and how He pleaseth. If it be not easier, it is certainly as easy, to make that to be again which once hath been, as to make that to be which before was not. When there was no man, God made him out of the dust of the earth, and therefore when he returns to earth, the same God can make him again."*

ALL MEN SHALL RISE AGAIN.

6. This will be without any exception, unless in the case of those who have already risen to a blessed life. Christ speaks universally when He says: *The hour cometh when all who are in the graves shall hear the voice of the Son of God. And they that have done good things shall come forth unto the resurrection of life,*

---

* Pearson. Analysis.

*but they that have done evil unto the resurrection of judgment.** And
St. Paul, in his Epistle to the Romans, says, *We shall all stand
before the tribunal of Christ.*† And when the Psalmist says that
the impious will not arise in the judgment, that is they will not
arise to a blessed life, and they will not be able to stand, or defend
their cause at the judgment seat.

THE TIME OF THE RESURRECTION.

7. The general resurrection is still future, and will take place
at the end of the world : immmediately before the general judgment. Holy Job,‡ and St. John,§ speak of the future resurrection
as something which is to happen on the last day. And this is the
common belief of the faithful. There are, however, some who
have already risen, and who are not again to die, but who will
appear in their glorified bodies at the general judgment, such we
believe to be the privilege of the Blessed Virgin. As to the bodies
of the saints that arose at the time of Christ's death, some with
St. Ambrose and St. Hilary, hold that they arose to an immortal
life, but St. Augustine, Ven. Bede, and others, hold that their
bodies again returned to the tombs. All, both good and bad, will
arise at the same moment. In a moment, in the twinkling of an
eye, at the last trumpet. Christ is the meritorious cause of the
resurrection of the just ; and His Resurrection will be the exemplary cause of their resurrection. The resurrection of all is attributed to the voice of Christ as to the instrumental cause, according to the words : *And all who are in the graves shall hear
the voice of the Son of God.*

THE STATE OR CONDITION OF MEN IN THE RESURRECTION.

8. Each soul shall resume the same body which it had in
this life. This is of faith. So that a man in the resurrection will
have the same flesh, bones, nerves, and all the other parts of the
body which he had before his death. This is clear from the words
of Job : *And I shall be clothed again with my skin, and in my flesh
I shall see my God. Whom I myself shall see, and my eyes shall
behold, and not another.*‖
It is also evident on the same grounds on which we believe
a resurrection—because, if either the same body should be joined
to another soul, or the same soul to another body, it would not be
the resurrection of the same man.

---

* St. John v. 28, 29.   † Rom. xiv. 5.   ‡ Job xix. 25.
§ St. John vi. 40, & xi. 24.   ‖ Job xix. 26, 27.

As to the conditions and qualities of those risen from the dead, we may ask, and answer the following usual questions :

Do those who, in life, or from their nativity, have been maimed, or deformed, arise with the same bodily defects ?

It is certain that the just will rise again without any bodily defect whatever. As to the wicked, it is not so certain ; but St. Thomas holds that they also will be free from natural bodily defects in the resurrection, inasmuch as the resurrection will be the work of God, and the works of God are perfect. Also, after the resurrection there will remain in man the power of all the senses—of hearing, seeing, &c., and their use ; because this belongs to the perfection of nature.

Will the Martyrs in their glorified bodies retain the wounds they received for Christ's sake ?

It is certain that in the glorified body of Christ His Five Wounds are retained ; but we are not obliged to admit the same in regard to the wounds of the Christian Martyrs. St. Augustine teaches that in the place of the wounds of the Martyrs a special brightness or glory will shine forth, so that their sufferings may be known.

IN WHAT AGE, AND SIZE, AND STATE, WILL MEN RISE AGAIN?

9. St. Thomas teaches that men will rise again in the size and form which they would have had at the age at which Christ arose, about the age of 33. And the reason he assigns is that God will repair a perfect nature ; but before or after that period nature is more or less defective.

All will not rise in the same height or size, but each will have that height or size which either he had, or would have had, at the age mentioned, all defects of nature being repaired. Because the restoration is not of the species but of the individual, and therefore will be proportioned to our individual nature without making each one a most perfect human being.

It is also Catholic doctrine to say, that the diversity of sex will be preserved in the resurrection, as this belongs to the perfection of the individual, and the species ; but as Christ has said : *In the resurrection they shall neither marry nor be married; but shall be as the angels of God in heaven.**

In the resurrection all the bodies of men will be immortal, according to the words of St. Paul : *For this corruptible must put*

---

* St. Matt. xxii. 30.

*on incorruption ; and this mortal must put on immortality.** But all bodies will not rise impassible. The bodies of the just will be impassible or incapable of suffering, but the bodies of the wicked will be passible : they will have to suffer all manner of torments worse than death ; always living, and as it were, always enduring the sorrows of death. In the words of the Apocalypse : *They shall desire to die, and death shall fly from them.*†

THE QUALITIES OR GIFTS OF A GLORIFIED BODY.

10. The bodies of the saints are to rise glorious and immortal.‡ By this is meant they shall have the four qualities of a glorified body—namely *Impassibility, Brightness, Agility,* and *Subtility.* These are founded on the words of St. Paul : *It is sown in corruption, it shall rise in incorruption. It is sown in dishonour, it shall rise in glory. It is sown in weakness, it shall rise in power. It is sown a natural body, it shall rise a spiritual body.*

By the quality of *Impassibility* is meant that the bodies of the saints will be henceforth incapable of corruption or any suffering. *It is sown* (or buried) *in corruption, it shall rise in incorruption.*

By the quality of *Brightness* is meant, that the bodies of the just shall rise in splendour which will be proportioned to each one's merits. *It is sown in dishonour, it shall rise in glory. There is one glory of the sun, another glory of the moon, and another glory of the stars ; for star differeth from star in glory. So also is the resurrection of the dead.*‖

By the quality of *Agility* is meant, that the bodies of the just will be able to pass from one place to another in an instant : *It is sown in weakness, it shall rise in power.*

By the quality of *Subtility* is meant, that the bodies of the saints, like the glorified Body of our Lord, shall be spiritualized ; and so will be able to pass, as He did, through closed doors, hard substances, &c. *It is sown a natural body, it shall rise a spiritual body.* The Blessed, by their supernatural power, will be able either to penetrate, or pass through other bodies, or resist them as they may wish.

"As four glorious gifts or qualities will be bestowed on the bodies of the saints in recompense of their virtues, so we may naturally infer that the bodies of the damned will be punished in some corresponding way. In place of *Impassibility,* they will be

---

* xv. 53.   † Apoc. ix. 6.   ‡ 1 Cor. xv. 42, 45.   ‖ 1 Cor. xv.

endued with a keen sensibility to pain: in place of *Brightness*, they will appear black and hideous, having all those vices and filthy passions to which they were subject during life depicted in their countenances; and in the place of *Agility* and *Subtility* they will become the prison-house of the soul, weighing down and clogging its spiritual capabilities and energies."*

* Companion to the Catechism. The General Judgment.

ARTICLE XII.

APOSTLES' CREED.	NICENE CREED.
The Life Everlasting. Amen.	And the life of the world to come. Amen.

CHAPTER I.

THE Athanasian Creed also expresses the same dogma : "And they that have done good shall go into life everlasting ; and they that have done evil into everlasting fire."

1. This life everlasting is not the same as the immortality of the soul ; but it is the joint life of soul and body, after the day of the Resurrection and the General Judgment. The soul never dies ; there is no such thing as annihilation ; in the next world soul and body, again united, will live for ever.

2. All men will not be in the same state in the world to come, as the Lord the Righteous Judge shall discern, and put a difference between the good and the bad. And as there shall be a Resurrection both of the just and of the unjust, so the Athanasian Creed says : *They that have done good shall go into life everlasting, and they that have done evil unto everlasting fire.*

As to the state of the lost souls hereafter, the Scripture is explicit. *The wicked shall be turned into hell, and all the people that forget God.** *Then shall He say unto them on the left hand :*

---

* Ps. ix. 17.

Depart from me ye cursed, into everlasting fire prepared for the devil and his angels.* They shall be cast out into that outer darkness, where there is weeping and gnashing of teeth.*

The punishment of the wicked will last for ever, for our Blessed Lord Himself declares : *Their worm dieth not, and the fire is not quenched.†* And the *second death ‡* means not annihilation, but separation from God : *they shall be punished with everlasting destruction from the face of our Lord and the glory of His power.§*

On the other hand, the everlasting life of the just will be spent in the light and enjoyment of God's own presence. *They shall be His people, and God Himself with them shall be their God. ‖ And His servants shall serve Him, and they shall see His face.***

In explanation of this Article of the Creed, we must dwell upon this two-fold state after death and the last judgment. The state of the wicked, and the state of the just—in other words : Hell and Heaven.

SECTION 1.

HELL AND ITS PUNISHMENTS.

3. The Hebrew *Sheol* and the Greek Αδης, translated into English, Hell, often signify the grave, or the place of departed spirits. Here was the rich man after death. The rebellious *angels* were also *cast down into hell, and delivered into chains of darkness.* (2 Peter ii. 4.)

The term hell is now commonly applied to the place of punishment in the unseen world. It is a place in which the reprobate and the demons suffer eternally.

4. *The existence of hell* is one of the principal mysteries or dogmas of our faith. We must first of all believe in God, and then that He is the remunerator ; that is, that God will reward the just for ever in heaven, and punish the wicked for ever in hell.

This dogma of faith may be proved from many places of the Holy Scripture. In the Parable of the Marriage Feast : then the King said to the waiters, *Bind his hands and feet, and cast him into the exterior darkness ; there shall be weeping and gnashing of*

'· St. Matt. xxii. 41,   † St. Mark ix. 44.   ‡ Apoc. xx. 14.
§ 2 Thess. i. 9.   ‖ Apoc. xxi. 3.   ** Apoc. xxii. 3, 4.

*teeth.** *Depart from me you cursed into everlasting fire, which was prepared for the devil and his angels.*† And in the Gospel of St. Luke, where it is said that the rich man died and was buried in hell.

5. *The place where hell is.* According to the tradition of the Church, the place of hell is subterraneous, which is in accordance with the scriptural manner of speaking in regard to this place of torment. Thus, in St. Luke's Gospel, it is narrated how the demons asked our Lord not to command them to go down into the abyss. It is not a dogma of faith that hell is in the bowels of the earth, or in its centre, although it would be rash and against the common notion of the faithful to teach the contrary.

The gates of hell, mentioned by our Saviour, signify the power of hell; for the people of the East call the palaces of their princes gates.

The Jews say there are three gates belonging to hell: the first is in the wilderness, and by that Corah, Dathan, and Abiram, descended into hell; the second is in the sea, for it is said that Jonas, who was thrown into the sea, cried to God *out of the belly of hell.*‡ The third is in Jerusalem, for Isaias tells us that *the fire of the Lord is in Sion, and his furnace in Jerusalem.*§ (1) Earth. (2) Water. (3) Fire. These are evidently three modes of death or destruction.‖

According to the references of the Old Testament, that place is deep (Job xi. 8), and dark (Job xi. 21, 22), in the centre of the earth (Num. xvi. 30; Deut. xxxii. 22), having within it depths on depths (Prov. ix. 18), and fastened with gates (Is. xxxviii. 10) and bars (Job xvii. 16). In this cavernous realm are the souls of dead men, the Rephaim and ill spirits (Ps. lxxxvi. 13., lxxix. 48; Prov. xviii. 14; Ez. xxxi. 17, xxxii. 21). In the New Testament the word *Hades*, like *sheol*, sometimes means the grave, or the unseen world; but it is used of the place of everlasting torments in St. Luke xvi. 23; St. Matt. xi. 23; 2 St. Peter ii. 4. And it is in this sense it is commonly understood by all Christians, and even Jews in the present day.**

The Pains of Hell.

6. The pains of hell are two-fold: the *pain of loss* and the *pain of sense.* The pain of loss is the privation of the vision of God in punishment of sin, together with an everlasting hatred of good, and the greatest sadness and dereliction of spirit.

---

* St. Matt. xxii. 13.   † Ibid. xxx. 41.   ‡ Jonas ii. 3.   § Isa. xxxi. 9.
‖ Calmet's Dict. Hell.   ** See explanation of the word in Article V.

The pain of sense is that which is perceived by the senses, and by the soul, caused by the fire, and the other physical torments of that state.

(a) The pain of loss is incomparably greater than any other pain or torment of hell ; because it is the more opposed to the greatest and the highest good ; and it is in that, that damnation essentially consists. For with God all other things could be endured.

It is true we have not on earth the vision of God, and its privation here does not cost us much suffering or sorrow ; but we must remember that it is not now due to us ; that it does not belong to this state, but it is that which is due after death, and destined for all men, and which the wicked will therefore feel as a privation and a penalty : because through their own fault they have lost so great a good, and are deprived of so much happiness. This may be illustrated by the example of a King, who, through his own fault, becomes dethroned and deprived of his Kingdom.

(b) The pains of the damned are not equal. All are punished according to the measure of their demerits ; according to the words of the Apocalypse,* *As much as she hath glorified herself, and lived in delicacies, so much torment and sorrow give ye to her, because* (in reference to the fall of Babylon) *she saith in her heart : I sit a queen, and am no widow ; and sorrow I shall not see.* Not even the pain of loss can be said to be equal ; for although as a privation of the vision of God it must of itself be equal, yet it can be said to be greater or less according to its cause and its effects. The greater the sins of any one, the greater will be the indignation and the wrath of God in rejecting such a sinner from His sight ; and the greater on that account will be the affliction of the lost soul, according to that which is decreed by the Divine power and justice, because the pain of loss is a privation of the vision of God in relation to sin, and to the punishments of Divine justice.

(c) *The fire of hell.* It was fire that consumed the burnt sacrifice and the incense-offering, beginning with the sacrifice of Noah (Gen. viii. 20), and continued in the ever-burning fire on the altar first kindled from heaven, and re-kindled at the dedication of Solomon's temple. It was the symbol of Jehovah's presence. and the in-

---

* Apoc. xviii. 7.

strument of His power, in a way either of approval or destruction. (Exod. iii. 2 ; xiv. 19, *et. seq.*)

According to the common opinion of Catholics, fire will be the instrument of the Divine justice in hell, and the fire of hell is real, material or corporeal fire. That as to its substance it is the same as our fire, but differing in its accidents and qualities. It is much more severe than our fire : it penetrates to the interior soul ; it is not bright but obscure ; it burns but does not consume, and it does not need fuel of any kind, but is included in itself and subsists by itself like the sun. St. Augustine, writing of it in his Commentary on the 57th Psalm, says, that it is more terrible and severe than anything which a man can endure in this life. This opinion is founded on the fact that Sacred Scripture in many places clearly asserts that there is fire in hell : *And shall cast them into the furnace of fire. Depart from me ye cursed into everlasting fire,* &c. Which expressions should be taken not in a metaphorical sense, but in their true literal meaning ; as there is no reason for a contrary interpretation.

From the texts of Scripture already quoted, we have to learn that not only the bodies of the wicked will suffer by the action of fire, but also lost souls and the demons. The fire was prepared for the devil and his angels. And in the Apocalypse it is said : *And there came down fire from God out of heaven, and devoured ; and the devil who seduced them was cast into the pool of fire and brimstone, where both the beast and the false prophet shall be tormented day and night for ever and ever.*[*]

Material fire could not naturally act on a spirit, but it can do so as the instrument of the divine power. Our bodies act on our souls in this life ; and God, in the other life, can cause fire to act immediately on the souls of the wicked and on the demons. There is a special difficulty in accounting for the manner in which the demons, who are often going about this world, suffer from the fire of hell. It appears that they are never free from its pains ; as the Angels, when they visit this world, never lose sight of the vision of God in heaven. It is probable that the fire of hell has, by divine dispensation, the power of afflicting and acting upon the demons, even when they are in the air around us. Its action is not confined to the limits of hell itself, but can act upon all the damned, no matter where they are, according to the words : *out of hell there is no redemption.* Its action and power is prevented by God from affecting others ;

---

[*] Apoc. xx. 9, 10.

and, therefore, whilst the devils around us are burning, their fire cannot affect us.

(d) *The worms, the darkness, the weeping and the gnashing of teeth.* In Isaias it is said : *The worm shall not die, and their fire shall not be quenched.*[*] And our Saviour, in St. Mark's Gospel, says : *It is better for thee to enter lame into life everlasting than, having two feet, to be cast into the hell of unquenchable fire, where their worm dieth not, and the fire is not extinguished.*[†] St. Basil, in his comments on the 35th Psalm, admits the existence of real worms and serpents in hell, which gnaw continually, and in an inexplicable manner, the bodies of the damned, without consuming them. On the other hand, St. Thomas understands the worms in a metaphorical sense, and takes them to mean the remorse of conscience, which is appropriately called a worm, as it is generated out of the corruption of sin, and tortures the soul, as a real worm would by gnawing within our body without ceasing. The reason assigned by St. Thomas for understanding the text in a metaphorical sense is, that after the day of judgment, and the renovation of the world, no such animals will exist, or mixed bodies, except the bodies of men. This reason does not hold with regard to the material fire, which is admitted by all as the means of hell's torments.

There will be in that place corporeal darkness ; *they will be cast out into exterior darkness.* This darkness, from the position of hell in the centre of the earth, is naturally enough concluded. That must be a dark place. But we are told that the darkness there is not complete ; there will be some kind of dark sulphurous light, so that the damned, for their greater misery and punishment, may be able to see, not clearly, but in thick confusion, the horrible scenes by which they are surrounded and tortured.

It is not difficult in such a place to suppose *weeping and gnashing of teeth.* Owing to the incorruptible state of the body, there will not be the real shedding of tears ; so that the weeping refers to moans and wails of the voices which continually go forth from the midst of the torments. The gnashing of teeth will be real, caused partly by the rage of the damned against God, and

---

[*] Isa. lxvi. 24.   [†] St. Mark ix. 44, 45.

partly from the intensity of the sorrows and pains which they have to suffer.

Finally, according to the teaching of St. Thomas, every kind of punishment will be found in hell, according to the different kinds of sin for which men are condemned; so that one who has sinned in many things, and in many ways, will be tortured by many and different kinds of punishments. It is supposed that the same fire will have the power of torturing in a variety of ways: for exciting thirst in the drunkards, hunger in the gluttons, &c. Sacred Scripture conveys the notion of the generality of these sufferings when it expresses the pains of hell by so many different kinds of torments.

7. *The eternity of the pains of hell.* The future liberation of the wicked and their purification, and the future liberation of even the devils and all the lost souls out of hell, and their admission into the Kingdom of heaven, after a long term of suffering, is an opinion attributed to Origen. Such an opinion is contrary to faith, and abhorred by every Christian.

The pains of the damned will last for ever. This is of faith, and is clearly proved from the texts of Scripture already quoted: *Depart from me you cursed into everlasting fire.* "It has been ingeniously contended that this text proves only that the fire is everlasting, not that the condemned are to suffer everlastingly in it. But this evasion cannot be reconciled with the conclusion of the discourse, in which it is said that their punishment will be everlasting: *And these shall go into everlasting punishment.** The same is taught in other passages. *The smoke of their torments shall ascend for ever and ever.† Whosoever was not found written in the book of life, was cast into the lake of fire—the lake burning with fire and brimstone. This is the second death.‡* How can life for ever be called a Second death? Because, answers St. Augustine, to live in everlasting suffering is rather death than life. For no death can be worse than that death which never dies."§

The wicked, after the day of judgment, will not be consumed or annihilated, but will remain alive in soul and body, to endure the torments to be inflicted on them by the justice of God for all the sins committed by them in the body. Souls are immortal by their very nature, and bodies will be rendered immortal at the general resurrection.

And as the reprobate shall never fail to endure the torments

---

* St. Matt. xxv. 41—46.   † Apoc. xiv. 11.   ‡ Apoc. xx. 15; xxi. 8.
Dr. Lingard's Notes *in loco.*

to their sins, so the justice of God will never fail to inflict those torments. They shall never live to pay the uttermost farthing; or, rather, no payment or satisfaction at all can be made there. One part of their misery is the horror of despair; and it were not perfect hell if any hope could lodge in it. The favour of God is not to be obtained when there is no means left to obtain it; in that world to come there is no place for merit, or satisfaction, or virtue. As the tree falls, so it lies; no change can be wrought in man within those flames, no purgation of his sin, no sanctification of his nature, no justification of his person, and, therefore, no salvation for him for ever.

The Scripture speaks in the same way of the duration of the pains of the wicked and the glory of the just, and as this will be eternal, so also will the pains of the wicked be. The same word is used alike in both cases.

8. St. Thomas assigns the following reasons to show us the equity of this duration of the torments of the damned:—

(a) Because mortal sin in a certain sense contains an infinite malice—inasmuch as God, who is infinitely good, is contemned by it—therefore it deserves to be punished by a penalty at least eternal in duration.

(b) Because the guilt remains for ever; this cannot be remitted without grace, which is not given after death.

(c) Because the person who sins mortally has the interpretative will of remaining in that sin for ever, inasmuch as he places himself in a state out of which he cannot get without the divine assistance; and inasmuch as he prefers the creature, for whose love he sins, to God.

(d) Because there is on earth a punishment for him who sins (by high treason, say,) against his king or country, for he is sometimes punished, as far as it is possible, for ever; thus by death, as St. Augustine says, they are for ever cut off from the society of the living. The same may be said of perpetual banishment. If an exile could always live, he would always remain an exile.

9. The pains of hell cannot be said to be infinite in intensity, because God alone is capable of an infinite action; and no creature could endure infinite suffering. They may, however, be said to be infinite in extent or in duration, as they are to last always. And the pain of loss, as well as the pain of sense,

CC

inflicted for mortal sins, will never be diminished or interrupted, although the accidental pains—such as the vexations of the demons, their reproaches, and the reproaches of others, can be subject to change and diminution.

10. Let us consider what must be the state of the soul as to its intellect and will in the midst of all these pains and horrors.

According to St. Thomas, the soul in hell will retain all its natural knowledge. It will know whatever it knew here on earth. It will consider the evil work which it did and for which it is condemned, and all the delightful goods it has lost; and by the thought of both it will be the more tortured. It will also know some of the things which go on here on earth, as the demons will manifest them to it; or as God will make them known to it at the particular judgment, or by some other special way. Thus the rich man who was buried in hell knew that his brothers here on earth were leading sinful lives.

In that state the lost souls will think of God, but only as the avenger and punisher, as St. Thomas teaches; and from this are born their depraved will and their hatred of God.

The same Saint teaches that, before the Day of Judgment those souls know that the blessed spirits are in a state of inestimable happiness. In the last judgment they will see the glorified bodies of the saints, and after the judgment they will be entirely deprived of the vision of the blessed. They will, however, retain the memory of their glory, which will only serve to their own sorrow out of envy for the happiness of the saints; and because they have lost the state of happiness which so many others have obtained.

In regard to the wills of the damned. We have first to state that the wills of the devils are entirely bad in such a way that they sin mortally by every act which proceeds from their own will; they are obstinate in sin as they have reached their term, in which they remain as to the same state of mind and will, because in all things they act out of pride and rebellion. As to men, it is held that every deliberate act of their wills is evil: because they also are obstinate and confirmed in evil, and they cannot desire that which is good, except through some perverse motive.

Neither the one nor the other will ever repent of their sins. They will hate sin because of the punishment which it has brought upon them; and when the expression "penance" is applied to the lost, it must be understood of their affliction because of the penalty of sin; but no sorrow for sin itself. They will have hatred towards God because of their punishments, and this hatred will cause many of them to blaspheme Him.

Finally, as the blessed no longer merit by their good works in heaven, and their essential glory is not increased by them ; so neither do the damned demerit by their sins, or deserve an increase of their punishments. The reason is because both the blessed and the lost are beyond the state of merit or demerit ; they have reached the term of their reward or punishment, and they are no longer capable of meriting or demeriting.

But the very will of the damned, and the sins committed through it, are a pain and a punishment to them ; as the goodwill of the blessed serves to their reward and happiness.

All the reasons assigned by infidels against an eternity of punishment are of no value, and they are not new, but as old as unbelief itself.

11. (a) " To say that God would condemn a poor creature eternally for the sake of only one mortal sin, is it not making God a cruel judge ? "

To this we answer that the number of those sins of a lost soul is only an accessory thing. God pardons *seventy times seven times ;* that is, an indefinite number of times, anyone who truly repents. If, then, anyone be condemned to hell for only one mortal sin, it is because such a one died freely in a state of final impenitence, with the knowledge and acceptance of all its consequences. He has laughed at the justice of God ; he has contemned His mercy. It is the sinner who has condemned himself, who has been his own executioner. God warned him often enough, but He does not interfere with the freedom of man's will, and therefore He let him go where he liked ; and thus his cry of despair will be for eternity, " the fault is mine ; it is my fault alone ! "

(b) But is it just that a sin of an instant should be punished by an eternity of suffering ?

Human justice does not take into account, and rightly so, the time which it takes a criminal to commit murder : but it punishes eternally by depriving the murderer of his life which he will never get back in this state. If an obstinate sinner should live eternally here on earth, he would always remain in evil, and be always deserving the same punishment. His sin, in his intention and will, is eternal ; and it is therefore just that the penalty last for ever.

(c) But is it possible that an infinitely good God would leave His creature in suffering for ever ?

There would be no eternal hell were it not that God is infinitely good, and that He loves His creatures in an infinite manner.

It is this love, contemned and trampled under foot to the last hour, which calls forth, on the part of God, the definite and final abandonment of the soul.

(d)   But could not God pardon the lost soul after it has made sufficient expiation ?

God would pardon the lost soul if it would repent.   The damned will never repent, and they will never repent because in that state they are incapable of repentance.   Their will was fixed in evil at death ; therein it will remain for ever, as it is no longer free to turn to good.

(e)   Should not God leave the damned liberty to merit, and offer them the grace of conversion, as He offers the sinner in this life?

That is to say that God should give the damned a new trial, or a new period of probation.   But on this supposition, either the damned will accept the grace of God, or they will refuse to accept it.   If they accept it they will be saved, and their portion and happiness will be the same as those just souls who faithfully observed the law of God in this life ; and from this it would follow that a man could live here on earth any kind of life— he could hate both God and man, and commit all manner of iniquity, and die with blasphemy on his lips, and depend on grace and repentance in the next life.   Or the lost souls would refuse to receive the grace of God, and again throw themselves freely into a state of sin ; then, to reclaim them, a third or fourth opportunity should be given, and so on indefinitely, which would be nothing less than a mockery of divine justice.

It is therefore conformable to the wisdom of God to limit the gift of His grace, and the time of merit and demerit, to the present life, and to establish after death a definite sanction, and to proclaim the evangelical maxim :   *as the tree falls there shall it remain.*

(f)   God knows beforehand those that will be lost.   Why, therefore, does He create them ?

God has created them for eternal happiness, and has given, or at least offered, them the means to obtain it.   If they are lost, it is solely by their own fault.   God has wise reasons for tolerating the evil which the wicked do on earth, and the damnation which is the result of it.   He obtains through its toleration great good ; for the elect, who are scandalized and persecuted by the wicked, a great harvest of merits ; and for Himself, a signal manifestation of His patience, His mercy, and His justice. In this question, as in many others, there are contained mysteries which will be unfolded or revealed in the life to come. Both the elect and the reprobate will then know and acknowledge that the judgments of God are true and just.*

THE PUNISHMENT OF CHILDREN WHO DIE WITHOUT BAPTISM IN A STATE OF ORIGINAL SIN.

12. Their state will be eternal or everlasting, and therefore we have to refer to it in treating of the life everlasting.

It is of faith that children who die in original sin suffer the pain of loss. This is proved from the words : *Unless a man be born again of water and the Holy Ghost, he cannot enter into the Kingdom of God.** We have also to remember that every mortal sin excludes from heaven, and original sin is mortal. Hence the opinion is improbable which says that these children will have nothing whatever to suffer either in the way of sorrow or affliction ; for they know that on account of that sin they are deprived of eternal happiness, which must naturally cause them sorrow and sadness.

There is a sharp controversy amongst Catholic authors as to whether children dying with only original sin suffer the pain of sense. St. Thomas teaches clearly that they do not. Punishment, according to him, in the next life is due only to personal sin.

Their state in the future life will be one of natural happiness, and in it they will be able to know and love God as the author of nature ; but inasmuch as they will be deprived of eternal happiness, we conclude the important and grave obligation of parents, doctors, nurses, and priests, to see that children are not deprived of the Sacrament of Baptism, and the guilt of those who neglect to have children baptized, or through neglect permit them to die without Baptism.

---

* Expos. Elementaire de la doctrine Catholique. par L'Abbé Moulin.
* St. John iii. 5.

SECTION 2.   (ARTICLE XII.)

HEAVEN.

1. What is meant by heaven.—2. The vision of God in heaven.—3. No created intellect can naturally see God as He is Himself.—4. A created intellect, aided supernaturally, can see God as He is in Himself.—5. The light of Glory.—6. The inequality of the Beatific Vision.—7. The cause and the result of this inequality.—8. Whether the Blessed comprehend God.—9. The object of the Beatific Vision.—10. The *accidental* Beatitude of heaven.—11. The aureolæ of glory.—12. The vision, love and fruition of God by the Blessed.—13. The inhabitants of heaven: (a) Human beings, (b) Angels, (c) The Immaculate Mother of God, (d) Christ in His Sacred Humanity.—14. The essential Beatitude of heaven.—15. The eternity of heaven, and the everlasting life of the Blessed.

1.   HEAVEN or Paradise is the place where the Angels and Saints enjoy eternal beatitude.   Hence they are called Blessed.

No one enters heaven who is not in a state of grace, free from all sin, mortal and venial, and who has not satisfied entirely the justice of God for the temporal punishment due to sin.

Heaven is the recompense of fidelity to the law of God, which commands us to believe in Him, to hope in Him, and to love Him.   This reward is God Himself, as He said to His servant, Abraham, *I am thy reward exceeding great.*

THE VISION OF GOD IN HEAVEN.

2.   There are three ways in which we can know God.   (a) Naturally, by abstraction, and from the effects of God's power which we behold.   (b) Supernaturally, by faith.   (c) Supernaturally, by the Beatific Vision, or by the Vision of God, which the blessed possess in heaven.

We have here to consider this last mode of knowing God, namely, by the Beatific Vision.   In this we must reflect :—

(a)   That the Vision of God is of such a nature that it cannot be received by the corporeal eye.   Our eyes, even when glorified, will not be able to see the essence of God :   *Whom no man sees or can see.**   As regards

---

* 1 Tim.

corporeal vision, man sees by the act of a bodily organ ;
but God is entirely simple, therefore, by such a corporeal act, His essence cannot be seen, as no act can
go beyond the nature of the power from which it
proceeds. The object of the Beatific Vision is outside
and beyond all the objects of corporeal vision; in
such a way that it would involve a contradiction to
suppose that the essence of God could be seen by
a bodily act. Such an act should be of necessity
spiritual, and the power from which it proceeds must
therefore be a spiritual one.

(b) A created intellect of its own natural force cannot see
God as He is in Himself.

3. This proposition was defined by faith in the Council of
Vienne, under Clement V., in the year 1311, against the Beguards
and the Beguins. These heretics taught (a) that a man in this
life could attain to such a degree of perfection that he could no
longer sin, or acquire any more grace. (b) That having once
attained this state he need not pray, nor would he be bound to
keep the commandments of the Church. (c) That man, even in
this life, could attain final beatitude in the same degree as in the
next life, and that every intellectual nature that has attained
its beatitude, is blessed in such a manner that, in order to
receive the Vision of God and to enjoy Him, it has no need of the
light of glory.

It is in the sense of the proposition stated against these
errors, that we understand the texts of Scripture : *No one knoweth the Son but the Father, neither doth any one know the Father
but the Son, and he to whom it shall please the Son to reveal Him.**
*Now this is eternal life : That they may know Thee, the only true
God, and Jesus Christ whom Thou hast sent.*†

The reason why a created intellect cannot of itself see God,
is because the vision of God, as He is in Himself, is Eternal
Glory and Supernatural Beatitude ; and it is of faith that man
cannot by his own power merit eternal glory, and that he cannot
of himself, and of his own natural power, attain beatitude.
Moreover, if a man cannot elicit an act of faith, hope, or charity,
or do any good supernatural act without the aid of God's grace,
it follows that he cannot elicit that supernatural act which is the
greatest of all, namely, the Beatific Vision, without any aid
from God.

* St. Matt. xi. 27.   † St. John xvii. 8.

St. Thomas says that, in order that anything may be known, there ought to be some proportion between the object that is known, and the subject knowing it, because no power can naturally go beyond its proportionate object. But between God, as clearly seen, and the created intellect, there is no proportion. The cognoscitive power corresponds to the perfection of the being, and no created being can attain to the perfection of God, or naturally see Him as He is in Himself.

4. The created intellect, aided supernaturally, can see God as He is in Himself, that is intuitively or clearly as to His essence and nature. This is of faith defined in the Council of Florence (1439), where it is defined that departed souls, entirely purified, are immediately received into heaven, and there see God Three in One as He is.

We have also numerous texts of Holy Scripture in proof of this doctrine: *Blessed are the clean in heart, for they shall see God.** *We see now as in a dark mirror, then we shall see God face to face,†* *even as He is.*

It is possible for men, by the supernatural aid of God, to obtain their beatitude ; but the intuitive vision of God constitutes the essence of beatitude, or is at least necessarily required for it ; according to the words of St. John : *This is eternal life that they know thee, the only true God, and Jesus Christ whom thou hast sent.*

We know that there is in us a natural desire to see God, who is the first cause of all things ; and this desire cannot be empty and fruitless, therefore it is right that it should be satisfied. Nature does not give a desire towards that which is impossible, and we should not wish naturally for beatitude if that were not possible for us.

The Light of Glory.

5. As the created intellect cannot see God intuitively, of its own power, and as it is of faith that men and Angels see God intuitively in heaven, it is necessary that something be given to the intellect to enable it to attain, or to receive, this vision. The medium by which the created intellect is raised up to see God intuitively is called the Light of glory. It is of faith that the Light of glory is required for the Beatific Vision of God, as defined in the Council of Vienne, in the condemnation of the errors of the Beguards and Beguins.

---

* St. Matt. v.   † 1 Cor. xii. 12.

In Thy light, says the Psalmist, *we shall see light*.* The reason why the light of glory is required, is that a created intellect is insufficient, and in itself unproportioned to the Vision of God. Therefore, it is necessary that it be elevated by some power, or quality, to enable it to receive that vision : and this is no other than the *Light of glory*.

From the doctrine here laid down, it follows that no one in this life can naturally see God. Christ only, during His life on earth, always had the Vision of God ; because He was always in the enjoyment of the Beatific Vision. He was at the same time a *comprehensor* and a *viator*.

As to the Vision of God, which was conceded to Moses and to St. Paul, Catholic doctors are not agreed as to the nature of this great privilege. Moses was the first doctor of the Jews, and St. Paul the first doctor of the Gentiles, and it is clear from Scripture that to them was conceded some special vision of God, different from all other prophets. It was not a permanent vision, but some extraordinary vision of the glory of God's Kingdom.

It follows also that in regard to the Vision of God there are two things to be considered, namely, on the part of the power or faculty that receives the vision, and on the part of the object, which is God. On the part of the faculty, namely, the created intellect, it is too weak of itself to receive the Vision of God, and therefore requires the elevation and the strength given it by the Light of Glory ; as far as God is concerned He is most luminous and visible, but the weak minds of His creatures require the Light of Glory to receive that vision, or to behold Him as He is in Himself. This vision is not natural, but proceeds from a supernatural principle, as faith does in this life ; and it is entirely supernatural as to its object, namely, the glory of God.

From the explanation here given we understand the *Light of glory* to be a certain supernatural quality, or habit, or principle, which strengthens and perfects the intellect in such a manner as to enable it to receive the vision of God. It has three functions to perform—(*a*) It strengthens the intellect to elicit the act of the Beatific Vision. (*b*) It disposes it to receive the essence of God under an intelligible form. (*c*) It enables the intellect to receive the full Beatific Vision of God. All three are included in the one notion or idea of that Light of Glory, namely, that it strengthens and elevates the intellect to see God intuitively, face to face, even as He is.

---

* Ps. xxxv. 10.

I may remark that in the Vision of God in heaven no created species comes between the soul and God. Such a species would be superfluous, because such a species is required only when the object is not present to the intellect, or is not sufficiently intelligible in itself because of its materiality. But in heaven the essence of God is immediately present to the soul, and God is entirely spiritual, and therefore intelligible in the highest degree, because altogether immaterial. Besides, no species, either created or createable, could represent God as He is in Himself.

God will by Himself unite Himself to the intellect in the Beatific Vision, and therefore no species of any kind will be required in this vision, as there will then be no medium whatever between the soul and God.

THE INEQUALITY OF THE BEATIFIC VISION.

6. It is of faith that the Blessed in heaven, by reason of their unequal merits, behold God, and receive His Beatitude in different and unequal degrees. This is defined in the Council of Florence, in *Decreto Unionis*, where it is defined that the souls of the Saints are immediately received into heaven, and there see God, intuitively One and Three, according to the diversity of their merits, one more perfect than another. And the Council of Trent pronounces an *Anathema* against any one who should deny that a just man merits an increase of glory by his good works. This inequality of Beatitude in heaven was taught us by our Divine Lord Himself in the words: *In my Father's house there are many mansions ;** and St. Paul tells us : *there are bodies celestial, and bodies terrestrial ; but one is the glory of the celestial, and another of the terrestrial. One is the glory of the sun, another the glory of the moon, aud another the glory of the stars. For star differeth from star in glory. So also is the resurrection of the dead.†*

It is, therefore, of faith that the Blessed behold God unequally, or in different degrees, some more perfect than others. This is against Jovinian, who taught that man's merits and sins were all equal, and therefore his rewards and punishments were equal also. And it is against the Lutheran doctrine, which asserts that as we are justified by Christ alone, irrespective of any merits of our own, and as the justice of Christ is equal for all, so the beatitude of the just will be equal in heaven. The vision of God is the wages or reward of the good, which we do

---

* St. John xiv. 2.   † 1 Cor. xv. 40, *et seq.*

here through God's grace, and is bestowed according to the merits of each just soul.

7. The moral cause of the inequality of glory and beatitude, is the inequality of good works and merits.

Its physical cause is the inequality of the Light of Glory. The power of seeing Him more or less perfectly depends on this light. All the beatific visions both in men and angels are of the same species or kind. They have the same formal object, namely, without any medium or species; and the same proximate principle from which the vision proceeds, namely, the Light of glory.

It does not follow from the doctrine of the inequality of glory, that those who see God less clearly are not completely happy and their appetite completely satisfied, because they well know that this glory corresponds to their merits, and they desire no more; all are inflamed by charity, and, therefore, in perfect conformity with the divine will in all things.

8. In connection with the Vision of God, the question is asked whether the blessed *comprehend* God. *Comprehend*, in its Theological sense, has two meanings. (a) It signifies the acquiring or the attaining to an object that is sought or desired, and in this sense it is of faith that God is comprehended by the blessed. It is in this sense that St. Paul speaks, when he says: *Know you not that they that run in the race, all run, indeed, but one receiveth the prize? So run that you may obtain.** (b) Comprehension means to know and see a thing adequately, that is to know it as much as it is knowable. It is the adequate knowledge of an object, and applied to God, it means to know His essence and all that it virtually or eminently contains. It would mean to know God as He knows Himself, in a perfect and infinite manner. In this sense God is incomprehensible to His creatures. Hence the prophet calls Him *great in counsel*, and *incomprehensible in thought.*† And the Apostle in his Epistle to the Romans, writes: *O the depth of the riches of the wisdom and the knowledge of God; how incomprehensible are His judgments, how unsearchable His ways.* The Council of Lateran (cap. fimiter) says: "We believe that God is incomprehensible. The reason of this is because He is infinite and immense. To comprehend Him would mean to know Him inasmuch as He is knowable, but no created mind could attain to such a perfect way of knowing God, inasmuch as it would mean to know Him in an infinite manner, which is not possible to a creature."

---

* 1 Cor. ix. 24.   † Jer. xxxii. 19.

THE OBJECT OF THE BEATIFIC VISION.

9. The Object of the Beatific Vision is two-fold, *formal or primary*, and *material or secondary*. The *formal* or *primary* object of Beatitude is that which is seen on its own account, and which constitutes the essential glory of heaven, and this is God Himself. The *secondary* object is that which is seen on account of the *primary*, and under it are included all the creatures which the blessed see. The accidental glory of heaven arises from the vision of the secondary objects, as the essential glory of heaven proceeds from the immediate vision of God Himself.

THE ACCIDENTAL BEATITUDE OR GLORY OF HEAVEN.

10. This arises, as I have said, from the vision or knowledge which the Blessed have of secondary objects, namely, creatures.

They see and know creatures in the *Divine Word*, that is, in the Divine Intelligence. God created all things by the Word, and He understands Himself by the Word. The knowledge which the blessed have is like the knowledge which God has of Himself and all other things. All creatures are contained in the Divine Word, as by that Word all things were made. Therefore, the blessed seeing the Word, see in it all things, or at least all things which relate to them in any special way.

The blessed do not see all the things which He has done or can do. His power is infinite, and, therefore, what He can do extends to infinitude; and if the blessed could see all that God can do, they would be able to comprehend God. Besides there are special things which God has reserved to Himself, and which the blessed can never know, unless God chooses to reveal them to them. These are: (a) Future contingent things, that is, those things which depend upon the free will of men. (b) The secrets of the heart, that is, the interior thoughts of the soul. (c) The day of the General Judgment. *Of that day and hour no one knows, not even the Angels in heaven.*

The Blessed see and know concerning creatures, whatever specially relates to them, because in heaven every just and honest desire will be satisfied. That we may classify what specially may be said to belong to the knowledge of the blessed, we have to consider them (a) in the order of grace (b) as parts of the whole universe, (c) as such a person, either private or public, as the case may be.

Under the first consideration the blessed will see and understand the mysteries of faith, which were revealed, and which they
believed in this life, according to the words : *As we have heard so
have we seen, in the city of the Lord of hosts, in the city of our God.*
Thus they will understand the mysteries of the Incarnation, of
Redemption, of Predestination, and all other mysteries connected
with the truths of faith.

Under the second consideration the blessed will see and
know all the different *genera* and species of things, and the principal parts of the universe—heaven and earth, the elements, the
heavenly bodies, &c.

Under the third consideration the blessed will know all that
belongs to that state or position which they occupied when
on earth. Thus, those who were Popes will know all that
belongs to the welfare of the whole Church ; bishops, what concerns the dioceses over which they presided ; Founders of
Religious Orders, all that concerns those Orders ; parents have
a knowledge of their families here on earth; relations and friends
know all that they desire concerning those they have left on
earth, and so forth.

The Blessed, besides this special knowledge which belongs
to them under the three-fold consideration, also know many other
things. Thus it is said that *there is joy in heaven upon one sinner
doing penance* ; and St. Paul says : *We are made a spectacle to the
world, to angels and to men.*

The blessed, therefore, know all the prayers that are
addressed to them ; and God reveals to them many other things
which may increase their accidental glory.

The qualities of glorified bodies. To this accidental glory
belong the qualities or gifts of the bodies ; to wit, *Impassibility,
Brightness, Subtility* and *Agility*, as explained in the Eleventh
Article.

THE AUREOLÆ OF GLORY.

11. Some souls will also have their accidental glory augmented by the addition of special heavenly and supernatural
gifts or qualities, called the *Aureolæ*, or small crowns of glory.

The souls in heaven retain their perfection and all their good
natural qualities and acquired sciences ; they retain also their
spiritual characters or marks of Baptism and Confirmation, and
in the case of ecclesiastics, that of Holy Orders. And to these
are added, in the case of some souls, special crowns of glory,
given in reward for certain victories gained through special

labours and sufferings here on earth. These are called the *Aureola* of glory.

They are three in number, namely, that of *Martyrdom*, that of *Virginity*, and that of *Doctorship*. The crown is given to Martyrs, because they obtain a victory principally over the world. To Virgins, because they obtain a victory principally over the flesh. To Doctors and preachers, because these obtain a victory specially over the devil. The rewards are referred to in Sacred Scripture. Of Martyrs, it is said, *Greater love than this no man hath than that he lay down his life for his friends.** Of Doctors, *he who will confess me before men, I will confess him before my Father who is in heaven.*† Of virgins, it is said, *they follow the lamb whithersoever he goeth.*‡ By these are signified special rewards to be granted hereafter for each of these victories. Besides these special gifts granted to Martyrs, Virgins and Doctors, there are other heavenly gifts which belong to all beatified souls.

12. These are the *vision*, *love* and *fruition* of the souls in heaven, which corresponds to the three Theological virtues.

The *Vision of God* is that which we have considered above. It corresponds to faith, and implicitly includes the other two, namely, love and fruition.

Love, which corresponds to and is of the same species as charity; and it is the convenience or suitableness of the vision which makes it valued and cherished.

Fruition. This is sometimes taken in the sense of love, but it means more than that here. It means the possession and retention of the thing loved. These supernatural gifts, as I have said, will belong to all the blessed.

13. Under the secondary object of beatitude we have to include the inhabitants of heaven. All concur in that beatitude. To be numbered with the blessed will add to our accidental glory in heaven. Our friends and companions there will be the inhabitants of heaven, and amongst them we may consider :—

    (a) *Human beings,* men and women like ourselves. There they will be without spot or blemish, purified and beatified, because now in that place into which nothing defiled can enter. There brothers and sisters once more meet; there children are re-united to their parents, and friends long separated by death become again associated.

---

* St. John xv.   † St. Mark viii.; St. Luke xii.   ‡ Apoc. vii.

In this class we have not only to contemplate companions, friends, and relations, but all the Saints of God : Those of the Old Law and those of the New, from the just Abel to the last Saints ; the Patriarchs, Prophets, Apostles, Patrons, &c.

(b) *Angels.* The choirs of Angels, or of so many pure and heavenly spirits. The millions and millions, and thousands of millions, that stand before the throne of God ; and amongst them those special Guardian Angels who watched over us in life.

(c) *The Immaculate Mother of God.* The Queen of heaven will welcome her children and receive them into the Kingdom of her Son.

(d) *Christ in His Sacred Humanity,* as He is at the right hand of the Father, in that Kingdom purchased by His precious blood ; where He still retains His Five Sacred Wounds, which shine with greater splendour and brightness than the sun. Our souls on entering heaven will hear from His Sacred lips those sweet words of welcome : *Come ye blessed of My Father, possess the Kingdom prepared for you.*

THE ESSENTIAL BEATITUDE OR GLORY OF HEAVEN.

14. This arises from the Vision of God.

The blessed in heaven see God, One in essence, and Three in Persons, as He is in Himself. This is of faith, as we learn from the Council of Florence, in the Decree of Union. They therefore see in God, His essence, the Divine Persons, and also His attributes both relative and absolute. The attributes of God and the Persons are not really distinct from the essence of God, and therefore they are seen by one and the same act as the essence is seen.

It is of this vision of God that St. John speaks when he says : *Dearly beloved, we are now the sons of God ; and it hath not yet appeared what we shall be. We know that when he shall appear, we shall be like to him ; because we shall see him as he is.*

The Beatific Vision corresponds to faith in this life, as it is its reward ; therefore the blessed will see in heaven everything which they believe here, and unless they were to see the attributes of God as well as His essence, their desire would not be fully satisfied ; and they would not be perfectly happy. These attributes they know by revelation here, and therefore it belongs to their happiness to behold them in heaven by the Beatific Vision.

According to St. Thomas the vision in heaven is *intuitive, quiddative*, or *essential*, and *beatific*, therefore it includes the essence and the attributes ; and moreover, as God is a pure act, when His essence is seen, His attributes and the Divine Persons must also be seen and be the object of that vision.   When, in the words of St. John, the blessed see God as He is, they see all, for all that is in God is one.

The everlasting life of the blessed is spent in the light of God's presence.   *They shall be His people, and God Himself shall be with them.**   *His servants shall serve Him, and they shall see His face.*†

This everlasting life is begun on earth according to the words of St. John : *Amen, Amen, I say unto you, that he that heareth my word and believeth in Him that sent me, hath everlasting life.*

It is continued and perfected in heaven.   And after the Resurrection and the Last Judgment, the whole man, body and soul, will enjoy this everlasting life.   *Then shall the King say to them on His right Hand : Come ye blessed of my Father, possess the Kingdom prepared for you from the foundation of the world.*

This happiness arises (*a*) from the perfection of the body, equal to the Angels, made like unto Christ, (*b*) from the perfection of the soul.   *There we shall know as also we are known ; and become conformed to the image of His Son.*   (*c*) From the perfection of the state of beatitude, for the blessed shall never hunger or thirst any more ; and there will be no need of the sun or of the moon to give them light and heat; *for the Lamb is the lamp thereof.* God Himself, the God of love, is the fount and source of the happiness of the blessed, and of His fulness we have all received.

After the last sentence, the elect will rise triumphant towards heaven, singing their eternal hymn of gratitude and love ; and the reprobate will sink into the depth of hell with the wicked.   An Angel shall close the depths of the horrible abyss, and place thereon the seal of God, which shall never, never be broken. Henceforth, Eternity shall everywhere reign.

While we are upon earth, standing as it were upon a narrow bridge, with heaven on one side and hell on the other, it is in our power to choose between the two.   By freely consenting to sin, we are choosing a living death in hell; but by persevering in a good and virtuous life, we are choosing life everlasting in heaven.

Life everlasting means, that if we serve God faithfully in this life, we shall be happy with Him for ever in Heaven.

---

* Apoc. xxi. 3. and xxii. 3, 4.

It is called *Life everlasting*, to teach us that after this life there is another, which will last for ever, and that the just shall enjoy eternal happiness in it.

The happiness of heaven is to see, love, and enjoy God in the Kingdom of His glory for ever and ever.

We cannot form a just conception of the happiness of heaven, for : *Eye hath not seen nor ear heard, neither hath it entered into the heart of man, what things God hath prepared for them that love Him.**

Amen means *so be it.*

We say *Amen* after the Apostles' Creed to express our firm belief in all that the Creed contains.

Life everlasting is not promised to faith alone, however firm it may be, but to faith that worketh by charity. It is necessary, therefore, that our lives be in conformity with our faith, in order to attain the noble end for which God made us : To KNOW, LOVE AND SERVE HIM HERE ON EARTH ; AND TO SEE AND ENJOY HIM FOR EVER IN HEAVEN.†

THE ETERNITY OF HEAVEN, AND THE LIFE OF THE BLESSED.

16. Its duration is as necessary as the life itself ; because, in order that all the above-mentioned rewards amount to a true felicity, there must be an absolute security of the enjoyment without any fear of losing it.

That this life is eternal we are assured by Him Who has purchased it for us and promised it to us. He often calls it eternal life ; and it is described to us in Scripture as a *continuing city, everlasting habitations, house eternal in the heavens ;* and it is expressed by *eternal glory, eternal salvation, an eternal inheritance, the everlasting Kingdom* of our Lord and Saviour, Jesus Christ.

And this eternity is explained in terms liable to no mistake : *If any man keep my word he shall not see death for ever.*‡ And *every one that liveth and believeth in Me shall not die for ever.*§ There : *God shall wipe away all tears from their eyes ; and death shall be no more, nor mourning, nor crying, nor sorrow, shall be any more, for the former things are passed away.*‖

This life eternal was purchased for us by the suffering and death of Christ : *who hath destroyed death, and hath brought to light life and incorruption by the Gospel.***

Let the thoughts of this eternity renew in us an earnest de-

---

* 1 Cor. ii. 9.   † Companion to the Cat. in loco.   ‡ St. John viii. 51.
§ St. John xi. 26.   ‖ Apoc. xxi. 4.   ** 2 Tim. i. 10.

DD

sire of heaven and of heavenly things, and of the enjoyment of that vision of God which alone can satisfy us ; let them withdraw our inclinations from earth and earthly things, and all the pleasures of this life, for we have not here a lasting dwelling-place, but we seek another ; let them encourage us to take up the Cross of Christ, and carry it with fidelity and perseverance, *reckoning that the sufferings of this time are not worthy to be compared with the glory to come, that shall be revealed in us.** *For that which is at present momentary, and light, of our tribulation worketh for us above measure exceedingly an eternal weight of glory. While we look not at the things which are seen, but at the things which are not seen : for the things which are seen are temporal, but the things which are not seen are eternal.*†

FINIS.

RECENT PUBLICATIONS.

—·⊷·—

THE CATECHIST;

Or, Headings and Suggestions for the Explanation of the Catechism
of Christian Doctrine.

By Rev. G. E. HOWE. 2 vols. 10s. net.

HEAVEN ON EARTH;

Or, Twelve Hours of Adoration before the Blessed Sacrament.

With Prayers for Mass, Vespers of the Blessed Sacrament,
Compline, etc.

By Rev. D. G. HUBERT. Cloth gilt, 2s. 6d.

ECCE HOMO.
𝔓assion 𝔐editations.

By Rev. D. G. HUBERT. With Preface by LADY HERBERT.

1s. 6d.

THE CONSOLER;

Or, Pious Readings Addressed to the Sick and all who are
Afflicted.

By Père LAMBILOTTE. Translated by Abbot BURDER. 3s. 6d.

R. WASHBOURNE, 18 PATERNOSTER ROW, LONDON.

BENZIGER BROS.: NEW YORK, CINCINNATI AND CHICAGO.

ROMAN MISSAL.

Adapted to the Use of the Laity.   In Latin and English.

Complete Edition, 1897.

With all the latest New Masses and Appendices for England,
Ireland, Jesuit, Benedictine, Franciscan, and other Religious
Orders.

With Supplement containing Masses for Week-days in Lent.

Soft morocco, red or gilt edges, 5s.; Rutland roan, gilt edges,
6s. 6d.; calf boards, red edges, 8s. 6d.; morocco boards, gilt
edges, 8s. 6d.; calf limp, red under gold edges, 8s. 6d.; morocco
limp, red under gold edges, 8s. 6d.; russia boards or limp, red
under gold edges, 10s. 6d.

POPULAR MISSAL.

For the Use of the Laity.   In Latin and English.

Abridged 1897 Edition of the above, with all the latest Masses
and Appendices as above.

Cloth, red edges, 2s. 6d.; soft morocco, red or gilt edges,
3s. 6d.; calf boards, red edges, 6s.; morocco boards, gilt edges,
6s.; calf limp, red under gold edges, 6s.; morocco limp, red
under gold edges, 6s.; russia limp or boards, red under gold
edges, 8s.

R. WASHBOURNE, 18 Paternoster Row, London.

BENZIGER BROS. : New York, Cincinnati and Chicago.

www.ingramcontent.com/pod-product-compliance
Lightning Source LLC
Chambersburg PA
CBHW031047110726
47900CB00003B/841